PRINCETON SERIES ON THE MIDDLE EAST

Bernard Lewis and Andras Hamori, Editors

THE NEW FACE OF LEBANON

To Afife, Chris, Adam, and Hadi

The New Face of
Lebanon

HISTORY'S REVENGE

William W. Harris

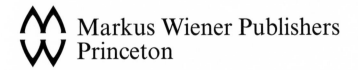

Markus Wiener Publishers
Princeton

Photo on page i: Beirut, 2005

Portions of chapter 8 previously appeared in William Harris,
"Bashar al-Assad's Lebanon Gamble," *Middle East Quarterly* 12,
no. 3 (June 2005), and are used in modified form by permission.

For information write to: Markus Wiener Publishers
231 Nassau Street, Princeton, NJ 08542
www.markuswiener.com

Library of Congress Cataloging-in-Publication Data

Harris, William W.
    The New face of Lebanon : history's revenge / William W. Harris.
        p. cm. — (Princeton series on the Middle East)
    Updated ed. of the author's "Faces of Lebanon," 1997.
    Includes bibliographical references and index.
    ISBN 1-55876-391-0 (alk. paper) — ISBN 1-55876-392-9 (pb.: alk. paper)
        1. Lebanon—History—Civil War, 1975–1990. 2. Lebanon—History—1990–
I. Harris, William W. Faces of Lebanon. II. Title. III. Series.
DS87.H3723 2005
956.9204'4—dc22   2005043517

Markus Wiener Publishers books are printed in the
United States of America on acid-free paper,
and meet the guidelines for permanence and durability
of the committee on production guidelines for book
longevity of the council on library resources.

■ CONTENTS ■

Trilingual Hizballah billboard that says "Israel must be destroyed"
in Farsi (Persian), Arabic, and English
(near Ba'albak, looking westward toward Mount Lebanon, January 1995)

■ PREFACE TO THE SECOND EDITION ■

"Last month I walked down to the devastated seaside street in Beirut where former Lebanese Prime Minister Rafik al-Hariri and 21 others were killed on February 10 in the most spectacular political assassination of contemporary times. It remains a little scene from hell, frozen by the requirements of the U.N.'s first ever murder investigation. The impressive crater created by one ton of TNT, the shattered buildings, and the general ruin represent a grim marker of the notion that murder is an acceptable way to conduct political business, a notion that the international community must stamp out once and for all."

So begins my op-ed piece published in the July 25, 2005, *Wall Street Journal*. The aftermath of the February 2005 murder of Rafik al-Hariri is a crucial test for both Lebanon and the United Nations, given the U.N. commitment in Security Council Resolutions 1595 and 1636 to track down the assassins and their masters. U.N. success in this task would be a huge boost for U.N. prestige in the Middle East, and for the credibility of multilateral action in international affairs. Equally, failure to crack the Hariri case would be a body blow for the international organization, significantly reducing its authority in the world's most important crisis zone. Failure would also announce that "murder pays," and would expose Lebanon to recrudescence of the Syrian hegemony it so unexpectedly escaped in 2005. In brief, the U.N. Security Council has fused its reputation with the future of a small Middle Eastern state, with no turning back.

The year 2005 was a pivotal historical moment for the Lebanese people, with the opportunity for a decisive break with three bleak decades—fifteen years of chaos followed by fifteen years of stifling command from Damascus. Lebanon taking its opportunity depends on whether or not Lebanese leaders can transcend their sectarian compartments. Sustained recovery of the country's fragile democracy and sovereignty further depends on the Franco-American and U.N. cover that Lebanon has acquired out of events triggered by the 2003 U.S. occupation of Iraq, and associated Syrian miscalculation. Lebanon's "cedar revolution" has not occurred in a vacuum—it is a fortuitous by-product of President George W. Bush's overthrow of Saddam Husayn, ironic considering Lebanese condemnations of the American unilateralism in Iraq that became multilateralism in Lebanon.

Renewed Lebanese "independence" offers a good vantage point

from which to evaluate Lebanon's post–Cold War circumstances, eight years after the original *Faces of Lebanon*. I have therefore written a completely new final chapter for the new edition, the first overview of the period of Syrian hegemony to appear in print. It is also the first published analysis of the current Lebanese/Syrian crisis, concentrating on the Lebanese and international aspects. Otherwise, I have undertaken limited updating and correction of other parts of the text. I have not, however, seen any reason to adjust my perspectives on the historical distinctiveness of Lebanon's complex of communities, on the indigenous sources of Lebanese sectarianism, and on substantial Lebanese as well as external responsibility for the breakdown of the country in the late twentieth century.

It is difficult to find anything positive about Syrian Ba'thist domination of Lebanon from 1990 to 2005. First, I don't agree that the Syrian presence enabled Hizballah's liberation of occupied southern Lebanon from Israel. The Israelis stirred up a Shi'i hornet's nest from 1983 onward, which gave Hizballah all it needed to run a successful resistance campaign. The Syrians even sought to delay Israeli withdrawal from Lebanon, because Israeli occupation of the "security zone" buttressed Syrian hegemony in Beirut. Second, I don't accept that Lebanon needed the Syrian army for "stability." The Syrian-Lebanese security apparatus of the 1990s repressed a civil society that was recovering momentum in the late 1980s. Damascus also encouraged divisiveness among the Lebanese as a control tactic. The argument that the Lebanese are wild people ready to fly at each other, requiring a disciplinary hand, is insulting, caricatures the war period, ignores the lessons taken on board by 1990, and is reminiscent of French mandatory tutelage. Third, I believe that Syria constricted Lebanon's reconstruction. Without Syrian hegemony, reconstruction would have proceeded more exuberantly, with enthusiastic Diaspora participation, less leakage of investment, and more foreign financial support. An independent Lebanon, reviving as a regional hub, would have been in an incomparably stronger position to mobilize international pressure against Israeli occupation. In sum, Ba'thist Syria stole fifteen years from the Lebanese people.

I am indebted to my publisher, Markus Wiener, for encouraging me to work on the new edition. I am also most grateful to Susie Lorand for her usual excellent editing, to Cheryl Fink for formatting and the imaginative cover design, to Diana Conway for publicity, and to

Professors Bernard Lewis and Andras Hamori for their backing as series editors. At the University of Otago I thank Professors Marian Simms and Rick Garside for their support. Finally, my wife and sons have been tolerant, as ever, of my writing diversions, with almost simultaneous second editions of both this book and *The Levant*.

Dunedin, November 2005

ACKNOWLEDGEMENTS

This book is the product of twelve years of experiences of Lebanon and the Lebanese, through a large part of Lebanon's war period and the unhappy aftermath. These experiences began in 1983–84 when I first visited Beirut as the recipient of a Rockefeller Foundation post-doctoral "international relations" fellowship. My thanks therefore go first to the Rockefeller Foundation for enabling me to establish the involvements that have finally led to this book.

I lived in Lebanon through much of the mid- and late 1980s, including more than a year as an academic staff member at the Haigazian University College, and otherwise as a visitor from the School of Advanced International Studies, Johns Hopkins University; Exeter University; and the Australian Defence Force Academy, University of New South Wales. My appreciation goes to all four of these institutions for facilitating my research interests in the Levant.

In Lebanon I have made many friends from all the major communities. They have contributed to my knowledge and appreciation of a country that has become, through them, part of my life. I particularly wish to mention the support, open-heartedness, and hospitality of Farid al-Khazen, Georges and Muna Assaf, Wa'il Kheir, Nabil Beydoun, Michael and Élise Bacos-Young, Joseph and Françoise Sfeir, Lionel Ghurra, Marc and Muna Ghurra, François and Joumana Kamar, Naji Aoude, Melhem Chaoul, Habib Malik, Ghassan Salameh, the Kaoukji and Na'amani families in Ra's Beirut, the Aramounis in Brumana, and the Chamouns in Zahla. I thank Michel Aoun, Faruq Abilama', Muhammad Beydoun, Asa'ad Germanos, Charles Ghustin, Salim al-Huss, Karam Rizq, Étienne Saqr, Elie Salem, Akram Shuhayyib, Ghassan Siblani, and Jubran Tuwayni for giving their time to talk with me. I am also indebted to the kindness of Wilma Cholokian of the Haigazian University College, Bulos Na'aman of Université Saint-Esprit, David Hirst of the *Guardian* newspaper, Francis Gallagher and Janet Hancock of the British Foreign Office, Antonio Pitol—Venezuelan Ambassador to Lebanon, Nadim Shehadi and Fida Nasrallah of the Centre for Lebanese Studies in Oxford, Magne Mikalsen, George Mead, and the late Dani Chamoun, whose tragic death in 1990 was a great loss to Lebanon.

In the Eastern Mediterranean beyond Lebanon, I have received vital assistance for my work on this book. I am especially grateful to the Dayan Center of Tel Aviv University for permission to use material from my annual chapters on Lebanon in the Middle East Contemporary Survey, 1988–95, and to my friends at the Dayan Center for their encouragement and for access to their unrivalled collection of primary sources in Arabic and Hebrew. In Israel, I thank Itamar Rabinovich, Asher Susser, Martin Kramer, Ami Ayalon, Amira Margalith, Edna Liftman, Haim Gal, and Uri Lubrani for their time and assistance. I acknowledge the hospitality of Richard Harper and John Woodhead at the British School of Archaeology in Jerusalem, the Grossman family in Ramat Gan, Ora and Irv Kaplan in Ramat Aviv, and Stuart Swiny and Vathoulla Moustoukki at the Cyprus-American Archaeological Research Institute in Nicosia.

The major part of the book was written while I was on leave in 1995–96. I had a pleasant and useful interlude in the United Kingdom in August 1995, for which I thank Tim Niblock and Gerald Blake at Durham University, and Donald and Pamela Richards in Oxford. Thereafter I was at the Near Eastern Studies Department of Princeton University, between September 1995 and February 1996.

At Princeton I am indebted above all to Bernard Lewis, whose advice and support has been indispensable to the publication of my work. I am very appreciative to Heath Lowry and the faculty and staff of the Near Eastern Studies Department for providing a most congenial environment for myself and my family. Sincere thanks are due to my publisher, Markus Wiener, for taking a very special personal interest in the book, and to Susie Lorand and Cheryl Fink, for their superb and painstaking efforts in the editorial and production work.

I finished the book on return to the University of Otago Geography Department. At Otago, I would like to acknowledge Brian Heenan and Ann Trotter for their help with funding, Peter Holland for his valuable suggestions as a tireless reader of the manuscript, and Bill Mooney for converting my tracings into beautiful maps. I also thank *al-Hayat*, *al-Safir*, and *Ha'aretz* newspapers for permission to use cartoons as detailed in the text, and Boris Kremer, Simon Bell, Dani Sfeir, and Travis Benson for help with photography.

The final comment must be reserved for my wife 'Afife, for my wife's family in Lebanon, and for Chris, Adam, and Hadi. They have been very tolerant, and have kept me going through the months of writing.—*University of Otago, Dunedin, New Zealand, August 1996.*

LEBANON AND THE WORLD

In 1991 a new word, "Libanisation," formally entered the French language, defined in Larousse as "processus de fragmentation d'un État, résultant de l'affrontement entre diverses communautés" [process of fragmentation of a state, as a result of confrontation between diverse communities]. The dictionary observed that the term "is tending to replace 'balkanisation.'" In 1994, after the Larousse definition was reiterated, a brief note in Lebanon's pre-eminent newspaper, *al-Nahar*, reported the annoyance of senior Lebanese religious personalities that their country should be the exemplar for the turbulence afflicting multicommunal states after the Cold War, most prominently in the former "Eastern Bloc."[1] "Libanisation" and its English equivalent, "Lebanonization," entered circulation at the end of the 1980s, when Lebanon was experiencing a severe outburst of violence and, with "national" governments on the two sides of Beirut, seemed to be facing official disintegration. In the media, this was of course dwarfed by the collapse of the Soviet Union and the changes in Eastern Europe, but the West's perspectives regarding the nationalist, ethnic, and sectarian outbreaks in these vast territories were influenced by interpretation of the long-running Lebanese crisis. Hélène Carrère d'Encausse's fine study, *The End of the Soviet Empire*,[2] published in 1990, referred to the "Lebanonization of the Caucasus" in analyzing the clash of Christian Armenians with Shi'i Muslim Azeris for command of the Armenian Nogorno-Karabakh enclave in Azerbaijan.

Why did the difficulties of a country as small as Lebanon, containing a collection of sectarian groups whose preoccupations would seemed to have little relevance beyond Lebanon's immediate neighbor-

1

hood, make sufficient impact in Europe and North America to spawn generic terminology for a major post–Cold War security issue? After all, even during the period in which Soviet military might "froze" the latent nationalisms of much of Eurasia, Lebanon was only one of many countries in which ethnic, communal, or sectarian loyalties sapped the legitimacy of the established order. The reason for Lebanon's high profile lay in a combination of Lebanon's singularity as a state, the fate of Beirut, which by the 1960s had become the "world-city" of the Middle East, and the attention drawn to the Eastern Mediterranean as a result of the creation of Israel, the Arab-Israeli conflict, the Palestinian issue, and Western concerns about Persian Gulf oil.

Among the independent states comprising the Arab world in the mid-twentieth century, Lebanon stood alone because of its Christian presidency, the high proportion of non-Muslims in its population (in the 1950s and 60s still about 50% if Druze are added to Christians), its Arab-Western cultural dualism, and the peculiarity of its so-called confessional democracy, which enabled the commercial and rural upper class to maintain control of the state. When the combination of internal complexities and external pressures made Lebanon a war theatre in the mid-1970s, the country possessed all the necessary features to make a high-profile impact on the West. The June 1967 and October 1973 Arab-Israeli wars already ensured a global fixation on Eastern Mediterranean affairs, and in this context Lebanon lay between the two regional powers—Israel and Syria—and provided the main base from which armed Palestinian organizations provoked the Israelis. Lebanon also presented itself as the pre-eminent meeting ground of Christendom and Islam in the Middle East, the refuge for all the radical and opposition movements of the region, and the chief cultural bridgehead of the West in the Arab world. This was a unique and explosive mixture.

Perhaps nowhere else in the world were so many cultural and political contradictions evident in such a small space as in the Lebanon of the 1970s. Three million people of seventeen officially recognized Christian, Islamic, and Islamic-derived communities inhabited a mere 4,000 square miles of largely mountainous topogra-

2

phy. Beyond the level of family, clan, and village, these communities were the primary focus of identity for the population, which was highly differentiated despite the Arab ethnicity and Arabic language of the overwhelming majority. No single sect numbered more than a third of the population, and three "great" communities from two religions each had a proportion of more than 20%—the Maronite Christians and the Sunni and Shi'i Muslims. This alone, even without all Lebanon's other particularities, was a highly unusual circumstance.

Lebanon's greatest contradiction, however, lay in its construction as a twentieth-century territorial state. The notion of a distinctive Mount Lebanon began life as an assertion of Druze and Maronite identity in Sunni Islamic surrounds, but in the nineteenth century the increasingly dominant Maronite Christians appropriated it as a vehicle for Maronite nationalist ideology. The concept meant little to the Sunnis, Shi'is, and Orthodox Christians incorporated into the expanded "Lebanon" established after the First World War by the French mandatory regime. Maronite nationalism, which integrated the long-standing communal consciousness of the Maronite Christian peasant population of Mount Lebanon with nineteenth-century ideas in favor of a Maronite-dominated polity, could never be a suitable foundation for the Lebanese state that emerged in the 1920s.

Only political pluralism, with each of the major communities feeling that it had a fair role in the country's identity and management, could make the new Lebanon acceptable to the bulk of its people. Nonetheless, Maronite leaders were determined to have political supremacy. In consequence, the Lebanese state amalgamated the outward form of political pluralism, most notably a sectarian carve-up of the cabinet, parliament, and bureaucracy, with the inner reality of primacy for the Maronite segment of the high bourgeoisie, which held the presidency and several strategic civilian and military posts. The rest of the upper class, especially the Sunni Muslims, received enough of a share in the spoils to be willing to provide cover for this state of affairs. In the first three decades of Lebanon's independence, from 1943 to 1975, the relationship of the Maronites to Lebanon resembled that of the Serbs to Yugoslavia or of the Russians to the Soviet Union, despite the differences in social structures and political philosophies. Demographic change and rising political awareness in the population from the 1950s onwards, especially with respect to Shi'i Muslims, challenged the Maronites, the Sunnis, and the high bourgeoisie, and guaranteed political instability.

Much of Lebanon's global impact in the periods before and after the collapse of civil order in 1975 related to the status, characteristics, and fate of Beirut, for which the rest of the country had become an appendage or extended suburb by the 1960s. Through the nineteenth century, after Bonaparte's incursion into the Eastern Mediterranean inaugurated European interventions in the Middle East unprecedented since the Crusades, Mount Lebanon's large Christian population and special ties with Western Europe assisted Beirut to develop from a minor port into the foremost link between the West and the "Mashraq"—the Arab East.

On this foundation, Beirut became the commercial and intellectual capital of the Arab world in the mid-twentieth century—a unique blend of the West and the Middle East, of Christendom and Islam. The combination of independent Lebanon's open political system, liberal capitalist economy, and spectacular landscape made Beirut a magnet for money, vacationers, and political refugees. In these respects, Beirut towered above the rest of the Arab world, the more so as other Arab countries fell under repressive authoritarian regimes.

A further ingredient in Beirut's ascent was the wealth of the Persian Gulf oil states. In the 1960s, the Arab states of the Gulf viewed Beirut as an effective, secure financial and services center, and valued Lebanon as a conservative state in an increasingly radical region—some of the same features that elevated Beirut and Lebanon in the mind of the West.

The glitter and cosmopolitanism that made Beirut a "world city" was, however, only one face of an extraordinary metropolis. Beirut's economic dynamism concealed the depressed condition of much of rural Lebanon, and stimulated a continuing population shift toward the capital. The new migrants of the 1950s and 60s were Muslim and Christian, although with an ever-growing Shi'i component, and they shared a hostility toward the high bourgeoisie which urban experience

4

only intensified. Beirut's suburbs, from the Maronite petit bourgeois concentrations of the east to the Shi'i "belt of misery" that grew from nothing to an encircling mass in a mere two decades, seethed with envy, grievance, and political radicalism. Two non-Lebanese elements exacerbated these dangerous conditions: the Palestinian refugee camps, centers of political mobilization in the 1960s, and the transient underclass of Syrian poor, a reserve labor pool that helped maintain an unemployment rate of at least 20% and kept wages low while prices soared. The high bourgeoisie took no heed of "street" discontents and, with the intrusion of the Arab-Israeli conflict after 1967, catastrophe became inevitable.

Beirut's descent into fifteen years of wars, militias, and sectarian fragmentation coincided with an important transition in world history. When Lebanon entered its long nightmare in the early 1970s, competition between the U.S. and the Soviet Union, secular ideologies, and the "balance of nuclear terror" dominated global geopolitics. The confessional conflicts of such places as Beirut and Belfast, in Northern Ireland, seemed secondary and archaic. When Lebanon's "second republic" began to emerge from the dust and rubble in the early 1990s, the Cold War had ended and an Islamic "challenge" supposedly complicated the new global hegemony of the capitalist West. Beirut's experience of state collapse, warlords, and militarized cantonization was being repeated in many places—Somalia, Angola, Liberia, Algeria, Iraq, Central Asia, and Yugoslavia. Such phenomena came out of the Cold War "icebox" as the chief geopolitical concern of the world community.

In the 1980s, metropolitan Beirut was a patchwork of militia jurisdictions, under the command of warlords who alternately fought and collaborated with one another. These warlords, from various social backgrounds, scorned the traditional political class, which still exerted influence through what survived of the state machine. The militias were blatantly sectarian and, through much grief and strife, compartmentalized the population into artificial homelands of religious communities. For the outside world Beirut demonstrated the fate of a great modern city if government agencies lost control. It warned of the aftermath of nuclear war or the ultimate implications of

5

social breakdown, and it conjured up images of the European Middle Ages.

Beirut's militia nerve-centers and fortresses—the *majlis al-harbi* ("war council") compound of the Christian "Lebanese Forces," the Junblatt family home in Wat' al-Musaytba for the Druze, and the Hizballah strongholds in the southern suburbs—constituted a modern version of the urban civil wars of Renaissance Italy. Lauro Martines, a leading historian of the Italian city states, observes that "the velocity of social change proved to be too much for harmonious development . . . As visual drama . . . the deadly competition among hostile blocs was best expressed by the soaring fortresses belonging to noble families."[3] The similar military functions of the ninety-seven-meter-high Asinella tower of medieval Bologna and the thirty-floor Murr tower of wartime West Beirut illustrated the family resemblance of the warring factions of twelfth-century Bologna and late-twentieth-century Beirut.

Lebanon's sectarian strife and temporary cantonization at a time of global transition, when it attracted attention as an extreme case of regime breakdown immediately before such cases multiplied across Eurasia, invited the coining of words like "Lebanonization." In the 1980s, Lebanon also featured prominently in another phenomenon that made a sensational impact in the West—Islamic radicalism and an associated surge of terrorism against Westerners and Western targets. Impulses from the new Islamic revolutionary regime in Shi'i Iran affected the Lebanese Shi'i community at a time when it was particularly susceptible to religious fundamentalism, when Shi'is were fed up with lack of access to power and disillusioned with leftist ideologies. Israel's incompetent handling of its relations with the Shi'is during its 1982–85 occupation of most of Southern Lebanon also boosted the Islamic radicals.

Events in Lebanon demonstrated both the ability of Islamic radical organizations to transfix Western politicians and media, and the practical limitations of a mode of thinking that had only minority support in its own milieu and lacked serious answers to the problems of a multicommunal society. Hizballah, the "Party of God," became the most potent political force among Lebanese Shi'is by the late 1980s. It represented the principal extension of the Iranian revolution in the

Arab world, posed a more bothersome military irritation for the Israelis than the Palestinians had been before 1982, and achieved household word status in the West through suicide bombings and seizure of Westerners as hostages. Incidents attributed to Hizballah or splinter groups extended from the 1983 demolitions of the U.S. embassy and U.S. Marine compound in Beirut through the kidnappings of almost two dozen American and European civilians in the mid-1980s to two huge car bomb explosions in Buenos Aires in the early 1990s.

For years, the word "Lebanon" held special dread for Western immigration officials and the security services of Western and Middle Eastern states—"Lebanon" signified a black hole of destruction, extremism and terror. Lebanese Shi'is, as migrants and travellers, had to put up with suspicion and harrassment, particularly from the Sunni-dominated Arab oil states of the Gulf.

However, despite its international bogeyman image, Hizballah could manage only a limited impact on Lebanon's affairs. It had nothing to offer the non-Shi'i two-thirds of Lebanon's population, and its impact within the Shi'i community owed more to the regime's scandalous neglect of the poor and Israeli bombardments than to the party's own attractions. By the 1990s, Hizballah was forced to the conclusion that it could not continue to defy Lebanon's cosmopolitan reality, and that it should find itself a niche within the political system if it wished to avoid suffocating in a largely hostile environment. Party leaders denied any ambition to impose an Iranian-style Islamic state, a central component of Hizballah's February 1985 program, sought dialogue with Christian religious personalities, and prepared for the prospect of having to coexist with Arab-Israeli peace arrangements. These adjustments suggested vulnerability and hardly marked Hizballah as a harbinger of the sort of collision between Islam and the West—a "next world war"—hypothesized in Samuel Huntington's "Clash of Civilizations?"[4]

Some of the new "Beiruts" of the 1990s—Algiers, Sarajevo, and Grozny—lay along the "fault line" separating Huntington's Islamic, Western, and Orthodox civilizations, a rough division of cultural zones running through the Mediterranean from end to end, bisecting the Balkans and cutting across the Caucasus and Central Asia. However, as bitter strife in Afghanistan, Pakistan, Georgia, Azerbaijan, Kurdistan, southern Iraq, the Yemen, and Croatia—not to mention Lebanon, Bosnia, and Algeria themselves—indicated, cleavages within Islam and conflicts among non-Muslims in the neighborhood of Huntington's "fault line" were just as pronounced as any "clash of civilizations." Lebanon's breakdown and warfare involved all these features, and if the term "Lebanonization" is to mean anything, it should warn against superficial generalization.

Huntington's "fault line" could be more usefully characterized as a huge zone of mosaic cultures, where modern territorial states have only poorly represented the underlying pattern of identities. Judeo-Christian and Islamic civilizations both originated in this zone, which in modern times has experienced an interpenetration of Western and Islamic influences that makes any "clash of civilizations" more a series of civil wars within *Dar al-Islam* than a showdown between Islam and the West. This zone also experienced the splintering of both Christendom and Islam into a bewildering variety of sects, causing widespread tensions.

Three religious orientations have been promoted by competing local imperial powers since the rise of Islam in the seventh century: Orthodox Christianity by Byzantium, Sunni Islam by a succession of authorities from the Umayyads to the Ottomans, and variants of Shi'i Islam by the Fatimids in Egypt and the Safavids in Iran. Within their territories, these empires tended to take a hard line against rival versions of their own faiths. The Byzantines adopted a hostile stance regarding Monophysites, Maronites, Armenians, and the Western Catholic "barbarians" of the Crusader period, hostility that was returned with interest, and the Sunni Muslim empires barely tolerated or vigorously persecuted Shi'i Muslims of whatever variety, an animosity that was also liberally reciprocated. From the eighteenth century onwards, some sectarian differences were sharpened by the interventions of several European powers in the Ottoman Empire. Habsburg and Russian power play in the Balkans emphasized Christian/Muslim and Catholic/Orthodox distinctions, and general European influence in the Eastern Mediterranean advantaged local

Christians in relation to Sunni Muslims and others, for example the Druze in Mount Lebanon.

Lebanon's late-twentieth-century crisis reflected this historical legacy, as well as developments such as the Franco-Maronite creation of Greater Lebanon, divergent demographic trends between communities, and the clash between Western secular ideologies and Islamism. Indeed, the same sort of background, with local variety, characterized the three most fractured subregions of the Mediterranean and Southwest Asia—the Levant, the Balkans, and the Caucasus. The local and external inputs into the tensions of these areas have been so intertwined that it is difficult to define anything as purely local or purely external, and the messiness of an interpenetration of civilizations seems the best way to conceive of the local jostlings. For example, the bulk of Bosnian Muslims have made clear their primary commitment to a European identity and their lack of interest in the sort of Islam represented by Iran or Saudi Arabia. Similarly, most Lebanese Muslims, through their lifestyles and political outlooks, have indicated unwillingness to be regimented by Shi'i or Sunni fundamentalism.

A study of the historical background of Lebanon's crisis, as well as the elaboration of the crisis itself, can serve to illuminate the conflicts of identity and interests more generally involved in the nationalist, ethnic, and sectarian assertions that assumed such prominence in the post–Cold War world. The fact that Lebanon's story is a particularly rich and varied tapestry, encompassing sectarianism and class conflict, secularism and religious radicalism, Islam and Christendom, the Orient and the West, Sunni and Shi'i, Israel and the Arabs and much else besides, makes it possible to draw many parallels with other places and contexts. The Lebanese "prototype" contained most of the elements of the newer crises of state viability in the 1990s, whether the collision of Westernism and Islamic revivalism in Algeria or the complex disintegration of Yugoslavia. Also, at least at the level of media generalization, "Lebanonization" had reasonable applicability in characterizing the factionalism of Georgia and other conflicts on the margins of the former Soviet Union.

Exploration of the similarities and divergences between Lebanon and Bosnia-Herzegovina, for example, might help in more general interpretation of problems of cohesion in multicommunal states in the post–Cold War era. Both cases entail communal differentiation into Christian and Muslim groups, absence of a dominant majority, effective cantonization, and intense external involvement. Sarajevo appears to mirror Beirut as a cultural mélange and a communally fractured city. In both cases particular personalities played critical roles, but in different ways: in Lebanon the social insensitivity of upper-class politicians, mainly Christians, contributed to a poisonous interaction of communal and class divisions over several decades; in Bosnia-Herzegovina, Serbian and Croat nationalisms were heated up in little more than a year by the posturings of the leaders of Serbia and Croatia. More broadly, the fact that Yugoslavia's semi-socialist order and Lebanon's liberal capitalism incubated similar crises is very instructive.

As for external interference, in both cases outside powers were involved in the collapse of order and the evolution of the crises. In particular, Syria's ambitions, strategic interests, and manipulative links with local parties in Lebanon might be compared with the plans and performances of Serbia and Croatia in Bosnia. As regards more distant powers, limited understanding led to unhappy outcomes—for example, European tinkerings in Yugoslavia in 1991–92, or the U.S.-sponsored Multi National Force in Lebanon in 1983. Otherwise, however, the roles of Serbia, Croatia, Russia, the E.C., the U.N., and NATO in Bosnia diverged significantly from the involvements of Syria, Israel, the Palestinians, the U.S., and Arab states in Lebanon.

The most noteworthy aspect of the Lebanese example—which its Bosnian counterpart appears to share—is that, fifteen years after domestic warfare ended, Lebanon's crisis has evolved rather than being resolved. Syrian interference in Iraq after the Anglo-American toppling of Saddam Husayn in 2003, and strategic errors in Lebanon in 2004, created conditions in which the international community and most Lebanese turned against Syria's post-1990 command of Lebanon. Syria withdrew from Lebanon in bad grace, Syrian-Lebanese relations entered a rancorous new phase, and a new sectarian dispute loomed, with many Shi'is having a different perspective on events from the rest of the population. Shi'is continued to feel that their influence did not reflect their weight, with the difference that, through the 1990s and into the new century, they were joined by the Maronites in this grievance. Hilal Khashan's 1992 study of the "Lebanese confessional mind,"[5] based on a postwar survey of student attitudes, uncovered continuing antipathy in intercommunal relations.

Faces of Lebanon: Context and structure of analysis

The main purpose of this book is to interpret the origins, nature and fate of the Lebanese state and society which emerged in their modern form during French mandatory rule in the Levant after 1920. The dominant theme is that of the interrelations of an extraordinary conglomeration of communities in Mount Lebanon and its surrounds (maps 1 and 4). The working out of these interrelations is relevant for all multicommunal societies.

A Lebanese entity initially took shape in the sixteenth century, in a tentative manner, as the local autonomy of Druze lords in Mount Lebanon. It reflected the laxity of Ottoman Turkish authority in a rural periphery of difficult topography. The Ottoman state tolerated such autonomy, on the part of rural leading families and its own provincial governors, as long as it received the required tax revenues and acknowledgement of its suzerainty.

The autonomy of Mount Lebanon became particularly well established because it embodied a unique combination of the independent-mindedness of a group of semi-feudal landlords with the autonomous will of two compact sectarian communities—the Druze and the Maronite Catholics. It was also buttressed from the outset by the connections of the Maronites, as the principal Catholic presence in the Eastern Mediterranean, with Western Europe—with the Vatican, France, and the Italian city states. A lasting viability was assured at the end of the sixteenth century by the powerful leadership of the Druze Amir Fakhr al-Din, who strengthened the European linkage and extended his rule beyond the coastal mountains. Although Fakhr al-

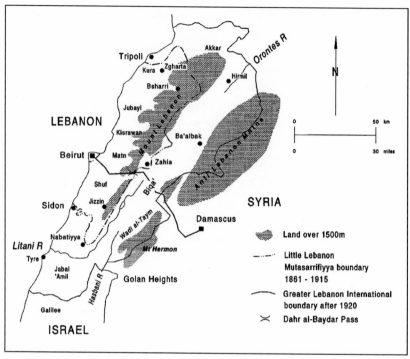

Map 1. Mount Lebanon, Little Lebanon, Greater Lebanon

Din overreached himself, and alarmed the Ottoman government into deposing him, the sociopolitical framework that became consolidated during his control of Mount Lebanon endured as the *imara* (emirate or "principality") of the Ma'n and Shihab families.

From the late eighteenth century on, the original Druze-Maronite symbiosis, with Druze primacy, was disrupted by increasing Maronite political assertion, based on demographic growth and advantages derived by Christians from nineteenth-century European penetration. This assertion also destabilized Mount Lebanon's feudal social system, a family network of Druze and Maronite landlords headed by the Shihab "princes," because it came from two elements outside the traditional leadership—the Maronite church and peasantry. Peasant sentiment shifted from feudal allegiances to Maronite communal identification, and Druze sectarian feeling strengthened in response.

12

In the mid-nineteenth century both the *imara* and the old social order collapsed in the midst of violent Druze-Maronite confrontations and Ottoman and European interventions. Mount Lebanon's autonomy survived—the Europeans, especially the French, checkmated Ottoman maneuvers to impose direct rule—but it mutated from a coterie of Druze and Maronite leading families into a pluralist association of sectarian communities. This second version of "Lebanon," formulated in 1861, had defined boundaries and was termed the *mutasarrifiyya,* or Sanjak of Mount Lebanon. It gave the Druze security and a measure of political participation, but its communal pluralism only mildly tempered the Maronite political ascent, which was grounded in the demographic and economic realities of the late nineteenth century.

Many Maronites conceived the *mutasarrifiyya* as the basis for an independent Lebanon that would be a Christian bastion and an outpost of Western Europe in the Middle East. Even those who recoiled from such isolationism and visualized Lebanon as a "bridge" between the West and the Middle East in practice advanced communal pluralism to mask Christian supremacy. The First World War, the demise of the Ottomans, and French and British hegemony in the Eastern Mediterranean provided the opportunity for the Maronites to get what they wanted.

In 1920, France promoted a third "Lebanon," referred to as "Grand Liban" or Greater Lebanon to distinguish it from the smaller territory of the *mutasarrifiyya.* Vigorously lobbied by Maronite and supporting interests, the French extended Lebanon's boundaries in all directions, to include almost the entire physiographic complex of the Lebanon and Anti-Lebanon mountains, with the intervening trench of the Biqa'. Maronite politicians aimed for an economically viable entity, with ports and wider agricultural possibilities, incorporating outlying Christian populations. However, the advent of Greater Lebanon also transformed the communal make-up of the Lebanese entity from the simplicity of a solid Maronite and Christian majority with a Druze minority and small Shi'i and Sunni presences into an intricate sectarian conglomerate. The new country incorporated Sunni and Shi'i Muslims numbering more than 40% of its population. Greater Lebanon was a Maronite concept for Maronite purposes but it was also a multicom-

Lebanon between Israel and Syria
(Ze'ev in *Ha'aretz,* 19 July 1993)

munal entity the majority of whose people did not share either the concept or the purposes. This book examines how such a contradiction affected the development of the modern Lebanese state, and how Greater Lebanon, despite its initial artificiality, did eventually come to mean something—not necessarily the same thing—to all its communities.

The book consists of three parts. Part One considers the fundamentals of Lebanon's geopolitical environment and sectarian and social composition. These comprise the underlying circumstances of the country's history and modern existence. First, it will be shown how Lebanon's topography, location, and population geography have influenced external involvements as well as local sectarian interactions. Second, Lebanon's deep problems of national identity and state legitimacy cannot be analyzed without assessing sectarian and class differentiation. Third, much of Lebanon's story is the story of its families and

The Lebanese and their regime
(Yasin al-Khalil in *al-Safir,* 15 January 1994)

clans and the changing orientations of its elite. Lebanon's evolution since the 1920s has depended on the maneuverings of its high bourgeoisie, and on the relationship of leading families to their sectarian communities.

Part Two discusses the fortunes of Greater Lebanon from the 1920s to the temporary disintegration and cantonization of the 1980s. It examines the slow coming together of high bourgeois elements in Greater Lebanon, and the successful establishment in the 1940s of the political framework of an independent state, a framework that was maintained with increasing difficulty in the face of socioeconomic change and unfavorable developments in Lebanon's Middle Eastern surrounds. By the 1970s, in a context of poor leadership and external interference, the political system could no longer contain the destabilizing consequences of social and sectarian discontent and shifting demographic balances.

Some of the factors in the temporary foundering of Greater Lebanon between 1975 and 1990 can be related to other crises of state viability, but others are specific to Lebanon and its Eastern Mediterranean context, making the formulation of "lessons" a treacherous enterprise. Interpretation of Lebanon's war in chapters 5 and 6 attempts to give new perspectives, as I believe that the impact of the Israeli and American interventions of the early 1980s has been exaggerated, whereas the economic collapse and declining popular toleration of militias in the mid-1980s, crucial for the dénouement of the war after 1988, have received inadequate attention.

Part Three analyzes Lebanon's affairs in the transformed global circumstances since the end of the Cold War. Ironically, as nationalist, ethnic, and sectarian problems in the old Eastern Bloc came out of the "icebox," Lebanon was subjected to imposed stabilization and an effort to downplay its unresolved crisis of identity, sectarian relationships, and socioeconomic imbalances. After General Michel Aoun's ill-fated bid to break the constraints of sectarianism and external pressures brought a final round of Lebanon's war in 1989–90, the country sank into torpor under Syrian overlordship.

PART ONE

Elements
of Lebanon

Roman ruins, Ba'albak, 1995

CHAPTER ONE

LAND AND GEOPOLITICS

From the Romans to the Ottomans

Mount Lebanon and its surrounds (map 1) have had a distinctive geopolitical significance since the Islamic conquest of most of the Eastern Mediterranean in the seventh century. Between the advent of Islam and the incursion of the Western European Crusaders in the eleventh century, modern Lebanon's mountains acquired their multisectarian demography and assumed strategic salience in regional power play.

A new Eastern Mediterranean world took shape when Islam burst out of Arabia and Byzantium retreated into Anatolia, with new patterns of religious and political differentiation. Through the first five centuries of the common era, under Roman and Byzantine rule, the region was under a single political authority. The zone of conflict between empires was generally in Mesopotamia, removed from the Mediterranean littoral. Also, as long as the Mediterranean basin remained a "Roman lake," no challenge to the regional order could come from the sea. In these circumstances Mount Lebanon had no more geopolitical relevance than Appalachia in the present-day U.S.

The great regional upheaval inaugurated by the Byzantine-Persian war of 605–628, which involved military movements unprecedented for centuries and opened the way for the Islamic takeover of Syria in the 630s, changed everything. The new Islamic empires of the Umayyads and the 'Abassids confronted Byzantium on a sea front that encompassed the whole Eastern Mediterranean, and a land front that fluctuated between Anatolia and northern Syria. Mount Lebanon commanded the central part of the Syrian coast and complicated access from the interior to the sea. The Umayyads introduced Persian Muslim settlers and the 'Abassids maintained Beirut as a major coastal garrison.[6] In later 'Abassid times the threat of Byzantine naval raids increased as Byzantium revived as a military power between the eighth and tenth centuries.

As for the land fronts, Mount Lebanon was at first relatively deep in undivided Muslim-dominated territory. This situation, however, proved ephemeral. In the tenth century, the central part of *Dar al-Islam* (the Islamic domain) fragmented between the Isma'ili Shi'i Fatimids, based in Egypt, and the 'Abassids and Seljuq Turks, based in Mesopotamia. The boundary zone fluctuated, but Mount Lebanon was usually part of it or close to it. In the tenth century Byzantine encroachment southwards put Mount Lebanon between Christian and Muslim powers as well as near an Islamic dividing line. In 975 the great Byzantine general John Tzimisces led an expedition as far as Caesarea, making a brief appearance in Beirut. Thereafter the Emperor Basil II (976–1025) maintained a strong Byzantine presence in the Orontes valley, immediately north of Mount Lebanon, and decisive Byzantine recession did not occur until the 1070s, not long before the Western Crusader arrival.

Mount Lebanon represented a buffer territory between the Fatimids and Byzantines (map 2), and both powers were generally too absorbed in their court intrigues to be bothered with extending effective authority into this area. The situation had important demographic consequences. In the late tenth century, after 350 years of Islamic rule, the majority of Mount Lebanon's people were heterodox Muslims, chiefly Twelver Shi'is. Orthodox Christians coexisted with Sunni Muslims in the coastal towns, and Maronite Christians occupied the higher mountain reaches of the far north. This pattern changed during the eleventh century. Believers in the divine status of the sixth Fatimid caliph, al-Hakim, came to the southern part of the mountain in the 1020s, fleeing into the fringe of *Dar al-Islam* to escape Fatimid persecution in Egypt after the disappearance of al-Hakim in 1021. Their followers became the Druze community, replacing Shi'is in several districts. At about the same time, the Maronites were reinforced by Maronite populations shifting south out of the

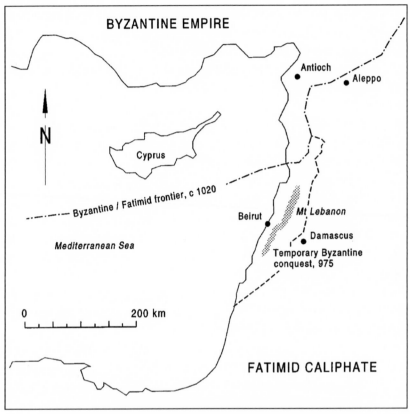

Map 2. The Byzantine-Fatimid Frontier at the time of the
Emperor Basil II (976–1025)
*Adapted from Chris Scarre, ed., The Times Atlas of Medieval Civilizations
(London: The Times, 1990)*

Orontes valley, where the Byzantines were hounding them as heretics.
Mount Lebanon's Twelver Shi'is became squeezed between the
Maronites and the Druze, and the scene was set for the multisectarian
interactions of the following millenium.

The next phase began with the defeat of the Emperor Romanus IV
by the Seljuq Turks at Manzikert in 1071. Decades of vicious factionalism in Constantinople after the death of Basil II, documented in

Michael Psellus's *Fourteen Byzantine Rulers*, had finally reaped their reward. As the Fatimids were themselves in decline, the last decades of the eleventh century saw a virtual power vacuum in Syria. The Seljuqs were preoccupied in Anatolia and Mesopotamia, and between Antioch and Palestine, where weakening Fatimid authority persisted, several smaller Islamic principalities jostled for precedence. Theoretically, Mount Lebanon and its neighborhood came under the rule of the Amirs of Tripoli and Damascus, as well as Fatimid suzerainty. Nahr al-Kalb (the Dog river), immediately north of Beirut, served as the Tripoli-Fatimid boundary. In practice, the Maronites, Shi'is, and Druze of the hills did as they pleased. The rulers were mainly concerned with the trade and taxes of the ports and fertile coastlands. However, the geopolitical vacuum in Syria, a wealthy region crossed by significant trade routes and located between major contemporary powers, could not continue.

Change came from an unexpected direction, certainly from the perspective of the local peoples. The shock to Byzantium at Manzikert and appeals to Western Christendom eventually brought an army of Crusaders to Constantinople in 1098. Because to relieve Eastern Christians was unviable as a rallying-call in Western Europe, where the "Greeks" were either unknown or disliked, the First Crusade had been assembled to restore Jerusalem to Christian control and for the more conventional attractions of plunder en route. Since the seventh century, Byzantium had not shown much interest in Jerusalem—Basil II could easily have seized it but never felt moved to do so—but the predatory tendencies of the Western "barbarians" ensured that the Emperor Alexius Comnenus was anxious to help them reach the Levant and leave Byzantine territory. The Emperor's daughter Anna noted: "The Latin race at all times is unusually greedy for wealth."[7] To Byzantine surprise, the Crusaders promptly overran the Eastern Mediterranean coastlands from Antioch to Gaza, capturing Jerusalem in 1099. Mount Lebanon's geopolitical status was immediately elevated, as it became the central part of the Crusader alignment facing the Muslims of the Syrian interior.

The Crusaders received their introduction to Mount Lebanon on their coastal march to Jerusalem. The Amir of Tripoli, adept at maneuvering between the Fatimids and Seljuqs, hoped to use the *Franj* (Franks) to rid himself of the Fatimids, and gave them free passage. For their part, the Crusader leaders were impressed with the prosperity of the ports and the fertility of the gardens around Tripoli, Beirut, Sidon, and Tyre.[8] After conquering Palestine, they consolidated their position to the north. Anna Comnena gives a vivid account of the tactics of Raymond of Provence outside Tripoli: "As soon as he arrived, he climbed and seized the summit of the hill which lies opposite the city and which forms a part of the Lebanon; it would serve as a fortress and he could cut off the water flowing down from the Lebanon into Tripolis ... After informing the emperor [Alexius] of these actions, Saint-Gilles [Raymond] asked that a very strong fort should be constructed there before bigger Muslim forces turned up from Chorosan."[9] Raymond's castle survives to the present as the citadel of Tripoli. Tripoli held out until 1105, when a large part of its population was massacred by Crusader troops, and Tyre until 1124.

From the outset, the Crusaders split Mount Lebanon between the County of Tripoli and the Kingdom of Jerusalem (map 3), using the old Fatimid boundary at Nahr al-Kalb. The main Crusader interests involved living off the local economy, overwhelmingly concentrated on the coastal strip, holding the north-south land communications, also along the coast, and preserving the entrepôt at Tyre, with nearby Acre a breakpoint for the trade in spices and other commodities from interior Asia to Europe. Tens of thousands of Frankish and Italian immigrants established themselves in the ports—a temporary intrusion of Latin Catholics among the Muslims and Eastern Christians.

The Crusader interests and presence, almost exclusively on the coast, involved the Mount Lebanon massif to the extent that the interests and presence could not be sustained without command of the coastal mountain range. In contrast to the chain of spectacular castles in the 'Alawi mountains further north—Krak des Chevaliers, Marqab, Sahyun, and others—the Crusaders built fortifications only at the northern and southern extremities of Mount Lebanon.[10] In the north they established the Gibalcar castle in the 'Akkar, to face Krak des Chevaliers across the Homs gap, and in the south they founded the formidable pile of Beaufort and the cliffside outpost of Cave de Tyron,

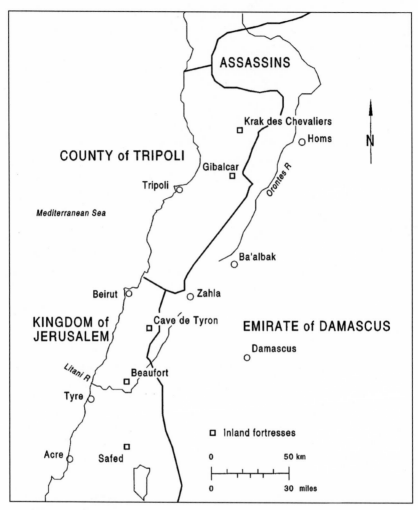

Map 3. The Crusader County of Tripoli and Vicinity, about 1150
Adapted from Marshall, 1994, pp. xii–xiii; Westermann's Großer Atlas zur Weltgeschichte
(Braunschweig: Georg Westermann Verlag, 1966, p. 65.)

above present-day Jizzin, to control the gap at the entrance to the Biqa' from Jabal 'Amil (map 3). Between Jabal 'Amil and the 'Akkar, they relied on the natural mountain wall on the west side of the Biqa', supplemented by observation points and spies. The great trench of the Biqa' served as the frontier between the Crusader states and whoever

24

ruled in Damascus, and the Latins kept to the western margin. The reaction of the mountain communities to their first taste of European Christian domination varied, although the Latins ruled with a light hand and rarely faced any trouble. The Druze stood aloof, the Maronites were split between those for and against a connection with Rome, and the Shi'is divided between quiescence and cooperation.

Although the Crusaders lost Jerusalem and most of the Palestinian interior in 1187, the alignment in the central sector—Mount Lebanon and the county of Tripoli—remained relatively static, despite Muslim incursions and warfare among the Latins themselves, until the second half of the thirteenth century. After defeating the Mongols at Ayn Jalut in 1260, the vigorous new Mamluk state which had replaced the Ayyubid successors of Salah al-Din in Egypt turned its attention to the surviving European territories in the Levant. The Mamluks led a militant resurgence of Sunni Islam, and Crusader collaboration with the Mongols guaranteed an aggressive Muslim riposte.

The Sultan Baybars first dealt with areas north and south of Mount Lebanon—Antioch and the Galilee—using new artillery and siege machines that Crusader fortifications could not withstand.[11] In the process, the Mamluks peeled away the redoubts flanking Mount Lebanon. In the 1260s they captured Safed—the major fortress in the Galilee hills—as well as Beaufort and Cave de Tyron, and in the Homs gap Gibalcar and Krak des Chevaliers fell in 1271. Baybars could not afford to leave these hostile outposts to his rear, across his lines of communication, when he attacked the coastal towns. The Hospitallers used Krak des Chevaliers as a base for raids on Homs and Hama, which was intolerable to Baybars, and Safed and Beaufort represented good forward positions for Muslim offensives against the ports of Acre, Tyre, and Sidon.[12]

After taking Gibalcar, at the extreme northern end of Mount Lebanon, Baybars wrote a letter to the Count of Tripoli, Bohemond VI, describing "how we moved the mangonels [ballistic siege machines] through mountains where the birds have difficulty in establishing their aeries . . . Our yellow banner has taken the place of your red one, and the sound of the church bell has given way to *Allahu akbar.*" Baybars informed Bohemond that "the remnants of your men have been released" to warn "the people of Tripoli . . . that only a little time remains in your lives . . . and to tell your churches and walls that the mangonels send greetings in anticipation of an early encounter."[13]

The Mamluks completed the destruction of the Latin east after Baybars' death, conquering the coastland of Mount Lebanon in the 1280s, including Tripoli in 1289 and finally Acre in 1291. The Latin population either was massacred or fled, in revenge for the atrocities of the First Crusade.

Under the Mamluks, the geopolitical situation of Mount Lebanon resembled that of the Umayyad period—once again deep within an extensive Islamic state, but exposed to sea raids. Through the fourteenth century two issues bothered the Mamluks in Syria—Shi'ism, because they were determined to uphold Islamic orthodoxy, and fear of European mischief-making. These concerns were conflated in Mount Lebanon, where the substantial Twelver Shi'i population of the Kisrawan overlooked a long stretch of the coastal road. European infiltration might be expected among both the Shi'is and the Maronites. After the Crusades, the Maronite clergy had a link with Rome, albeit tenuous, and the Latins kept a strong base in Cyprus.

The Mamluks favored the Druze as agents to help secure the hinterland of the coastal ports, and ignored their heresy as long as it was not openly displayed. The Druze obliged. The Mamluks were conciliatory toward the Maronites, leaving them to the control of their clan leaders, or *muqaddims*. Initial rebelliousness was swiftly defused or quashed. The Twelver Shi'is, however, met the religious zeal of their new rulers with truculence, and the Mamluks sent military expeditions into the Kisrawan in 1299 and 1305. After 1305, the Sultan Nasir brought 300 Turcomans into the Kisrawan as fief-holders, to secure the coast between Beirut and Tripoli. At this time the Mamluks re-established Tripoli in a more defensible site, fortified Beirut, and connected Beirut with Damascus by a line of signal posts as an early warning system.[14]

From the early fourteenth to the late fifteenth century Mount Lebanon did not cause the Mamluks any significant difficulty. In the event, the Europeans made no serious moves, whether from Cyprus or further afield, and the late fifteenth century land frontier with the expanding Ottoman state was distant until the sudden Mamluk collapse in 1516. The Mamluks exploited Druze amenability by cutting timber in the Shuf hills and quartering troops,[15] forcing villagers to destroy the trees to end the visitations. Some Druze became rebellious toward the end of Mamluk rule, but this had no effect on the Ottoman perception of the community as an ally of the Mamluks.

Mount Lebanon, Little Lebanon, Greater Lebanon

Mount Lebanon—The Imara

In 1516, the Ottoman Sultan Selim I reached out of Anatolia to seize the whole territory of the decayed Mamluk state in a single campaign. Mount Lebanon proved a headache for the Ottomans from the first days of their capture of Syria.

The Druze in particular did not adjust readily to the change of authority, mainly because they were immediately subjected to the same religious hostility that the Mamluks had displayed toward Twelver Shi'is. Under the administrative system of millets, whereby Christians and Jews had legal autonomy in personal status matters (most notably marriage, divorce, and inheritance), Druze and Shi'is were required to behave as Sunni Muslims, at the same time as Ottoman religious officials in Damascus and Aleppo excoriated them, even promulgating *fatwas* (legal opinions) inciting the killing of Druze.[16] Such virulence especially characterized the first decades of Ottoman rule in Syria, and the Druze rebelled repeatedly from 1518 to 1585.

For the Ottomans, Mount Lebanon was a security problem in a sensitive location. It abutted the coast, was open to fresh European interest from the sixteenth century on, and was the southern end of a chain of important towns in the Syrian interior—Aleppo, Hama, Homs and Damascus. The inland towns represented a strategically vital axis for Ottoman control of the Eastern Mediterranean, and for land communications with Egypt and the holy cities of Mecca and Medina. Insubordination and foreign penetration directly to the west of this axis could become a strategic threat, and the Ottomans experienced both phenomena in Mount Lebanon through the sixteenth century. The Druze kept up their insurrections for so long in part because of their communal cohesion and the mountainous topography, but even more because the Venetians who controlled Cyprus from 1468 to 1571 supplied them with large quantities of firearms superior in range and caliber to equivalent Ottoman weaponry.[17]

The Ottoman capture of Cyprus in 1571 did not have any noticeable quietening impact on Mount Lebanon, and in 1585 the Ottomans organized a very large force to suppress the Druze. The governor of Egypt, Ibrahim Pasha, gathered contingents from all the eastern provinces of the empire, and after subjugating the Shuf was made chief minister in Istanbul. Mount Lebanon may not have been a "mountain refuge," but it was a tough enough environment with a peculiar enough population in a sufficiently salient location to give it unique strategic prominence in the Ottoman east.

Three conditions underscored this prominence after 1585. First, Ibrahim Pasha's campaign contained rather than stabilized the Druze issue. Frictions persisted, the governor of Damascus was unable to exercise his authority in a large part of the mountain, and the danger of a further flare-up remained. Second, when the energetic Shah 'Abbas I became ruler of the Persian Safavi empire in 1587 the Ottomans had to contend with a serious challenge from the east. The Safavis had made Persia a Shi'i domain in the early sixteenth century, assisted by Shi'i *'ulema* (singular *'alim,* religious scholar) from Jabal 'Amil, the Shi'i area on the southern fringes of Mount Lebanon. The Ottomans were nervous about the allegiance of the Shi'is around Mount Lebanon, the largest Twelver Shi'i presence in the depth of Ottoman territory. The Shi'i factor complicated the Druze problem on the flank of Damascus. Third, the European Catholic Counter-Reformation had as a side-product an increased Vatican activism regarding the Maronites, the main "Catholic" community in the Middle East. The relationship between Rome and the Maronite patriarchs established in the twelfth century atrophied under the Mamluks, and in 1585 the Vatican moved to revive it by founding a Maronite college in Rome, for the education of Maronite clergy.

Henceforth the Ottomans faced external influences from both

28

Europe and Persia in Mount Lebanon. The Maronites hardly figured in Ottoman priorities in the sixteenth century, but they eventually posed a major threat to the territorial integrity of Ottoman Syria. Although Kamal Salibi, in his *House of Many Mansions* (1988), argues that Mount Lebanon did not stand out from other parts of Syria in political terms, this is difficult to reconcile with the fact that no other area of the Eastern Mediterranean presented the Ottomans with such a multiplicity of challenges through several centuries.

In 1590, to settle Druze affairs and to guard against Shi'i subversion, the Ottoman governor of Damascus appointed the leading Druze strongman, Fakhr al-Din Ma'n, as subgovernor for the *sanjak* (district) of Sidon-Beirut.[18] He had gained Ottoman confidence by stabilizing the Shuf and organizing tax payments. However, Fakhr al-Din took advantage of disputes between the governors of Damascus and Tripoli and the rebellion of 'Ali Janbalad in Aleppo to extend his rule into the Kisrawan and the Galilee. He welcomed Italian and Vatican influences and favored local Christians, encouraging Maronites to migrate southwards into the Matn and the Shuf. By 1613, the Ottomans had become sufficiently suspicious of Fakhr al-Din's ambitions and European penetration to launch an expedition against him, shrinking Ma'nid authority back to the Shuf. Fakhr al-Din departed for Italy, spending five years in Tuscany, and the Druze country returned to the anarchy of the late 1580s. The Ottomans had little choice but to restore him in 1618. He then intensified his European and Christian connections and seized lands deep in the governorate of Damascus, as far as Palmyra. Istanbul could not ignore such encroachment on the main inland axis of Syria.

Fakhr al-Din was finally deposed by a large army in 1633, but over half a century he had inaugurated new phenomena in Mount Lebanon. He created an alignment of Druze and Maronite leading families that became the backbone for 150 years of local administrative autonomy under the Shihabs, and he nurtured a Maronite-European interaction that was to define Maronite identity as this community became the leading sectarian element in the mountain. These phenomena had no counterpart elsewhere in Syria.

It has virtually become an orthodoxy among historians (Chevallier, 1971; Salibi, 1988; van Leeuwen, 1994) that the Ma'ns and Shihabs were unexceptional in Ottoman Syria, but this ignores both the longevity of the Ma'n/Shihab *imara* (principality) and the peculiarities of the Druze-Maronite context. Certainly, the *imara* was not a one-man episode like the cases of such eighteenth-century regional bosses as Jazzar Pasha or Zahir al-'Umar, and the equivalence asserted by van Leeuwen is inappropriate.[19]

Crystallization of Mount Lebanon's administrative autonomy, under the governors of Sidon and Damascus, and its extension to the greater part of the mountain, took more than a century. The Ma'ns did not resurface as the preeminent family of the Shuf until the 1660s, and their Shihab relatives who succeeded them in 1697 at first administered only southern Mount Lebanon. The Shihabi *imara* acquired its full territorial form in the late eighteenth century, when it wrested the tax farm function for the Maronite north from the Shi'i Hamadas. The fact that the *imara* was nothing more than a local lord having limited financial and judicial functions, constrained both by lesser lords beneath him and by Ottoman governors technically above him, was less significant than the social prestige of the Shihabs and the encouragement their *imara* provided for Maronite political development and French and Vatican influences.

Maturation of the *imara* coincided with Shi'i unrest in Jabal 'Amil, immediately to the south, in the 1770s—the most significant Shi'i "troubles" since the days of Fakhr al-Din. These conditions in Mount Lebanon coincided with the real beginning of the Ottoman Empire's struggle for existence against European pressures. In 1774, the Ottomans were defeated after an eight-year war with Russia, and forced to sign the humiliating peace of Küçük Kaynarca. During the war the Ottoman governor of Egypt had rebelled and sent forces as far as Damascus before being overthrown. Shortly after the war the Persians, who had been quiescent for some decades, raided Anatolia and briefly occupied Basra in Mesopotamia. Consequently, in 1775 Istanbul gave full powers to a tough Bosnian, Ahmad Jazzar Pasha, to do whatever he saw fit to maintain Ottoman sovereignty in Syria. With the Persian ruler Kerim Han Zand raiding across the eastern frontier in 1774-76, Jazzar Pasha initially concentrated on smashing the Shi'is of Jabal 'Amil, suspected as a "fifth column" for both the Persians and

Russians. His expeditions were so effective that the Shi'is were not heard from again in Ottoman times.

However, Jazzar Pasha had less success in the more formidable task of deflating the Maronite-Druze *imara*. For a few years he managed to subjugate the resourceful Bashir II Shihab, invested as amir in 1788, by force and vigorous intervention in the internal affairs of the mountain. He revived direct Ottoman rule in Beirut, which had come under Shihabi control in the mid-eighteenth century, and played between Bashir II, other Shihabs, and the Druze chiefs (see chapter 3). Bashir II regained room for maneuver as soon as Jazzar Pasha died in 1804. Despite efforts by later Ottoman governors to curb or remove him, he consolidated his position and preserved the *imara* by demonstrating his indispensability for maintaining order in Mount Lebanon.

Bashir II ensured that the *imara* lasted long enough into the nineteenth century for the political, economic, and demographic evolution of the Maronite community to reach a point at which direct Ottoman rule became no longer possible. Bonaparte's invasion of Egypt in 1798 and his subsequent incursion into Palestine, despite his being checked by Jazzar Pasha and checkmated by the English, changed the strategic environment in the Eastern Mediterranean. Both the British and French became much more involved in the Ottoman east—the British because they viewed French and Russian actions in the late eighteenth century as a challenge on the route to India, and the French because great power competition increased the significance of their new connections with Egypt and their old ones with Mount Lebanon.

Beirut and Mount Lebanon attracted the great powers as the primary base for their interests in Syria—the port and mountain offered the central position on the regional coast, the gateway to Damascus, and the main trading facilities via the local Christian merchants. The large Christian population presented a tempting territorial foothold. At the same time, European interventions, investments, and connections greatly disturbed intercommunal relations by favoring Maronites and other Christians. In Mount Lebanon, Orthodox and Maronite traders prospered as middlemen, the Maronite peasantry improved their incomes by producing silk for export, and educational opportunites mainly benefited the Christians. The Sunnis of the coast and the Druze of the mountain found themselves falling behind in economic and demographic terms from the 1820s onward.

After 1830, Mount Lebanon acquired a geopolitical significance unparalleled even in the Crusader period. First, the rise of Muhammad 'Ali in Egypt after the French invasion, Muhammad 'Ali's repudiation of Ottoman overlordship in 1832, and the takeover of much of Syria in the 1830s by his son Ibrahim Pasha, put Mount Lebanon in a frontier location between regional powers—an echo of the Fatimid-Byzantine configuration. This in turn heightened Anglo-French rivalry: the French favored Muhammad 'Ali's Egypt and the British sought restoration of Ottoman sovereignty. Second, energetic Egyptian administration in Syria and encouragement of European trade interests elevated Beirut's status as the regional entrepôt. Third, Bashir II's efforts to degrade the Druze leadership, his elimination of the Druze chief Bashir Junblatt in 1825, and his alliance with the Maronite church—all for political rather than sectarian purposes—stirred Druze antipathy toward the amir and the Maronites, and mixed dangerously with Druze economic jealousies.

Sectarian tension surfaced in Mount Lebanon's society simultaneously with the mountain becoming a front line for regional and great power intrigues. Fakhr al-Din and the Shihabs had established a political setting that eased Maronite consolidation—Bashir II's importunities were thus bringing the mountain principality to an end when it had already outlived its usefulness for the Maronites. Mount Lebanon on the brink of the upheavals of the mid-nineteenth century, out of which emerged the formalized autonomy of the *mutasarrifiyya*, foreshadowed the Greater Lebanon of the 1970s.

Little Lebanon: The Mutasarrifiyya

Mount Lebanon's strategic salience and its utility to the Egyptians caused the demise of the Shihabi *imara*. Ibrahim Pasha found Mount Lebanon's financial and human resources indispensable to maintaining the Egyptian hold on Syria, especially as a government more intrusive than the Syrian population was accustomed to tolerating made Egyptian rule increasingly unpopular in the late 1830s. Ibrahim Pasha exploited Bashir II as a revenue-gathering agent, requiring heavy taxes from Mount Lebanon, and in 1838, when the Egyptians could not contain a Druze insurrection south of Damascus, he demanded that Bashir II conscript thousands of Maronites to uphold Egyptian authority. Bashir II knew the destructive implications of such action for communal coexistence, but he had no choice but to join the Egyptians to crush Druze rebels in Wadi al-Taym and around Mount Hermon. Ibrahim Pasha also used the *imara* to control the Shi'is, putting Bashir II in charge of Jabal 'Amil without any consultation with Shi'i chiefs. In sum, the Druze opposed Egyptian occupation from the outset, the Shi'is were quickly alienated, and by 1839 taxation and confiscation of weaponry aroused Maronite popular rejection. Bashir II's Egyptian option, an asset in the 1820s, in the end doomed him.

As for European interest, the British watched carefully for an opportunity to have the Egyptians removed from Syria, especially following Ibrahim Pasha's rout of an Ottoman army in northern Syria in 1839, which indicated Ottoman incapacity. Mount Lebanon, the flank of Damascus, was the obvious Egyptian weak point, and a Maronite revolt was the obvious means to justify great power military intervention in Beirut. In early 1840 British agents pressed the Maronite patriarch to defy Ibrahim Pasha, while the Egyptians provoked Lebanese civilians with disarmament and conscription. Maronites and Druze jointly rebelled; the British organized a convention of the Ottoman government and European powers to demand Egyptian evacuation of Syria; and in September 1840 a British-Austrian-Ottoman force landed in Junya, under British direction. Egyptian authority in the Syrian interior collapsed, Bashir II went into exile, and the Ottomans resumed their administration of the region.

The Maronite-Druze combination against Ibrahim Pasha and Bashir II was a brief aberration caused by special circumstances. The Ottoman return, far from presaging orderly government, guaranteed almost immediate Maronite-Druze hostilities and prolonged destabilization. In the first instance, Druze landlords evicted by Bashir II more than a decade before followed Ottoman officials back to Mount Lebanon, a reappearance which the Ottomans had to endorse. Maronite peasants refused to recognize these lords and fighting erupted. In general, the Ottomans wished to impose direct provincial administration on Mount Lebanon after the eviction of Bashir II, and to dispense with the use of local landlords as administrative agents. However, the fact that the Ottomans had returned under British auspices compromised their prestige, and reduced them to trying to realize their objective through backstage maneuvers among the landlords and the great powers. The Ottoman manipulations, discussed in chapter 3, could only have destructive effects in an atmosphere charged with sectarian tensions and friction between peasants and landlords.

Turbulence in Mount Lebanon after 1840 continued to involve the contending interests of the great powers, particularly Britain and France. The French, smarting from the reverse inflicted on their Egyptian friends and worried about British commercial penetration, nurtured their relationship with the Maronites, encouraging Christian truculence. Against this, a sympathetic British posture stiffened Druze and Ottoman determination. The Austrians and Russians also meddled on their own accounts, the former competing with the French among local Catholics and the latter posing as champions of Orthodox Christians.

In Syria as a whole, the extension of secularization and European-style government reforms threatened the institutionalized Sunni Muslim superiority. It did little to elevate the Ottomans as a power in relation to the Europeans, but greatly inflamed Muslim resentment of local Christians throughout the Ottoman East. Warning signs of the consequences of sectarian disequilibrium came with anti-Christian riots in Aleppo in 1850; as with Maronite-Druze friction in Mount Lebanon these also reflected non-Christian sensitivity regarding urban Christian commercial prosperity. As the double governorate of Maronites and Druze fell to pieces through the 1850s in Mount Lebanon, regional as well as local conditions pointed toward sectarian troubles.

The Maronite-Druze warfare of 1860, in which the Christians were devastated despite their preparations and numerical weight, is examined in chapter 3. The main geopolitical implications involved the conflict's spillover into a week-long massacre of Christians by Sunni Muslim mobs in Damascus in July 1860, a second European military intervention in Mount Lebanon in 1860-61, and the new twist given to Ottoman-European relations by the establishment of an internationally recognized Lebanese entity.

At great power insistence the "little Lebanon" that had existed in geographically fluid form since the seventeenth century became a proto-state with fixed boundaries (map 1). Druze responsibility for atrocities led to the Christians being more than compensated in the new political arrangements, which in their finalized form reflected the Christian demographic superiority.

Haggling among the British, French, Russians, and Ottomans produced institutions accommodating sectarian pluralism and a measure of popular representation. According to an 1864 amendment to the initial *règlement organique* of 1861, the Ottoman governor, a Catholic from elsewhere in the empire, would be assisted by an advisory council of twelve members, with a Christian majority of seven and the communal balance in the hands of the two Orthodox members, satisfying Britain and Russia. Villagers would vote for a local headman *(shaykh)* and these headmen would vote for councillors in multimember districts. A district would have a predetermined number of councillors, in several cases from more than one sect, each of whom would be subject to the votes of all headmen, of whatever sect. Thus, although Maronites were underrepresented on the council, Maronite headmen in Maronite majority areas could heavily influence the election of councillors from other sects.

This system, which reflected Maronite peasant assertion from the 1820s onward as well as great power intrusion, was unprecedented in Ottoman administration and proved a prototype for sectarian pluralism in twentieth-century Lebanon. It replaced the quasi-feudal order of the *imara* and the old leading families lost their former political and legal status. Some of these families retained their political weight in a less formal way by infiltrating the bureaucracy of the new system. The governor had the Arabic title *mutasarrif*, literally "administrator," and the new entity was termed the *mutasarrifiyya*.

Engin Akarli, in *The Long Peace*, discusses how the interactions of the governor, the administrative assembly, and the first real "electorate" established foundations for the major political institutions of

Greater Lebanon in the 1920s. He also demonstrates how the Ottoman regime, through the governor, played a crucial role in stabilizing sectarian pluralism and enabling Mount Lebanon to put behind itself the upheavals of the mid-nineteenth century. He emphasizes the contrast with the divisive effects of French activities after 1860, especially French encouragement of the sectarian particularism of the Maronite church.

One would expect Ottoman archives—Akarli's main source—to highlight some perspectives and not others, regardless of their richness and variety. The Ottoman agenda was to preserve Ottoman sovereignty, still with the ultimate objective of disposing of the administrative oddity represented by the *mutasarrifiyya*. The *mutassarrifiyya* contradicted the preferred trend toward a more uniform imperial political system. After their sterile manipulations of the mid-nineteenth century, ending in the disaster of 1860, the Ottomans came to see it as in their interest to behave in a manner which would make the empire more acceptable to Mount Lebanon's Christians, and would reduce the Maronite impetus to turn to Western Europe. Akarli recognizes this, but does not let it get in the way of rehabilitating the Ottoman role in the formation of modern independent Lebanon—the Ottomans of course had no interest in creating any "Lebanon," pluralist or otherwise.

Several things need to be remembered by proponents of the virtues of the *mutasarrifiyya* and its Ottoman suzerain. At the most elementary level, the *mutasarrifiyya* would never have existed without the intervention of France and the other great powers. In particular, French pressure played a vital role in producing the 1864 arrangements, the basis for all the subsequent "pluralism." The 1864 regulations may not have been the outcome desired by the French, due to British influence, but they were even less the outcome wished by the Ottomans. As for admirers of the "secular state builders" of the *mutasarrifiyya,* who see regression with trends in twentieth-century Lebanon,[20] it was plainly easier to indulge secularism, tolerance, and pluralism in a situation where Maronites had a secure majority and Christians an overwhelming preponderance of 85% of the population. Facile "lessons" should not be translated to the much more complex sectarian context of modern Greater Lebanon, where the Maronite clergy and the French have not been the only sources of self-righteous "confessionalism."

Anyway, the *mutasarrifiyya* was geopolitically unstable in ways that made its continuation unlikely, even without the First World War. On the one hand, the area involved did not include Beirut, the channel to the outer world, or an adequate agricultural and economic base. Beirut had a Christian majority and could have been incorporated, together with much of the Biqa', without putting Christian dominance into question. Extension of the *mutasarrifiyya* to Beirut and the Biqa' was favored by the Christian pluralists of the administration and "town" as well as being an insistent demand of the hard-line Maronites of the church and "mountain." Sooner or later such aspirations promised conflict with the Ottomans and a drive for independence. On the other hand, the very existence of the *mutasarrifiyya* and the "Lebanonism" it implied cut across the precepts of the Arab nationalist ideology emerging in Ottoman Syria in the late nineteenth century. This Arab nationalism aimed at either a single state for all Arabs, or a single state in geographical Syria.

Western penetration via Beirut increased uncertainty about the future. This related far more to the general European and American influences on local social outlooks and sectarian relations than to the cruder French political intrusion highlighted by Akarli. The founding of Western educational institutions, most notably the Syrian Protestant College (later the American University of Beirut) in 1866 by American missionaries and St. Joseph's University in 1875 by French Jesuits, favored Christians and part of the Sunni bourgeoisie. More broadly, Western concepts of nationalism, liberalism, and socialism fed into local discontents and ideologies, providing the intellectual underpinning for both Arabism and Lebanonism (see chapter 2 for further discussion). Maronite distinctiveness was emphasized by increasingly elaborate cultural and commercial links with Europe and North America, accompanied by the large-scale out-migration from the 1860s onward. The emigration created a Lebanese diaspora in the West which by the mid-twentieth century exceeded the population of Lebanon, and which up to this point was overwhelmingly Christian. The emigration also indicated that the *mutasarrifiyya* lacked the resource base to support its people.

Apart from a benign posture regarding Mount Lebanon, in the hope that Christians could be persuaded to see the *mutasarrifiyya* as unnecessary, the Ottomans tinkered with the administration of the provinces of Beirut and Damascus, in order to strengthen imperial authority. Between 1865 and 1887, the Ottomans combined the two units into a single *vilayet* (province) of Syria, with its capital in Damascus. Beirut was downgraded to being the seat of a *sanjak*, subordinate to Damascus. The sultan and his officials wished to reduce Beirut's distinctiveness and to force it to look more toward the Syrian interior.[21] Beirut's merchants, both Christians and Sunnis, complained bitterly about the inconvenience of dealing with Damascus for government business. Beirut's expansion and links with the West went ahead regardless of such administrative devices, and in 1887 the Ottomans relented. After some debate, they reinstated the province of Beirut, thereby reinforcing Beirut's status in relation to the Syrian interior. This could only strengthen the logic of one day combining Beirut and the *mutasarrifiyya* in a larger "Lebanon."

In summary, by the first decade of the twentieth century, territorial change in the Levant seemed a definite possibility, whether for abolition of the *mutasarrifiyya* in line with Ottoman or Arabist preferences or for its expansion in response to Christian interests, particularly if backed by great powers. The First World War brought both outcomes in swift succession. After entering the war in October 1914 on the side of Germany and Austria-Hungary, the Ottoman regime lost little time in ridding itself of the *mutasarrifiyya,* so making plain the real extent of its concern with Mount Lebanon's sectarian pluralism. In June 1915 the Ottomans instituted direct rule, under the harsh military administration of Jamal Pasha, based in Beirut. At the same time, the British and French gradually established an understanding regarding their respective roles in the Eastern Mediterranean in the event of an allied victory. The so-called Sykes-Picot agreement of May 1916 implied the restoration of a special regime for Mount Lebanon, extended to Beirut and other areas. Britain recognized special French interests in coastal Syria. The understanding involved separation of coastal and interior Syria, both under French tutelage, with a boundary line in the Biqa'.

Indeed, before the war the French had concluded that their railway investments and commercial penetration in interior Syria required them to be ready to assert political domination in the event of an Ottoman collapse (Shorrock, 1970). Simultaneously, by the early twentieth century the British viewed Palestine and southern Mesopotamia as part of a strategic bridge between the Mediterranean and their Indian empire. Sponsorship of an Arab kingdom and a Jewish national home, as in the 1915 Hussayn-McMahon correspondence and the 1917 Balfour declaration, became components of the British concept. This was the background out of which an enlarged Lebanon emerged in 1920, as one of several new political units under French and British overlordship in the Eastern Mediterranean.

Greater Lebanon

In the April 1920 San Remo peace settlement between Turkey and the allies, after the Ottoman defeat by the British in 1917–18, France acquired a League of Nations mandate to control Mount Lebanon and interior Syria, and to guide the people of these lands toward political independence in some indeterminate future. The French took charge amid much agitation. The mandate dashed Arab hopes for immediate independence in a state covering the eastern Arab world, hopes encouraged by the British. Arab nationalism, until 1918 a weak movement of intellectuals and upper-class politicians disgruntled with Turkification after the Young Turk coup in Istanbul in 1908, received a massive boost from the brief experience of Arab independence under the Hashemite amir Faysal in Damascus between 1918 and 1920. Faysal's "kingdom" was eliminated by a French invasion in July 1920. Furthermore, new mandatory political boundaries promised to disrupt the historical economic hinterlands of such cities as Aleppo, Tripoli, and Damascus; British support for a Jewish "national home" under their Palestine mandate aroused Muslim and Christian suspicion throughout the Levant; and the French arrival occasioned a bitter rift between Maronite and non-Christian elements over the fate of Mount Lebanon.

In 1918–19, the Maronite patriarch, Ilyas Huwayyik, conducted discussions with French officials for an expanded Lebanese entity, which

would become a predominantly Christian state with Maronite preemi-
nence. In territorial terms, the Little Lebanon of the *mutasarrifiyya*
would be translated into a Greater Lebanon incorporating the fringes of
Mount Lebanon to the north, east, and south. Starvation and isolation
in the mountain during the First World War determined many
Maronites to seek a more secure agricultural base, which meant control
over the Biqa' valley and the anti-Lebanon range flanking the Biqa'.
Creation of an economically viable state to the benefit of all its inhabitants was the primary public argument; inclusion of Beirut and Tripoli
would secure trade with the Arab interior, and southward extension
would cover the Litani River, a valuable water resource. A firm foothold
south of the Litani was a particular French concern, in the context of
initial uncertainty regarding the geographical divide between the French
and British spheres (see chapter 4). Christian merchant families, for
example the Greek Catholic Pharaons, had lands in the fringe areas,
which also contained Maronite settlements.

Even among Maronites, Huwayyik's "Greater Lebanon" caused
controversy. Maronite members of the administrative council of the
mutasarrifiyya, including the patriarch's brother, rejected Huwayyik's
arrangement with the French (Akarli, 1993). They did not object to territorial expansion, but they viewed France's pretensions to dominate the
new Lebanon under an international "mandate" as impudent—after
half a century of autonomy Lebanon had a right to immediate independence. Ironically, hostility to France brought a coalescence between
these "Lebanonists" and Arab nationalists in Damascus. A few weeks
before its overthrow by General Gouraud, Faysal's regime accepted a
bigger Lebanon in exchange for a joint demand for independence.
Desperation propelled both parties. The French promptly arrested and
exiled the council members, before moving against Faysal. A different
sort of Maronite dissension came from the prominent Francophile
politician Emile Edde. Edde opposed geographical expansion altogeth-
er, expressing concern about the demographic implications of the patriarch's Greater Lebanon for the Christians.

The really vociferous opposition, however, came from the Muslims
of the areas to be added to Mount Lebanon, and from Syrian
Arab nationalists, including Christians in Beirut and Damascus. The

Sunni Muslims of Beirut and Tripoli feared long-term subordination in a Christian-dominated polity; the prospect of rule by local Christians was, if anything, worse than European colonialism. For Sunnis it meant an almost unimaginable inversion of the natural order of their universe. The Shi'i Muslims of the Biqa' and Jabal 'Amil, in the south, did not know about the Sunni trauma of losing sociopolitical supremacy, but clan leaders faced loss of autonomy, and Christian hegemony could only be distasteful. Syrian Arab nationalists felt forced to accept the peculiarities of the *mutasarrifiyya,* in a grudging manner, but they denounced its expansion into areas which had always been administratively distinct from Mount Lebanon. The Biqa', for example, was historically part of the Ottoman province of Damascus.

On 1 September 1920 the French implemented the Huwayyik scheme, the primary preference of the Maronites, and officially converted "Little Lebanon" into Greater Lebanon, establishing the boundaries of the modern Lebanese state. At the same time, the French backed pluralist arrangements for representation of the communities in legislative and executive organs under the High Commission of the mandate. As a result, Sunni and Shi'i grievances against Lebanon's existence slowly subsided, and the relative harmony of the *mutasarrifiyya* was able to be replicated, for a time and to a degree, in the more complicated sectarian mosaic of the new Lebanon.

During the 1930s, the Sunni political and commercial leadership drifted into cooperation with its Christian counterpart; the partnership was unbalanced in favor of the Christians, but Sunnis had enough of a voice in decision-making for the situation to be tolerable. Sunni personalities acquired a bigger government role than would have been the case in a Greater Syria, and came to see the merit of being big fish in a small pond. Shi'is, as a geographically peripheral, socially fragmented, and disproportionately poor community, could not yet exert political weight commensurate with their numbers, and found themselves dominated by Sunnis as well as by Christians. The new Lebanon at least brought the Twelver Shi'is of the Levant into a single state, and thus ultimately had its advantages. One day they too could be big fish in a small pond.

Overall, despite the possibilities for economic viability and communal pluralism, twentieth-century developments were not propitious for the Lebanon created by France in 1920. First, sectarian identifications and frictions highlighted by European influences in the nineteenth century had only begun to work themselves into the politics of emerging new Middle Eastern states. After the Maronite-Druze breakdown of 1860, sectarianism, whether or not peacefully managed, became the main obsession of Lebanese political life, debilitating the Lebanese political entity.

Second, Greater Lebanon relieved the economic and spatial limitations of Mount Lebanon at the cost of problematic new geopolitical features. The *mutasarrifiyya* of Mount Lebanon was anchored by a Maronite majority of 54% inside a larger Christian one of 75%[22]—Greater Lebanon brought in Sunni and Shi'i populations almost equivalent to the Maronites, had no majority sect, and did not exhibit any stable demographic balance between sects. Estimates by the French mandatory authorities in 1920–21 indicated a Christian proportion of 53% in Greater Lebanon, with Maronites slightly less than one-third of the total population.[23]

Beirut's overwhelming supremacy in the new Lebanon was an equally important source of instability. The French made Beirut the center for the High Commission for both Lebanon and Syria, concentrated their infrastructural investment in Beirut, and promoted the service and tourist sectors in Greater Lebanon's economy, which implied favoring the port-capital and neglecting the rural peripheries. Beyond Beirut, benefits primarily went to the old *mutasarrifiyya*, the capital's immediate hinterland and with its Maronite majority the core of France's cultural and strategic interest in the Levant. These circumstances accentuated the distinction between Greater Lebanon's largely Christian "center," which dominated officialdom as well as the economy, and its largely Sunni and Shi'i new territories. They also inaugurated a population shift from the peripheries into the center that was to destabilize social and sectarian relations.

Between 1921 and 1932 Beirut's municipal population more than doubled, from 77,820 to 161,382,[24] raising its proportion of the country's residents from 13% to 21% and setting the trend toward a metropolitan agglomeration of more than one million people by the late 1960s, or about 40% of Lebanon's population. Through the 1920s the Christian proportion of Beirut's residents increased from 45% to 52%, because of the arrival of Armenian refugees from Anatolia, while the Sunni percentage decreased from 42% to 32%.[25] However, the near-doubling of the Shi'i proportion from 4% to 7% presaged a fundamental change in Beirut's makeup that was soon to disturb both Christians and Sunnis.

Last but not least, Lebanon's expansion had regional implications. The new territories were added at the expense of interior Syria, certainly from the perspective of Damascus: in early 1995, I heard a Syrian diplomat refer to modern Lebanon as an "alleged" entity. These territories also became of strategic significance in the Arab-Israeli conflict after 1967.

Lebanon and the Middle East after 1967

Lebanon achieved independence from the French in 1943, and through much of the following half century it was the cockpit of the eastern Arab world. Lebanon held an uncomfortable intermediate position in two great issues convulsing the Middle East. In physical terms, it occupied a sensitive segment of the Arab-Israeli confrontation line, flanking both Israel and Syria. In cultural and economic terms, it functioned as the principal link between the Arab world and the West. Lebanon had an open political system and a free-wheeling liberal capitalist economy in a region where autocracy and state socialism prevailed; it acted as a magnet for dissident and radical Arab political groups, and aroused suspicion from Arab nationalists as being a cat's-paw of the Western great powers. These factors in turn elevated Lebanon's significance in the Arab-Israeli conflict, especially from 1967 on.

The 1967 war, with the humiliation of the Arab states, energized a confrontation that had been largely quiescent since the emergence of Israel in 1948–49. After 1967, the Palestinian Arabs appeared as an autonomous element, disruptive for both Arab regimes and Israel, and inter-state military competition escalated. For Israel, Lebanon presented challenge and opportunity. Its weak regime and political diversity made it the principal haven for Palestinian guerilla organizations, but also opened doors for Israeli penetration behind the Arab lines. For Arab regimes Lebanon was troublesome: a base for subversive probing by external powers, by Israel, and by Middle Eastern Islamic and secular radicals.

In several respects the Middle Eastern geopolitical dispositions of the late twentieth century—the first fifty years of the modern Arab state system—came to echo the dispositions of nine centuries earlier, when Crusaders, Byzantines, and Muslims engaged in their multi-cornered play for regional advantage. External interventions, regional power centers competing in the Levant, Islamic geopolitical fragmentation—all these had vaguely similar contours. Here, however, the similarity ended. Late-twentieth-century technology and population pressures gave a meaning to distance, space, and resources unknown in earlier periods. On the highly compressed front between Syria and Israel, Lebanon offered room for maneuver where the two powers could test each other with little risk of wider warfare. Lebanon's heightened strategic significance, particularly from 1967 to the 1990s, is best considered from the perspective of the relationship between the Middle Eastern political alignments of the period and Lebanon's internal characteristics.

The Middle East of the late twentieth century could be loosely divided into three geopolitical subregions (map 4), each with its own concerns, but with mutual interactions. The Eastern Mediterranean encompassed Egypt and the Levant, and interests concentrated on the Arab-Israeli confrontation. The Gulf was defined by oil, and by the local rivalries between Saudi Arabia, Iran, and Iraq. The third subregion at first meant only Turkey, the large rump state that survived the Ottoman collapse, with the main issues being Turkey's position on the NATO front line with the Soviet Union, and its suspension between the Middle East and Europe. The Soviet collapse in the early 1990s transformed both the subregion and the issues: Turkey became more involved with the Caucasus and Turkic Central Asia, which raised questions regarding its role between Europe, Central Asia, and the eastern Arab world, and regarding interactions with Iran.

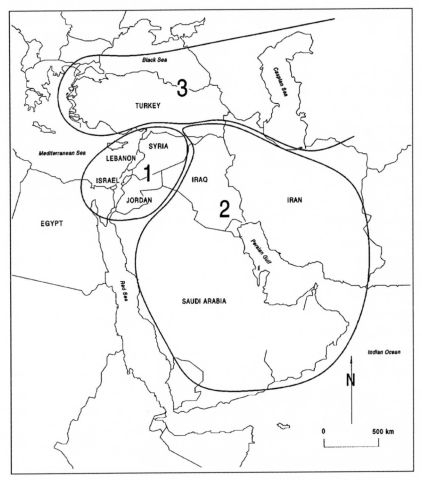

Map 4. Geopolitical Subregions of the Middle East, Late Twentieth Century:
(1) The Levant; (2) The Gulf; (3) Turkey/Caucasus

Lebanon and Turkey

Lebanon has had only a subdued relationship with Turkey, mediated through Syria, a state which the Turks viewed unfavorably until 2000. Excepting the Gulf oil countries, Turkey had little time for its former Arab provinces. Ba'thist Syria under Hafiz al-Asad resented Turkey as a Western outpost, maintained boundary grievances, and behaved provocatively when the Syrians thought they could get away with it. Lebanon became involved because, in the 1980s, Syria opened the Biqa' valley to Kurdish Labor Party (PKK) guerillas, who mounted an increasingly serious rebellion against Turkish authority in eastern Anatolia. In the early 1990s, the Turks intimated they might bomb the Biqa', and reminded Syria of its water vulnerability by cutting the flow of the Euphrates, Syria's primary source, to fill the new Ataturk dam. The water affair affected Lebanon, as there was little doubt about where Syria would turn for alternatives if it felt constrained.

In October 1998, Turkish patience finally expired, and Ankara threatened war if Damascus did not secure the Syrian-Turkish border and expel PKK chief Abdullah Öcalan. The Beirut regime backed Syria, but there was a thrill of anticipation among many Lebanese. Hafiz al-Asad chose to bow to superior power. Syria signed a security agreement with Turkey, closing PKK operations in Syria and the Biqa'. Turkey pushed for inclusion of Lebanon in the formal arrangements, but Beirut simply referred the Turks to Damascus. After 2000, Bashar al-Asad sought better relations with Ankara, an interest reciprocated by Turkey. At the same time, Turkey valued Lebanon for its commercial expertise, aware that Syrian viability depended on the Lebanese banks.[26] In 2005, Turkey prepared to reassess its involvements in the light of the U.N. inquiry into the Hariri murder, and in June 2005 Recep Tayyip Erdoğan made the first-ever visit to Lebanon by a Turkish prime minister.

Lebanon and the Gulf

Lebanon had more significance for the regional powers of the Persian Gulf. In the 1960s, Lebanon was a bourgeois capitalist outpost in a new sea of Arab state socialism, and thus a valued associate of the shrunken band of conservative Arab monarchies. Beirut had a prominent role as a financial center between the Arab oil shaykhdoms and the West, and Mount Lebanon beckoned as a summer retreat for the oil-rich. When chaos and militias took over in Beirut after 1975, Saudi Arabia showed an interest in salvaging the old regime, and a strong aversion to the secular and religious radical forces that found a fragmented Lebanon a congenial base. Both the Saudis and the

Americans were concerned about perturbations in the hinterland of the oil reservoir.

Saudi Arabia's dilemma was that to deal with Lebanon it had to operate through and alongside Ba'thist Syria, which knew how to be pragmatic as long as it was paid off. A complex balance of competition and collaboration evolved between Saudi Arabia and Syria, the mix varying with Syria's interpretation of its interests. During the 1980s, the rise of Islamism in Beirut and the reduced influence of conservative Lebanese politicians alarmed the Saudis, and the Syrians exploited these trends for leverage. At the end of the 1980s, the recession of Syria's Soviet patron threatened an erosion of Syria's position, but the 1990 Iraqi invasion of Kuwait and the subsequent American-led war against Iraq allowed Damascus to make itself useful on the fringes of the Western camp. Even as the Saudi-sponsored Ta'if meeting of Lebanese parliamentarians in October 1989 paved the way for a revival of conservative politics in Beirut, the Syrians secured Saudi and American approval for strategic hegemony in Lebanon. Syria exploited the West's confrontation with Iraq to eliminate the autonomy of Christian East Beirut, which had been an annoying conduit for Iraqi, Saudi, and Israeli influences. Syria also paraded its links with Iran to present itself as a possible restraint on Islamic radicalism in Beirut. Lebanon worried Saudi Arabia because its Shi'is attracted revolutionary Iran.

For Saddam Husayn's Iraq, Lebanon became the means for revenge on the rival Syrian Ba'thists for helping Iran in the 1980–88 Iran-Iraq war. In the late 1980s, Iraq liberally supplemented the arsenals of Lebanon's Christian sector, and encouraged its leadership to defy Syria. This fed into General Michel Aoun's "war of liberation," which challenged not just Syria, but also American and Saudi interests in stabilizing the Eastern Mediterranean. The Ta'if conference was Saudi Arabia's reply, and thereafter the Iraqi connection with Lebanon vanished with Iraq's defeat in the 1991 Gulf war.

Before 1979, the Shah's secular regime had little enthusiasm for Iran's ties, as a largely Shi'i country, with Shi'i communities in the Arab world. Lebanon thus hardly figured in the Iranian government's world view. In the 1980s, under Islamic revolutionary leadership, almost everything changed; the only constant was Iran's assertion of itself as the primary power of the Gulf, although now with an interest in the transformation of other Middle Eastern regimes into anti-Western Islamic states. Despite economic difficulties and exhaustion following the eight-year war with Ba'thist Iraq, the Iranian impetus to change the Middle Eastern political scene survived into the early 1990s. The main development through the 1990s was some decline in energy, with economic constriction enforcing a more flexible approach regarding the West and Arab oil states. In the regime's internal disputes between more and less pragmatic personalities the former slowly gained ground, but Iran maintained a prickly demeanor.

In the world view of revolutionary Iran the Shi'i connection with Lebanon had a multifaceted resonance. First, Jabal 'Amil in southern Lebanon had supplied expertise to assist Iran's conversion to Shi'ism in the sixteenth century, and there was a continuous interchange of religious scholars between the two countries. Musa Sadr, who propelled the Shi'i community into the Lebanese political mainstream in the 1970s and founded the mildly reformist Amal movement, came from Iran, although with an old Lebanese family background. Second, the Lebanese Shi'i community, Lebanon's largest sect by the 1960s yet politically disadvantaged, represented a strategic base for Iran in the heart of the Arab world, to the west of unsympathetic Arab regimes. Third, Lebanon's Shi'is lived on the Arab-Israeli front line. Iran rejected the existence of Israel and, more important, preferred the Arab-Israeli conflict to persist as a source of instability in the Middle East, a situation convenient to Iran's regional strategy.

Like Saudi Arabia, revolutionary Iran had to collaborate with the Syrians in Lebanon. Iranian access to Hizballah, the Lebanese party that spearheaded local Iranian influence, ran through Damascus, and Syrian military power could either buttress or paralyze Iranian operations. Iranian and Hizballah military facilities sheltered under a Syrian umbrella in the central Biqa' valley. For the Syrians, the "strategic alliance" with Iran elevated Syria's bargaining weight with the West, the Saudis, and Israel. To a degree it softened the impact of removal of Syria's Soviet cover, and offered disruptive possibilities if Arab-Israeli developments did not proceed according to Syrian tastes. For its part,

Iran might acquiesce in Syrian and Lebanese arrangements with the Israelis, but it was determined to preserve its Eastern Mediterranean foothold. In the early 1990s, Iran encouraged Hizballah to tie itself into the Lebanese official apparatus, via the 1992 parliamentary elections, and contributed financially to Hizballah's social programs. Lebanon remained important to Iran's assertion of itself on the international stage.

Lebanon in the Eastern Mediterranean

After 1967, geopolitical conditions in Lebanon's Arab surrounds involved increasing strains, emphasized by unresolved political and social frustrations and the authoritarian behavior of governments. Regimes, however imposing, were insecure because of shaky legitimacy in the face of pan-Arab, pan-Islamic, or sectarian sentiments, because of rule by minority elements, or because of incapacity to satisfy popular aspirations. The presence of Israel, the plight of the Palestinians, and the dichotomy between oil-rich Arabs and their poorer brethren all contributed to geopolitical confrontation.

From 1967 to 1990 the leading eastern Arab autocracies—Syria, Iraq, Egypt, and Saudi Arabia—reacted to insecurity by either jostling for precedence or groping for solidarity. Despite many attempts at mediation, it proved impossible to bridge the gap between the rival Syrian and Iraqi Ba'thists, which became a venomous personal contest between Syria's Hafiz al-Asad and Iraq's Saddam Husayn. Saudi Arabia and Egypt stood apart from others because of their close relations with the United States. In the 1980s, the Iran-Iraq war forced Iraq together with Western-oriented Arabs, but for Saddam Husayn this was a temporary expedient. After 1990, the context changed radically with the disappearance of the Soviet Union, the global supremacy of the United States, and the swift Western smashing of Iraq in the 1991 Gulf war. American determination to do something about Arab-Israeli affairs propelled Syria into coordination with Egypt and Saudi Arabia. As never before, Syria had to ponder the viability of its balancing act between making openings to the West and playing a spoiler role— Lebanon was an important lever both in Syria's hands, and in the hands of others against Syria.

Eastern Mediterranean geopolitics in the late twentieth century had distinctive features. Most notably, there were two levels of Arab-Israeli affairs. First, three countries counted as Middle East regional powers—Egypt, Israel, and Syria. After the 1979 Israel-Egypt peace treaty, the main strategic competition in Arab-Israeli affairs was between Israel and Syria. However, the main Arab-Israeli issue, reconciling the future of the Palestinian Arabs with Israeli security concerns, involved secondary Arab powers—the Palestinians, Jordan, and Lebanon. Ba'thist Syria sought to dominate the Palestinians, Jordanians, and Lebanese, and thus monopolize Arab decision-making, but it lacked the capacity to achieve this. Syria was poorly located to influence developments in the main Arab-Israeli arena, which encompassed Israel, the West Bank and Gaza territories, and Jordan. The 1990–91 advances in Syrian control over the Lebanese and over the Palestinians in Lebanon enhanced Syria's weight, but not in any decisive respect.

Lebanon held an important position in Arab-Israeli affairs. Notwithstanding geographical displacement from the Israel-Jordan axis, it lay between the two regional powers of the Levant—Israel and Syria—and its topography and demography were of considerable concern to both states. Lebanon's combination of commanding mountains with a long central valley reaching almost from northern Israel to central Syria had security implications for both its neighbors, especially in view of the difficulties of military breakthrough on the short, highly fortified Golan Heights front. In the case of a large-scale war, always a possibility in the 1970s and 80s, the Israelis had the option of a flanking thrust up the Biqa' valley, avoiding Syria's Golan defenses. For a "two-theater" war Israel possessed the superior technological and organizational facilities, in addition to having shorter lines of communication. Mount Hermon and the anti-Lebanon mountains would disconnect Syrian efforts on the Golan from those in the Biqa', and Syria lacked the command and control capability to coordinate two theaters effectively. At the least, Syria required a substantial military deployment in the Biqa' as long as the Arab-Israeli confrontation continued.

The communal heterogeneity of the Lebanese population also offered challenges to both Syria and Israel. Lebanon's demographic intricacy contributed to weak central government, particularly after the 1967 Arab defeat stimulated contradictory political demands from Muslims, Christians, and local Palestinians. Weak government meant that Lebanon became the only portion of the Arab front with Israel where Palestinian organizations could operate relatively freely, provoking the Israelis, irritating the Syrians, and briefly, between 1976 and 1982, building a "state within the state." Up until the mid-1980s Israel devoted much attention to Beirut, where the Palestinian political-military leadership established itself, and where Christian autonomy presented opportunities for diverting the Arabs, especially the Syrians. Thereafter, following elimination of the Palestinian "state within the state" by Israel and Syria, Israeli difficulties in dealing with the Lebanese Christians, and a rising Shi'i challenge to Israel in southern Lebanon, Israel restricted itself to securing its northern border.

Israeli and Syrian concerns regarding Lebanon were to a degree asymmetrical. Israel's interest in Lebanon inflated and deflated in relation to Lebanon's importance for the Palestinians, but events in Lebanon were never a threat to Israel's existence. Even the implications of full Syrian hegemony in Lebanon were diluted for Israeli observers by the belief that Lebanon was a diversion for the Syrians. Managing a buffer zone on Lebanese territory for defensive and strategic purposes continued to be a major Israeli enterprise after the mid-1980s, but Israel's heartland was a little removed from its northern front, and Israel could afford to shrink Lebanon in its strategic perspective through the 1980s.

The situation for Ba'thist Syria was different. Lebanon directly flanked the Syrian capital and nerve-center at Damascus, and represented a hotbed of sectarian, Arab, and foreign influences that might subvert the Ba'thist state, even apart from the Israeli dimension. For Syria, conceding Palestinian autonomy in Lebanon meant the prospect of war with Israel at a time and in circumstances chosen by others, a threat to Syria's whole role in Arab-Israeli matters and to Syria's pan-Arab prestige, and an invitation to the Syrian Ba'th's domestic and Arab enemies to make trouble. Allowing Lebanon to disintegrate irretrievably into militia and sectarian statelets, which almost happened between 1976 and 1989, had exactly the same implications, as well as creating a dangerous precedent for Syria, which is like Lebanon a multicommunal agglomeration. Syria also had to watch Iranian penetration, as even a long-standing "strategic ally" might not be so convenient in different circumstances. In consequence, Syria aspired from 1976 onward, when its army entered Lebanon to deter the Palestinians, to control the Lebanese regime in Beirut, and to convert Lebanon into a Syrian satrapy. Unlike Israel, Syria did not feel it could accord Lebanon less significance in its strategic perspective, or withdraw its attention from Beirut to the borderlands.

Short distances and regional resource limitations, particularly regarding water, have added to the sensitivity of Lebanon's position between Israel and Syria. In a landscape where, in the 1990s, only a few tens of kilometers took one from Israeli towns to Hizballah, Palestinian, and Iranian revolutionary guard bases, and then to the Syrian army and the Syrian capital, the two regional powers had rigid security requirements. In some respects air forces and surface to surface missiles have abolished distance, but in ground warfare, whether regular or irregular, advantage over an opponent still depends on geography and terrain. Indeed, in some ways the mobility and technology of the late twentieth century enhanced the value of vantage points, territorial forward projection, and topographic barriers. The Syrian presence in the Biqa' and the anti-Lebanon range up to the forced 2005 withdrawal showed that Damascus believed in such value. An Israeli-Lebanese-Syrian understanding concerning Lebanon needs to comprise solid international guarantees, disbandment of all armed groups in favor of the Lebanese state, and removal of all regional influences from Lebanon. Such an understanding is vital to Lebanon providing a real buffer between Israel and Syria.

Finally, regional population growth and resource problems affected Lebanon's relationships eastward and southward after 1967. Mount Lebanon receives a bountiful rainfall, and Lebanon has a visible water surplus in a semi-arid region where, in the late twentieth century, water supplies have come under pressure from rapidly increasing populations. Israel, the Palestinians, Jordan, and Syria all look ahead to difficulties, although of varying severity, and they collectively stand in contrast to Lebanon's more fortunate status. Most Arab accusations have concentrated on Israel's intentions respecting the Hasbani sources and the Litani river. However, Syria has probably had a stronger long-term interest in Lebanese water. The main reasons have been that Syria's population is set to increase from about 16 million in 2000 to more than 25 million by 2020—by far the largest demographic increment in the Levant; Syria shares water sources with Lebanon, most notably the Orontes river; and Syria penetrated deeply into Lebanese affairs in the 1990s. A lot depends on water sharing between Syria and Turkey, which remains uncertain.

Lebanon's strategic geography in the late twentieth century

Lebanon may be divided into three zones, representing its historical components and its strategically relevant internal features in the late twentieth century:

(a) The outer peripheries of the south and the Biqa', the bulk of the territories added to Little Lebanon in 1920;

(b) Mount Lebanon and its coastal slopes, which constituted the Little Lebanon of the *mutasarrifiyya* and the heartland of the preceding mountain autonomy;

(c) The coastal cities of Beirut, Tripoli, and Sidon, like the peripheries politically separated from the mountain until the French mandate.

Map 1 illustrates these zones.

The peripheries comprise the borderlands of most immediate significance to Syria and Israel. They encompass the Shi'i rural areas and the principal Lebanese rivers: the Litani in the south and the Orontes sources in the north. The Biqa' has had historical associations with Damascus and central Syria, and in the pre-statehood days of the Jewish Yishuv some in the Zionist movement indicated an interest in southern Lebanon up to the Litani. No Israeli or Syrian government has ever made official annexationist claims, but that has not prevented Lebanese suspicions, especially as the Israeli and Syrian presences in these areas began to seem indefinite in the 1980s. More diffuse ideas about "Greater Syria" undoubtedly threaten the Lebanese political entity, but such notions come as much from within Lebanon as from Syria.

Shi'i populations in the borderlands became important for Syria and Iran in the 1980s, for manipulation in Lebanese, Arab, and Arab-Israeli contexts. Israeli occupation of southern Lebanon between 1982 and 1985, originally to remove Palestinian bases but prolonged to extract peace terms from Lebanon, turned local Shi'is against Israel, creating a strategic asset for other Middle Eastern powers. After Israel retreated to the border "security zone" in 1985, Shi'i radicalism overshadowed continuing concerns about the Palestinians.

For Syria and Iran, Shi'is are distributed conveniently between a concentration abutting Israel, in southern Lebanon, and another population in the central and northern Biqa', well placed for logistics and organization. This situation has been useful for exerting pressure on both Israel and Beirut. For instance, in 1983 Shi'i suicide bombers attacked the Western multinational force in Beirut, seen by Damascus as detaching the Lebanese regime from Syrian influence. By the late 1980s, however, Damascus began hinting about quietening militant proxies for American and Saudi rewards. For Syria there was a delicate balance between the Shi'is being an asset or an embarrassment.

Two topographic features of the peripheries have special connotations. First, without a Syrian-Israeli peace settlement, the broken hill country of southern Lebanon makes the Israeli border vulnerable to guerillas. In March 1978 the Israelis moved into Lebanon, and refused to retreat all the way to the international boundary until hostile armed factions disappeared. Second, the great trench of the Biqa' exposed Damascus and central Syria to the Israelis. After 1976 the Syrians extended their military alignment, including armored units, well south into the flanks of the Baruq mountains, in the vicinity of Jizzin, and into the hills that divide the Biqa' from the upper Jordan catchment. Israel expelled the Syrians from these locations in 1982, and Syria was unable to restore tripwire positions across the southern entrance to the Biqa'. Israel retained the Jizzin highlands through its proxy militia, the South Lebanon Army (SLA), and shifted the tacit "red lines" against Syrian regular forces a little northward compared with before 1982. Also, Syria did not wish to face the Israelis directly, leaving this to local elements. In the early 1990s Syria had little forward cover for its forces in the central Biqa', which did not encourage it to be flexible

Israel's 1982 invasion of Lebanon—Israel Defense Minister Ariel
Sharon "guiding the perplexed," Ze'ev in Ha'aretz, 25 June 1982.

about military redeployment before making a settlement with Israel.

Mount Lebanon—the coastal upland block from the massif of Qurnet al-Sauda' in the north to the Shuf highlands in the south—is important because it dominates land communications, commands the Beirut metropolitan area and contains the Maronite and Druze core areas. One reason the Syrians disapproved of the Maronite and Druze autonomous zones of the 1980s involved the constraints they put on Syrian access to Beirut and the Lebanese regime. Even though Druze leader Walid Junblatt generally bowed to Syrian wishes, the Druze Shuf overlooked both the Syrian dispositions on the coastal side of the mountain, and the main coastal road from Beirut to the south. Druze links with Palestinians, Israelis, and others from this location irritated Damascus. The Maronite "canton," while it lasted, kept a critical portion of the Lebanese regime out of Syrian hands. Reduction of Christian autonomy in East Beirut and its mountain hinterland was complicated not only by the area's foreign connections, but also by the combination of rugged, well-vegetated terrain with dense urban settlement. Syria launched its decisive blow, in October 1990, only when the Christian sector was already weakened by a vicious internal war.

The mountain also overlooks the Biqa', and limits the approach to Beirut from the east to one main road across the Dahr al-Baydar pass, with a subsidiary road over a higher pass from Zahla. At 1,500 meters above sea level, Dahr al-Baydar can be closed by snow for days at a time in winter, which sometimes constrained Syrian operations in the Beirut region during the war years. On the Biqa' side of Mount Lebanon, the predominantly Christian city of Zahla is located at a sensitive point beside the approach to Dahr al-Baydar. In 1981, when the East Beirut enclave tried to extend itself into Zahla, intruding on the nerve center of Syria's military deployment, the Syrians reacted violently.

As for command of Beirut from Mount Lebanon, the American-led multinational force of 1983–84 quickly learned how difficult it is to maintain a presence in the Lebanese capital when unfriendly parties hold adjacent high ground. Between 1982 and 1987, when Syria was militarily absent from Beirut, Damascus found the wedge of coastal mountain seaward from the Dahr al-Baydar pass invaluable for influence on the capital, whether for links with West Beirut, overawing East Beirut, or monitoring and separating the Maronite and Druze mountain areas. In the provisions for Syrian redeployment in the 1989 Ta'if Agreement, Damascus sought to retain this advantage

Each of the big coastal cities has exhibited problematic geopolitical features in the late twentieth century. After 1949 Beirut, Tripoli, and Sidon all hosted large Palestinian refugee camps that became Palestinian military bases after 1967. The Syrians put an end to Palestinian autonomy in the suburbs of Beirut and Tripoli in the late 1980s. The Sidon camps, closer to Israel and unthreatening to Syria when 'Arafat's influence contracted after his 1993 agreement with the Israelis, continue to be a law unto themselves. Sidon's present strategic significance largely relates to these camps, but Tripoli and Beirut have had other noteworthy characteristics.

The Tripoli Sunnis have been a strategic problem for the Syrian Ba'thists since the 1970s—ironic, as local leaders condemned the 1920 separation of Tripoli from the Syrian interior. The problem concerns sectarian frictions in Ba'thist Syria, where many Sunnis deeply resented the 'Alawi minority's command of the state; in the late 1970s Tripoli became a center for subversion of Syria, with Sunni fundamentalist, Iraqi Ba'thist, and 'Arafatist Palestinian presences. Tripoli elements supported the 1979–82 Muslim Brotherhood rebellion in northern Syria, which was crushed with the March 1982 razing of the "old city" of Hama. Thereafter Syria dealt with Tripoli. In the two sieges of November 1983 and September 1985, with attacks by Palestinian and Lebanese proxies backed by Syrian artillery from the adjacent Kura district and Turbul hills, Syria defeated religious zealots and other troublesome parties, most prominently Yasir Arafat. Since 1986, the northern Lebanon Sunnis have not disturbed Damascus, although they detest Syrian 'Alawis. Strategic perspectives would probably change if Sunnis again took power in Syria.

Metropolitan Beirut, as the center of an anarchic polity, a liberal economy, and a media and publishing industry unique in openness and variety in the Arab world, fundamentally challenges the Arab interior, where these things have been organized very differently. In the late twentieth century, Syria could not close its western flank to competitors unless it dominated the Lebanese capital. For Damascus an unsupervised Beirut meant an open door for Palestinian, Israeli, Islamic, Western, and Arab regime influences, all disquieting. Such an open door was incompatible with Syria's strategic hold on the Biqa' and northern Lebanon, vital to the prestige and security of Hafiz al-Asad's regime.

From a Damascene perspective, various disturbing phenomena appeared in Beirut between 1975 and 1990: Bashir Jumayyil, with his Israeli links and his 1981 Zahla probe; 'Arafat's Palestine Liberation Organization (PLO) and its 1983 Tripoli foray; the 1982 Israeli invasion, with an abortive attempt to install an Israeli-oriented Lebanese regime; the 1983–84 American intervention, so incompetent as to enable its easy elimination; General Michel Aoun's 1989 "war of liberation," supported by Iraq; and Iran's influence in the Shi'i community. Most of these parties parading across the Beirut stage aimed to affect Arab-Israeli balances, and thus the general geopolitics of the Eastern Mediterranean—certainly the case with the Israeli, American, 'Arafatist, Aounist, and Iranian maneuvers. Slightly different circumstances and shrewder operations by Syria's opponents might have destabilized Syria's strategic posture and even the Syrian regime itself, with dramatic Middle Eastern repercussions.

The 1991 Gulf war and the end of the Cold War created enough of a Syrian-American-Saudi convergence in the early 1990s for the Syrian Ba'thists to shackle Beirut to their own agenda. However, with its diverse population of two million people, Beirut was too complex and too used to a multiplicity of influences to be caged for very long by a small and unstable power like Ba'thist Syria.

CHAPTER TWO

SECTS AND IDENTITIES

What distinguishes the Lebanese?

The Lebanese people exhibit a commonality and identity like that of such cohesive "nationalities" as the English or French, and a fragmentation into mutually distrustful groups similar to such multicommunal conglomerates as the former Yugoslavia, Malaysia, or Sri Lanka. Arab countries can be placed at different points on a spectrum between the Egyptians, a people with a distinctive collective consciousness, and historically new creations of Western colonial intervention like Iraq or Syria. Even now, after 85 years of Iraqi and Syrian geographical existence, it is questionable whether one may refer to "Iraqi" and "Syrian" peoples, rather than simply to state apparatuses occupying certain Arab territories. Modern Lebanon, uniquely, can be located at both ends of the spectrum—it is at once Egypt, Iraq, and neither. It is also at once firmly Arab and assertively separate in ways that transcend even the Egyptian case.

Two features of Lebanon's physical geography help to explain the cultural intricacy of the Lebanese. First, the Lebanese mountains have been a gathering place for sectarian minorities. Communal diversity persisted in this vicinity, historically an "island" in a Sunni Islamic "sea," less because the topography discouraged imperial armies than because Mount Lebanon lay away from major urban centers. Also, the natural compartmentalization of the mountains, with the alternation between Mount Lebanon, the Biqa', and the anti-Lebanon ranges, or between upland blocks (the 'Akkar, the Kisrawan, the Shuf, Jabal 'Amil), has ensured substantially autonomous evolution of the individual sectarian groups, as well as particularism based on clan and locality.

Second, open access from the Mediterranean, combined with a large Christian population, led to a cultural interchange with Europe and North America, through the nineteenth and twentieth centuries, which affected the mass of Lebanese, Christian and non-Christian, to an extent not paralleled elsewhere in the Arab world. This interchange helped to create a far-flung Lebanese diaspora population now greatly exceeding the number of Lebanon's own residents. After the creation of Greater Lebanon, and especially during the war years after 1975, Shi'i and Sunni Muslims came to develop diaspora communities and connections almost as prominent as the older external ties of their Christian countrymen. In the 1990s, there were perhaps seven million people of Lebanese origin outside Lebanon, overwhelmingly in the West, compared to less than four million Lebanese residents. At least as much of Lebanon's cultural orientation derives from interaction with the host societies of the diaspora, as from Arab associations.

Lebanon's delicate balancing acts between Islam and Christianity, and between the West and the Middle East, have determined its cultural outlook. In Lebanon, Christians are still almost 40% of the resident population—nowhere else in the Arab world are they more than 15%. Despite the fact that multicommunal states are a normal feature of the Middle East, no other Arab country approaches Lebanon's kaleidoscope of religious communities, with five sects each making up more than 5% of local Lebanese residents, and no community constituting more than 35% of the population. Lebanese Muslims interact much more than other Middle Eastern Muslims with local Christians, at all levels of society, and the depth and variety of these interactions affect their attitudes. Many Lebanese Shi'is, for example, have adopted Christmas almost as a festival of their own, and even Hizballah gives central importance in its program to a *modus vivendi* with Lebanese Christians. On the other hand, sectarian sensitivities have dominated public and private discourse as in no other late-twentieth-century Arab society—the conflict between secularism and Islamism that has assumed centrality elsewhere in the Middle East is in Lebanon only one dimension of the discourse concerning religion and politics, affecting and affected by the wider intersectarian debate. Lebanon's wars after 1975 emphasized the necessity of intersectarian coexistence for common survival, sharpening a "multicultural" Lebanese identity, but at the same time accentuated sectarian orientations. Contemporary Lebanon reflects both developments.

Lebanon's political system since the 1920s has integrated Western representative concepts and local social tradition in a very distinctive way. Within a framework of transplanted parliamentarianism, genuine electoral contests, and extensive public freedoms, political behavior has been determined not by Western-style ideological and party allegiances, but primarily by old feudal, family, and sectarian loyalties. Despite demands for changes in representative balances, strong popular adherence to this hybrid political model was not broken by its inability to maintain peace and consensus after 1975. Imposition of Syrian authoritarian influences after 1990 was an aberration of alien origin and questionable longevity.

Samir Khalaf (1987) gives an insight into the Lebanese integration of representative politics with clientelist and sectarian influences. He doubts the viability of any other means of operating Western-style democracy where attachments to clan and religious community still overshadow cross-cutting associations, such as social class or unions and professional organizations. Khalaf also notes the disadvantages of politics centered on patronage networks and personality contests: negation of the wider public interest, avoidance of serious public issues, and discouragement of national unity. Nonetheless the system, with its Western dimension in the 1926 Constitution and its traditional social dimension in the 1943 National Pact, successfully mediated sectarian frictions and provided relatively stable government until the 1970s. In the midst of moralizing about Lebanon's civil strife, it should be remembered that no other Arab country has ever matched Lebanon's parliamentary record, or evolved anything resembling Lebanese confessional democracy.

Lebanon's existence, albeit with vague and varying boundaries, since the Druze feudal chief Fakhr al-Din established an autonomous area under Ottoman overlordship in the 1620s, has buttressed Lebanese identity, although it has also been a source of dispute. It is important that some form of Lebanese entity predated European colonial interventions, creating a pedigree that cannot be claimed by such citadels of modern Arabism as Syria and Iraq, from which Lebanon has been abused as an unnatural product of French colonialism. A shared historical tradition goes beyond Lebanon's historical core in the coastal mountains, extending to the Tripoli and Biqa' areas, for example regarding the hereditary feudal social order, somewhat different from Ottoman rural society in most of what is today termed Syria. In addition, many of the present-day Biqa' Shi'is are descendants of people displaced from Mount Lebanon by the Mamluks and Ottomans. Greater Lebanon was therefore not an entirely illogical development. Besides, for the Shi'is of Jabal 'Amil the choice in the 1920s was not between Greater Lebanon and Damascus, but between Lebanon and the Jewish Yishuv.

However, Lebanon's historical autonomy is more central for Maronites and Druze, as the leading participant communities, than for other sects, and between Maronites and Druze the nature and implications of proto-Lebanon have been strongly disputed. For Druze, the original *imara* of Fakhr al-Din became gradually usurped by Maronite Christians, owing to demographic and economic trends. Maronites have used long-standing mountain autonomy to claim that their community has been the primary feature of a Lebanon also distinguished by its "Christian" personality—not an argument endearing to other sects. Like many things about Lebanon, the historical legacy is ambiguous.

Kamal Salibi (Shehadi and Mills, 1988) correctly observes that the themes and forces characterizing developments in the neighborhood of Mount Lebanon during the nineteenth and early twentieth centuries were similar to those at play more broadly in the Arab territories of the Ottoman Empire, although he glosses over significant variations in detail and intensity. His implication that Mount Lebanon's history stands out from that of the rest of the Arab east only on the level of "Ottoman administrative irregularity" is much more debatable, and contradicted by his own portrayal of the unusual coherence and energy of the Maronite Christian community. As Salibi indicates, Maronite fears and ambitions supplied the connecting thread in the historical progression from Mount Lebanon's tentative *de facto* autonomy, through the Little Lebanon of the *mutasarrifiyya,* to Greater Lebanon and the modern Lebanese state. Nowhere else in the Arab world was there an indigenous non-Islamic population with such organizational will, geographical compactness, and political potency. In few other places anywhere has there been such a variety of intercommunal chain reactions set off by the self-assertion of such a group, from the mid-nineteenth century onwards.

Sect and class

Most scholarly analysis has tended to interpret Lebanon's social evolution from one of two perspectives regarding the relationship between the vertical divisions of society, meaning sects and clans, and the horizontal divisions, meaning socioeconomic classes. One approach treats sect and class virtually as separate phenomena, emphasizing the weakness of class identification and its subordination to family and sectarian attachments (Khalaf, 1987). Against this, the second approach reduces sect to an extension of class formation with, for example, Shi'i Muslims heavily concentrated in the poorer strata and Christians heavily overrepresented in middle and higher strata (Barakat, 1979). Both perspectives offer useful insights, but both also distort Lebanon's reality.

A third approach would be to accept that, since the time of the *mutasarrifiyya,* Lebanon's population has experienced a duality of strengthening socioeconomic differentiation and intensifying sectarian orientations. This perspective does not require sect and class to be viewed as primary and secondary, in either direction. Sectarian attitudes have been much influenced by socioeconomic relations, within and between sects—the social discontents of the lower orders have exacerbated sectarian prejudices. I once heard an upper class Sunni refer to poor Shi'is as "dirt." Quite simply, the communal and socioeconomic dimensions are difficult to disentangle from one another.

For the Lebanese population in general a marked pyramidal socioeconomic stratification evolved between the 1840s and 1975, with rural to urban migration and the growth of Beirut as a great commercial entrepôt for the Middle East. A small ruling class of urban commercial families and rural chiefs held the apex of the pyramid and manipulated the political system. The old feudal leadership of the countryside moved into the expanding government apparatus. A 1961 French study, quoted by Barakat,[27] showed that 4% of Lebanese took a third of national income. This 4% came from all sects, but overall Christian dominance may be inferred, and with Sunnis greatly outweighing Shi'is among Muslims. The same study categorized 50% of Lebanese as poor or very poor, taking only 18% of national income. Shi'is may well have been a half of this broad base of the pyramid, but there were also large Maronite and Sunni segments. In between stood the relatively new moderately endowed groups, ranging from petit bourgeois shopkeepers to middle managers, middle-rank civil servants, and professionals. These elements were disproportionately Christian, and probably disproportionately non-Maronite, reflecting Christian educational advantages.

Between 1975 and the early 1990s—the war years—income gaps widened and the majority of residents became much poorer. The ruling class eventually incorporated militia leaders, war profiteers, and mafiosos, to add to the older rural, commercial, professional, and religious components. Non-Christians, including Shi'is, became better represented, although at an obvious cost—by 1990, the ruling class was more unsavory and less democratic than before the war years. It was also, in income terms, even further separated from the ordinary Lebanese; a 1992 study claimed that 450 individuals alone held 55% of all assets in Lebanon's banking system, as a result of financial redistribution away from the lower and middle strata with the collapse of the national currency after 1985.[28] The political consequences, explored in chapter 8, were well illustrated by the insensitive and anti-democratic performance of the restored Lebanese central regime of the early 1990s.

As for the rest of the socioeconomic pyramid, the central part contracted and the base expanded. War and currency depreciation devastated Lebanon's middle class, with many people forced to leave the country and many others impoverished. This meant a significantly attenuated buffer of the "middle sort" between the insouciant super-rich and the angry poor. Bourgeois emigration visibly reduced the Orthodox Christian and Armenian communities and sapped the demographic weight of the Christian sector. Lebanon suffered a terrible loss of trained and educated manpower; even return migration with peace and economic recovery would only partially compensate, as most of the emigrants quickly established roots and investments in their new countries.

Meanwhile, through the 1980s, the proportion of the population in lower income bands steadily inflated. Reliable statistics do not exist, but surveys of the one-third of Lebanese who became refugees point to 50% being below the standard of the minimum wage,[29] a level roughly equivalent to the lowest category of the 1961 study, which then covered 9% of the population. Effects of the process may be detected in the popular mobilization behind new political movements at the end of the 1980s— the Islamic call of Hizballah, for Shi'is, and the romantic nationalist appeal of General Michel Aoun, particularly for Maronites but also for others. Socioeconomic slippage of a large part of the Maronite community alienated it from traditional and militia leaderships by 1988. This recalled the Maronite peasant uprisings of 1820 and 1840, discussed in chapter 3.

Sectarian and class considerations intermingled in social relations after Lebanon's independence in 1943. Between 1943 and 1975 the context was massive rural-to-urban migration and concentration of the population in Greater Beirut. In both the Christian and Islamic sectors the old leadership, dominantly Maronite in the former and dominantly Sunni in the latter, faced the problem of incorporating an enlarged and more politically aware "street" into the political game.

For the Maronite poor and petit bourgeois who occupied new quarters in the eastern parts of the capital, resentment of their own upper class was balanced by fear of non-Christian challenges to the overall Maronite political advantage, an advantage that held them a little above the bottom of the heap. They thus gravitated toward right-wing organizations with paramilitary offshoots such as Pierre Jumayyil's Kata'ib party, especially after the first breakdown in the government system in 1958. Sectarian solidarity was maintained by a combination of such new organizations with Maronite church activity and older-style patronage arrangements. However, solidarity in a more complex Maronite society had a price—it stoked the fires of communal chauvinism and weakened the ability of the old Maronite upper class to relieve political tensions through compromises with its non-Christian counterpart.

In the Islamic sector the movement of Shi'i poor from Lebanon's peripheries in the Biqa' and the south to the environs of the capital represented Lebanon's largest internal migration. Many of these people became more educated without improving their economic circumstances, and they inhabited a "belt of misery" that included the southern suburbs and eastern extensions in Naba'a and Karantina. Their attitudes toward the established order conflated socioeconomic and sectarian resentments—wealth tended to be identified as Christian and Sunni. Such resentments coalesced with the general influence of pan-Arabism and socialism on Shi'i and Sunni youth, threatening the authority of the traditional non-Christian leadership, which was disproportionately Sunni.

The traditional politicians tried to absorb unwelcome militant tendencies, aimed ultimately at sweeping away the Muslim part of the ruling class, by demanding revision in the 1943 Christian-Muslim power sharing agreement, and more Lebanese attention to Arab causes, primarily the Palestinian issue. This was not enough to prevent Muslim political fragmentation—gang bosses, often originally middlemen for upper-class patrons, asserted their autonomy and linked with radical Palestinian groups—but it was enough to contribute to a growing rift between the Christian and non-Christian segments of the regime.

After 1975 sectarianism appeared to reign supreme, as the country and its capital split physically between predominantly Christian, Muslim, and Druze areas, as large-scale refugee movements brought segregation of the communities, and as triumphant militias fanned sectarian bigotry to secure their power bases. For many Muslims and Druze, East Beirut and the central part of Mount Lebanon became like another planet, which they did not visit for years at a time. Similarly, many Maronites did not dare set foot in West Beirut, the Biqa', or much of the south.

However, in the second phase of the war period, during the 1982–1988 term of President Amin Jumayyil, economic deterioration united the bulk of Lebanese in deepening misery. After the reunification of Beirut in late 1990, common socioeconomic grievances became conspicuous among the lower orders, directed at the high bourgeoisie rather than from one sect against another. Sectarian identification had not diminished, but fifteen years of destructive turmoil in a small space had perhaps taught the inescapability of a common destiny.

Sectarian communities

Apart from minority immigrant groups making up about 6% of the population, chiefly Armenians and Kurds, the Lebanese have a common Arab ethnic background. Communal differentiation has been by religious sect, and more broadly between Christian and non-Christian. In this book, non-Christian refers to Islam and its heterodox offshoots. Variation in custom, historical tradition, and social behavior accounts for a considerable rigidity in communal identity, although there is also a strong shared Arabic culture and historical experience. For example, the Lebanese legal system contains no provision for non-religious treatment of personal status issues; for such important matters as marriage and inheritance, Lebanese, unless they leave the country, must go to the religious law courts of their various sects. Christians in general have clung to favorable sectarian allocations in the political system, fearing that the alternative would be Islamic political domination. Muslims have consistently rejected secularization of the legal system, on the model derived from the Christian West, because this would challenge Islam's role in society.

In the late 1980s Christians were less than 40% of the resident Lebanese population of about 3.5 million.[30] Estimates putting the Christian proportion above 40% do not incorporate hemorrhage by out-migration with the collapse of the middle bourgeoisie after 1985. Conversely, non-Christians comprised more than 60% of Lebanese residents, encompassing Muslims (about 59%) and the heterodox Druze and Alawis (about 6%). Despite demographic shifts in favor of

Muslims, especially Shi'is, estimates claiming a non-Christian proportion above 65% are exaggerations. The demographic evidence is discussed in the next section. Because there has been no census since 1932,
all figures are debatable approximations.

The seven major sectarian communities divide between two tiers as
regards demographic and political weight. Three "great" communities—
the Shi'i Muslims, the Maronite Christians, and the Sunni Muslims—
each contain more than 20% of Lebanese residents, and hold the principal regime offices *(ta'ifiyya al-fi'a al-uwla)*. Four other communities—
in descending demographic order: Orthodox Christians, Druze, Greek
Catholics, and Armenians—occupy a second tier, with subsidiary stakes
in the regime.

A presentation of the main distinctive features of the major communities now follows (see also Betts, 1979 and 1985; Gordon, 1980;
Moosa, 1986; Salibi, 1988; Halawi, 1992; J. Harik, 1994), with pre-1975
geographical distributions depicted on map 5.

Maronite Catholics
(in 1990 about 21% of resident Lebanese)

Lebanon would not exist without the Maronites, as the country is
an expression of the determination of this compact and relatively coherent mountain population to achieve political insulation from its Islamic
surrounds. The Maronites arose out of the Monothelite controversy of
the early seventh century, when the Byzantine emperor Heraclius tried
to achieve a compromise between Orthodox and Monophysite
(Egyptian Coptic and Syrian Orthodox, also known as Jacobite) views
about the relationship of human and divine natures in Christ. The compromise laid down that Christ had two separate and equal natures but a
single will, thus incorporating elements from both the "two nature"
(Orthodox) and "single nature" (Monophysite) perspectives. Monothelitism was adopted only by groups of Christians in northern Syria, in
the neighborhood of Homs, Hama, and the Orontes valley. The monks
of a monastery of Marun professed the doctrine, and a John Marun was
a leader of the Monothelites in the late seventh century; the term
"Maronite" probably derives from one or both of these names.

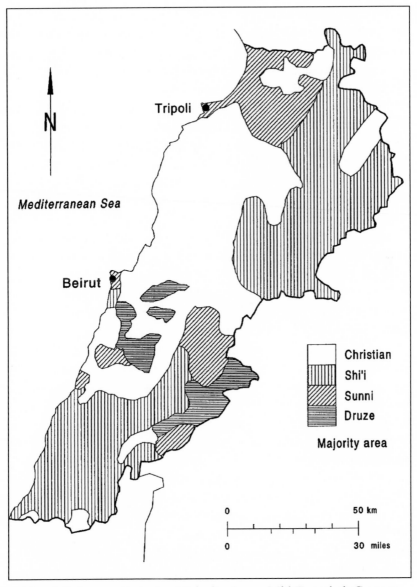

Map 5. Lebanon: Sectarian Majority Areas, Mid-Twentieth Century
Abstracted from Tübinger Atlas des Vorderen Orients (TAVO), Sheets A VIII 7
(Lebanon: Religions) and A VIII 9 (Lebanon: Christianity), Tübingen, 1979

Maronites were present in northern Mount Lebanon from the seventh century. They even asserted local autonomy under their church and village chiefs in the first centuries of Islamic supremacy in Syria. However, the mountains inland from Tripoli did not become the main Maronite home until the tenth century, when Orthodox hostility after the Byzantines reconquered parts of northern Syria from the Muslims caused Monothelites to shift southwards in order to remain in Islamic territory. The Maronites were largely restricted to the hinterland of Tripoli and Jubayl until the late Middle Ages. Thereafter their population slowly grew and spread through the Kisrawan and Matn areas in the seventeenth century, reaching Jizzin in the far south of the Lebanon range in the nineteenth century.

In 1180, while the Crusaders occupied Mount Lebanon, the Maronite patriarch accepted the supremacy of the Pope and established a formal link with the Roman church. However, Maronites continued to maintain Monothelite and Monophysite beliefs, considered heretical by the Vatican, until the sixteenth century. After about 1450, the Vatican sent a series of Franciscan and Jesuit missions to Lebanon to investigate "abuses and errors" (Moosa, 1986). As late as the 1590s the Maronites were found to be influenced by Syrian Orthodox views about the single divine nature of Christ, which had even displaced Monothelitism. Only at this point did the Vatican manage to instill sufficient ecclesiastical discipline to establish the Maronites as the prototype Uniate church. The term Uniate indicates full conformity with Roman doctrine, whether on the two natures of Christ or other matters. Otherwise the Maronites kept their Syriac ritual and distinctive religious hierarchy, headed by the Maronite patriarchate. The Maronite church, with its openness to the West, considerable land resources, powerful sense of mission, and promotion of education, has greatly contributed to the dynamism and independent-mindedness of the community in recent centuries.

Historically the Maronites have been rural and isolated, but in the nineteenth century some were drawn into commercial functions as a result of Western economic penetration, and thereafter they established a strong presence in Beirut. In 1975, the Maronites made up the great majority of the population in all of northern Mount Lebanon, with a strong presence in the Shuf and Jizzin mountains to the south, and extensions in the Biqa' and the 'Akkar hills. Maronite communities beyond the Christian heartland of Mount Lebanon were of course badly affected by the disruptions of the war years after 1975.

Other Christians
(in 1990 about 14% of resident Lebanese)

The non-Maronite Christians, particularly the Orthodox, have interacted more widely with other Middle Easterners and been historically less connected with the Christian West than the Maronites. By far the biggest of these sects (half of the total) is the Orthodox church, the direct heir of Byzantine tradition. Lebanese Orthodox, and a somewhat larger number in Syria, are under the jurisdiction of the Orthodox patriarch of Antioch, who resides in Damascus—unlike all other heads of major Lebanese Christian sects, who live in the vicinity of Beirut. The church is a sister organization to the Greek Orthodox, the Russian Orthodox, and the other Arab Orthodox under the patriarch of Jerusalem, although unlike the patriarchate of Jerusalem the Antiochene church has indigenous Arab—not Greek—leadership. Arab Orthodox, including Lebanese adherents, have an urban orientation and historically have been partners with Sunni Muslims in the traditional commercial class of the Arab east. In 1683 a portion of the Orthodox decided to join Rome as a Uniate church, like the Maronites. Many came to Mount Lebanon from the Syrian interior, especially Aleppo, where their original church made life difficult for them. They retained Orthodox ritual, set up their own patriarchate, and became known as Greek Catholics, now about 4% of Lebanon's population.

Armenians, who represent another 3%, came to Lebanon and Syria primarily from eastern Anatolia in 1918–20, after their aspiration to recover their Medieval statehood out of the wreckage of the Ottoman downfall was disappointed, and after a series of terrible massacres at the hands of Turks and Kurds. They arrived in Beirut as refugees, and the Maronite leadership promptly ensured that they were officially treated as Lebanese, to buttress the Christian sector. To the present, the Armenians have maintained their own special sort of dual existence—as an integral part of the Lebanese entity, and as members of a far-flung Armenian nation. In the Beirut suburb of Burj Hammoud, 50,000 Armenians have sustained an Armenian language press, Armenian radio stations, and Armenian paramilitary parties. Even in the 1990s, Arab Lebanese regard broken Arabic speech as an Armenian attribute. The largest number belong to the ancient Armenian Gregorian Orthodox church, and there are sizeable groups of Armenian Catholics and Protestants.

In 1975, non-Maronite Christians were at least 60% of Greater Beirut's Christian population, and probably one-quarter of its total inhabitants. The Orthodox were half of Tripoli's 20–25% Christian fraction, and the Greek Catholics formed the largest community in the 90% Christian Biqa' city of Zahla.[31] Outside main towns these sects generally ranked as secondary to the Maronites, although the Orthodox had their own rural area in the Kura, near Tripoli, and were important in the 'Akkar, Matn, and Shuf districts of Mount Lebanon, while Greek Catholic villages were prominent in the north Biqa' and east of Sidon.

Twelver Shi'i Muslims
(in 1990 about 35% of resident Lebanese)

Between the Islamic conquest and the eleventh-century Crusader invasion of the Levant, the majority of the people then living in what is now Lebanon became Muslims, but away from the coastal towns, in common with a wider rural trend in Syria, Twelver and Isma'ili Shi'ism were most popular, as a reaction to the Sunni urban ruling class. Shi'a simply means the faction of the Caliph 'Ali, cousin and son-in-law of Muhammad, who confronted those who emerged as the "Sunni" elite of the early Islamic world. Shi'ism acquired a tradition of martyrdom and resistance to established Sunni authority when 'Ali's son Husayn rebelled and was killed at Kerbala. For Shi'is, 'Ali and Husayn were the first of a line of Imams—saintly personalities who provided, in a sense, cosmic poles of their times, although they were not of divine status. Twelvers believe in a line of twelve Imams, while Isma'ilis believe in seven; the deviation occurred after the sixth Imam,

72

Ja'far al-Sadiq, who founded the Shi'i Ja'fari school of religious law. For Twelvers the last Imam went into hiding, and will reappear to put the world to rights at the end of the human age. Shi'is tend to regard mainstream Islamic history after 'Ali as a wrong path, under illegitimate regimes.

By Crusader times, Twelver Shi'is were the main population in the hills south of Mount Lebanon, in much of the Biqa', and also in large parts of central Mount Lebanon later dominated by the Maronites and Druze. In the sixteenth century, they supported Iran's transition to Shi'ism, and thereafter their connection with the Iranian Safavid empire, chief Middle Eastern enemy of the Ottomans, made them a suspect element from the Sunni Ottoman perspective. Twelver Shi'is were pushed out of the Kisrawan and the Shuf by Maronite and Druze expansion, and a late-eighteenth-century Ottoman punitive expedition ransacked Shi'i religious institutions in their southern heartland of Jabal 'Amil. Such experiences left them with little empathy for either Maronite or Druze visions of Lebanon, and little interest in Sunni Muslim authority, whether Ottoman or Arab.

When Twelver Shi'is came under the modern Lebanese state they were a geographically peripheral population, disunited by clan rivalries and oppressed by their own feudal lords in a manner other communities had largely left behind. Only in 1969 was management of Shi'i legal affairs finally separated from the Sunni judicial system, when Musa Sadr succeeded in having parliament establish a Higher Shi'i Islamic Council.

Sunni Muslims
(in 1990 about 24% of resident Lebanese)

Sunnis have always been the dominant component of the Islamic world. In their view, they are the keepers of Islamic orthodoxy, following the *sunna* (custom) of Muhammad, the first four caliphs (three of whom are cursed by many Shi'is), and the early Islamic community. Sunni Islam's social framework is elaborated by four great schools of religious law, which vary somewhat on interpretation: the Hanafi, Hanbali, Maliki, and Shafi'i. Sunnis have no place either for an elevated status for the Caliph 'Ali (who is mentioned in the Shi'i profession of Islamic faith) or for the Shi'i tradition of Imams, a tradition that affects both Shi'i religious law and psychological orientation. Lebanese Sunnis follow the relatively flexible Hanafi law school, with personal status matters and *waqf* (religious endowments) under the *dar al-ifta'* (office of legal opinions) headed by the Chief Mufti of the Republic.

Sunnis have always represented a minority in the vicinity of Mount Lebanon, although for most of the period after the advent of Islam, up to the First World War, the ruling regime of the Levant derived from their co-religionists. Historically, they were the primary community of the coastal towns of Beirut, Tripoli, and Sidon, where they took part in commerce and local government. In Beirut they became outnumbered by Christian rural migrants by the mid-nineteenth century, and during the past two decades also by Shi'is. In 1975, Sunnis perhaps still held the position of metropolitan Beirut's largest sect, were at least 75% of the population of Tripoli, Lebanon's second city, and dominated Sidon. Outside the port cities, they made a significant showing only in the far north, a corner of the Shuf, and parts of the Biqa'. Because they lacked an extended territorial base, the Sunnis were strategically disadvantaged compared with Lebanon's "mountain" communities— the Maronites, Druze, and Shi'is. This was to be a significant weakness after 1975.

Druze and 'Alawis
(in 1990 about 5% and about 1% of Lebanese residents, respectively)

The two heterodox offshoots of Shi'i Islam in Lebanon have virtually nothing in common with each other. Druze have played a central role in the history of Mount Lebanon for centuries, while 'Alawis became noticeable in Lebanese affairs only after the late 1960s, when members of their community seized and retained the leadership of the Syrian regime.

The Druze were heirs to the early footholds established by Isma'ili Shi'ism in the Levant. A small group who regarded the sixth Isma'ili Fatimid Caliph in Egypt, al-Hakim (996–1021), as a manifestation of God on earth, proselytized successfully in parts of the Lebanon and anti-Lebanon ranges in the eleventh century. Druzism, named after Darazi, an early follower of al-Hakim, secured a strategic location in the Shuf hills, in the central part of Mount Lebanon, counted a majority of the leading medieval feudal families of the mountain among its adherents, and between the fourteenth and eighteenth centuries was the dominant sectarian affiliation in Mount Lebanon's rural social order, before displacement by the Maronites. As a community, the Druze closed their gates to new converts after only a few decades, and later relied on intense communal solidarity and military prowess to compensate for small numbers. As a faith, Druzism favors a neo-Platonic view of God as an impersonal universal intellect, embraces reincarnation, and rejects the traditional "pillars" of Islam such as fasting and set prayer times. It is thus regarded as grossly heretical by orthodox Muslims.

Details of religious knowledge have always been guarded by a class of religious initiates, termed *'uqqal* (wise men), and have not traditionally been disseminated among the lay Druze population, termed *juhhal* (ignorant people). In the fifteenth century, the position of *shaykh al-'aql* (chief of wisdom) emerged as the spiritual headship of the community, in the hands of the Buhturi family. Because the *shaykh al-'aql* inevitably deals with secular and political matters he has not necessarily been from the highest rank of *'uqqal,* who prefer to maintain their ascetic, mystical orientation and avoid the diversions of the ordinary world. After 1825 the position was split between the Junblatti and Yazbaki factions (see chapter 3), creating a double spiritual leadership.[32] In 1962 the *shaykh al-'aql* became a government official responsible for the legal affairs and religious property of the Druze community, equivalent to the Sunni Chief Mufti, and in 1970 Kamal Junblatt and Majid Arslan, as factional chiefs, agreed on de facto reunification. In other words, there would be only one *shaykh al-'aql* at any one time. Ideally, the *shaykh al-'aql* serves as a channel between the religious initiates and the wider Druze community and between Druze political factions, as well as representing the community to outsiders. In practice, he has generally been limited by factional rivalry.

Lebanese 'Alawis, confined to the Tripoli area, are a minor southward extension of the 'Alawi community of the Mediterranean coastal mountains in northern Syria. 'Alawi belief involves a development of Twelver Shi'ism, principally elevation of the Caliph 'Ali to divine status. In 1972, the Lebanese Shi'i leader Musa Sadr gratified Syrian President Hafiz al-Asad by formally recognizing 'Alawis as Shi'is, and therefore as Muslims. After 1976, many Syrian 'Alawis moved into northern Lebanon under the cover of the Syrian military presence, raising local Sunnis' fears about the security of their landholdings.

Lebanese concepts of Lebanon

Since the inauguration of the Little Lebanon of the *mutasarrifiyya,* in the 1860s, the Lebanese have evolved contrasting ideas regarding the role and identity of the modern Lebanese polity, concepts loosely related to sectarian identities. At the two ends of the spectrum are what has been termed "Lebanonism," a view of Lebanon as something detached from its Arab neighborhood, and "Arabism," conceiving Lebanon as a temporary aberration, eventually to be dissolved into Arab unity, perhaps first in a Greater Syria.

Lebanonism implied asserting the mythology of Phoenician origins and of attachment to the West. Mostly it was a cover for what could be labeled Maronite nationalism—Lebanon as a vehicle for the Maronite community, with a back seat for the Druze, and other Christians brought along as ballast. The post-1918 metamorphosis of Little Lebanon into Greater Lebanon both expressed and contradicted Lebanonism, as separation from the Arab and Islamic worlds could hardly be reconciled with incorporation of large additional Muslim populations. Most Maronite leaders had a short-range perspective, confident that they could lord it over the enlarged domain (Zamir, 1985). When this confidence declined, as after 1975, Little Lebanon resurfaced as an option in some quarters, under its new cover of "federalism."

Arabism originated with the Christian intellectuals of late-nineteenth-century Beirut who played a major part in formulating modern pan-Arab nationalism, influenced by European ethnic nationalism. The main premise was freedom from Ottoman Turkish rule, with the com-

76

monality of the Arabic language and the Arab origins of Islam. Arabism acquired its particular Lebanese significance in the 1920s, when Greater Lebanon brought masses of unwilling Muslims into a Christian-dominated polity. These Muslims slowly came to accept the fait accompli of Greater Lebanon, but most remained deeply suspicious of Maronite orientation toward Europe, and they viewed Lebanon as an integral component of the Arab world. Arabism, in the sense of questioning Lebanon's permanence as anything other than an Arab "region" *(qutr)*, was strongest in the heyday of Arab nationalism from the late 1950s to the 1970s, with its Nasirite and Ba'thist outgrowths. The concept has appealed most to Sunnis, whose co-religionists are the overwhelming majority in the rest of the Arab world, but it has also always had adherents in all the other communities.

The central tendencies among both Christians and non-Christians have been more accommodatory than the extremes would imply, but wide gaps in comprehension persist. For most Lebanese Christians, including the urban and cosmopolitan Orthodox, there has been a sense of precariousness as minorities in an Islamic Middle Eastern environment, a fear of slippage to powerless subordination—a modern *dhimmi* position. Unfavorable demographic trends in the twentieth century have intensified Christian sensitivity. In one vital respect, the sophisticated notions of political and cultural pluralism espoused since before the French mandate by the supple Orthodox and Maronite commercial class of Beirut did not vary from the cruder Lebanonism of the Maronite mountain. Pluralism, no less than Lebanonism, was intended to mark Lebanon off from its neighborhood but, in the instance of pluralism, not to cut it off. Christian advocates of a multicommunal polity wanted to carry enough Muslims with the idea to ensure the viability of a distinctive Lebanon.

Most non-Christians, although in recent times reconciled to a distinctive Lebanon, have regarded Christian pluralist ideas as subterfuges to perpetuate unjustifiable Christian political advantages. Muslims have broadly acknowledged the principle of communal partnership in governing a sovereign Lebanese state, but with institutionalized power-sharing only at the highest political level, and this arranged in such a way as to reflect Lebanon's late-twentieth-century reality of a resident non-Christian majority.

After 1975 the picture was complicated by changes at both ends of the Lebanese spectrum. First, Islamic radicalism displaced secular Arabism as the main offering at the absolutist end of the non-Christian ideological range. Arabism and socialism, which theoretically allowed Muslims and Christians to meet as equals, gradually lost ground because of disillusion with Arab republican regimes, and the electrifying effect on Lebanese Shi'is of the establishment of a Shi'i Islamic regime in Iran in 1979–80. The 1985 charter of the Shi'i Hizballah (Party of God) was unambiguous about its blueprint for a restructured Lebanese entity: "we call upon everyone to opt for Islamic government, which alone guarantees justice and honor for all, and alone can block any new attempt by imperialism to infiltrate our country."[33] Second, Islamism hurt advocates of pluralist power-sharing in the Christian sector, and Lebanonism gained ground in the guise of sectarian federalism. The federalists of the Lebanese Forces militia had little interest in pluralist formulae for powerful central government, and wanted Lebanon split between autonomous cantons.

Perhaps the most significant single feature of the late 1980s and early 1990s, covered in Part Three of this book, was the failure of the extremist formulations to prevail, even in the Shi'i and Maronite communities. The intricacy of Lebanon blocked the Islamic and federalist approaches, as it also hindered Arabism, and the war that nourished the extremes also confounded them.

Islamic radicalism was itself hopelessly split between Shi'i and Sunni versions; Sunni religious fundamentalists made allies of convenience for Hizballah, but their schemes had no place for Lebanese ayatollahs. Hizballah's initial model for an Islamic republic with a Khomayni-style supreme religious guide, despite apparent populism, could never hope for more than a partial Shi'i following—a ceiling of 10–20% of Lebanon's population. Many Sunnis were stirred by the Iranian revolution, as a blow against Western interests, but the Shi'i dimension quickly became repellent to them. Within the Shi'i community, the internecine fighting of 1988–90 between the Hizballah and Amal militias damaged Hizballah's reputation. In 1992, Hizballah dropped Islamic government from its official program, gave more prominence to a common front with "oppressed" Christians, and generally recognized Lebanon's cultural variety in a manner unheard of among Islamic radical movements elsewhere in the Arab world.[34] Lebanon was no Egypt or Algeria.

As for the Christians, in 1988–90 the Aounist adventure (chapter 7) disposed of both federalism and cantons in two years of storm and fury. General Aoun's non-sectarian nationalism capitalized on wartime social shifts, principally the impoverishment of the Maronite middle and lower classes, to re-emphasize a common Lebanese fate. The economic degradation of the late 1980s indicated that the federalists could not offer a viable future for ordinary Maronites. Although Aoun's Christian militia enemies succeeded in crippling the Aounist enterprise, they also wrecked their own "Little Lebanon." Restoration of central government authority came on the only possible basis—sectarian pluralism—but unfortunately as a regime subservient to Syria.

In the end, the existence of Maronites, Shi'is, and Druze as 60% of modern Lebanon's population, with a common position as sectarian minorities in the wider Sunni Arab environment, probably ensures the permanence of the Greater Lebanon created by the French to gratify the Maronites, whatever happens with Arabism and Islamic movements in the Arab world. Indeed, Greater Lebanon has become of most potential benefit to the Twelver Shi'is who were brought into it in 1920 as a marginal political factor, but who formed its largest sect fifty years later. Incorporating the Shi'is of the south and the Biqa' into Lebanon made them the only large Lebanese community with no demographic extension into Syria or Israel. Greater Lebanon provided an excellent territorial base for the Shi'is of the Levant, isolated from coreligionists in the Gulf, to aspire for a leading role in a state. The mass of Shi'is thus have had good reason for loyalty to Greater Lebanon, as demonstrated by their instinctive support for the Lebanese army, even an army under Maronite command, and good reason to oppose Lebanon's weakening either by sectarian cantonization or by Israeli, Syrian, or wider Arab domination. Paradoxically, Shi'i political organizations became instruments of creeping Syrian hegemony in the 1980s, contradicting longer-term Shi'i concerns. This was encouraged by the Lebanese Maronite and Sunni establishments' disdain for Shi'is, by Shi'i views of Israeli and Palestinian pressures on their community, and by the Syrian president's careful cultivation; otherwise it was not a natural development.

The problem among Maronites, Shi'is, and Druze has been that although all have had an interest in Lebanon, it has not been the same interest in the same Lebanon. By the late 1970s, many Maronites had doubts about a Greater Lebanon within which they were one of several elements, rather than pre-eminent, and most Druze had never favored Greater Lebanon to begin with. Mount Lebanon meant something for Druze, and presumably many would not have objected in the 1920s to the emergence of a modern "Little Lebanon," in which they would have had a more powerful demographic and political position. Fifty years later, however, the Christian militia concept of an isolationist, Maronite-ruled Mount Lebanon was totally rejected, in part because of justified apprehensions about Kata'ib intentions to submerge the Druze of the Shuf.

In Greater Lebanon, the Druze had new Muslim associates to face the Maronites, as the old mountain relationship soured after the mid-nineteenth-century Druze-Maronite hostilities. This balanced the reduction in the Druze proportion of the population from 15% to 7% in the transition from the *mutasarrifiyya* to a larger polity.[35] Also, Druze and Shi'is alike stood aloof from the special Maronite association with France; they wished freedom of maneuver, for which Lebanon had its conveniences, but not separation from the Islamic Middle Eastern context. Lebanon's special degree of Westernization of course did influence Druze and Shi'i identity, and even that of the Sunnis, but non-Christians tried to avoid according it centrality in their image of themselves. In any event, regardless of such differences, in the late twentieth century Greater Lebanon was the only Lebanon available, and those who wanted political distinctiveness in the Arab world had to make do with it.

Demography and politics

Modern Lebanon's constitutional order up to the 1989 Ta'if arrangement, based on a combination of the 1926 written constitution and the unwritten 1943 National Pact, represented a compromise among leaders of the communities brought together into one polity by the French mandate. From the outset, politics, communal demography, and socioeconomic developments could not be disentangled from one another. The point of departure for arguments about communal power balances was the 1932 census, which showed a marginal Christian majority of 51%, compared with the Christian proportion of 75% in the *mutasarrifiyya*. Also, "confessional democracy" was a concoction of the traditional political class of the various sects, in particular reflecting a slow pragmatic convergence between the Maronite and Sunni establishments. This meant later problems in accommodating social forces outside the traditional political arena.

The 1926 constitution defined the authority of different components of government—the presidency, the cabinet (council of ministers), the parliament (chamber of deputies), the judiciary—without defining sectarian distributions. The 1943 National Pact, the foundation stone of independent Lebanon (el-Khazen, 1991), involved an understanding about which sects would hold what in the government, army, and bureaucracy. In essence, the Maronites hung onto the maximum possible prerogatives compatible with keeping non-Christians in the political system, while the Sunni leadership dominated non-Christians. In the Maronite-Sunni deal, the former held the powerful executive presidency, in the French style the primary arm of government, while the subordinate but strategic post of prime minister was reserved for the latter. The Maronites also made sure of precedence in the military and security institutions. The Shi'is were given a condescending nod with the allocation of chairmanship of parliament, in protocol terms "the second presidency," but in 1943 a position more of shadow than of substance. In the single-chamber parliament the ratio of six Christians for every five Muslims and Druze prevailed, each multimember electoral district to have seats divided between sects (17 were officially recognized for this purpose) in rough proportion to population. Even in the bureaucracy, merit considerations operated in the framework of the 6:5 rule, and of preserving sectarian quotas.

Through the decades after the 1932 census, differential natural increase and emigration rates shifted the population ratio of Christians to non-Christians against the Christians, while political allocations remained frozen according to the 1943 dispensation. Although the delicacy of the balance in the 1932 census meant that Maronite-dominated regimes thereafter avoided holding another census, enough can be derived from sample studies, the 1970 government survey of the economically active population, and the 1988 Hariri foundation food distribution, to give some indication of population growth, differential natural increase between sects, and emigration. Two analyses using such sources (Soffer, 1986; Faour, 1991) suggest a Christian decline from 51% in 1932 to 35–40% by the late 1980s. Both studies have disappointing aspects: Soffer underestimates Shi'i natural increase, compared with Sunni Muslims, and understates the impact of post-1975 hostilities on the Shi'i community, which stimulated emigration; Faour deals only with the gross Christian-Muslim comparison, with no individual consideration of even the three major sects.

Work by Joseph Chamie on sectarian fertility differentials (Chamie, 1977), based on data from the 1970 government survey of 30,000 households and the 1971 national fertility and family planning study, enables one to check on the trend reported by Soffer and Faour, as well as to consider individual sects more closely. The statistical raw materials are the 1932 census, the population estimates constructed from the 1970 government survey and the 1988 Hariri food distribution, and the 1970 sectarian total fertility rates given by Chamie. The population estimates suggest approximate growth rates for Lebanon's population: 2.8% per annum for 1932–70, and a somewhat lower 2.6% for 1970–88. Problems with the 1988 estimate, discussed below, mean that the 1970–88 growth rate is probably too high, but there is little dispute from analysts about the preceding period. Chamie's fertility rates point to the possibility of notional growth rates for sects from the 1932 base, if one varies these around the general population growth trend to the same degree 1970 sectarian fertility rates varied around the general population fertility rate. Such an equivalence projects the 1970 fertility pat-

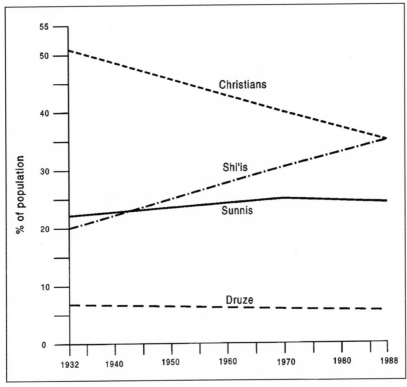

Figure 1. Trends in Sectarian Proportions among
Lebanese Resident in Lebanon, 1932–88

*(My calculations as detailed on pp. 82–85, based on fertility rates as in
Chamie, 1977, p. 368; Hariri Foundation estimates as in Faour, 1991, p. 636;
1932 census statistics as in Zamir, 1985, p. 98)*

tern back to 1932, and excludes the impact of intersectarian variation in out-migration. Specifically, it assumes that lesser Christian-Muslim fertility gaps for earlier decades, and higher Christian out-migration, roughly cancel each other out—which may be close to reality.

Even with these assumptions, it is interesting that updating sectarian populations from 1932 to the late 1980s using notional sectarian growth rates, extrapolated from Chamie's fertility investigation, produces sectarian proportions of the population very similar to those

	Lebanese resident population	data sources	% Maronite	% other Christian	% Sunni	%Shi'i	% Druze	Demographic Changes
Mutasarrifiyya								
1911	414,858	census	58	21	4	6	11	Enlargement of Lebanon; disproportionate losses in mutasarrifiyya with famine, 1914-18
Greater Lebanon								
1921	609,069	census	33	22	21	17	7	1920s: Maronite slippage, Shi'i increase, Armenian refugee influx
1932	782,415	census	29	22	22	20	7	
1943	1,046,421	official estimate	52% Christian		48% non-Christian			No census after 1932. Trends: Christian and Druze decline, Shi'i rise
1970	2,265,000	adjusted Ministry of Planning survey	about 42% Christian?		about 58% non-Christian?			Growth rate somewhat depressed by war, 1975-90 (accelerated out-migration more significant than casualties
1990	3,500,000	Hariri Foundation	21	14	24	35	5	

Table 1. Lebanese Resident in Lebanon: Numbers and Sectarian Proportions, 1911–90
(Chamie, 1977; Faour, 1991, pp. 632, 636; Zamir, 1985, p. 98: my calculations as shown in figure 1.)

extracted by Faour from the 1988 Hariri "head count." One arrives at the same Christian to non-Christian ratio of 35 to 65—via a separate route. This gives a little confidence for going beyond Faour, to suggest developments for the individual sects, from 1932 through 1970 to the late 1980s.

Figure 1 and Table 1 depict an evolution of considerable political importance. The most prominent feature cuts across the dividing line between Christian and non-Christian: The Shi'i community grew from one-fifth of Lebanon's population in 1932 to over one-third half a century later, to overtake both the Maronites and the Sunnis, the leading partners in political sectarianism. This was as pregnant with disruption for Sunni-Shi'i relations as it was across the Christian-Muslim spectrum; the Sunni-Shi'i ratio in the general population has changed from 23:20 in 1932 to 24:35 in 1988. Otherwise, the Maronites declined from 30% to 21%, other Christians from 21% to 14%, and the Druze dipped below 5%. The Christian to non-Christian ratio went from 51:49 to 40:60 by the early 1970s; in other words, within the period of greater statistical reliability.

Some observations and qualifications need to be made regarding the demographic evolution. First, the trend through the war years is less reliable than that up to the early 1970s, because of suspicion that the 1988 Hariri count somewhat exaggerated the total population. One accusation was that because households knew the underlying purpose of the food distribution included assessment of reconstruction aid requirements, people felt encouraged to inflate household size, and that distribution workers, although alerted to the problem, could not hope to screen out all such inflation.[36] However, this does not necessarily upset the Christian-Muslim proportions. Second, the agreement on sectarian percentages between the 1988 Hariri count and estimates for 1988 based on Chamie's work is reached without any reference to sectarian variations in out-migration—a notable curiosity given that Christians historically have had a greater propensity to leave than non-Christians. For the late twentieth century, it may be that the large departures of Shi'is and Sunnis during the war years have substantially reduced the imbalance. Over the longer period, it is probable that casting 1970 fertility rate differences back several decades has been unfair to the Christians, but that the effect in exaggerating the non-Christian proportion of the population has been approximately balanced out by higher Christian emigration. Whatever the case, I conclude that the Christian proportion of Lebanon's population in the mid-1990s must be very close to 35%, and assertions that it is significantly different are not justified.

Steady slippage in the Christian share of the resident population has raised tricky questions about Lebanon's relations with the Lebanese diaspora, which remains more than 50% Christian. Certainly Lebanon's internal balances cannot be treated in isolation; aside from the millions of people of Lebanese origin overseas, many of whom maintain Lebanese citizenship rights through paternal descent, more than 300,000 left to live abroad between 1975 and 1990.[37] Some hundreds of thousands might return if full peacetime conditions were restored; the impact on internal sectarian percentages is unpredictable. Maronite leaders oppose alteration of diaspora citizenship rights, whereas Shi'is and Sunnis frown upon potential political participation by people more than a generation removed from Lebanon.

Demographic change, however, has lessened the salience of the Christian-Muslim distinction, and emphasized a more intricate set of cleavages. In recent decades sectarian distinction has become triangular, between Christians, Shi'is, and Sunnis. The Shi'i rise has sharpened Shi'i-Sunni friction, and the Christian contraction has caused Maronites and other Christians to gravitate into a more cohesive communal block. Christians as a whole today have about the same demographic weight as Shi'is—35%. The Druze are the odd ones out, oscillating in their outlook, the only constant being the survival imperative.

Further, the rise of militant political movements in the urban lower and lower middle classes of both the Christian and the Islamic sectors through the 1950s and 1960s fragmented the population at all social levels, exacerbating antagonisms between and within sects. For Christians the pull at "street" level was toward the radical right, as instability in the Arab world, with the overthrow of conservative pro-Western regimes, made Maronites feel threatened. For non-Christians the general pull was toward reforming the political system to enhance the Muslim role. The Maronite and Sunni political establishments, the pillars of the

National Pact, steadily lost authority to new forces and were tugged in different directions by "street" demands. Struggles between old politicians and aspirants coming up from below, and among the new political forces themselves, caused a bewildering oscillation of coalescence and splitting for the individual communities, above all for Shi'is and Christians. The consequences were well demonstrated by the multiplicity of inter- and intrasectarian hostilities after 1975.

The Shi'i community burst onto the political stage in the early 1980s, and this decisively shattered the non-Christian sector. Israeli-Palestinian hostilities in southern Lebanon through the 1970s caused mass flight of rural Shi'i poor from the south to the Beirut suburbs. In consequence, the Sunnis lost their majority in predominantly Muslim West Beirut to the Shi'is, a change emphasized by the parallel influx of Shi'is forcibly uprooted from old Shi'i neighborhoods in what was becoming Christian East Beirut. Demographic upheaval ended the political quiescence of a large part of the Shi'i population, and also reduced the traditional co-option of Shi'is by non-Shi'i political parties. In the mid-1970s Musa Sadr supplied a center of gravity previously absent in the community (Ajami, 1985), and Shi'is came to see themselves as threatened or subordinated by Palestinians, Maronites, and Sunnis alike.

In the 1980s politically active Shi'is, a growing portion of the community, rebelled against their environment. Israel's removal of much of the Palestinian apparatus in 1982, followed by Israeli-Shi'i frictions and enforced Israeli retreat, allowed new Shi'i communal militias, little noticed in the 1970s, to take charge in much of the south and West Beirut, in uneasy collaboration with the Druze. The transformation scared the Sunni, Druze, and Christian bourgeoisie of West Beirut, especially when the 1984 takeover of West Beirut by Shi'i and Druze militias brought an invasion of Sunni and Christian bourgeois districts by Shi'i poor from the southern suburbs. The Sunni upper and middle class of Beirut, latterly propped up by the Palestinians, was temporarily marginalized. Even the Sunni "street" in such lower class areas as Basta felt the reduction in their community's demographic and political weight.

Sunni-Shi'i antagonism became inflamed in 1985, when the Shi'i

Amal militia laid siege to the Palestinian refugee camps. Sunni spokesmen lost no time in expressing sympathy with the Palestinians; Sunni Chief Mufti Hasan Khalid referred sarcastically to the Shi'i "dispossessed." I was in West Beirut at the time, and heard one Shi'i taxi driver quote a popular saying to mock Sunni discontent with shifting circumstances: "The dogs bark, but the caravan moves on." [38]

Shi'i coherence, however, being very recent was also very fragile. Shi'i assertion, and behavior as if the community was already a Lebanese majority, which it was not, invited a damaging setback. This occurred in the late 1980s with fragmentation of the community encouraged by the Syrian Ba'thists, who harnessed the Shi'is to their drive for domination over the Lebanese. Among the Shi'is, Syria aided the secular Amal militia as pressure on the Palestinians and the Maronite-dominated regime, and supported Iranian penetration and Islamism to push out Western interests and the Israelis. The Shi'is thus acquired two heads—Amal and Hizballah—and the interplay of Syria and Iran helped precipitate bitter warfare between the Shi'i militias in 1988–90, tearing the community apart at the moment of its greatest salience in Lebanese affairs. For Syria, the Shi'is had by then served their immediate purpose, and there was no haste to settle the hostilities. With the 1989 Lebanese constitutional reform, Damascus returned to playing with the Christians and the Sunnis.

Lebanon and Syria

Greater Lebanon was never entirely accepted by the Syrian state that emerged out of the French mandate for Lebanon and Syria as a truncated rump of *Bilad al-Sham*—"the country of Damascus," or "of the north"—a territory encompassing all the Levant, and often thought of as geographical Syria. *Bilad al-Sham* has on no occasion formed a political unit, always having been either split up, or part of something larger. During Ottoman times, it—or the alternative term "Syria"—referred to a region with a broadly common Arabic dialect, history, climate and landscape, but the Ottoman regime divided it into a number of provinces. None of this prevented those who ruled

Damascus after 1943, particularly the pan-Arab Ba'thists after 1963, from regarding the Lebanese, Jordanian, and Palestinian Arabs as rightfully subordinate to the new Syrian political entity, even if political "coordination" was conceived as the supremacy of one state over others, rather than a crude will for a single state.

Culturally, Lebanon and Syria grade into one another; the Palestinians and Jordanians have not had quite the multiplicity of family and sectarian connections with Syria as have crisscrossed the Lebanon-Syria border. Lebanon's Sunni Muslim, Orthodox Christian, and Armenian communities could hardly be disentangled from their Syrian brethren, even as they developed a Lebanese sentiment and a distaste for Syrian authoritarianism. A large fraction had close relatives in Damascus, Homs, and Aleppo. Lebanon's Maronites and Druze also have substantial numbers of coreligionists in Syria, but the intensity of interaction has been significantly less. Only the Shi'is have had almost no communal interest across the border, and the new Shi'i leadership of the 1980s set up the closest ties of all with Syria's 'Alawi-Ba'thist combine, partly because Damascus was the way station between Lebanon and Iran. Certainly, if independent Syria had evolved a political and economic system remotely resembling the liberalism and openness of Beirut, much of Lebanon's distinguishing character would not have been so distinctive. Syria, however, made no equivalent evolution; it has become a significantly different society, with a significantly different modern history. Syria and Lebanon may grade into one another, but what one may term their social and political "centers of gravity" are mutually alien.

The distinction between Lebanon and Syria may be discussed at two levels. First, the modern states vary fundamentally in their sectarian mixtures and the demographic relations of the communities—in other words, in a most basic aspect of their social geography. In Lebanon, three communities exist in a rough balance, although not demographically equal, and even in the late twentieth century no single sect is more than 35% of the population. In Syria, Sunni Muslims are at least two-thirds of the population, and no other community reaches 15%, not even all the Christians added together. Further, the West has had much less effect on the cultural orientation of the Syrian communities, including the Christians, leading to real divergences in mentality between Beirut and Damascus, including for Muslims. Aside from the Western impact, the special case of Lebanese Twelver Shi'i outlooks does not have a real parallel within Syria.

Second, the trend toward a rigid autocratic regime in Damascus contrasted with Lebanon's semidemocratic political tradition, which managed to survive into the 1990s. The rise of 'Alawi lower-middle-class personnel, via the armed forces and Ba'thist ideology, to dominate the Syrian state and overturn the old upper class, created a modern Syrian history as removed from that of Lebanon as Russian history is from French history. The underlying Sunni-'Alawi theme of contemporary Syrian affairs—the story of two-thirds watching one-eighth, a small minority, moving from subordination to paramountcy—simply cannot be related to Lebanon's own multisectarian experience.

Because of such contrasts, Lebanese-Syrian relations in the late twentieth century could not be an easy matter, despite the rhetoric about "twins" and "one people in two states." The huge divergence in political and economic character, and in international relationships, especially at the popular level, overshadowed, even eroded, cultural familiarity. Also, the behavior of the Syrian army in the areas of Syrian military deployment in Lebanon after 1976 did not encourage many Lebanese, whatever their community, to view Syria with much favor. The 1991 Treaty of Brotherhood, Cooperation and Coordination subordinated Lebanese decision-making to the requirements of the Syrian regime; for the vast majority of the Lebanese people it was a product of *force majeure* that had to be tolerated for the duration of prevailing power relations in the Eastern Mediterranean. Otherwise it meant nothing to them. Once, in the mid-1980s, I traveled in a service taxi from Damascus to Beirut with some members of the Shi'i Amal militia. After crossing the border, the militiamen expressed relief in strong language at "leaving the dictatorship." Up to 2005, conditions have not changed.

Aerial view of Beit ad-Din, the palace of Amir Bashir Shihab

Mahsubak ana ismi fulan
Min ahsan ayla bi lubnan
Wa murashah nafsi nayyib
Awal band min arba'in
Bikhalli as-sama tshatti tahin
Wa al-ard tnba' benzin
Bila rusum wa dara'ib
Bas intakhibuni na'ib

At your service, my name is such-and-such
From the best family in Lebanon
And I present my candidacy for parliament
As my first of forty promises
I shall have the sky rain flour
And the earth give forth benzine
Without fees or taxes
Just elect me a deputy

—*'Umar al-Za'ni* (1895-1961)

CHAPTER THREE

FAMILIES AND RULERS

The place of "family"

Families and clans remain the foremost elements in the lives of individual Lebanese. Personal associations and social activities continue to center on extended families to a notable degree for a society that has successfully adapted itself to the operations and philosophy of Western capitalism. Lebanon's twentieth-century history demonstrated that a population's adjustment to modern urban living and new modes of production need not diminish the "primordial" ties of family, village, and sect (Khalaf, 1987).

The combination, however, has had a high price, because concentration on family loyalties has retarded the development of wider social responsibilities and political associations, vital for the proper functioning of a modern state. The implications may be detected in a wide range of phenomena, including the exaggerated role of formalized family associations in civil society, the malignant presence of patronage networks in the state bureaucracy, the absence of significant issue-based parties in a political system still dominated by personal or sectarian connections, and the alarming public indifference regarding environmental pollution and urban planning in a small, densely populated country.

Family connections and sectarian identity are difficult to disentangle from one another, because marriages have overwhelmingly been within sects, and political interactions between sects have principally been the interactions of leading families, at least until very recent times. The fact that the family worlds of the vast majority of Lebanese are

93

contained within sectarian boundaries has reinforced sectarian orientations, and the fact that "family" has always been the focal point of
Lebanese life has implied that contacts and alignments between leading
families have historically been the main mechanism of sectarian coexistence.

The pecking order of families and clans within and between sectarian communities has altered through Lebanon's history since the imposition of Ottoman authority and the emergence of the *imara* in the sixteenth century. This has reflected the broader shifts in geopolitical, economic and sectarian conditions discussed in chapters 1 and 2. The composition of the Lebanese ruling class of the late twentieth century
reflected a combination of historical legacies: (a) survival of major landed families—*muqata'jis*—from the period of the Ma'nid and Shihabi
imara; (b) emergence of new names in Mount Lebanon through Shihabi
recruitment and Maronite clerical and peasant activism after the mid-
eighteenth century; (c) concurrent growth of the commercial class of the
coastal towns due to expanded trade opportunities and European influence, with Christians favored but also involving the Sunnis; (d) advantage taken of administrative reform, political stability, and economic
openings in the *mutasarrifiyya* and the Ottoman Levantine provinces
after 1860; and (e) ferment in the middle and lower classes, particularly
for Shi'is but also for Maronites and Sunnis, with Lebanon's commercial
florescence in the mid-twentieth century.

Establishment and decay of the *iqta'i* (quasi-feudal) social order, 1516–1840

After the expulsion of the Crusaders in the thirteenth century, the
Mamluk rulers of the Levant, as already noted, favored the Druze in
Mount Lebanon and intermittently persecuted the Maronites and Shi'is.
For a brief period in the mid-fifteenth century the sway of the Arslan
and Buhturi families of the Banu al-Tanukh tribe, both enjoying good
relations with the Mamluks, extended from Tripoli to the Galilee.[39]
When the Ottoman Turks defeated the Mamluks and seized geographi-
cal Syria in 1516, they did not acknowledge any special role for the

Arslans or Buhturis, and the southern part of Mount Lebanon was in a state of insurrection for much of the sixteenth century.[40] In 1590, the Ottomans turned to a Druze district chief, Fakhr al-Din Ma'n, as their agent, appointing him *sanjakbey* (see chapter 1) of Sidon. The Ma'n family stemmed from Beduin Arabs who had settled in the Shuf hills in the eleventh century.

Between 1590 and 1633, Fakhr al-Din established an autonomous domain much bigger than modern Lebanon, including the Biqa' and interior Syria as far as Palmyra, giving him sufficient revenues to support an effective private army. In the process, he turned against the Ottoman governor of Damascus, promoted relations with Europe, favored local Christians, and eventually appeared as if he might subvert Ottoman overlordship in much of the Eastern Mediterranean. In 1633, the Sultan Murad IV mounted a military campaign and overthrew him. However, before his removal and execution Fakhr al-Din inaugurated two family alignments that were important for the next phase of Mount Lebanon's history.

First, he cultivated a link with the al-Khazens, a leading Maronite family who were at the forefront of the seventeenth-century Maronite settlement of the Kisrawan district, not far to the north of the Ma'nid core area in the Shuf. This Ma'n/al-Khazen link was the formative element in the coalescence of Druze and Maronite rural tax-farmer families *(muqata'jis)* to form the intersectarian quasi-feudal social system that characterized Mount Lebanon between the sixteenth and mid-nineteenth centuries. Acquisition of extensive lands in the Kisrawan enabled the al-Khazens to dominate the Maronite community through the seventeenth and eighteenth centuries. Their patronage and intervention also led to the Maronite church becoming centered in the Kisrawan, thus reducing the influence of the Shi'i Hamada shaykhs who controlled the Maronite north in this period. Al-Khazen authority waned only in the late eighteenth century, with fragmentation of family landholdings, disunity between the family branches, indebtedness to moneylenders, and social change among Maronites (for detailed treatment, see van Leeuwen, 1994).

The most important implication of the collaboration between Fakhr al-Din and the al-Khazens was the boost it gave to Maronite territorial expansion and to Maronite commercial and cultural relations with Western Europe, mediated by the al-Khazens as "French consuls" after 1658. Members of the al-Khazen family joined Fakhr al-Din in exile in Tuscany in 1613–18, where they contributed to his credibility with the French, the Italians, and the Vatican. Ironically, facilitation of a Maronite "ascent" by the Ma'n/al-Khazen association also led to developments that would later undermine both the al-Khazens and the Druze-Maronite *muqata'ji* order.

Second, Fakhr al-Din made an alliance with the Kurdish chieftain 'Ali Janbalad, who took Aleppo and briefly defied the Ottomans in the early seventeenth century. Janbalad's situation in the relatively open terrain of northern Syria was much less stable than that of Fakhr al-Din, and the Ottomans recaptured Aleppo in 1607. Janbalad fled into Anatolia, but members of his family settled in the Shuf under Ma'nid protection, where their name changed slightly to Junblatt. The Junblatts became accepted as Druze shortly thereafter, although no record exists regarding exactly how this happened—an unusual occurrence so many centuries after the closure of the sect to new members. Marriage into the Banu al-Tanukh certainly helped.

By the mid-eighteenth century shrewd family alliances, land acquisition, and the personal qualities of individual Junblatts led to the family becoming the leading Druze name of Mount Lebanon. A Shaykh 'Ali Junblatt joined the ranks of the foremost *'uqqal*—religious scholars—as well as being acknowledged as the principal *muqata'ji* of the Shuf. At the beginning of the nineteenth century the Junblatt "tax farm" in the Shuf, Jizzin and neighboring districts encompassed 200 villages with 30,000 inhabitants—compared with the 31 villages with 13,000 residents which were the responsibility of the older Abu Nakad family.[41]

After Fakhr al-Din's downfall in 1633, the Ottomans shrank the Ma'nid realm back to southern Mount Lebanon, dimensions within which they found the *imara* useful as a device for indirect rule and tax delivery, and did not consider it a threat. In 1697, the Ma'nid family line failed to produce a male heir, and a majority of Druze leaders agreed to transfer the *imara* to the Shihab family, related to the Ma'ns by marriage and pre-eminent in Wadi al-Taym, the original Druze stronghold on the western flank of Mount Hermon. Interestingly, both the Ma'ns and Shihabs began their tenure of the *imara* as Sunni Muslims—the Ma'ns by dissimulation and the Shihabs with more conviction. Although the Ma'ns were undoubtedly Druze in the sixteenth century, even Fakhr al-Din was careful to maintain a Sunni public face. At least up to the eighteenth century, the Ottomans would not have sanctioned local autonomy under non-Sunni management, and the Druze adapted to this circumstance.

At the outset, the Shihabs had authority in only part of Mount Lebanon. Their rule extended northward into predominantly Maronite areas only as far as the Kisrawan, where they depended on the al-Khazens. The rest of the coastal mountain range, the ports of Tripoli, Sidon, and Beirut, the valley of the Biqa', and the southern hills of Jabal 'Amil were technically under the direct command of the Ottoman governors of Sidon and Damascus. The governor of Sidon, on behalf of the Sultan, formally invested each Shihabi amir, or "prince," with his right to rule, but the Shihabs sometimes operated as equals of the governors. The resulting competition prevented any single strongman from achieving regional hegemony, and probably represented an Ottoman device to safeguard imperial authority and revenue extraction—in this sense the Shihabi *imara* was certainly part of the "system."[42]

Further, in the surrounds of the *imara* away from the coastal plain, the governors tolerated the existence of local fiefdoms under Shi'i rural bosses, although the latter did not have the status of the Shihabs. The Shi'i Hamada and Harfush families held sway and collected taxes in the north Biqa', and from Hirmil the Hamadas gained control of the main Maronite areas of northern Mount Lebanon between the sixteenth and late eighteenth centuries. South of the *imara*, another set of Shi'i clans— those of al-Asa'ad, al 'Ali al-Saghir, al-Sa'b and al-Munqir—dominated the Shi'i population of Jabal 'Amil from Mamluk times, asserting themselves from strongpoints in rough hill country, including from old Crusader sites (for more detail, see Halawi, 1992).

The Shihabs took two steps during the eighteenth century that consolidated their supremacy and strongly influenced the relative positions of families in the social hierarchy. Early in their rule, they had to face a factional challenge from within the Druze community. The challenge arose from a long-standing division of leading Druze families into two groups, termed "Qaysi" and "Yamani" in reference to an Arab tribal split early in Islamic history. Such terminology gave respectability to what was otherwise simply a struggle for precedence (Betts, 1987). The Ma'ns and Shihabs adhered to the Qaysi faction, while the 'Alam al-Din family, one of whom had been the leading chief of the Shuf in the twenty years after Fakhr al-Din's fall, led the Yamanis. The 'Alam al-Dins refused to accept the succession of Haydar Shihab in 1707, and in 1711 the Shihabs, most notably supported by the Junblatts, routed the Yamanis at Ayn Dara', near the Dahr al-Baydar pass between Beirut and the Biqa'. The Ayn Dara' outcome greatly elevated the Junblatts, especially as many 'Alam al-Dins and other Yamanis left Mount Lebanon to settle in a hilly area of southern Syria subsequently known as the Jabal al-Druze.

Later in the eighteenth century the Shihabs became involved in the affairs of northern Mount Lebanon, leading to a major territorial expansion of the *imara*. In the 1750s, Maronite and Sunni peasants rebelled against their Shi'i Hamada overlords, and by 1759 they had expelled the Hamadas from Bsharri and the 'Akkar.[43] Both the northern Maronites and the Hamadas sought assistance from the *imara*—the Maronites asked the al-Khazens to persuade Amir Mansur Shihab to intervene against the Hamadas, without discernable effect, and the Hamadas turned to the Yazbaki Druze faction to restrain Mansur.

The Hamada attempt to exploit the new Druze factionalism among the victors of 1711—in which the Yazbaki group, particularly the Abu Nakads and 'Imads, tried to undercut the ascendant Junblatts—backfired. The Junblatts reacted by allying with Yusuf Shihab, Mansur's rival for leadership of the *imara*. This was arranged through Yusuf's energetic advisor, Sa'd al-Khuri, and represented a bid to curtail both Mansur and the Yazbakis. The northern Maronites gave Yusuf Shihab tax money to take to the governor of Damascus. In 1764, backed by the Junblatts, Yusuf asked the governor for appointment as tax farmer for the area, in place of the Hamadas. The governor readily obliged, and for a time the extended *imara* had two rulers—Yusuf Shihab in the north and Mansur in the south. In 1770, Yusuf took charge of the whole of

Mount Lebanon.

Enlargement of the *imara* created new family and communal balances. At the upper social level, the number of *muqata'jis*—local chiefs who collected taxes, administered justice, and raised troops on behalf of the amir—increased, and relative weightings changed, both between Druze and Maronites and among Maronites. The Druze retained the advantage, especially in the higher ranks (amir, muqaddam, prominent shaykhs), but in diminished form. Druze leading families included the Arslans (amir), Muzhirs (muqaddam), Junblatts, 'Imads, Abu Nakads (upper level shaykhs), Talhuqs, 'Abd al-Maliks and 'Ids (shaykhs). The Abilama's, who like the Shihabs and Arslans had held amir rank for centuries, were originally Druze but in the eighteenth century were converting to Maronite Catholicism. Maronites, previously only represented by the al-Khazens and Hubayshes of the Kisrawan, became a majority of middle and lesser shaykhs, with the appointment of several northern village landlords as *muqata'jis*—the al-Khuris, Dahdahs, Karams and Abi Sa'bs. Apart from the Druze and Maronites, there were only the Shi'i Hamadas (ranked immediately after the amirs) and the Orthodox 'Azars (lesser shaykhs), both of the north (I. Harik, 1968; Salibi, 1965).

For several decades, until the early nineteenth century, strong nonsectarian loyalties of peasant to *muqata'ji* prevailed, and Druze landlords even encouraged Maronites to move south as tenants, and supported land development by the Maronite church. However, the growing Maronite majority in the enlarged *imara,* Maronite migration into the Druze territories of the Matn and the Shuf, even as far as Jizzin, and autonomist sentiments among the Maronite clergy and peasantry, all promised disruption for the social system and for Maronite-Druze relations. This was presaged by adjustment by the Shihab amirs themselves. In the late eighteenth century some of the Shihabs, like the Abilama's, became Maronite. The religious allegiance of the ruling line wavered, with rumors of secret conversions offset by occasional public reiteration of Sunni Islam.

In any case, the Shihabs increasingly favored Maronite interests, and employed Maronite commoners as assistants and scribes. In the late eighteenth century, this provided a new route for family elevation, the best known cases being those of Sa'd al-Khuri and Jiryis Baz. Baz, son of a scribe for Amir Yusuf from the Shuf village of Deir al-Qamar, rose to become the personal assistant *(mudabbir)* of Amir Bashir II, and helped determine the affairs of the *imara* in the first years of the nineteenth century.[44] The Druze chieftains were not happy with the drift of events, but the situation was obscured until the 1820s by dissensions among both Druze and Maronites, and by the continued dependence of the amir on Druze leaders for the viability of his authority.

Between the late eighteenth century and the 1840s, the Maronites attained their ascendancy in Mount Lebanon as the other two mountain communities—the Druze and the Shi'is—suffered a decisive decline. This was mainly during the period of Amir Bashir II Shihab. Collisions between Shi'i chiefs and the Ottoman governor of Sidon, and between Druze *muqata'jis* and Amir Bashir, which went badly for leading Shi'i and Druze families, formed the background to the intercommunal shifts.

The Shi'is of Jabal 'Amil prospered in the seventeenth and eighteenth centuries from the export of high quality cotton, returning higher tax revenues than Mount Lebanon.[45] In the early eighteenth century they came under the influence of a powerful Galilee tax farmer, Zahir al-'Umar, whom the Ottomans had great difficulty in containing when he allied himself with the Russians and rebellious Egyptians in the 1770s.[46] Forced to appoint Zahir governor of Sidon in 1774, the Ottomans deposed and killed him in 1776 immediately after making peace with Russia.

The new governor of Sidon, Ahmad al-Jazzar, lost no time in settling accounts with the major Shi'i chief, Nasif al-Nassar, who had been Zahir's leading local supporter. Al-Jazzar, the "butcher," subdued the Shi'is with great ferocity, and their headmen were either executed or forced to flee. At about the same time the cotton trade collapsed. A semblance of stability returned only after al-Jazzar's death in 1804, when al-Nassar's son arranged for surviving local chiefs to resume their official roles, but the shock reduced Jabal 'Amil to a backwater, a situation that did not change for more than a century.

Druze factionalism, manipulated by Amir Bashir, led by 1825 to a situation in which the Shihab ruler could escape from the influence of Druze leading families, particularly the Junblatts. From the outset of his rule, in 1788, Amir Bashir was aligned with the powerful Shaykh Bashir Junblatt and lacked a firm Maronite base, because the Maronites of the north favored the family of Amir Yusuf Shihab. Amir Bashir used his connection with Bashir Junblatt to reduce other Druze chiefs, mainly from the Yazbaki faction. He destroyed the Abu Nakads of Deir al-Qamar and greatly weakened the 'Imads. In 1808 Amir Bashir conspired with Bashir Junblatt and even remnants of the Yazbakis to have his overly influential advisor, Jiryis Baz, murdered.

As a result of these maneuverings, Bashir Junblatt came almost to monopolize political authority among the Druze. In 1820, Amir Bashir needed Junblatt's support to overcome a Maronite popular uprising, the *'amiyya*. The next year, however, when the amir was briefly forced into exile in Egypt after confronting the governor of Damascus, Junblatt tried to undercut him. On his return, Amir Bashir determined to dispose of Junblatt, and carefully cultivated the Maronite church and Yazbaki Druze. Junblatt appealed to northern Maronites, but rising sectarian sentiment counted against him.

In 1825, Amir Bashir, commanding a largely Maronite force with a contribution from the Ottoman governor of Sidon, defeated Junblatt's largely Druze force at Mukhtara, the Junblatt family seat in the Shuf. Junblatt was thereafter imprisoned in Acre, where he was strangled on the orders of the governor of Damascus. Junblatt's downfall and Amir Bashir's new Maronite alignment permanently altered the politics of the *imara* in favor of the Maronites. The events also illustrated new twists in Ottoman "divide and rule" policies—Istanbul apparently calculated that its interests would be best protected by Amir Bashir as the most effective local force, which proved a mistake.

As for the Maronites themselves, significant developments occurred in community leadership from the late eighteenth century on. After a Vatican-sponsored church council in 1736 that considered the role and organization of the Maronite church, the religious hierarchy slowly became less influenced by *muqata'ji* families such as the al-Khazens and the Shi'i Hamadas. It paid more attention to the concerns and education of the wider Maronite population. The political interventions of patriarch Yusuf al-Tiwwan (1796–1808), who aligned with Jiryis Baz, illustrated the change.

More broadly, Jubayl and the north regained some of their weight in Maronite affairs with the rise of the new *muqata'jis*—the Dahdahs, for example, took over Hamada lands—and rural property development by the Lebanese Order of monks. The Lebanese Order was founded in about 1700 and became a major factor in the more dynamic role of the church later in the century.[47]

Amir Bashir's decision in 1820 to impose new taxes on the Maronite peasants via the *muqata'jis,* because of a demand for extra revenue from the governor of Sidon, provoked an upheaval. Exemption of the Druze, owing to Junblatti influence, led to Maronite resistance. Bishop Yusuf Istfan, secretary to patriarch Yuhanna al-Helou (1809– 23), encouraged the peasantry to refuse the taxes and to select village representatives *(wukala')* as their spokesmen in dealing with the amir. This involved rejection of Maronite *muqata'ji* authority, especially that of the al-Khazens, then allied with the Junblatts, and assertion of communal "public interest," a notion probably borrowed from the French revolution. Significantly, the peasants had allies other than the church. They received financial support from the Christian artisans and traders of Beirut, Zahla, and Deir al-Qamar.[48] For some decades Christian traders had been exploiting the financial embarrassments of the older *muqata'ji* families, who were struggling to cope with Bashir II's tax demands, and increasingly needed credit.

In the 1820s Amir Bashir had no choice but to adapt to the new balances in the Maronite community. The most prominent consequence was the amir's close relationship after 1825 with the new Maronite patriarch, Yusuf Hubaysh (1823–45). Hubaysh came from a minor *muqata'ji* family, yet promoted alignments that subverted the old social system. Muhammad 'Ali's rebellion in Egypt against the Ottoman central government in the 1820s and the Egyptian occupation of the Levant through the 1830s encouraged communal and leadership changes in Lebanon. Amir Bashir allied himself with Muhammad 'Ali, and his value to the Egyptians depended on his ability to "deliver" the Maronite population.

Hubaysh and other church leaders thus had a free hand to indulge in their version of social engineering, which involved strengthening Maronite sectarianism by cutting Maronite-Druze links, whether among peasants or between peasants and *muqata'jis*.[49] After 1832, this took place in a permissive environment—the Egyptians favored Arab Christians for the sake of higher tax returns, commercial interactions with Europe mainly benefited Christian entrepreneurs, and some senior Shihabs finally committed themselves to Maronite Catholicism.

In the 1830s the connection between the Maronite amir and the Maronite patriarch became the principal political axis of Mount Lebanon. The church aimed for a Christian *imara* based on Maronite communal solidarity, with the Druze subordinated and the Egyptian-Ottoman confrontation exploited to extract greater local autonomy. The Egyptian objective of more effective central authority therefore implied tension, as it involved constraints as well as benefits for Christians.

Toward the end of the 1830s, Egyptian demands for taxes, peasant labor, and military conscription stimulated Maronite peasant rejection of both Egyptian rule and Amir Bashir. The amir and most Maronite *muqata'jis* opposed rebellion, while the church wavered in the face of the popular upsurge. One member of a *muqata'ji* family—François al-Khazen—played a prominent role in encouraging the peasants, while new names emerged from the peasantry itself as organizers of a second *'amiyya* (revolt) in 1840—from the 'Aql, Abu Samra, al-Shantiri, and Shi'i Daghir families.[50] Patriarch Hubaysh, concluding that a Christian *imara* under Egyptian patronage was an illusion, joined the peasants and repudiated Bashir II. European military intervention in September 1840 terminated Egyptian rule and restored the Ottomans.

Decisive disruption, 1840–60

Between 1840 and 1861, leadership and family influences in Mount Lebanon and adjacent areas were much affected by a prolonged political crisis. By 1842 the Shihab family's pre-eminence came to an end because of Druze hostility, the incompetent performance of Bashir III, and the Ottoman will for direct rule. The Ottoman authorities played between different social and sectarian groups to render local autonomy unworkable. They exacerbated divisions without achieving stable overlordship. The Ottomans sponsored the return of Druze *muqata'jis* exiled in 1825, principally the Junblatts, Abu Nakads, and 'Imads. Once re-established in their Shuf lands, these *muqata'jis* sought to reassert control over the local Maronite peasantry. The peasants resisted, supported by the church, leading to a succession of Maronite-Druze clashes between 1841 and 1845.

In response, the Ottoman government split Mount Lebanon into two districts, the double *qa'imqamiyya,* with the north under a Christian governor from the Abilama' family and the south under a Druze Arslan—the two princely families next in rank after the Shihabs. The Christians and Sunnis of Beirut and Tripoli and the Shi'is of the Biqa' and Jabal 'Amil remained under direct rule by Ottoman provincial governors. The arrangement contradicted the interests of important social elements and paved the way for new upheavals.

In both parts of Mount Lebanon, appointed councils formally took judicial and tax collection functions out of the hands of *muqata'jis,* but in practice the old leading families retained effective power over the peasants. Both Druze and Maronite *muqata'jis* viewed the administrative adjustment as a threat, and they subverted it. In the south, the chief Druze families, abetted by the Arslan governors, overrode the Maronite and Druze representatives *(wukala')* appointed to give the population direct access to local government. In the north, despite the recent history of peasant uprisings, the Maronite rank and file had no such representatives and endured resurgent domination by al-Khazen shaykhs and other *muqata'jis,* who reduced the district council to impotence (for more detail, see I. Harik, 1968).

At the same time as social and sectarian gaps widened in the mountain, interaction intensified between Mount Lebanon and the coast, particularly Beirut. This reflected the commercial rise of Beirut from the 1820s on, through the Egyptian and *qa'imqamiyya* periods, which led to Christian migration from mountain to town and merchant penetration of the mountain. Beirut, secondary to Tripoli and Sidon before 1800, had a central position in relation to the *imara* and its silk exports after Yusuf Shihab displaced the Hamadas as tax-farmer for the north in the

1760s. The Shihabs favored Beirut because they could appropriate port revenues after about 1750, while Sidon and Tripoli remained firmly in the hands of the Ottoman governors. Christian traders, particularly Orthodox and Greek Catholics, benefited by far the most from the nineteenth-century trade between Western Europe and the Eastern Mediterranean, concentrated on Beirut (Fawaz, 1983). However, several Sunni Muslim families also profited, especially through their trade links with the Syrian interior.

A set of town-based names became prominent alongside those of Maronite and Druze *muqata'jis*—non-Maronite Christians such as the Sursuks, Pharaons, Tuwaynis, Bustros, Fayyads, Mudawwars, Abelas, and Bassuls; Maronites including the Lahhuds, Asfars, and Bazes; and Sunni Muslims such as the Bayhums, Barbirs, al-Yafis, and Fakhuris (older-established) or the Salams and al-Wazzans (newly emergent). Some of these families had interesting external origins: the Sursuks derived from southern Turkey, the Bustros had appeared in Lebanon from Cyprus in the late sixteenth century, and the Bayhums, an offshoot of the Itani clan, were descended from Spanish Muslims who came to the Eastern Mediterranean in medieval times.[51] The al-Yafis and Fakhuris had particularly notable religious associations, the former with upper-class family extensions in the main towns of interior Syria and the latter being made guardians of hairs of the prophet Muhammad by the Sultan 'Abdulaziz in 1862.[52]

As regards their interests in Mount Lebanon, the Christian merchant houses owned or acquired rural lands, and invested heavily in silk production for export. *Muqata'ji* families found it difficult to maintain their lifestyles in the new money-based society after about 1750, and in the nineteenth century were compelled to align themselves with urban merchants to whom they would otherwise never have given a moment's attention. The al-Khazens took loans from the Lahhuds and Tabets, the Abilama's from the Asfars, and the Arslans from the Bazes.[53] The Sunni Bayhums established mountain connections in several directions: financial partnerships with the Junblatts and other Druze and Maronite *muqata'jis*, a close family relationship with the Maronite Shihabs and joint land purchases with the Orthodox Bustros.[54] Some *muqata'ji* families adapted to the new conditions, making their own commercial and real estate investments in Beirut.[55] In this way the Druze Arslans and Junblatts "came to town" and built the base for their political viability in the twentieth century.

Transformations in social and family balances contributed to the outbreak and outcome of the violence that convulsed Mount Lebanon between 1858 and 1861. In brief, Ottoman favoring of the Abilama' family in the north of the double *qa'imqamiyya* inaugurated a succession of crises climaxing in the 1860 Maronite-Druze war. Ottoman preference for the Abilama's after 1845 provoked the al-Khazens, who refused to cooperate with the Abilama' governorship. This tussle allowed a reassertion by the Maronite peasantry, bitter about new impositions from the *muqata'jis,* who were in turn trying to sustain their financial and social standing vis-à-vis Beirut.

The Abilama' *qa'immaqam* (administrator) looked to the church, the peasants, and the French for support; members of the al-Khazen and Hubaysh families joined with the British to promote an alternative Abilama'. In the late 1850s, the political order collapsed throughout northern Lebanon, and villagers in Zahla and the Kisrawan took the opportunity to elect local leaders and defy the Abilama's and al-Khazens alike. Further north—in the Maronite hinterland of Tripoli—the populist movement was commanded by a maverick *muqata'ji,* Yusuf Karam of Ihdin, who had his own concept of a new Maronite-dominated Lebanese entity.

In 1858–59 the al-Khazens and others fled to Beirut and the Kisrawan passed into the hands of various village bosses, for example the Sfayrs of 'Ajaltun, but with the initiative mainly seized by an illiterate farrier, Tanyus Shahin. According to two authors,[56] the local Ottoman authorities and the French consul adopted a permissive attitude toward this third and most dramatic *'amiyya.* Some Ottoman officials apparently viewed chaos positively, as an opening for direct rule, while the French hoped to resuscitate the Shihabi *imara.*

Peasant control of the Kisrawan exacerbated communal tensions in the Arslan-ruled south of the *qa'imqamiyya,* where the class divide between peasants and leading families was also a sectarian divide between Maronites and Druze. The changing balance between Beirut and the mountain, with the ascent of merchant families, also disturbed intercommunal relations. It represented a Christian advance, which had obvious implications for future political leadership, and within the Maronite community it reinforced the decline of old allies of the Junblatts such as the al-Khazens. These developments increased the nervousness of the Druze *muqata'jis,* and made them even more determined to hold down the local peasantry.

For their part, the Maronite peasants of southern Mount Lebanon felt provoked by the attitude of the Druze *muqata'jis* and exhilarated by the Kisrawan rebellion. Ominously, Maronite communal exclusivity propagated by the clergy through the early nineteenth century ruled out a class combination with the Druze peasantry, who were easily mobilized by the Druze leadership for a sectarian showdown. Both sides had been amassing weapons since the troubles of the early 1840s, and both manipulated connections in Beirut—Maronite activists extracted contributions from sympathetic Christian bourgeois elements, and Druze *muqata'jis* looked to Sunni Muslim leaders and townspeople. Sectarian sentiment fed back and forth between mountain and town, although many non-Maronite Christians and Sunnis tried to insulate themselves from the affair. Ottoman officials in Beirut and Sidon avoided involvement, but exhibited partiality toward the Druze. Almost every element in the Lebanese social equation of early 1860 indicated the likelihood of a Maronite-Druze collision, and a few incidents and skirmishes ignited the conflagration of June–July of that year.

Maronite activists anticipated that their fourfold numerical superiority (about 50,000 fighters compared with 12,000 for the Druze) would enable them to crush their opponents, and incited the Druze by aggressively mobilizing their followings.[57] In reality, major deficiencies on the Christian side outweighed their advantages in wealth and numbers. Most significantly, rapid growth had made the Maronite community an unwieldy conglomerate, encompassing a multiplicity of leaders and prominent families with diverse concerns. The old *muqata'ji* families had no stomach for a fight with their Druze counterparts; the Christian merchant families, substantially non-Maronite, had intercommunal interests and no political impetus; the church hierarchy, including the supposedly belligerent Bishop Tubiya Aoun of Beirut, discouraged violence; and the new populist leaders of Kisrawan and the north had their own agendas, which did not favor adventurism in the mixed Druze-Christian districts. Yusuf Karam headed for the Matn with a large force, but halted there because he did not yet wish to burn his bridges with the Ottomans. Tanyus Shahin was out of his depth in the affairs of regions outside his home district.

The Christians of the Shuf, Jizzin, Zahla, and the Biqa' thus faced the Druze alone, with a few village leaders and no coordination whatsoever. Ottoman garrison commanders stood aside from Druze operations and massacres, and previous provocations of the Biqa' Shi'is by the Zahlawis gave the Druze useful allies for overrunning Zahla. The fact that the Shuf had been the seat of the Shihabi administration, as well as a strategic location for commerce in the southern part of the mountain, meant that a prosperous Christian population had become established in the nineteenth century at Deir al-Qamar, in an indefensible position. This and other isolated Christian villages in the Biqa', with large populations of Orthodox and Greek Catholics as well as Maronites, invited depredation. The Druze had good interior lines of communication, a compact base in the Shuf, and competent command under Sa'id Junblatt. The results over only four weeks were devastating: 11,000 Christians dead; many thousands of refugees from the mixed districts and the Biqa' crowded into Beirut; 200 villages sacked.[58]

However, the very scale of the defeat and massacres, compounded by the killing of 8,000 Christians by the Muslims of Damascus in July 1860, brought European intervention. The establishment of a committee of the Great Powers, a French military expedition, and Istanbul's determination to save Ottoman sovereignty by sternly punishing those responsible for the massacres, together allowed the Maronites to take political advantage from military disaster. The new autonomous Mount Lebanon that emerged from the deliberations between the Great Powers and Istanbul was, at least in its adjusted 1864 form, under firm Christian command. Some Maronites protested the importation of a non-Lebanese Christian governor, the fact that their representation on the administrative council never fully reflected their numbers, and the limited geographical extent of the *mutasarrifiyya*. On the other hand, the new entity provided a starting point for schemes aimed at a larger Maronite controlled Lebanon.

Whatever their setbacks between 1840 and 1861, the Christians, among whom the Maronites predominated, had such superior numbers and resources by mid-century that they could not be other than the central factor in any autonomous political regime. Imprisonment and dispersal of Druze *muqata'jis* in 1860–61, despite the brevity of exile for those deported, also helped set the scene for Christian political primacy in the "Little Lebanon" of the late nineteenth century.

Consolidation of the ruling class, 1860–1920

In the sixty years before the creation of Greater Lebanon in 1920—the period of the *mutasarrifiyya* in Mount Lebanon—family and social networks operated in three political arenas: the Christian-dominated autonomous area of the mountain; the coastal urban centers of Beirut, Tripoli, and Sidon; and the mainly Shi'i rural peripheries of Jabal 'Amil and the Biqa', like the mixed Sunni-Christian coastal cities under normal Ottoman provincial government but with distinctive family and leadership characteristics.

In the *mutasarrifiyya,* the pattern of family connections emerging from the mid-century collapse of the old order assumed the form out of which the political system of twentieth-century Greater Lebanon evolved. The close involvement of the Christian and Sunni merchant families of Beirut in the affairs of the mountain continued, because Beirut functioned as the de facto capital of the *mutasarrifiyya.* Association with the mountain, a Christian majority after 1850,[59] and the trade with Western Europe distinguished Beirut from Tripoli and Sidon. The latter two cities were dominated by traditionalist Sunni families with mixed Arab and Turkish ancestry. These families operated in the government, religious, and traditional commercial sectors, following the usual pattern of the Syrian hinterland. Tripoli had good links with the Syrian interior, whereas Sidon had its long-standing administrative and port functions usurped by Beirut, causing leading local families to move to the new metropolis. As regards the Shi'is of the peripheries, prominent families remained a very limited circle of clan leaders in the

109

tribalized society of Ba'albak-Hirmil, or rural landholders and religious scholars in Jabal 'Amil. These areas stagnated in social development terms, and became marginalized in relation to the mountain and the coastal cities. Their Shi'i populations distinguished them from the Sunni Syrian interior.

Mark Twain [Samuel Clemens], in *The Innocents Abroad*, provides brief but perceptive observations on the contradictions of the Beirut of 1867, caught between several worlds. He was impressed by "women of Beirout," who "cover their entire faces with dark-colored or black veils, so that they look like mummies, and then expose their breasts to the public." Twain also noted the case of a "young gentleman," probably an Orthodox Christian, who volunteered to act as guide, then demanded payment—"The Consul was surprised when he heard it, and said he knew the young fellow's family very well, and that they were an old and highly respectable family and worth a hundred and fifty thousand dollars!"

From Beirut, Twain trekked through the Biqa' to Ba'albak. He had nothing good to say about social conditions for Shi'i villagers in the lands beyond the *mutasarrifiyya:* "The Pacha of a Pachalic does not trouble himself with appointing tax-collectors. He figures up what all these taxes ought to amount to in a certain district. Then he farms the collection out. He calls the rich men together, the highest bidder gets the speculation, pays the Pacha on the spot, and then sells out to smaller fry, who sell in turn to a piratical horde of still smaller fry. These latter compel the peasant to bring his little trifle of grain to the village. . . It must be weighed, the various taxes set apart . . . But the collector delays this duty day after day, while the producer's family are perishing for bread; at last the poor wretch, who can not but understand the game, says, 'Take a quarter—take half—take two-thirds if you will, and let me go!' " Twain commended the people, "who often appeal to the stranger to know if the great world will not some day come to their relief and save them." (*The Innocents Abroad*. New York, Library of America edition, 1984, pp. 342–343, 350–351.)

Crystallization of new social realities in the *mutasarrifiyya,* with abolition of the legal functions of the *muqata'jis,* was delayed by years of disorder in the Maronite northern districts. Yusuf Karam, the only *muqata'ji* to indulge in populist mobilization, dissented from the Ottoman-European accord. In 1860 Karam acted as an Ottoman agent in the Kisrawan, forcing Tanyus Shahin to accept government authority and appointment as a local administrator. In return, Karam wanted a Lebanese entity extending beyond the mountain, and hoped to become its governor. The *mutasarrifiyya* and its initial Armenian Catholic *mutasarrif,* Daoud Pasha, disappointed Karam and his partisans.[60] Karam's support went beyond local Maronites to include Orthodox of the Kura, Tripoli Sunnis, and the Shi'i Harfush clan of the northern Biqa'—an illustration of connections between the coast, the mountain, and the Biqa'. Karam launched rebellions in 1864 and 1867, and was finally defeated and forced into exile by Ottoman troops.

As the *mutasarrifiyya* stabilized after the Karam episode, the composition of the upper social levels reflected three factors: acquisition of government office, trade-based wealth, and the influence of the Maronite church—in descending order of importance. Most former *muqata'jis* competed vigorously for administrative functions, especially district governorships, which they could use to maintain patronage networks in the absence of *iqta'i* authority. Junblatts and Arslans alternated as *qa'immaqams* in the Shuf, and the Shihabs, al-Khazens, and Karams aspired to similar posts further north.[61]

The new administrative apparatus, however, did not only permit *muqata'jis* to survive as local lords in new clothing. It also provided an avenue for promotion of second-level Maronite mountain families who had begun to register themselves from the late eighteenth century on through ascent in the church, administrative assistance for the Shihab amirs, and expansion of landholdings. The al-Khuris, Chamouns, and Faranjiyyas, families that later provided presidents of Lebanon, exemplify this category.

The al-Khuris stemmed from the Mubaraks, who produced noted seventeenth-century bishops, and the Salihs, recognized as a minor shaykhly family (Ma'luf, 1907). From this background, Sa'd al-Khuri emerged as amir Yusuf Shihab's chief advisor. In the mid-nineteenth century, Bishara al-Khuri, from a closely related branch of the family, became a much-respected judge, and his son, Khalil Bey, rose to be Secretary of the Arabic office, one of the primary positions in the *mutasarrifiyya*. Khalil's son Bishara became a leading politician under the French mandate and first president of independent Lebanon.

As for the Chamouns, a less spectacular trajectory led to a similar endpoint. The family can be traced back to the Jubayl district in the north, as an offshoot of the Saqr clan, which entered the written record with Father Istifan Saqr, a leading Maronite monk (Ma'luf, 1907). Through the eighteenth and early nineteenth centuries the Chamouns spread to Zahla, Ba'albak, and Deir al-Qamar in the Shuf. The Deir al-Qamar branch produced Nimr Chamoun Efendi, a senior official in the finance department of the *mutasarrifiyya*. His son, Camille, entered parliament under the mandate, and in 1952 succeeded Bishara al-Khuri as president.

The Faranjiyyas, with the Mu'awwads and Duwayhis a locally important clan below the *muqata'ji* level in Zgharta, inland from Tripoli, also registered themselves beyond their neighborhood when a Sulayman Faranjiyya became a district *(nahiya)* administrator under the *mutasarrifiyya*. Sulayman's son Qadib ran for parliament in 1929, in a bitter contest with a French-supported candidate. Qadib's followers killed nineteen Senegalese troops of the French mandatory security forces in an incident near Tripoli, and Qadib became a deputy by popular acclaim. Qadib's son Hamid was a widely respected member of the government in the late 1940s and 50s, particularly as foreign minister, but was crippled by a stroke in October 1957. Another son, Sulayman, first attracted media attention in July 1957 through a feud with the Duwayhi clan that climaxed with the gunning down of 23 people in a church in the village of Mizyara—Sulayman was in charge of the Faranjiyya side at the shoot-out. The authorities issued an arrest warrant for him, interpreted by the Faranjiyyas as revenge by President Chamoun for their opposition activities. Sulayman fled to Syria, where he received sanctuary in the home of Hafiz al-Asad, then a rising air-force officer. Sulayman became Lebanon's fifth president in 1970.

Trade, property purchase, and entry to Western-style professions, byproducts of Lebanon's multiplying links with Western Europe, helped

112

"The Rock"—Kata'ib leader Pierre Jumayyil,
billboard on a building in Ashrafiyya, Beirut, 1986

elevate such families during the *mutasarrifiyya*. The cases of the
Jumayyils and the Eddes illustrate these aspects of the process particu-
larly well. The Jumayyils first appeared in the written record, like the al-
Khuris and Chamouns, via the clerical institutions. A Bishop Filibus
Jumayyil became patriarch in 1794, and a priest named Daniel
Jumayyil, who died in 1847, was famous for his learning in canon law
(Ma'luf, 1907). The family moved south from Jaj to Bikfaya in 1545,[62]
and built up respectable landholdings in the Upper Matn by the nine-
teenth century. Amir Bashir II awarded them shaykhly status. Under the

113

mutasarrifiyya, the Jumayyils entered the professions and established business links with Egypt, where they operated a cigarette factory.[63] Dr. Shaykh Amin was the father of Pierre, a pharmacist who later founded the Kata'ib party, and the grandfather of Bashir and Amin, Lebanese presidents in the turbulent 1980s.

The Eddes followed a parallel path from country to town through business and the legal profession. Like the Chamouns and Jumayyils, they originated in the Jubayl district. The family's most noted early-twentieth-century member was the leading Beirut lawyer Emile Edde, Francophile and integrated into the commercial elite of Ashrafiyya, who headed the Maronite opposition to Bishara al-Khuri during the French mandate.

By these routes a whole collection of families, generally from leading clans in Christian villages, joined the Maronite and Druze *muqata'jis* and older Christian and Sunni merchant families at the summit of the society of Beirut and the *mutasarrifiyya.* In the mountain this diversifying upper class was flanked by the Maronite church hierarchy, which had provided an initial stepping stone for many members of the new high bourgeoisie. The church buttressed whoever shared its vision of Lebanon as an independent Christian state. The *mutasarrifs,* with firm Ottoman backing, did their best to restrict the social and political influence of the church.[64]

Although the coastal cities were politically distinct from the *mutasarrifiyya,* and headed by Sunni Muslim and Orthodox Christian families as opposed to the Maronite-Druze combination of the mountain, their societies increasingly coalesced with that of the *mutasarrifiyya.* Sunnis who had established local seniority through religious leadership, Ottoman political favor, or trade with Damascus and Aleppo had to adjust to new circumstances. This meant participation in external trade, closer involvement with Christians and Europeans, and real estate investment.

Sidon gradually became little more than an outlier of Beirut. The al-Sulh family, for example, with extensions in Ba'albak as well as a strong position in Sidon, shifted its attention to Beirut in the late nineteenth century. The al-Sulhs were exceptional among Sunni leading families in their involvement in Ottoman imperial administration outside

Lebanon, which gave them broader horizons.

The Sunni merchants of Beirut prospered, but were outstripped by the Christians. Beirut's Sunni and Christian elites both invested heavily in the education and social welfare of their respective communities, one product being the Maqasid society, established in 1878, involving most of the leading Sunni families (Fawaz, 1983; Johnson, 1986; Halawi, 1992). A century later this was still one of Lebanon's principal educational and medical institutions, dominated by the Salams from 1909 onward. The Bayhums, Salams, al-Sulhs, and others enabled Beirut's Sunnis to enter the twentieth century as a major component of Beirut's society, but not as more than a large, powerful minority.

Of the coastal cities, Tripoli's position and character changed the least through the late nineteenth century. Tripoli preserved its autonomy as a port city and remained overwhelmingly Sunni. Substantial communal homogeneity helped one family, the Karamis, to emerge as clear leaders among the urban bourgeoisie by the early twentieth century. The Karamis owed their elevation to their religious eminence, several members of the family being chief muftis of Tripoli, as well as to property holdings and commerce. Tripoli's continued position as the primary outlet for the northern part of Mount Lebanon gave the Karamis a solid basis for participation in the politics of Greater Lebanon after 1918, beginning with 'Abd al-Hamid Karami, chief mufti in the 1920s. Other leading families included Sunni property holders, such as the Muqaddims, Jisrs, 'Awaydas, and Mir'ibis, the last being the most eminent landholders of the rural 'Akkar, and Orthodox Christian traders and moneylenders, for example the Khlats, Burts, and Nawfals.[65] Orthodox Christians played a disproportionate role in the urban economy from the early nineteenth century on.

As in Mount Lebanon, Ottoman administrative reform had repercussions for the leading families of the Shi'i peripheries. However, their insulation from the commercial dynamism of Beirut meant change did not go beyond some recirculation in the elite, which remained relatively small and undiversified. Abolition of the old Ottoman system of using local chiefs as intermediaries for government, together with the more active provincial administration of the post-tanzimat period, whether from Damascus or Beirut, meant that leading landed families had to establish themselves inside the official apparatus to retain their status among the population. Only some managed to do this, such as the Sunni al-Sulhs, who had estates near Nabatiyya, the Asa'ads and Zayns of Jabal 'Amil, and the Hamadas of the Biqa'. As with the Christians of the *mutasarrifiyya,* new people entered the Shi'i leadership of Jabal 'Amil by acquiring official positions. These came from the ranks of lesser landowners and grain merchants. In the hinterlands of Sidon and Tyre the 'Usayran and al-Khalil families became steadily more influential. In Ba'albak, which like Jabal 'Amil had shrunk from relative prosperity into obscurity after the late eighteenth century, friction with the Ottoman authorities brought the eclipse of the Harfush family and the rise of the Haydars, favored by the Ottomans.[66] The Hamadas held their ground in Hirmil, together with satellite clans like the Ja'afars.

Ottoman governors played between older and newer members of the elite, and virtually no social movement occurred outside this restricted arena, in contrast to developments in Beirut and the mountain. The Shi'i religious class, which was subordinated to Sunni authority and had been badly treated by Jazzar Pasha in the late eighteenth century, was fragmented, politically quietist, and under the thumb of the rural bosses. Its social role could not be compared with that of either the Maronite church in the mountain or the Sunni judicial structure in the coastal cities.

Continuity and change in the elite of Greater Lebanon, 1920 on

Establishment of Greater Lebanon in 1920 brought together the coastal cities, the mountain, and the Shi'i peripheries into a single political entity, separated from the Syrian interior. The elites of the three zones, differing in background and sectarian composition, were now compelled to relate to one another in the same political arena. Reactions to the fait accompli imposed by France and Maronite leaders from Mount Lebanon varied greatly.

Most of the Christian elite of Beirut and the mountain were delighted, and looked forward to being the central element in the broadened upper class of Greater Lebanon. The Sunni bourgeoisie of Beirut and Tripoli were shocked and, together with some Orthodox Christians, stood against what they regarded as an illegitimate product of European colonialism.

Druze leaders expressed opposition, but realized that they could not overturn the French mandate. They decided to get what they could for themselves and their community, while verbally supporting Arab nationalism. The Junblatts accepted the French whereas the Arslans, led by Shakib Arslan, emphasized Arabism. The politically aware minority among the Shi'is was similarly divided. The chief landlords and clan bosses, torn between their ties with the Syrian interior and their expectation of spoils from collaborating with the French, chose the pragmatic path of the Junblatts. In contrast, educated younger Shi'is, who had been caught up in the Arab nationalist movement of the late Ottoman period, chose rejection and rebellion in the 1920s.

In a way, French mandatory authority eased a coalescence of elite elements to form a new Lebanese ruling class, albeit poorly integrated, by the 1940s. French authority, because of its alien character, could be more easily tolerated by non-Christians than outright political domination by local Christians. Also, unpopular mandatory policies, such as monopoly control over tobacco purchases from growers, provided opportunities for Maronite, Sunni, and Shi'i leading families to come together on particular issues.

In order to contain Islamic hostility to Greater Lebanon, the French and the Maronite proponents of a multiconfessional Lebanon played on the ambivalence of the Shi'i rural leadership. In 1926 the mandatory regime accorded Shi'is the right to have their own judicial system for personal status matters (the Ottoman Empire had always refused to recognize the distinctiveness of non-Sunni Muslims). Members of the Shi'i elite, for example from the Zayn, Haydar, and Hamada families, entered the parliaments of mandatory Lebanon from the first elections in 1922.

In contrast to the Shi'is and Druze, most leading members of the Sunni elite of the coastal cities boycotted the institutions of Greater Lebanon for almost fifteen years. However, the Sunni political stance was not uniform, and eroded with time. The principal early exception to the boycott, Muhammad al-Jisr, from a notable Tripoli family, even presented himself for the presidency in 1932, having gained sufficient Maronite support to win. Jisr's action precipitated a crisis and French suspension of the constitution, but it demonstrated the possibility of Maronite-Sunni political combination.

The Salams of Beirut and 'Abd al-Hamid Karami of Tripoli were more rigid in their Syrian unionism than other Sunni pan-Arabists and high bourgeois leaders, such as Riyadh al-Sulh, 'Abdallah Bayhum, and Khayr al-Din al-Ahdab. The high water mark of Sunni bourgeois rejectionism was the second "conference of the coast," hosted by Salim Salam in his Beirut home in early 1936, which demanded reintegration of the coast and the Biqa' with Damascus.

Against this, other Sunnis had entered the administration by the mid-1930s and were moving toward an understanding with the Maronite high bourgeoisie. 'Abdallah Bayhum accepted the job of Secretary of State between 1932 and 1937, a period of direct French rule. Khayr al-Din al-Ahdab succeeded him with the 1937 restoration of constitutional government, as Lebanon's first Sunni prime minister. Riyadh al-Sulh avoided any official role but cultivated contacts with the Maronite political leadership, prodded by his cousin Kazim al-Sulh.[67]

A number of factors favored a gradual Sunni-Maronite convergence. First, Maronite acceptance of a moderate Orthodox personality, Charles Debbas, as Lebanon's first president signalled flexibility from the Christian upper class. During Debbas's term, from 1926 to 1932, both he and the French exhibited openness to the Islamic leadership. Second, French suspension of the constitution in 1932 gave the Maronite bourgeoisie its first cause for disenchantment with French hegemony, providing common ground with Sunnis. Third, by the early 1930s interest in Lebanon on the part of the upper-class Arab nationalist politicians of interior Syria was declining. These politicians negotiated with France in 1936 for a Franco-Syrian treaty without making their grievances over Greater Lebanon a critical issue,[68] and ceased to nourish Sunni disaffection in Beirut and Tripoli. Fourth, Sunni coastal leaders soon realized that they would have more influence in a Lebanese entity than in a Greater Syria. Fifth, much of the Sunni upper class attended Catholic schools, which gave them personal connections with the Maronites to add to those derived from business interactions. Riyadh al-Sulh, for example, went to the Lazarite school in 'Ayntura and the Law Faculty of St. Joseph's University.[69]

The basis for a modus vivendi between the Sunni and Christian elites evolved during the presidency of Emile Edde after 1936—an irony because Edde embodied the "mountain" perspective of Lebanon as a Maronite homeland, still the chief orientation of the Maronite clergy. Just as the strident Arabism of the 1936 Sunni "conference of the coast" paralleled a pragmatic trend among Sunni leaders, Maronite particularism coexisted with compromising tendencies in the Christian sector. The modus vivendi of the elites arose from an understanding between Riyadh al-Sulh and Bishara al-Khuri, who represented the pluralist Christian outlook of Beirut. Al-Sulh and al-Khuri converged on confessional power-sharing in an independent Lebanon acknowledged to be Arab, but with a special connection with the West.

The French themselves ensured majority Maronite support for independence by their behavior during the Second World War. First, the 1936 Franco-Lebanese treaty remained unratified by the French, and in September 1939 France again suspended the constitution, citing the exigencies of war. British pressure forced de Gaulle's Free French to accept Lebanese parliamentary elections in 1943, but in November of the same year, when the new Lebanese regime headed by al-Khuri as president and al-Sulh as prime minister had parliament delete privileges for the mandatory power from the constitution, French troops arrested leading regime personalities. The six detainees—al-Khuri, al-Sulh, 'Abd al-Hamid Karami, Camille Chamoun, Adel 'Usayran, and Salim Taqla—represented a broad spectrum of the elite elements of Greater Lebanon. This small group encompassed Maronites, Sunnis, and a Shi'i and almost the full range of elite ideological orientations. Demonstrations against the French action brought the Maronite paramilitary Kata'ib movement of Pierre Jumayyil together with the most activist Arab nationalists among the Muslims. France performed the unintended service of assisting upper-class coalescence across Greater Lebanon's sectarian communities and between the coast, the mountain and the peripheries.

The 1943 National Pact, an upper-class power-sharing consensus, reserved the positions of president and prime minister for the Maronites and Sunnis respectively, involved a sectarian share-out of official posts, and accorded the Shi'i and Druze leading families the minimum necessary to attach them to the system. The pact, examined in more detail in chapters 2 and 4, inaugurated three decades of stability for the high bourgeoisie, from 1943 to 1975. The mid-twentieth century marked the apogee of the so-called *zu'ama* (singular: *za'im*)—the rural and urban "big men" who controlled Lebanon by dispensing money, jobs, and favors, by manipulating networks of client politicians, and by exploiting family, sectarian, and regional allegiances. About 250 families monopolized parliament, and the Maronite and Sunni elites of Mount Lebanon, Beirut, and Tripoli dominated the system, with Maronite primacy. A few Shi'i *zu'ama* managed the peripheries, in line with their stake in the regime.

Even after 1975, when Lebanon reaped the consequences of failure to address decades of accumulating social and political strains, no revolutionary transformation affected a ruling class that had already outlived its counterpart in Syria. The impact of fifteen years of civil strife between 1975 and 1990 on the Lebanese elite was far less than that of the Ba'thist coups of the 1960s on the Syrian ruling class. Lebanese leaders had not left security institutions like the army open to takeover by disaffected elements, and Lebanon's sectarian compartments made it difficult for radical movements to have an impact outside their "home" communities. In the 1990s, the membership, economic orientation, social attitudes, and political behavior of the high bourgeoisie were a recognizable continuation from the 1940s.

Two significant developments, however, should be noted. Change in upper class membership principally involved a new and larger Shi'i elite, reflecting the increased economic weight of the community. Older Shi'i leading families were joined by a host of nouveaux riches, rising out of a new Shi'i middle class that in turn represented a mid-twentieth-century awakening of the peasant population of the peripheries. Much of the new Shi'i wealth derived from entrepreneurial endeavors in West Africa, North America, and the Gulf oil states. Also, the prominence of Shi'i militias in the 1980s and Syrian backing helped open the upper class to a Shi'i influx. In general, these nouveaux riches shared the free market proclivities and social mores of the pre-existing high bourgeoisie, which absorbed them without altering its basic character. The Christian, Sunni, and Druze components of the elite were less disrupted. Some militia operatives, wartime businessmen, and professionals ascended from lower social levels, especially in the Maronite community, but as with their Shi'i fellows the ascent changed them more than it changed the class they entered.

A relative of my wife went to the Ivory Coast in the 1980s as a tailor. Through hard work and personal connections he won a contract to produce uniforms for the local security forces. He turned this into a substantial business, enabling him to invest in property in both Lebanon and the Ivory Coast.

Many Shi'i businessmen are impatient for a regional peace settlement, anticipating broad new opportunities in commerce and tourism. They are not enthusiastic about Hizballah's vision of the future.

The most dramatic new feature in the 1990s was not so much change in the high bourgeoisie as a whole, but the highly selective staffing of the government and regime—selection by Syria and, a little later, by billionaire Prime Minister Rafiq al-Hariri. The president, prime minister, and parliamentary speaker of the mid-1990s were all from new middle-class families of the mid-twentieth century.

After 1990, a majority of ministers and senior officials had either militia or nouveaux riches business and professional backgrounds. A number happened to be from older leading families—for example, Walid Junblatt, Sulayman Tony Faranjiyya, Michel Edde, 'Umar Karami, and 'Ali 'Usayran—all given the nod by Damascus. Others would have been social nobodies without Syria and the wartime militias—for example, 'Abdallah al-Amin (a Shi'i Ba'thist), Muhsin Dallul (also a Shi'i, and Syria's man in Junblatt's Progressive Socialist Party), Nasri Khuri (a Maronite Syrian Social Nationalist appointed secretary-general of the

Syrian-Lebanese Higher Council), and Elie Hubayqa (a Maronite from the Lebanese Forces who had aligned himself with Syria). A few, for example Amal leader Nabih Barri, combined diaspora business activities with militia connections in their rise from the middle class or below.

Finally, Rafiq al-Hariri contributed a private elite network, promoting his employees and partners into senior regime positions. Most, like Hariri himself, were self-made men from the relatively new middle bourgeoisie. Generally they had prospered outside Lebanon, in the Gulf or the West, from the 1970s on. Hariri's network included Fuad Sinyora (Sidon Sunni, and associate in Hariri's business empire), Farid Makari (Kura Orthodox, launched into commerce via Hariri's Oger company in Saudi Arabia), and Yasin Jabir (Nabatiyya Shi'i, with trade, construction, and hotel enterprises in the United Kingdom, Lebanon, and elsewhere).

Such personnel shifts are substantially altering the profile of the upper class. It should be noted here that leaders of the most popular opposition movements—General Michel Aoun and the Hizballah commanders—also do not derive from older secular and religious leading families. However, the *zu'ama*—Salams, Karamis, Asa'ads, Jumayyils, Chamouns—retain their client networks, even if reduced, and have considerable staying power. Renowned old "shaykhly" or "princely" families, such as the al-Khazens and the Abilama's, still have great public prestige long after their political eclipse. Even before 1975, only a small minority of the upper class could be said to date back to the "traditional" ruling families of the late eighteenth century. The remainder represented the accretions and adjustments of two centuries of great geopolitical and socioeconomic flux. The late twentieth century—Lebanon's war and its aftermath—continued the trend.

PART TWO

Greater Lebanon, 1920–89

The three Jumayyils: Amin ("The Rock"),
Pierre, Bashir (Ashrafiyya, 1986)

Since the *imara* of Mount Lebanon collapsed in 1840 there have been three major disruptions in Lebanon's modern history, separated by intervals of 55 years: 1860–1915 and 1920–1975. First came the crisis of the mid-nineteenth century, and the transformation of the *imara* into the *mutasarrifiyya*. The second disruption involved the First World War, the abolition of the *mutasarrifiyya,* and the demise of the Ottoman Empire. It ended with French intervention and the creation of a new, expanded Lebanon.

Flaws in the political and economic foundations of Greater Lebanon contributed to a brief crisis in 1958 and to a prolonged break-down in the 1970s. The upheavals between the "civil war" of 1975–76 and General Michel Aoun's wars in 1988–90 marked the third great disruption in Lebanon's history. The outcome was a constitutional agreement extracted from Lebanese parliamentarians by Saudi Arabia, Syria, and the U.S. in the Saudi city of Ta'if in October 1989. This terminated the Maronite-Sunni National Pact under which the Greater Lebanon of the French mandate had become an independent Lebanon in 1943. Unlike the two earlier disruptions, the post-1975 wars did not bring yet another "new" Lebanon—instead they produced a de facto confederation with Syria.

After 1920 the leaders of Greater Lebanon needed to integrate the lands and populations added to the *mutasarrifiyya,* and to establish a common understanding of the meaning of the new state. The same issues faced a variety of such states emerging from the wreckage of the Ottoman and Habsburg Empires. In Lebanon, integration was achieved at the high bourgeois level. The 1926 constitution and the 1943

National Pact provided the necessary sectarian political compromise while the free market service economy assured a congenial environment for the elite. Political and economic common interests also extended to a growing middle class in Beirut and its environs, although this did not lead to a common view of the nature and purpose of the state.

Otherwise, the political and economic order of Greater Lebanon had deeply divisive implications. First, the upper and middle classes were themselves unbalanced in sectarian terms, being disproportionately Christian and with Sunnis outnumbering Shi'is. Second, in the context of the Shi'i demographic surge and other social changes discussed in chapter 2, Greater Lebanon's sectarian political allocations became increasingly controversial. Third, manipulation of patronage networks by upper class cliques, mixed with populist politics among Muslims and Christians in a rapidly growing Beirut, produced a witch's brew of discontents. This brew bubbled away beneath the crust of high bourgeois "confessional democracy." Fourth, far from integrating the coast, mountain, and peripheries of Greater Lebanon, the merchant republic only emphasized the distinction between the former *mutasarrifiyya* and the largely Muslim, especially Shi'i, areas tacked onto it in 1920.

For all these reasons, the regime configuration of the 1940s could not persist indefinitely without either redefinition or violent disruption. However, the dialectic of Islamic demands and Maronite insecurities, added to the rigid determination of the ruling class to preserve its privileges, made a peaceful political adjustment unlikely. The predominantly Sunni leadership of the Islamic sector could only cope with intensifying pressures from below by deflecting them toward the Christians. In turn, Christian bosses who considered compromise risked being outflanked by Christian radicalism.

The Lebanese high bourgeoisie was rescued from the fuller elaboration of this scenario by the Palestinians and Israelis. Arab-Israeli intrusion after 1967 enabled the ruling class to blame "foreigners," "Zionism," and "Syria" for Lebanon's ills. Nonetheless, Lebanon's political elite cannot escape responsibility for the storm that broke upon Lebanon in 1975.

My treatment of Lebanon's war years after 1975 in chapters 5 and 6 emphasizes the period following the 1982 Israeli invasion. This is partly because there are detailed accounts of the early war years by other authors (for example: Salibi, 1976; Rabinovich, 1984; Goria, 1985; Johnson, 1986; Kassir, 1994; El-Khazen, 2000). Their interpretations also deal with the lead-up to the 1975–76 "civil war," so that here a summary should suffice. I analyze developments after 1982 in more detail for several reasons, including my own experience of Lebanon, which dates from 1983; the greater relevance of the later period for the outcome of the war in the 1990s; and the fact that the existing literature for Lebanon in the 1980s is fragmentary and inadequate.

Above all, there has been no properly balanced, integrated assessment of trends among Christians and Shi'is, the two stellar giants of Lebanon's sectarian constellation in the late twentieth century. Another gap in the literature involves Lebanon's economic slide in the mid-1980s, which directly affected the viability of militia cantons and precipitated new populisms—Aoun for Christians and Hizballah for Shi'is. As for the Syrian-Lebanese dimension of Lebanon's crisis, there has been insufficient recognition of the fact that in the 1980s the struggle for Lebanon was conducted between Maronite leaders in East Beirut and Hafiz al-Asad in Damascus—not between Christians and Muslims, and certainly not between Christians and Shi'is.

Indeed, if Lebanon's war period has any connecting thread—from its beginning in Ayn al-Rumana on 13 April 1975 to its dénouement when the Syrian army entered the presidential palace in Ba'abda on 13 October 1990—it must be the emergence, maintenance, and collapse of the autonomous Christian entity run from East Beirut by a fractious collection of Maronite communal bosses. East Beirut and its hinterland were the core of Greater Lebanon from 1920 until the Maronites blew themselves apart at the end of the 1980s. Through the war years East Beirut was the chief internal antagonist of the "Islamic and nationalist" militias, the PLO, and the Syrians, and the chief Eastern Mediterranean ally of Israel and—in the end—of Ba'thist Iraq. Even when the spotlight was on the Palestinians, Shi'is, and Israelis, East Beirut was there in the background as the largest and most powerful "canton." Even when it was being ignored by the media, East Beirut was the major Lebanese player: enticing Israel in the early 1980s; frustrating Syria from the late 1970s to the late 1980s; holding tight to critical regime institutions such as the presidency and army; and raising the spectre of Lebanon's dismemberment. Finally, in 1989–90, it was a "Götterdämmerung" in East Beirut that cleared the way for a new phase in Lebanon's history.

Government Buildings (the "serail") from the French mandatory period under reconstruction, Beirut, 1995

CHAPTER FOUR

A HOUSE ON SAND, 1920–67

The French Mandate and the molding of Greater Lebanon, 1920–46

The geopolitical features and institutional framework of the Greater Lebanon that became independent Lebanon in 1943 were a creation of French policy between the world wars, French interaction with the local sectarian leaderships, and British intervention at the beginning and end of the mandatory period—all with a measure of continuity from the "little Lebanon" of the *mutasarrifiyya*.

First came the territorial dispensation of 1920, a product of Maronite lobbying, French interests, and British acquiescence based on alliance considerations. As noted in chapter 2, the Maronites and French generally agreed on expansion of the *mutasarrifiyya* to incorporate the western Biqa' with Ba'albak and Hirmil, the partially Christian 'Akkar hills which comprised the far northern extension of the Lebanon range, and the cities of Beirut and Sidon. Maronite hard-liners headed by patriarch Huwayyik wanted Tripoli as an outlet for the extended northern mountain region of the new Lebanon. On the French side the only discordant note came from Robert de Caix, chief assistant to the first French high commissioner for Syria and Lebanon, General Henri Gouraud. De Caix, precisely because he wanted Lebanon to be a solidly Christian entity, opposed the extended boundaries and stressed the sectarian complications. However, he was overridden by Gouraud and by Maronite lobbying in both Paris and Beirut (for more detail, see Zamir, 1985).

The French themselves were the main element in setting the eastern boundary deep into the anti-Lebanon range, as part of the policy to reduce and weaken the new Syrian entity based on Damascus. France also played the senior role in incorporating the Shi'i areas south of the Litani river, suggested as Lebanon's southern boundary in December 1919 negotiations with Faysal.[70] After toying with the notion of a separate Shi'i entity on the model of ideas for the 'Alawi and Druze areas of the new Syria, the French evidently concluded that integration with Greater Lebanon was the best way to assert France's presence in the border region facing the British presence in Palestine. This outcome was probably influenced by successful British pressure to have the Sykes-Picot boundary moved northward in the Galilee hills, to satisfy Jewish interests regarding the Hula valley.

French policy toward Greater Lebanon had a dualistic quality that reflected contradictory French impulses as well as contradictions in the nature of the new entity. The working out of this dualism greatly affected the character of independent Lebanon.

General Gouraud himself represented a romantic impulse that conflated historical links with the Maronites, a sense of Catholic commonality, and the strategic calculation that Mount Lebanon's Christians provided France with a solid bridgehead in the Eastern Mediterranean. More broadly, a powerful combination of religious, commercial, and bureaucratic interests converged in France to demand French political primacy in the Levant: the main Catholic religious orders, who had educational and cultural involvements with the Maronites and other Levantine Catholics; the chambers of commerce of Paris, Marseilles, and Lyons, which represented the large French investments in railways, ports, and trade; and senior officials and military officers, including de Caix and Gouraud, who saw control of the Levant as buttressing French colonialism in North Africa.[71] The "colonial lobby" strongly penetrated the French Assembly and, partly influenced by Lebanese Catholic activists in Paris, supported the concept of Greater Lebanon as a Christian-dominated state. Despite sometimes difficult relations, France thus generally encouraged Maronite politicians and the Maronite church to view Greater Lebanon as a sphere ordained for their primacy.

This backdrop of French policy was complicated by other considerations: Greater Lebanon had a non-Maronite majority, a fact made crystal clear by the 1932 census, and France had a powerful pragmatic interest in reconciliation with the non-Maronite population, particularly the estranged Sunni Muslims but also Shi'is, Druze, and Orthodox Christians. After the Druze and Arab nationalist revolt in interior Syria in 1925–26, France needed to look to the viability of its position in both Lebanon and Syria. Also, secularism and anticlericalism were prominent in France's "Third Republic," and on occasion these cut across the Catholic connection. In 1926 the first civilian high commissioner, Henri de Jouvenel, proposed transferring Tripoli from Lebanon to Syria.[72] De Jouvenel aimed to placate Arab nationalism, but he was supported by Maronites like Emile Edde who were worried about demography. The initiative wilted in the face of wider Maronite hostility, and was never repeated. In the mid-1920s the Maronite church and others opposed the anticlerical high commissioner Maurice Sarrail, watching suspiciously for signs of policy revision regarding Greater Lebanon.

Pragmatism and concern for stability colored French management of local politics. This was demonstrated by the decision in 1922 to preserve and expand the relatively balanced multisectarian voting system of the *mutasarrifiyya*. Further, the second French high commissioner, General Maxime Weygand, took care to ensure that major sects received major government posts—amenable Sunnis were appointed vice president of the initial Representative Council (1922–25) and thereafter to cabinet level positions even when the bulk of the Sunni leadership boycotted the mandatory regime. The decision of Fuad Junblatt at the outset of the mandate to shift the orientation of his Druze faction from Britain to France generally resulted in a solicitous attitude toward the Druze by French mandatory authorities. Fuad's wife, Nazira Junblatt, who took over leadership of the Junblatti faction after Fuad's assassination in 1921, reportedly commented: "You British have told us that the country would be handed over to the French, so it is with them that we have to make arrangements."[73] The French cultivation of Shi'i neo-feudal leaders has already been mentioned in chapter 3.

The most important institutional developments took place in

1926–29, as part of the French response to the disturbances in Syria. These disturbances, which began in the Jabal al-Druze of southern Syria in July 1925, spilled into Lebanon in November 1925 when a Druze-led force crossed into the Hasbaya and Marj'uyun areas from the Hawran. Many local Christians fled, and it took some weeks for the French to contain and defeat the rebels.[74] The Shuf Druze and most southern Lebanon Shi'is stood aloof from the affair, despite the Arab nationalist agitation of the Arslans.

In December 1925 de Jouvenel, who had just become high commissioner, asked the Representative Council to draft a constitution for Lebanon.[75] The council appointed a committee, which met in Beirut, received suggestions from Paris, and produced a consitutional document in May 1926. In a process similar to the evolution of the *règlement organique* in the early 1860s, the Representative Council adopted this document and amended it in light of the circumstances in 1927 and 1929. French constitutional practice came together with the ideal of Lebanon as a Christian-Muslim partnership promoted by the Latin Catholic banker Michel Chiha, secretary of the drafting committee. The document provided for a strong presidency and an equitable allocation of regime posts between the sects. Definition of the sectarian allocation was left to oral understandings, but it was taken for granted by the French and most Christians that the presidency would become a Christian preserve.

The mandatory power, in the person of the high commissioner, retained ultimate executive and veto authority for the meantime. Indeed, the autocracy of the high commissioner itself became a legacy for independent Lebanon, as indicated by the executive assertiveness of presidents Bishara al-Khuri and Camille Chamoun. Constitutional amendments up to 1929 reduced parliament from two chambers—cumbersome in a small country—to a single House of Deputies, and stretched presidential tenure to a nonrenewable six-year term. The parliament was accommodated in a spacious building in the "star square" *(sahat al-najma)* of downtown Beirut. Except when suspended by the mandatory power in 1932–34 and 1939–43, it assembled regularly until the collapse of public order in 1975.

Apart from the constitutional and electoral framework of "confessional democracy," firmly in the hands of the high bourgeoisie and weighted toward the Maronites, the French mandate also determined the character of Lebanon's bureaucracy and established rudimentary security forces. The local officialdom inherited from the *mutasarrifiyya* was diversified under the French, although kept relatively small. The mandatory bureaucracy comprised the French-staffed high commission, an overarching authority for Lebanon and Syria with common functions for the two countries, most notably security and customs, and Lebanon's own government departments, locally staffed but supplemented with French advisors. Educational and medical services, however, continued to be largely left to private or sectarian provision, which greatly favored the Christians (Owen, 1976).

The administration could be reasonably efficient, as in the depression years of the early 1930s,[76] but French supervision added habits of paternalism and authoritarianism to the clientelism and corruption already well developed during the *mutasarrifiyya*. The Ottoman governors had themselves sometimes set the tone, as when Nassib Junblatt had to pay bribes to the wife of Muzaffar Pasha in 1903–4 to maintain his appointment as *qa'immaqam* of the Shuf.[77] In the late 1920s Bishara al-Khuri used his cabinet position as minister of the interior, with its possibilities for dispensing jobs and favors, to begin building the network of clients that was to serve him well when he became president of the republic. Such features made the bureaucracy perfect for cocooning the upper class, but highly unsuitable for answering Lebanon's social and development requirements.

As for the security forces, the French recruited local military units in Lebanon and Syria that were consolidated in 1930 as the Troupes Spéciales du Levant, subordinated to the main French force of the Armée du Levant. Maronites provided the bulk of the Lebanese contingent, about 6,000 out of a Syrian-Lebanese total of more than 22,000 in 1944, when the Lebanese and Syrian elements had to be disentangled from one another into separate armies. More generally, division of the common functions of the high commission, especially customs, disturbed Lebanese-Syrian relations into the 1950s.

French dealings with the Maronite community, the leading element of Greater Lebanon, had significant implications for Lebanon's political evolution. The French did not wish to be overly dependent on any one Maronite political tendency, nor did senior French mandatory officials wish to become too much involved with the sectarian exclusiveness of the Maronite "mountain." In consequence, in the mid-1920s the French assisted the emergence of two Maronite blocs by balancing between the two most active Maronite political personalities, the lawyers Emile Edde and Bishara al-Khuri. Both Edde and al-Khuri were francophile, but Edde looked to an indefinite French protectorate over Lebanon as a Christian homeland whereas al-Khuri joined with his brother-in-law Michel Chiha in conceiving the French mandate as the starting point for an independent Lebanon that could only give Christians long-term security under the umbrella of Christian-Muslim collaboration. After Lebanon acquired its constitutional framework in 1926, Edde organized his following into a faction later termed the "National Bloc" while al-Khuri used his more elaborate patronage connections to bring allies and supporters together into a "Constitutional Bloc," formalized in 1934. Edde's espousal of an organic tie between Lebanon and France obviously appealed to the French, but al-Khuri's sectarian pluralism conformed better with the practical requirements of managing the mandate.

Through the 1930s the French interaction with the Maronite and Sunni communities had the effect of bringing Maronite and Sunni leaders closer together on the common theme of seeking French departure. Al-Khuri's Constitutional Bloc offered a connection between Maronite Lebanon and Greater Lebanon that eased the functioning of the mandate, but al-Khuri himself wanted to terminate French control. Many Maronites became truculent vis-à-vis French authority as they sensed that its usefulness was passing. In the early 1930s, for example, patriarch Antun Arida had cordial exchanges with Arab nationalists in Damascus on the basis of common hostility to French policies. In November 1936, a Maronite pharmacist, Pierre Jumayyil, founded a strong-arm youth movement, the Kata'ib (Phalange), partly out of concern that the French might retreat before the Sunni pressures to dismember Greater Lebanon which reached a climax after Salim Salam's 1936 Conference of the Coast. Jumayyil's followers almost immediately came into conflict with the mandatory authorities, who regarded them and the less coherently organized Sunni Najjada movement as threats to public order. The French refused to recognize either group as a political party, and French troops intervened against the Kata'ib's 1937 aniversary parade. Casualties included Pierre Jumayyil—a useful image boost for the Kata'ib chief.

Notwithstanding its emphatic "Christian" orientation, the Kata'ib was one of a series of organizations in mandatory Syria and Lebanon influenced by European fascism: The Steelshirts and the National League among Syria's Sunni Arab nationalists, and the Kata'ib, the Najjada, and Antun Sa'ada's Syrian Social Nationalists (SSNP) in Beirut. These movements appealed to younger Lebanese and Syrians from the growing petite bourgeoisie because of their emphasis on discipline, force, and nationalist identities. After the mandate the Kata'ib developed a sophisticated program linking its Lebanese nationalism with social reform, but it remained an almost exclusively Christian party.

The declaration of emergency rule in Lebanon in May 1932 and interference by the mandatory authorities in Lebanese elections and parliamentary activities in 1934 caused strong grievances in the al-Khuri camp. Camille Chamoun, one of three founding members of the Constitutional Bloc, observed: "The high commissioner, jealous of the least Lebanese initiative, lost no opportunity to affirm his omnipotence . . . Electoral lists were cooked up [*un véritable 'cuisine'*] between the French and Lebanese authorities on the one hand, and the candidates on the other. Generally, apart from vetoes dictated by higher politics— or personal antipathies—the authorities supported the candidates most preferred by public opinion, because their success required the least effort."[78]

After parliament elected Edde president in 1936 with a majority of one vote, the Constitutional Bloc devoted itself to crippling the administration. This situation was clearly conducive to coalescence between al-Khuri and leading Sunnis, and a loose coalition in favor of an independent Lebanon became a real prospect before the outbreak of the Second World War. Sunni separatist agitation, which did not and could not have a practical program, peaked with the 1936 Conference of the Coast, which was really separatism's death rattle. At that time Kazim al-Sulh pointed the way ahead by writing that the conference needed a dialogue with the Christians, not the French high commissioner.[79]

Edde's administration collapsed in April 1941, unable to cope with wartime dislocation, especially following the defeat of France and the advent of the Nazi-aligned Vichy regime. In June 1941, alarmed by German links via the Vichy-controlled Levant with coup leaders in Iraq, the British army invaded Lebanon and Syria, quickly prevailing over Vichy forces after some initial difficulties in Southern Lebanon and on the Golan Heights. The British, who did not want to be distracted by problems with the local population, urged de Gaulle's Free French to promise independence to Lebanon and Syria in advance of the operation. De Gaulle did this only with bad grace,[80] and the Free French contingent which accompanied the British and Commonwealth forces hastened to assert political control in Beirut and Damascus. The French declared Lebanon and Syria "independent" in November 1941, but also reiterated the powers of the mandate, emptying the declaration of practical meaning. This step both exasperated the British and provoked the local population, and in February 1942 Britain sent General Edward Spears to watch the French and to press them toward fulfilling their commitment.

Spears played a vital role in bringing Riyadh al-Sulh and Bishara al-Khuri together in 1942–43 to establish the Maronite-Sunni compromise known as the National Pact. Al-Sulh contributed the relatively new Sunni perspective that acceptance of Greater Lebanon need not contradict aspirations toward ultimate Arab unity, as long as the Maronite leadership accepted Lebanon's "Arab face." Al-Khuri contributed the view of most of the Christian high bourgeoisie that Lebanon could not be viable without a Muslim political role and a close relationship with other Arab states, but with the proviso that Muslims must accept Lebanon's distinctiveness and openness to the West. These outlooks were knitted together in a delicate double balance: no alliances with the West vis-à-vis no involvement of Lebanon in Arab integration schemes, and executive authority divided between a Maronite president and a Sunni prime minister. Al-Sulh conceded a Maronite political advantage for the sake of a unified approach to independence and to protect the Sunni commercial stake in Lebanon's bridging function between the West and the Arabs.

The British presence enabled parliamentary elections in September 1943 that produced a majority in the House of Deputies for Bishara al-Khuri as president. Al-Khuri asked al-Sulh to form a government, and al-Sulh formally outlined the National Pact in an October 1943 ministerial statement. The French persisted in rearguard actions against independence, most notably the arrest of Lebanon's most senior politicians in November 1943, thereby making Lebanese hostility to the mandate almost universal. Apart from insuring that the French understood that their time had passed, General Spears contributed some of the specific details of the National Pact, particularly the 6:5 Christian/non-Christian allocation of parliamentary seats. Lebanon and Syria adamantly refused treaty arrangements with France, and the last French troops left Lebanon in late 1946.

Two presidencies and a crisis, 1946–58

Lebanon's National Pact system operated without disruption until May 1958, through the periods of presidents al-Khuri and Chamoun, although there was a trend toward destabilization. Lebanon's affairs during these twelve years may be characterized in terms of two paradoxes. First, the upper class, with its rural semifeudal and urban commercial components, maintained its social position and command of the regime regardless of sectarian strains. At the same time, however, bitter political infighting between upper-class factions eventually brought a collapse of public order. Second, while Syria and Egypt witnessed the demise of parliamentarianism, Lebanon's "confessional democracy" acquired a measure of popular respectability. Election procedures were venal and elitist, but they involved genuine intersectarian collaboration and public participation. Nonetheless, the National Pact steadily lost legitimacy. These contradictions provided the backdrop for the crisis of May–October 1958 and its "Shihabist" outcome (the best English sources for more detailed information on the events are Hudson, 1968; Salibi, 1976; Goria, 1985; Johnson, 1986; and Alin, 1994).

Bishara al-Khuri has been credited with successfully implementing the double balance of the National Pact, as well as being a major participant in its formulation. Certainly his presidency, from 1943 to 1952, took independent Lebanon through its teething stage. On the other hand, al-Khuri's enthusiasm for unfettered liberal capitalism and his abuses of presidential power confirmed unattractive features of Greater Lebanon already visible under the Mandate, features incompatible with multisectarian equilibrium.

In politics, al-Khuri's Constitutional Bloc dominated the electoral map through astute alliances with a few great *zu'ama* who organized "grand lists" of parliamentary candidates in large constituencies—the five administrative governorates. These included Ahmad al-Asa'ad (Shi'i) in the south, Sabri Hamada (Shi'i) and Henri Pharaon (Greek Catholic) in the Biqa', Rashid Karami (Sunni) and Hamid Faranjiyya (Maronite) in the north, Majid Arslan (Druze) in Mount Lebanon and Riyadh al-Sulh (Sunni) in Beirut.[81] The initial opposition, chiefly the Eddes, was restricted to Mount Lebanon. Using vote-buying and other tactics carried over from the Mandate, al-Khuri's machine secured an overwhelming victory in the 1947 parliamentary elections, which al-Khuri promptly exploited to amend the constitution and gain a second presidential term "for one time only." As a result, Maronite presidential hopefuls from his own camp, most notably Camille Chamoun, turned against him. Al-Khuri's partnership with a highly respected prime minister, Riyadh al-Sulh, only partly obscured the fact that his assertion of presidential power undermined the internal balance intended by the National Pact and set an unfortunate precedent.

In economics, al-Khuri and his circle believed that the class they represented should be unrestrained in its investment of the profits made from allied wartime spending in the Levant, and should be free to make money by whatever means it pleased. The outcome was the minimal tax, minimal tariff, and strong currency regime of the so-called "merchant republic." Al-Khuri and the other leaders of Beirut's commercial sector were highly unsympathetic to state spending on social welfare or to any encouragement of industry and agriculture, which implied state intervention and regulation of foreign trade. Beirut thus continued to develop as a great center of Middle East regional services, real estate speculation, and tourism, on the basis of an erratic economic boom that lasted into the 1960s.

The costs of the boom were stagnation and infrastructural neglect everywhere beyond the metropolis and Mount Lebanon. A predominantly Christian elite with a Sunni appendage absorbed the profits, and a disproportionately Shi'i and Sunni mass was hit by the inflation and unemployment produced by the "free market." Furthermore, the expansion of Beirut's middle class was also biased toward Christians, not simply because of the Christian "head start" in education and ties with the West, but also because the "trickle-down" from the free market was a sectarian "in-house" effect—Maronite, Orthodox, or Armenian employers tended to hire Christians, preferably their own people.

From the first days of independence, al-Khuri's "merchant republic" helped Lebanon on the road to social and sectarian trouble in the late twentieth century. Peripheries remain neglected in 2005; parts of the Shi'i south have benefited from the recent Shi'i rise, but Tripoli is depressed and there is grinding poverty in the Akkar, the north Biqa', and southern Beirut.

More immediately, al-Khuri drifted into trouble from 1948 onwards, for both political and economic reasons. As an aspirant social reformer, the young Druze leader Kamal Junblatt found the regime uncongenial after a brief spell as a minister, and joined al-Khuri's enemies. Not surprisingly, the regime also faced labor union problems, with notable communist influence.[82] In 1949, the Palestine debacle marked the end of a short cozy phase in which Lebanon could easily manage openness to both the West and the Arabs, Arab states at that time being uniformly conservative and Western-aligned. Through the 1950s, rising Arab radicalism made Lebanon's balancing act more and more problematic. In 1950, the customs union with Syria collapsed over the contradiction between Lebanon's laissez-faire trade policies and the Syrian trend toward autarchy. The disruption of the transit trade through Beirut was a blow to both economies. In July 1951, al-Khuri lost his prime ministerial prop when Riyadh al-Sulh was assassinated in Jordan by a member of the Syrian Social Nationalist Party.

Even al-Khuri's electoral allies could not prevent his parliamentary majority from slipping in the 1951 elections, and the coalescence of upper-class opposition with street protests unnerved the regime. Chamoun, Junblatt, Edde, and senior Sunni politicians made a loose combination in favor of vague reforms—their divergent outlooks precluded a specific program. Administrative corruption and press censorship caused Prime Minister Sami al-Sulh to desert al-Khuri in September 1952, and a general strike indicated public isolation of the president. General Fuad Shihab, anxious to preserve the unity of Lebanon's new army, declined to intervene on the streets, and on 18 September 1952 al-Khuri stepped down, his majority in the House of Deputies proving irrelevant to his survival.

Parliament then elected Camille Chamoun as president. Chamoun had eclipsed Emile Edde as the leading opposition Maronite, and his public front of mild reformism, mixed with defense of Arab perspectives during his terms in the late 1940s as Lebanese ambassador to Britain and the United Nations, gained him sufficient Muslim as well as Christian credibility to defeat Hamiḍ Faranjiyya in the parliamentary vote. Chamoun was also the candidate favored by Britain and the U.S. Chamoun, however, did not come from the ranks of the traditional rural *zu'ama* or the merchant elite—his background was middle class rather than high bourgeois—and he lacked the personal power base and alliances that Bishara al-Khuri had been able to mobilize. The coalition that brought him to the presidency fell to pieces almost immediately. Kamal Junblatt denounced him as a fraud; leading Sunnis demanded a census, a Muslim vice president, and constitutional change; and the more conservative *zu'ama* obstructed administrative reform.

In 1952–53 Chamoun had grave difficulties forming governments, and resorted to emergency decrees to implement fragmentary reforms. These included female suffrage, more independence for the judiciary, extensive personnel changes in the bureaucracy (opposed because they cut across clientelist connections), and public takeover of some basic services, for example electricity. Upper-class hostility to the modest administrative shakeup did not bode well for the future.

In response, Chamoun asserted presidential authority. He aimed to displace most senior *zu'ama* and their clients from the House of

Deputies, and to promote new people who would owe their seats to presidential patronage. He began by adjusting constituency arrangements for the 1953 parliamentary elections, increasing the number of electorates from 9 to 33, and reducing the number of seats from 77 to 44. Twenty-two constituencies would have only one member each, and *zu'ama* could therefore no longer manipulate "grand lists" of candidates in multimember constituencies. Chamoun's targets included Maronites like the Faranjiyyas as well as Muslims like Ahmad al-Asa'ad and Sa'ib Salam and the Druze leader Kamal Junblatt. He quickly attracted the accusation that he sought to subordinate prime minister and parliament to an autocratic presidency, thereby abrogating the Maronite-Sunni balance of the National Pact. Sectarian friction surfaced early in Chamoun's presidency with Muslim calls for equivalence in administrative appointments, still biased toward Christians in violation of a constitutional requirement. Sunnis and Shi'is were more interested in sectarian power relations than in bureaucratic efficiency.

From 1954 on, external influences intensified Lebanon's internal polarization. The Arab world divided between states which continued close relations with the West, such as Iraq, Jordan, and Lebanon, and forces in Egypt and Syria that emphasized radical republicanism and Arab nationalism and opposed Western alignments. The regional power struggle, principally between Gamal Abd-al Nasir's Egypt and Hashemite Iraq with their contending Arab union schemes, became conflated with international Cold War rivalry. Nasir stirred Arab mass opinion with his stand against what he perceived as relics of Western colonial domination, such as the residual British interest in Egypt and attempts to pull Arab countries into anti-Soviet defense pacts. For Nasir, relics of colonialism soon included conservative regimes sympathetic to the West. For many Lebanese Muslims, Chamoun's pre-presidential espousal of Arab causes now came to be viewed as hypocrisy and trickery; Chamoun of course saw no contradiction.

For Arab nationalists, Chamoun stepped out of the closet once and for all when he and Prime Minister Sami al-Sulh visited Turkey in April 1955 and appeared to endorse the so-called Baghdad Pact, whereby Iraq was linked to the West-leaning, non-Arab "northern tier" of the

Middle East. The pair were treated to demonstrations and a boycott by leading Muslim *zu'ama* when they returned to Beirut. Thereafter Chamoun aroused further fury, chiefly among Muslims, with his tacit acceptance of the Eisenhower doctrine for U.S. assistance to Middle Eastern states threatened by "communism," and his November 1956 refusal to expel the British and French ambassadors after the Anglo-French invasion of the Suez canal zone. On these foreign policy issues, Lebanese opinion split into two camps roughly coinciding with differing attitudes concerning internal affairs. Each perceived the other as breaking the two balancing formulae of the National Pact for Lebanon's external relations and sectarian power sharing. On the one hand, most Muslims—especially urban Sunnis—saw a tilt toward the West and Maronite hegemony. On the other hand, Chamoun and most Christians—especially Maronites—saw Nasirite interference in Lebanon's internal affairs and denigration of Lebanon's sovereignty. Chamoun behaved forcefully, but it would be unfair to blame him overmuch: given Lebanon's make-up and the Middle Eastern environment of the 1950s, the internal schism was inevitable.

The real question was whether political dexterity and commonality among the high bourgeoisie could contain factionalism and prevent a breakdown of public order. This proved to be the case through the mid-1950s, but the situation took a decisive turn for the worse after early 1957, partly because of the approaching 1958 presidential election. Chamoun undoubtedly felt that he had not been given a fair chance to make his mark since 1952, that Lebanon's existence was threatened, and that circumstances required firm management. His regime frontally challenged rival *zu'ama* in the 1957 parliamentary elections in ways that put previous manipulation in the shade. An imaginative gerrymander created constituency boundaries that splintered the support bases of leading opposition politicians. Junblatt and Sa'ib Salam lost their seats while Chamoun's Shi'i ally Kazim al-Khalil defeated Ahmad al-Asa'ad's list in the south. Chamoun's embittered opponents assumed that he intended to have the new House of Deputies re-elect him as president, in the style of Bishara al-Khuri; Chamoun refused to comment.

Inter-Arab tensions reached new heights in the aftermath of the

Suez affair. Nasirite agitation led to a virtual state of siege in Lebanon, at least from the government perspective, while the Americans involved themselves in an abortive attempt to overturn the weak regime in Damascus.[83] The Syrian Ba'thists appealed to Nasir, and in February 1958 Syria and Egypt came together in the United Arab Republic (U.A.R.), under full Egyptian command. The union convulsed the Islamic sector in Lebanon, as the majority of Sunnis and Shi'is favored submergence in the Arabist tide. Chamoun, backed by the bulk of the Christian street, was absolutely determined to preserve Lebanon. In early 1958 only a small spark was needed to ignite widespread violence.

On 8 May, unknown assailants killed an anti-regime Maronite journalist in Tripoli. Public order instantly collapsed in Tripoli and Muslim sections of Beirut, as riots extended into mobilization of gangs and small militias by radical parties—Nasirites, the Ba'th and Communists—and the street agents *(qabadays)* of opposition *zu'ama.* Opposition elements were loosely linked in the National Front, an initiative of Kamal Junblatt. Despite their mutual antipathy, the Kata'ib and SSNP rallied their followers in support of President Chamoun: pan-Arabism was the enemy of both the Lebanonists and the proponents of Greater Syria. General Shihab kept the army out of the conflict, and Chamoun did not ask him to intervene. After a few weeks of heavy fighting, government authority became restricted to central Mount Lebanon and the eastern part of Beirut—the Christian heartland. All the areas added to Mount Lebanon in 1920 came under the control of their local *zu'ama,* in defiance of the regime, and weaponry and volunteers infiltrated into the north and the Biqa' from the Syrian province of the U.A.R.

The events were only prevented from taking on a fully sectarian coloration by the cross-sectarian extensions of the two alignments, and by the mediation of a "third force" of Christian and Muslim politicians. The Druze split between the old Yazbaki and Junblatti factions, with Majid Arslan remaining with Chamoun and defending the airport from Junblatt's followers. In June, Arslan retired from the arena after Druze shaykhs arranged an inter-Druze truce. As for Sunni West Beirut, Prime Minister Sami al-Sulh stood by Chamoun, but he was isolated and his decision finished his political career. In the south, Kazim al-Khalil of Tyre also kept his alliance with the president, but was forced to flee to Beirut. In contrast, the most prominent family of the north, the Faranjiyyas, opposed Chamoun, especially after the regime sponsored the Duwayhi family in Zgharta in the 1957 elections. A few other Christian personalities, such as Henri Pharaon and Charles Helou from al-Khuri's Constitutional Bloc, stayed out of the confrontation and participated in a "third force," together with some second-rank Sunnis, for example Fawzi al-Huss. Maronite patriarch Bulos Meouche, suspicious of Chamoun's ambivalence about seeking a second term, kept his distance from the president.

At the outset, Chamoun requested that the U.S. Administration consider intervening under the Eisenhower doctrine.[84] The U.S. stalled, hoping that the crisis might deflate without its involvement, and required that Chamoun declare that he would not seek re-election. On 30 June Chamoun complied with this condition, having also appealed to the U.N. Thereafter President Eisenhower and Secretary of State Dulles both acknowledged an obligation that would be difficult to abandon, despite concerns about entanglement in local sectarianism. Fighting subsided by early July, by which time U.N. observers had arrived to report on the sources of the disturbances. However, it seemed unlikely that internal mediation could repair the rift in the upper class or calm the quasi-revolutionary mood on the streets of Tripoli and West Beirut. The opposition demanded immediate removal of Chamoun from the presidency and equal representation of Muslims and Christians in parliament. A possibility thus existed that Greater Lebanon would dissolve into its original components, with the peripheries being absorbed by the U.A.R. and a Christian mini-state emerging in Mount Lebanon and East Beirut. Apart from the relative passivity of the Palestinian refugee camps, the 1958 conflict was a "dry run" for the far more devastating 1975 collapse, and demonstrated that Lebanon did not need intrusion of the Arab-Israeli conflict to come to grief.

In 1958, Lebanon was saved by a coup in Iraq. On 14 July, army officers led by General 'Abd al-Karim Qasim overthrew the Hashemite monarchy, thereby terminating the Baghdad Pact and removing the

West's major ally in the Arab world. President Chamoun immediately asked for American troops, and this time the U.S. wasted no time. American Marines landed in Beirut the day after the Iraqi coup, and in the following days the presence increased to 14,000 men. The U.S. intervened to demonstrate Western will to an audience far beyond Lebanon, but in order to extricate itself creditably was compelled to deal with the grubby details of Lebanon's own crisis. A high-ranking U.S. envoy, Robert Murphy, sent on a fact-finding mission, swiftly took over mediation from the ineffectual "third force." By late July, after energetic persuasion, he had established a compromise. General Shihab, the only Maronite leader acceptable to both camps, would submit himself to parliament as a presidential candidate, thereafter taking over from Chamoun at the formal end of the *'ahd* (presidential period) on 24 September. The House of Deputies endorsed Shihab as president on 31 July.

On assuming the presidency, Shihab asked the opposition Sunni *za'im* of Tripoli, Rashid Karami, to form a government. Karami's choice of ministers, weighted toward the opposition and excluding Chamounists, was taken as a humiliation in the Christian sector. This, added to Nasir's approval of Shihab and Karami and the kidnapping of the assistant editor of the Kata'ib newspaper *al-'Amal,* sparked a second round of warfare in Beirut that became openly sectarian. The Kata'ib and the SSNP defied the new regime and traded fire with Muslim groups between 19 September and 17 October in the most violent phase of the 1958 conflict. This flare-up, however, did not derail the U.S.-brokered settlement, as its instigators did not aim to displace the new president. Meanwhile, U.S. troops departed in stages between August and October, after a 21 August U.N. General Assembly resolution calling on Arab states not to interfere in one another's internal affairs.

A final cease-fire came when Shihab and Karami agreed to shelve the proposed government, and Shihab appointed Karami at the head of an emergency cabinet of four members—two Muslims and two Christians, incuding Kata'ib leader Pierre Jumayyil. After 2,500 deaths, an equilibrium of "no victor and no vanquished" prevailed.

"Shihabism," 1958–67

President Fuad Shihab gave Lebanon its first and only experience of a military man in the presidency and systematic regime intervention in favor of socioeconomic justice. Shihab, a member of Lebanon's most illustrious family and distantly connected to Amir Bashir II, had risen rapidly in the officer corps through the Mandate, trained in France, and become the founding commander of independent Lebanon's army. Through the 1950s he had paid special attention to unity in the ranks and the proficiency and education of his officers; he gave Lebanon a force widely underestimated because it was small and held back from being used, but which was one of the most skilled and professional armies in the region.

Shihab was aloof, cautious, contemptuous of the factional antics of civilian politicians, and behind his anodyne public posture very much conscious of his historical role. Acutely aware that the 1958 upheaval reflected potentially disastrous social and sectarian dichotomies, as president he adopted policies aimed at a measure of income redistribution, Christian-Muslim parity in the bureaucracy, and economic and infrastructural development in the peripheries—citadels of insurrection in May–October 1958. In trying to implement his program, Shihab faced the same dilemma that had absorbed Chamoun's energies and brought down al-Khuri—the absence of a stable power base for the Lebanese presidency in the face of factional interests. Lebanon had no large Western-style political parties to contain factionalism and anchor the executive politically. Shihab naturally avoided the failed approaches of al-Khuri (manipulation of a grand coalition of *zu-ama*) and Chamoun (confrontation with much of this coalition). Shihab's method was to insulate himself from the old-style politicians without colliding with them, and to implement his policies through his own network in the military institution, the intelligence organs (principally military intelligence, known as *al-maktab al-thani* or the *deuxième bureau*), and new parts of the bureaucracy. Such an approach required a reliable majority in parliament, which implied use of the *deuxième bureau* to sap the client networks of potentially troublesome *zu'ama*. This combination of mild étatism, a social welfare drive, and security service influences within a civilian regime is what is meant by "Shihabism." The army itself grew from 10,000 to about 15,000 men during Shihab's presidency.[85]

Shihab's social reformism and attention to the Islamic sector was bounded by a fundamental commitment to the 1943 National Pact, and hence could not ultimately be satisfactory to Sunnis or Shi'is. However, when added to a strong tilt toward friendly relations with Nasir's Egypt, his internal program enabled swift pacification of Lebanon's day-to-day affairs. Despite the belligerence of some *zu'ama* in 1958, the depth of the factional rift and mass discontent came as a rude awakening to most of the upper class. For a time, politicians were willing to cooperate for the sake of economic stability and self-interest. In this context, the high bourgeoisie still had the capacity, when it was not at war with itself, to hold the lid on pressures from below. Consequently Lebanon had a breathing space into the mid-1960s.

Further, Syrian secession from the U.A.R. in 1961, after three years of subordination to Cairo, dampened Arabist enthusiasms among Lebanese Muslims. Indeed, having survived the Nasirite surge in 1958, Lebanon's integrity was not again to be challenged by Arab nationalism. The late-twentieth-century threats to the country from within and without had a different complexion.

As regards policy initiatives, Shihab imposed an equal distribution of high-level administrative posts between Christians and non-Christians, a significant boost for the latter. Government expenditure was increased, from about 11% of GNP in 1956 to about 23% in 1964,[86] creating a brief equivalence with the social democracies of Western Europe. The regime founded a central bank for more leverage over the economy and new agencies for planning, statistics, regional development projects, and social security, staffing these institutions with competent technocrats. The fact that Lebanon had no central bank until 1964, twenty years after independence, is a revealing indicator of the ad hoc procedures of the "merchant republic."

Interestingly, the Kata'ib played a special role in the creation of the first social security system for the Lebanese population, to be funded by employer, employee, and government contributions. Most distinctively, substantial resources were diverted to public works, roads, education, and agricultural investment, especially the combined irrigation/hydro-electric scheme on the Litani river. Such resources went mainly to the peripheral Shi'i areas—Southern Lebanon and the Biqa'—although Pierre Jummayil, as Minister of Public Works, made sure that Mount Lebanon was not neglected.

Shihab began his term with such widespread endorsement that he easily secured a sympathetic majority in the 1960 elections for the House of Deputies. The 1958 emergency cabinet lasted only until October 1959, when Raymond Edde resigned after frictions with Pierre Jumayyil—the Eddes had never had any time for the Kata'ib, which they and other upper-class Maronites regarded as uncouth. After 1960 Shihab created more and more cabinet posts to satisfy different factions; he operated with Junblatt's Progressive Socialist Party (PSP), the Kata'ib, Kamal al-Asa'ad's conservative Shi'i bloc, and most Sunni politicians, and used Sa'ib Salam as well as Rashid Karami as prime ministers. In his early years, virtually the entire Islamic leadership was prepared to work with him, the opposition being confined to estranged Christians such as Chamoun, Raymond Edde, and the SSNP. The latter was decimated by the security apparatus when it attempted a coup in December 1961.

Shihab's approach gradually stirred resentments. He wanted ministers to watch one another in multifactional governments while he shifted real decision-making elsewhere, into his inner circle of military cronies and technocrats. The fact that Shihab's confidants were generally from the middle rather than the upper class, and often displayed hostility toward *fromagistes* (cheese-eaters—Shihab's own term for many politicians), did not help.

By 1961 Prime Minister Sa'ib Salam found that he couldn't manage Kamal Junblatt, one of his senior ministers, and resigned when Shihab declined to back him. Salam later had the same experience with Junblatt in the 1970s, under President Faranjiyya. Karami served as prime minister for the remainder of Shihab's 'ahd and, with interruptions, through most of Helou's presidency up to 1970. Salam joined Shihab's opponents. In the run-up to the 1964 parliamentary elections, Shihab's machine endeavored to enlarge the room for maneuver for a Shihabist successor and to establish a base for Shihab's own return.

Tactics included *deuxième bureau* enticement of West Beirut *qabadays,* and subversion of the campaigns of Chamoun and Edde to retain their seats. This seamy, provocative dimension of Shihabism contributed to serious bourgeois disenchantment by 1964, expressed in assertion of economic liberalism against étatism, condemnation of the political role of military personnel, and a backlash in the Christian and Sunni "center" against favoring the peripheries.

Shihabism faltered after 1964, under the second Shihabist president, Charles Helou. Helou had solid qualifications—he had been a well-known Beirut journalist, an associate of Michel Chiha, and the main organizer of the "third force" in 1958—but he lacked the authority of his patron, even after he successfully resisted manipulation by Shihab's associates. In any case, even Shihab would have been hard put to navigate between the Scylla of upper-class requirements for an end to state intervention in the economy and the Charybdis of "street" agitation. The basic weakness of Shihab's program involved the continuing primacy of the commercial and landed elite in Lebanon's economic and political life. Any coalescence of old-style politicians as an opposition would paralyze the regime, as began to happen in 1967 when Pierre Jumayyil joined Chamoun and Edde in the anti-regime *hilf* (tripartite alliance). In short, the "merchant republic" was always supreme.

Greater Lebanon after half a century

Regardless of the upper-class compromises of the National Pact and "confessional democracy," Lebanon experienced gradually rising unhappiness from the mass of its population after the 1940s. Discontent had a strong sectarian dimension, because of shifting demographic balances and the unequal distribution of resources between the communities. Confirmation of the "merchant republic" as Lebanon's model in the late 1940s and the Shihabist experiment in the early 1960s greatly increased the likelihood of eventual social and political breakdown. The rapacious profiteering of the "merchant republic" could only have disastrous implications, whereas Shihabism was a damage control exercise that ended by doing more harm than good. Despite Shihab's étatism, the share of agriculture in the economy declined through the 1960s, and industry barely held its own as a poor relation of the service sector. Capital investment in agriculture displaced sharecroppers and laborers from the land, and education improvements enhanced the attractions of "town" and radical politics at a time of deteriorating urban living conditions and limited employment prospects for poorer people. The changes of the 1960s undercut the peasant support base of Shi'i rural bosses in a way that also destabilized the existing political system. Shihabism needed more time, but was never likely to get it.

This was the reality of the "Switzerland of the Middle East" even before the 1967 Arab-Israeli war and Israeli and Palestinian intrusions. Because of the main trend toward breakdown, Lebanon's positive features—habituation with parliamentary processes and experience of public freedoms and intersectarian cohabitation—were at risk.

In sum, the convergence of Christian and Muslim elites in the 1930s gave Greater Lebanon a more or less integrated upper class, and this upper class wielded enough patronage and had enough common self-interest to contain pressures from below for four decades. The elite, however, refused to acknowledge any social responsibility toward the Lebanese population—thereby offering no safety valve for rising social forces—and was predisposed to destructive factionalism at critical times, as in May 1958.

CHAPTER FIVE

INTO THE ABYSS, 1967–86

The approach of war

Despite a limited role in the 1948–49 Arab-Israeli war and the presence thereafter of over 150,000 Palestinian refugees on Lebanese territory, Lebanon had little to do with Arab-Israeli affairs up to 1967. Lebanon had an armistice agreement with Israel along a recognized international boundary, with no complications such as demilitarized zones or involvement within the lands of the former British Mandate for Palestine. The Lebanese government felt little impetus to excoriate Israel, unlike the more radicalized republican regimes of Egypt and Syria. The Palestinian refugees, mainly crowded into squalid refugee camps on the fringes of Beirut, Tripoli, Sidon, and Tyre, were content to let Arab states and armies take the lead in confronting "the enemy." For almost two decades Palestinians barely registered on the Lebanese political scene, and the Lebanese authorities took care to ensure that their penetration of Lebanese life did not go beyond investments by the Palestinian bourgeoisie and provision of cheap labor. Even Palestinian economic success aroused jealousy from the Lebanese elite, as was demonstrated by the 1966 collapse of the Palestinian-owned Intra Bank. In the 1960s Intra became Beirut's largest private financial institution, and a variety of Arab and foreign interests combined with Lebanon's central bank and Lebanese businesses to promote a crippling run on Intra's liquid assets.

The Arab defeat in the 1967 war against Israel changed all this. In reaction to the discrediting of Arab regular armies, various Palestinian military organizations established themselves among the refugee camp populations in countries neighboring Israel. Palestinians almost immediately began raiding across the June 1967 cease-fire lines, especially from Lebanon and Jordan. Israel held the governments hosting Palestinian military groups responsible for Palestinian operations within and beyond the Middle East. On 30 December 1968, after the hijacking of an El Al airliner to Athens, Israeli commandos raided Beirut international airport and destroyed thirteen Middle East Airlines aircraft. Israel's policy was to make conditions sufficiently unpleasant for the Lebanese and Jordanian regimes that they would be forced to move against the Palestinian camps. Certainly by 1969 the Palestinian factions, under the umbrella of the Palestine Liberation Organization (PLO), posed more of a challenge to these regimes than they did to Israel.

The Palestinian-Israeli hostilities overshadowed Charles Helou's presidency in its last three years. They finished off the Shihabist reform effort, already stymied since Shihab's departure in 1964. Palestinian activity also began to erode Lebanese sovereignty on the borders with Israel and Syria as well as around the camps in the main coastal cities. This re-exposed Christian-Muslim dichotomies in the regime that had been veiled since 1958 by Shihabism and cross-sectarian political maneuvering.

At the popular level, most Christians felt threatened by Palestinian assertion, regardless of the fact that Israel was its main target. Palestinians in Lebanon amounted to about 8% of the country's population, they were 85% Sunni and only 15% Christian (virtually all non-Maronite), and now that they had become politically energized they could play a critical role against Maronite pre-eminence. Maronite leaders as diverse as Kata'ib leader Pierre Jumayyil, former president Camille Chamoun, and northern rural boss Sulayman Faranjiyya demanded that the Palestinians be curbed. They especially emphasized the dangers to state institutions and sovereignty.

At this early stage, most non-Christians were not sympathetic to these concerns, although upper-class Sunnis like Sa'ib Salam and the al-Sulhs were unenthusiastic about Palestinian radicalism. Populist movements in Lebanon's Islamic sector—in the late 1960s being of the secular left rather than the religious right—linked with Palestinian

152

counterparts and made no secret of the fact that they envisaged a Lebanese-Palestinian alliance as a lever to force Christian leaders to accept constitutional change. The Druze chieftain Kamal Junblatt, pursuing his personal campaign against the Maronite and Sunni establishments, placed his Progressive Socialist Party (PSP) at the head of a collection of populist parties with Palestinian connections. Junblatt's National Movement, established in 1969, encompassed the Syrian Social Nationalists (SSNP), the Ba'thists, the Communist Party, and several Nasirite offshoots. Their chief Palestinian associates were George Habbash's Popular Front for the Liberation of Palestine (PFLP), Na'if Hawatmeh's Popular Democratic Front (PDFLP), and the Syrian-controlled Sa'iqa group. The rapidly expanding membership of these parties largely involved young Shi'i migrants to Beirut from the south, entranced by revolutionary rhetoric.

As with Nasirite Arabism in the 1950s, Sunni leaders had little choice but to adjust to street pressures. However, they themselves wanted a shift in the regime's balance, identified with the Palestinian cause, and stood against having Lebanese security agencies do what they saw as Israel's work.

President Helou and the army command were caught between the opposed Christian and Islamic sentiments aroused by Palestinian assertion. As Palestinian activity intensified in early 1969, Shihabist officers favored action to salvage regime prestige. In April 1969, clashes erupted between the army and Palestinian fighters, and Kamal Junblatt censured Prime Minister Rashid Karami and Muslim ministers for their hesitation to break with the president. In October, General Emile Bustani ordered his troops to cut Palestinian supply routes from Syria, but this brought Syrian military infiltration, caused Prime Minister Karami to dissociate himself from the regime, and precipitated a street rebellion in Tripoli.

Lebanese, Syrian, and Palestinian opposition made it plain that the army could not suppress the Palestinian organizations. President Helou and General Bustani caved in; on 3 November 1969 Bustani signed the "Cairo agreement" with PLO leader Yasir 'Arafat, by which Lebanon acknowledged PLO supremacy within the refugee camps, pledged itself to facilitate Palestinian access to the border with Israel, and in return received only the vaguest PLO affirmation of Lebanese sovereignty. Karami reactivated his performance of prime ministerial functions, but Christian hard-liners were furious, while the "Islamic and nationalist" camp felt emboldened further to test the regime. As for the Palestinians, the path was set toward a "state within the state."

In 1970, major domestic and regional developments made the violent disruption of Greater Lebanon significantly more likely. Within Lebanon, the August presidential election produced a surprise— Sulayman Faranjiyya. The front runner, ex-president Shihab, pulled out in the final weeks, probably fearing that he could not manage the country in increasingly adverse circumstances. The other leading Maronites—Pierre Jumayyil, Camille Chamoun, Raymond Edde, and Ilyas Sarkis as Shihab's stand-in—canceled one another out, leaving Faranjiyya to surface as a compromise candidate. Faranjiyya was an inflexible proponent of laissez-faire economics, and resented Shihab and Karami for excluding him from government after 1961. He had become minister of the interior under Helou in 1968, opposed the Shihabist security apparatus in the 1968 parliamentary elections, and built up a strategic position as a Maronite with good ties with Muslim politicians like Sa'ib Salam and Kamil al-Asa'ad as well as with Jumayyil and Edde.

Ironically, Kamal Junblatt, who had been an ally of Shihab, gave Faranjiyya his one-vote margin in parliament over Sarkis, because Junblatt wished to have a president in his debt—not a Shihabist who might improve state authority. Faranjiyya managed to present himself simultaneously as a liberator of the high bourgeoisie from Shihabist constraints, as a friend of Syrian President Hafiz al-Asad who would be indulgent toward the left and the Palestinians, and as an upholder of Maronite prerogatives and Lebanon's sovereignty. This was to prove a disastrous combination.

The turning point for Lebanon in the wider Middle East came in September 1970, only weeks before Faranjiyya's election, when King Husayn of Jordan went to war with the Palestinian forces encamped on his territory. Two consequences ensued.

As regards the Palestinians, thousands of PLO militants crossed into Lebanon, where Faranjiyya was lax about border supervision

154

despite his rhetoric about sovereignty. Lebanon became the only territory from which Palestinians could pursue an autonomous confrontation with Israel: the urban refugee camps, with about 200,000 residents, offered rearward infrastructure; the most permeable of Israel's front lines invited infiltration; and the Lebanese state was paralyzed by contradictory sectarian outlooks.

As regards Syria, a misconceived Syrian military intervention against King Husayn led to a coup in Damascus by Defense Minister Hafiz al-Asad, who seized the presidency. Asad provided Syria with its first stable regime in two decades, and Damascus was soon able to give consistent, unprecedented attention to its Lebanese flank. Up to 1975 Syrian influence tended to encourage Palestinians to defy the Lebanese state. Overall, after 1970 Palestinian, Israeli, and Syrian pressures on Lebanon visibly tightened.

Far from fortifying the regime to face these challenges, President Faranjiyya chose policies that weakened his own administration and destabilized society. He promptly purged the state's intelligence-gathering organ—the *deuxième bureau*—and elevated a friend from Zahla, Iskander Ghanim, as army commander. The removal of Shihabist officers meant virtually destroying the state's eyes and ears regarding Palestinian, Syrian, and Israeli activities. It also gave greater freedom to local radical parties including the SSNP, Ba'thists, and Communists, legalized by Kamal Junblatt as interior minister just before the 1970 presidential election.

At the same time, Faranjiyya undermined the delicate relationship between the presidency and the Sunni prime minister. He turned away from Prime Minister Sa'ib Salam when the latter was attacked by Kamal Junblatt. Salam declined to offer Junblatt a ministerial position, and Junblatt accused him of working to protect Maronite privileges and not preparing the army to stand against Israel. Faranjiyya satisfied Junblatt by not imposing any serious constraint on the activities of the left and the Palestinians.

In April 1973 Salam demanded the resignation of General Ghanim after an unopposed Israeli commando raid on Beirut, and resigned when Faranjiyya backed his army friend rather than his prime minister. To avoid appointing Rashid Karami, whom he disliked, Faranjiyya chose to replace Salam with Amin al-Hafiz, a second-rank Sunni from Tripoli. The Sunni establishment regarded this as an attempt to disenfranchise Sunni leaders just when they were also losing their popular influence to radicals and Palestinian groups. Although Faranjiyya was quickly forced to turn to the more respectable al-Sulh family, his behavior in the early 1970s compromised trust and working relations on the Maronite-Sunni political axis.

As regards socioeconomic affairs, Salam's appointment of a government of younger reform-minded technocrats in November 1970 seemed to be a positive indicator. At this time the service economy was entering a new boom, with enhanced Gulf oil revenues flowing into the banking system and a surge in real estate speculation. Faranjiyya, however, would not allow ministers to address social grievances, which were exacerbated by economic growth benefiting only a fragment of the population. Proposals to strengthen public education, reform public health, and overhaul a blatantly unfair tax system were all opposed by the president himself, who took the side of business friends. The affected ministers soon resigned.

Between 1970 and 1973 the so-called boom in fact imprisoned the majority of Lebanese, especially Muslims, in a trap of high inflation, falling real incomes, and labor competition from several hundred thousand Syrian immigrants. Industry and agriculture continued to stagnate while fortunes were made in services and property. The technocrats quickly faded from view, and some ministers favored incompetent cronies and promoted bribery and corruption in a manner that recalled the days of Bishara al-Khuri. The president's son Tony Faranjiyya, who became minister of posts and telegraph under Taqi al-Din al-Sulh in 1973, was reputed to be one of the worst offenders.

President Faranjiyya had no sensitivity whatsoever to the destructive effects of high bourgeois capitalism, monopolies, and official venality, or to the fierce hostility of Lebanon's poor, above all in the Shi'i community. He dismissed privation in a banal fashion, noting the presence of televisions and refrigerators "even in the slums"[87]—a close parallel to equally grotesque remarks in January 1995 by President Ilyas al-Hirawi, who denied that Lebanon faced a social crisis in the mid-1990s because the Lebanese possessed "two million cars."[88] Indeed the

156

economic policies of the early 1970s and mid-1990s resembled each other, the principal difference being that the Syrian army placed a lid on social discontent after 1990.

By 1974 price rises, especially for land, throttled the speculative boom. A downturn hit the construction industry, constricting an important safety valve for poorer job seekers. Inflation, however, surged, with 1974 price rises of over 100% for staple foods.[89] Interestingly, in the 1970s, prewar Lebanon and prerevolution Iran shared this background of boom and recession, accompanied by relentless inflation, weak employment generation, and widening skews in income distribution. Strikes, labor unrest, and student protest became regular events in Lebanon. The protests sometimes turned violent, as with repeated clashes between students and police in Beirut in January–February 1973, did not produce any concessions from the regime, and generally contributed to public alienation.

The insecurities of living in an overheated and socially unbalanced economy affected Muslims and Christians differently. In the Islamic sector, such insecurities buttressed the revolutionary left and helped radical Lebanese and Palestinian organizations to link with street level gang, clientelist, and criminal networks hitherto dominated by conservative Sunni bosses and the Shihabist *deuxième bureau.*[90] Among the mass of Maronites, economic frustrations fed into the growing sense of being a community under siege, in an environment where events were out of control. This aided the populist right—Jumayyil's Kata'ib, Chamoun's National Liberal Party (NLP), and their paramilitary offshoots—to appear as the only stable reference point for Christians adrift.

In May 1973 creeping Palestinian takeover of parts of suburban Beirut and provocations of the army by leftist Palestinian groups such as the PFLP, the PDFLP, and Sa'iqa—covered by Junblatt's National Movement—forced President Faranjiyya to take action. When the PDFLP kidnapped several Lebanese soldiers on 1–2 May, the army launched its largest operation against the Palestinians since 1969, surrounding the Beirut refugee camps. Clashes quickly involved 'Arafat's Fatah, the main PLO group; the Palestinians shelled the airport; and Faranjiyya had the air force bomb the camps. These developments also forced Syria's President Asad into the open, but against the Lebanese regime. Syria sent Palestinian units to occupy an area of Lebanese territory near Rashayya and closed its border with Lebanon, imposing an economic siege. Within two weeks Faranjiyya adjusted to the requirements of his friend in Damascus, suspended army operations, and made an accord with the PLO in Beirut's Melkart hotel that reiterated the 1969 Cairo agreement.

This second humiliation of Lebanon's army was more momentous than the 1969 episode because the Palestinian military apparatus had grown so much in the intervening years. In particular the army was impotent to do anything about the conversion of the Palestinian refugee camps of Tel al Za'atar and Dubbaya into armed strongholds, threatening communications between largely Christian East Beirut and its Maronite mountain hinterland. Most Christians could not fathom what this had to do with any struggle against Israel. Kata'ib leader Pierre Jumayyil tried to distinguish between Palestinian radicals who interfered in Lebanon's social and sectarian affairs and the "honorable resistance" of 'Arafat's Fatah, but in reality he and NLP leader Camille Chamoun concluded after May 1973 that they had no alternative except to ready their followers for hostilities. The multiplication of shipments of weaponry into the Christian sector in turn precipitated a local arms race with the parties linked to the National Movement.

From mid-1973 to early 1975, paramilitary factions in both the Christian and the Islamic sectors increasingly marginalized the Lebanese state, and there was a steady trend toward chaos. The aftermath of the October 1973 Arab-Israeli war did not help. Greater international respectability for the PLO through 1974, for example 'Arafat's reception at the U.N. in November, irritated Israel and many Lebanese Christians, whereas negotiations between Israel and Egypt, added to contacts between Israel and some Maronites, disturbed the Syrian regime and many Palestinians and Lebanese Muslims. Predictably, the tempo of Israeli-Palestinian clashes quickened through 1974, with Israeli air raids on the PLO in Beirut in December. Many more Shi'is fled their villages near the Lebanon-Israel border, arriving in the capital to swell dissatisfaction in Beirut's "belt of misery" and inflate Maronite fears of a threat to the political order. After Faranjiyya's regime ignored his demands in late 1973 for public investment in southern Lebanon and attention to the plight of its inhabitants, the popular Shi'i leader Musa Sadr held a rally of 75,000 Shi'is in Ba'albak on 17 March 1974 during which he launched his own political faction—the Movement of the Deprived, which was later to become the paramilitary Amal movement.

Maneuvering among Lebanon's political leaders, also involving 'Arafat's Fatah, in the last months before breakdown in 1975 illustrated both the divisive and the integrative roles of the upper class. Unfortunately divergence of interests and perspectives had gone too far for any consensus to be restored. President Faranjiyya and Prime Ministers Taqi al-Din and Rashid al-Sulh maintained cordial relations with the Maronite "right" and the National Movement "left," but did not satisfy either side's requirements. Faranjiyya drifted closer to Jumayyil and Chamoun on the matters of Palestinian encroachment on Lebanon's sovereignty and defense of Maronite political prerogatives, but remained open to Junblatt and the Syrian regime. Junblatt's influence in the regime peaked with Faranjiyya's appointment of his reform-minded friend Rashid al-Sulh as prime minister in November 1974, but Faranjiyya chose al-Sulh because he had no real power base and could not challenge the president's ministerial friends. Junblatt's influence thus had no chance of bringing any peaceful adjustment of sectarian political allocations.

Faranjiyya's predilection for weak prime ministers and his dealings with the Maronite "right" alienated upper-class Sunnis and Maronites. Sa'ib Salam and Rashid Karami, foes through the 1960s, came together in late 1974 with Raymond Edde, who had a personal score to settle with the Kata'ib over his brother Pierre's displacement from an East Beirut parliamentary seat, to form the *tahaluf* (alignment) against the regime. Salam and Karami now converged with the Shi'i Musa Sadr and the Druze-led National Movement in demands for revision of the National Pact, more power for the Islamic sector, and reduction of the power of the Maronite presidency.

The convergence, however, was only superficial, as all sorts of crosscurrents prevented any serious Islamic cohesion. In early 1975 Karami even hinted that he might support a crackdown on the Palestinian armed presence if Jumayyil considered limited change in the Maronite-Sunni political balance, but Jumayyil did not respond.[91] Musa Sadr did not trust either the Sunni high bourgeoisie or Junblatt, as he knew that they all looked down on Shi'is—he maintained his own channels to the Christian sector, particularly to senior religious personalities. Junblatt intimidated Salam and Karami by using his radical and Palestinian partners to undercut street support for Sunni politicians, particularly Salam, and his personal ambitions prevented smooth relations with Sunni or Shi'i leaders.

Yasir 'Arafat prefered to keep his Fatah out of Lebanese controversies, and had a reasonable modus vivendi with conservative Maronites, including Pierre Jumayyil, but his preference could not be sustained. On the one hand, Fatah was the backbone of the Palestinian infrastructure which Maronites wanted curbed. On the other hand, Junblatt and the Palestinian radicals needed the military weight of Fatah in any showdown with Maronite militias, and they would thus do everything possible to involve Fatah in fighting.

The fragmentation of the Lebanese political elite amplified street tensions, especially after a major clash between the Kata'ib and the PFLP around the Tel al-Za'atar camp in July 1974. In early 1975 two incidents caused a fundamental rupture between the Maronite "right" and the leftist-Palestinian alliance.

On 28 February the Nasirite leader Ma'ruf Sa'ad, an associate of Junblatt, was mortally wounded by gunfire during a demonstration of fishermen in Sidon against a monopolist fishing concession to a company headed by Camille Chamoun. Army intervention then sparked fighting between troops and gunmen, some from the Palestinian Ayn al-Helwa camp. These events well exemplified the intertwining of social discontent with Lebanese-Palestinian affairs. Sunni leaders, headed by Salam, denounced the army and the regime, sought Rashid al-Sulh's resignation as prime minister, and demanded an end to Maronite domination of the army. Junblatt tried to calm matters, to avoid embarrassing his friend Rashid al-Sulh. Jumayyil and Chamoun patronized large counterdemonstrations in East Beirut against any shift in the sectarian political dispensation.

On 13 April the shooting of several Kata'ib personnel at an Ayn al-

Rumana church was followed by the killing of 27 Palestinians on a bus stopped by Christian militiamen. This led to fighting between the Kata'ib and Palestinian factions across much of suburban Beirut, with 300 dead in three days.

Thereafter Fatah wanted to cool the situation, but Junblatt decided on escalation. His National Movement declared a boycott of any government containing Kata'ib representatives, whereupon Kata'ib and other Christian ministers immediately left Rashid al-Sulh's cabinet, depriving it of a parliamentary majority. Junblatt had in fact destroyed the position of his prime ministerial ally, who resigned on 15 May, virulently condemning the Kata'ib. Junblatt also achieved a broad consolidation of Christian support for the Kata'ib, presumably the opposite of his intention. On the other side, President Faranjiyya's attempt to introduce a military government provoked the Sunni and Shi'i establishments as well as the National Movement. Clashes continued, as both the Kata'ib and agents provocateurs in the Islamic sector had an interest in inflating their respective roles.

By mid-1975 the atmosphere was too poisoned for any reconciliation. The Christian and Islamic sectors separated sharply on the central issues: the sectarian foundations of the Lebanese state, the power balance between the sectarian communities, and the Lebanese-Palestinian relationship. Syria's Hafiz al-Asad was deeply concerned by the turmoil, and on 25 May Foreign Minister 'Abd al-Halim Khaddam visited Beirut as Syria's mediator, inaugurating a personal association with Lebanon that has lasted twenty years. Under the pressures of the early 1970s, Lebanon succumbed to its internal contradictions.

Palestinian salience, 1975–82

Successive rounds of heavy fighting between April 1975 and October 1976, the so-called "civil war," established the main geopolitical features of wartime Lebanon: de facto disintegration into militia and Palestinian fiefdoms, with a fluctuating Syrian presence, and de jure continuation of the state and territory of Greater Lebanon, the shadowy state apparatus remaining mainly in the hands of the old elite.

The New Face of Lebanon

On the ground, the Kata'ib and other Maronite militias sought to carve out a geographical position enabling them to block constitutional change and sustain their military viability against the Palestinian and Islamic militias. The PLO sought to hold its camps and bases, while Junblatt's National Movement and "rejectionist" Palestinians aimed to smash the Lebanon of the 1943 National Pact.

In the first few months Beirut was a messy patchwork of fronts and zones of influence, with local clashes in much of the rest of the country, especially in the north and the Biqa', with Sunni Tripoli and Christian Zahla as notable hot spots. Between October 1975 and February 1976 both sides began simplifying their territories by eliminating opposition enclaves and outliers, at great cost in lives, destruction, and the flight of refugees. The mostly Sunni Nasirites of the Murabitun militia entered the fray, pushing the Kata'ib out of the hotel district of West Beirut; Christian forces overran the Shi'i suburb of Naba'a and the Palestinian, Shi'i, and Kurdish enclaves of Karantina and Maslakh in East Beirut; and the National Movement expelled the Christians of Damur, Camille Chamoun's stronghold on the Shuf coast south of Beirut airport.

About 100,000 Shi'is were forced to leave East Beirut, and perhaps 10,000 Christians fled Damur. Kata'ib operations against Palestinian camps and the full military involvement of the PFLP, PDFLP, Sa'iqa, and other PLO elements all ensured Fatah entry to the hostilities. Various atrocities, including the murder of Christians in the Biqa', the "Black Saturday" targeting of Muslims in East Beirut, the massacre of 1,500 Palestinians, Shi'is, and others in Karantina and Maslakh, and the revenge killings of hundreds of Christians in Damur, increasingly subverted sectarian coexistence, although most Lebanese did not wish the damage to become irreparable. For example, despite his belligerence, Kamal Junblatt preserved the peace between Druze and Christians in the mixed districts of the Shuf.

President Faranjiyya had to accept Rashid Karami as prime minister after May 1975. Karami insisted on constitutional reform and refused to approve army intervention in the hostilities, but he maintained communications with Maronite leaders and worked to keep his multisectarian government in being. Faranjiyya was uncooperative. To protect his status as a Maronite *za'im*, he felt he could not diverge from the uncompromising posture adopted by Jumayyil, Chamoun, and the head of the Maronite monastic orders, Charbel Qassis. He hosted meetings of Maronite war leaders, who in early 1976 came together as the "Lebanese Front"; and his own militia followers in Zgharta and Ihdin, commanded by Tony Faranjiyya, became embroiled in fighting with the Sunni militiamen of Tripoli—Karami's home town.

Hafiz al-Asad stepped into this situation in late January 1976, immediately after the Karantina and Damur battles. Syrian-aligned Palestinians of the Palestine Liberation Army (PLA) were sent from Syria into the Biqa' to prevent Zahla from being used as a base to extend Maronite militia territory eastward, Khaddam assured Junblatt and 'Arafat that the Cairo agreement would be upheld, and Asad invited Faranjiyya and Karami to Damascus in early February to establish a political compromise. The outcome was Faranjiyya's "Constitutional Document," which proposed a modest adjustment to the National Pact in favor of the Islamic sector, primarily equivalence with Christians in parliament, but otherwise left the Maronite political advantage intact. The Maronite-Sunni monopoly of the two chief offices of state would remain, and there was no mention of army reform. Asad's objective was to convince the Christians that they could trust Syria, and thereby to wean them away from their Western orientation and from any scheme for an "isolationist" Little Lebanon. The approach bore a faint resemblance to the Ottoman stance toward the Maronites in the late nineteenth century. At the same time Syria would take care of the interests of the Muslims and Palestinians, thereby patronizing a new consensus under Syrian pre-eminence.

It was not to be. Syria's self-serving interpretation of the interests of the parties was of course not that of the parties themselves. Jumayyil and Chamoun were pragmatic enough to see advantages in flattering Asad—the Kata'ib envoy, Karim Pakradouni, was useful at this stage and later in presenting the accommodationist face of the Christian sector[92]—but they had no intention of delivering Christian Lebanon to Syria. Syria's immediate difficulties, however, came from Kamal Junblatt and his Palestinian allies. Junblatt regarded the Faranjiyya-Karami arrangement as appeasement of the Maronite bosses and an affront to himself. As a Druze, he remained barred from the highest state positions. The "Constitutional Document" also ignored the repeated demands of the National Movement for abolition of political sectarianism.

In February–March 1976 a crisis in the army gave Junblatt his excuse to pursue a "military solution." After the dismantling of Shihabist influence in the late 1960s, the Islamic sector had lost faith in the impartiality of Lebanon's army. The failure of the "Constitutional Document" to dilute Maronite supremacy in the army command led a Sunni officer, Lieutenant Ahmad Khatib, to promote a split in the officer corps, with a large body of Muslims breaking away to form a "Lebanese Arab Army." Instead of offering an amnesty and treat-ment of grievances, as advised by his army commander, Faranjiyya branded the dissidents as deserters. On 14 March, Junblatt demanded Faranjiyya's resignation and launched a military offensive by the National Movement, the PLO, and Khatib's followers to destroy the Lebanese regime. Palestinian sentiment against the Maronite militias gave 'Arafat little choice but to join him. The National Move-ment–Palestinian alliance quickly captured important terrain in the Matn hills above East Beirut, and the Maronites faced a major defeat.

Asad could not tolerate such defiance of Syrian efforts in favor of a settlement. Junblatt's "military solution" also threatened to bring radical and Palestinian domination of Lebanon, which promised a future of uncontrollable escalation with Israel and unsupervised intrusion of Arab elements unfriendly to Syria's Ba'thists—Iraq, Egypt, Libya, and others. Another consequence, no less dire, might be a conclusive Maronite alignment with Israel. Syria would lose its hold on its western flank, with prestige and practical implications inside Syria that would surely shake Asad's power base. Faranjiyya's survival and an orderly transition to a new Lebanese presidency in September 1976 were thus connected to the stability of the Syrian regime. Junblatt went to Damascus on 27 March after insistent summonses from Asad, but refused to bow to Syrian desiderata.

Syrian military intervention was now inevitable, and proceeded with the approval of President Faranjiyya. The fact that the Syrian plan encompassed upholding the National Pact regime, disciplining the

Palestinians and the Lebanese left, and generally calming Lebanon ensured a sympathetic response from the Americans, who were embarrassed by the predicament of Lebanon's status quo forces but determined not to be pulled into a repetition of May 1958. U.S. receptiveness helped to persuade the Israelis to stand aside, despite misgivings about an extended Syrian deployment to Israel's north. The price for Israel's acquiescence, transmitted to Damascus via Washington, involved several "red lines": no Syrian forces south of Sidon, no use of Syrian air power in Lebanon—bombing of the Palestinians might set a precedent for bombing of others later—and no introduction of surface-to-air missiles to Lebanese territory.

Syria intervened in three stages from April to October 1976, accompanied by a mounting bitterness between Asad and 'Arafat's mainstream PLO leadership that was never to be erased, even during the short rapprochement of the late 1970s. Syrian troops first moved openly into the Biqa' in mid-April, but Asad was reluctant to acknowledge a direct confrontation with Junblatt and the PLO. Syria thus deployed Sa'iqa as cover in the coastal cities. This was enough to relieve East Beirut, but not to subordinate the left and the Palestinians. Nonetheless, Syria's political clout was sufficiently enhanced to permit the May election of Asad's candidate, the Shihabist Ilyas Sarkis, as the next Lebanese president, in a parliamentary gathering in the Biqa' town of Shtura.[93] In June the Syrian army finally attempted directly to impose its will on the coastal regions. Syrian forces made little headway against the PLO, with a sharp reverse near Sidon. In a lengthy speech on 20 July, Asad condemned PLO involvement in Lebanese internal disputes—"The Palestinians fighting in Mount Lebanon are definitely not fighting for Palestine"; required Palestinian recognition of Damascus as the policy-making center—"We in Syria will always remain the heart of Arabism"; and asserted a unity of Syrian and Lebanese interests—"Because our history is one, our future is one and our destiny is one."[94]

The Maronite militias took the opportunity of Syrian pressure on the PLO to attack the Tel al-Za'atar Palestinian camp. Tel al-Za'atar fell on 12 August after a two-month siege. Perhaps 3,000 Palestinians, mostly civilians, died in the siege and its aftermath, and the Syrian regime came under fierce criticism throughout much of the Arab world for facilitating the militia operation. More significantly, the move against the PLO stirred discontent among Syria's Sunni majority, already resentful of political domination by the heterodox 'Alawi minority. As for the Maronites, the capture of Tel al-Za'atar secured access from East Beirut to Mount Lebanon, allowing the consolidation of a compact Maronite heartland.

In September 1976, Pierre Jumayyil's ambitious younger son Bashir brought East Beirut's paramilitary groups—the militia wings of the Kata'ib, the NLP, George 'Adwan's Tanzim, and Etienne Saqr's Guardians of the Cedars—under a joint military command headed by himself. This Kata'ib-centered alignment was termed the Lebanese Forces (LF). Simultaneously East Beirut's war leaders formalized their collaboration in a joint forum chaired by Camille Chamoun and known as the Lebanese Front.[95] Such Christian actions while Syria warred with the PLO and much of the Islamic sector further damaged Syria's Arab reputation.

Asad could not afford to get bogged down. In the two weeks before Sarkis replaced Faranjiyya in the Ba'abda presidential palace, on 23 September, Syrian forces made their third and largest assault on PLO- and National Movement–held areas. By this stage much of the Islamic sector was in Asad's pocket: the Sunni and Shi'i establishment adjusted to Syria's wishes at the time of the "Constitutional Document"; Musa Sadr, who, like Faranjiyya, had a good personal rapport with the Syrian president and who was tiring of Palestinian impositions on the Shi'is, had no difficulty in distancing himself from the PLO; and leftist movements like the pro-Syrian Ba'th and the SSNP deserted Junblatt.

The Syrian army gradually overwhelmed its opposition, but rather than pursue unilateral action Asad now accepted wider Arab involvement in peacekeeping. At a special summit of six Arab states in Riyadh the Syrian president ingratiated himself with the Saudis by assenting to an Arab deterrent force in Beirut. This proved a shrewd move. Syria largely recouped its pan-Arab credentials and got Arab approval for its military presence in Lebanon. A few thousand troops from various Arab countries arrived to join the 40,000 Syrian troops in Lebanon, but within a few months their home governments tired of the enterprise and Syria was left to its own devices. The Syrian army deployed in both West and East Beirut, 'Arafat and the PLO soon learned to live with the new situation, and relative stability prevailed until mid-1978.

Kamal Junblatt alone refused to accept the realities of power, and even put out feelers to the Maronites for war against Syria. On 16 March 1977 he was assassinated in the Shuf, and most observers believed Damascus to be responsible. In the heat of the moment, however, some Druze preferred to blame local Christians, and about 170 Maronites were murdered. Coexistence in the Shuf was disrupted in favor of the "revenge" sentiments "going back 140 years" which Asad had ascribed to Junblatt in his July 1976 speech.[96]

From East Beirut's perspective, Syria had served its purpose by late 1976 and Christians did not want the Syrian army in their area. Maronite leaders were suspicious of the restoration of relations between Damascus and the PLO through 1977, while the Syrians did not like the multiplying connections between East Beirut and Israel. In fact, East Beirut had been divided regarding its 1976 dealings with Damascus. Some in the Kata'ib and the old political establishment believed Lebanese Christians had to come to terms with their Arab environment. Others, including the Chamouns, saw the Syrian opening as an evil necessity to escape disaster in the "civil war." The rising young Bashir Jumayyil detected opportunities to play Israel off against Syria—a dangerous game, but Bashir had the presidency of the republic in his sights. On the "street," Syrian troops added to their unpopularity by interfering with smuggling and displaying pictures of Asad.[97]

In Ba'abda, President Sarkis initially fulfilled Syria's expectations of him as a pliable man who could cooperate with senior Muslims under a Syrian umbrella. Sarkis brought in a banker friend, Salim al-Huss, as prime minister. Sarkis and Huss set up a colorless cabinet of technocrats in December 1976, and the government thereafter ruled by decree and clamped down on the press. However, Sarkis's location in East Beirut, surrounded by Maronite strongmen, and his need to appear autonomous to his Maronite community, insulated him from Asad's supervision. He developed a good personal relationship with Bashir Jumayyil, and by 1978 was drifting away from his Syrian patron.

Constrained by the Syrians in Beirut after October 1976, the PLO returned its attention to the front with Israel in southern Lebanon, neglected through the 1975–76 "civil war." In the interim, Israel had tightened border defenses against infiltration and developed friendly relations with Christian militiamen in several small areas on the Lebanese side. Otherwise, the PLO held sway south of the Syrian deployment, although relations with Shi'i Lebanese were becoming problematic. On 11 March 1978, a Palestinian unit from Lebanon landed on the Israeli coast and seized a bus between Haifa and Tel Aviv. Carnage ensued when Israeli commandos stormed the vehicle to release the passengers.

The new Likud government of Menahem Begin responded by sending large Israeli ground forces into southern Lebanon, pushing the PLO away from the border. The Israeli advance stopped at the Litani river, leaving the main Palestinian infrastructure in Sidon and Beirut untouched. The flight of tens of thousands of Lebanese and Palestinians toward Beirut brought swift international condemnation of the Israelis. At an emergency meeting, the U.N. Security Council passed Resolution 425 calling for full Israeli retreat and prevention of Palestinian provocations. The U.N. established an Interim Force in Lebanon (UNIFIL), to be stationed between the Litani and the international border to oversee implementation of Resolution 425. In the event, the Israelis prevented full UNIFIL deployment by creating a security cordon along the border patrolled by a small proxy militia of Christians and Shi'is under a Lebanese army major, Sa'ad Haddad. UNIFIL became sandwiched between the PLO and Haddad, and Palestinian guerillas restored some bases in the midst of the U.N. area, in the so-called "iron triangle" (map 6). Israeli-Palestinian clashes continued as if UNIFIL did not exist, and by 1981 the PLO had enough artillery and multiple rocket launchers to mount a significant July bombardment of Israeli territory from positions north of the security cordon. For Israel it was a case of unfinished business.

Israel's "Litani operation" had its most significant repercussions not in southern Lebanon, but on relations between East Beirut and Damascus. It took place amid an important reversal of alliances within Lebanon: the 1977 modus vivendi between Syria and the PLO became a rapprochement in 1978, after Egyptian President Anwar Sadat's November 1977 visit to Jerusalem indicated that Egypt was leaving Asad and 'Arafat to confront Israel by themselves. For Lebanon's Christians these developments magnified Israel's status as the leading regional power of the Eastern Mediterranean, and the "Litani operation" showed that Israel intended to exert its weight on the Arab-Israeli northern front.

For Bashir Jumayyil and Camille Chamoun the time had come to break free of Syria. Sulayman Faranjiyya, however, refused any link with Israel or any disruption of his friendship with Hafiz al-Asad. Faranjiyya regarded Israel as responsible for Christian Lebanon's problem with the Palestinians,[98] and reacted angrily to militia associations with the "Zionist enemy." A split thus loomed between East Beirut and the Maronites of the north. Tensions rose as the Kata'ib tried to intrude on Faranjiyya's home turf in the Kura and Zgharta, with clashes between Kata'ib personnel and the Faranjiyya family's militia, the Marada. On 13 June 1978, a Kata'ib unit killed Faranjiyya's son Tony and other family members, sparking warfare between East Beirut and Syria.

Syrian forces swiftly took command of the northern Maronite territories, including Bsharri and the Qadisha valley, home to many Kata'ib personnel. Ex-president Faranjiyya made it plain that a long-term vendetta henceforth existed between himself and the Jummayyils. Syrian artillery pounded the surrounds of East Beirut, and a war of attrition commenced between Syrian troops and the LF militia in the densely inhabited Ashrafiyya district of the capital. International pressure, vigorous Maronite resistance, and Israeli warnings persuaded the Syrians to suspend their "punishment" in October 1978, and the Syrian army withdrew from East Beirut. Damascus lost both President Sarkis, who tendered his resignation in July in the knowledge that Asad had no alternative, and the Christian part of the Lebanese army. The Christian sector became a de facto Little Lebanon at the heavy cost of the detachment of the Maronite north.

Map 6 depicts the fragmentation of Lebanon in 1979–81, like 1977 a lull between storms. The lull ended with the 1981 Zahla crisis and an Israeli-Palestinian outburst in southern Lebanon, preludes to the 1982

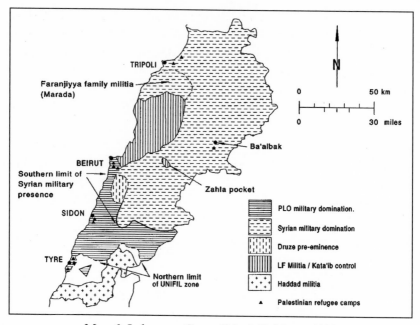

Map 6. Lebanon: Geopolitical divisions, 1980

Israeli invasion and a succession of upheavals which only subsided after the 1986 collapse of the Syrian-promoted Tripartite Agreement. Apart from the Syrian presence in much of the country and Israeli influence in the southern border zone, two entities held center stage: the Palestinian "substitute homeland" (*al-watan al-badil*), as it was derisively described by Lebanese, and Maronite "Little Lebanon."

From its headquarters in West Beirut the PLO busied itself with turning its political and military wings into a proto-state with a conventional army. Deference to Asad diminished as Syria's domestic circumstances worsened after 1979. A well-financed infrastructure in Beirut and a territorial base in southern Lebanon gave the PLO unprecedented prominence in the Arab world. As for the Lebanese factions in West Beirut, Junblatt's National Movement dissolved after his death, and a bewildering variety of militias and gangs competed violently in the shadow of the PLO. Walid Junblatt maintained his father's

PSP and, to the surprise of many who viewed him as an erratic playboy, proved an effective Druze leader. The Shi'i Amal movement emerged as the biggest Lebanese Muslim faction, counting perhaps 5,000 militiamen, but was poorly organized. Ibrahim Qlaylat's Murabitun remained an effective Sunni militia, but with only about 1,000 fighters could not compare with its rivals in other communities, even the PSP and Amal. Overall, the high-handed attitude of 'Arafat and the Fatah command and the arrogance of the PFLP and the rest of the Palestinian "left" alienated Lebanese Muslims more and more, but they were impotent until some great shock changed the power balance.

In East Beirut the primary development was Bashir Jumayyil's achievement of effective Christian leadership, even displacing his father and Camille Chamoun. Bashir's LF was the most powerful Lebanese militia, able to face the PLO or the Syrians. Relative order prevailed in the Christian sector, albeit produced by illegal authority and protection rackets. Superficially, Kata'ib ideology shifted toward Christian separatism, with less heard about social reform or coexistence, but both Bashir and his father looked to the leadership of Greater Lebanon—not "Little Lebanon."

For Hafiz al-Asad the resilience of the PLO and East Beirut coincided with rebellion by the Sunni Muslim Brotherhood inside Syria. From the 1979 massacre of 'Alawi military cadets in Aleppo to the March 1982 takeover of the old city of Hama by the Brotherhood, the whole future of Asad's regime seemed in question. Events in Syria were intimately bound up with the Lebanese situation: the rebellion reflected the unpopularity and economic costs of Syria's role in Lebanon and, in an inversion of Syria's behavior in Beirut, both 'Arafat and the Maronites meddled in Syria's domestic affairs by aiding the Brotherhood. As the PLO slipped out of the controls Syria had imposed in 1976–77 and Bashir Jumayyil colluded with Israel, the fears of Syrian Ba'thists regarding subversion of their western flank seemed to be becoming realized. Asad could do little until he suppressed the Brotherhood, but the 1979–82 regime crisis strengthened Syria's determination through the 1980s that it must impose itself in Beirut.

For Israel the state of affairs on the northern front at the outset of the 1980s encouraged intervention. The Syrian regime appeared both vulnerable and rigidly hostile—Asad was substantially building up Syria's military capabilities while the Brotherhood was threatening Ba'thist Syria from within. It did not require genius to perceive future danger and present opportunity. The 1979 peace treaty with Egypt gave Israel a lot of flexibility regarding the eastern Arab world. Many Israelis felt that this circumstance would not last indefinitely, and took the November 1981 assassination of Egypt's Anwar Sadat as a reminder of the uncertainties of the region. In Lebanon, Bashir Jumayyil beckoned, which attracted the Mossad (Israel's external intelligence organization) if not more skeptical minds in the Aman (military intelligence). Meanwhile the entrenchment of PLO infrastructure within Lebanon presented itself as an increasing nuisance.

Even a cautious centrist government of Israel would have been tempted to adopt a "forward" policy. Instead, adventurers commanded Israel through the early 1980s. Re-elected in June 1981, Begin's Likud took an aggressive turn. More careful politicians, most notably Ezer Weitzman and Moshe Dayan, were gone, and the energetic hard-line new defense minister, Ariel Sharon, determined security policy, fully backed by the like-minded Israel Defense Force (IDF) chief of staff, Rafael Eytan. For Sharon, Bashir Jumayyil and East Beirut were the key Arab instrument that Israel could use to crack Syria and transform the geopolitics of the Levant. The fact that Bashir viewed Israel in similarly instrumentalist terms—in the service of a personal and Maronite agenda—did not bode well for the relationship.

Bashir ended the 1979–81 lull with his project in early 1981 to attach the Christian militia pocket in Zahla (map 6) to East Beirut by a road across Mount Sannin. As Zahla abutted Syria's forces in the Biqa', this could only bring a fierce Syrian response. For Bashir the issue involved a test of his Israeli connection. However, it is unjust to represent the LF leadership as the sole agent provocateur, since the Syrians had been attempting for some years to subject Zahla to their authority (Harris, 1985).

In April 1981, the Syrians put Zahla under siege and lifted troops to the mountain heights by helicopter. The Begin government interpreted the latter move as a Syrian infraction of the Israeli "red line" regarding Syrian air power and shot down two helicopters. Asad immediately introduced surface-to-air missile batteries to the Biqa', a clear crossing of the "red lines," and a major Israeli-Syrian clash loomed. American and Soviet diplomacy defused the crisis, but Asad kept the missiles in place, leaving the Israelis unsatisfied, and Bashir was encouraged by Israel's embroilment in looking ahead to the 1982 Lebanese presidential election.

The 1981 Zahla events helped to integrate the issues of East Beirut's tussle with Syria and the future of the PLO presence. The threads were brought together by Ariel Sharon after he became Israel's defense minister in June 1981. Sharon evolved a "grand plan" (Schiff and Ya'ari, 1984; Rabinovich, 1984) to strike north as far as Beirut, demolish the PLO and Syrian positions in Lebanon, and dominate the 1982 Lebanese presidential election. Sharon hoped to have Bashir Jummayyil at the head of an Israeli-oriented Lebanese regime. His approach had crucial flaws: reliance on a single Lebanese personality, Bashir's intention to use the Israelis while keeping Arab lines open, and the lack of an Israeli consensus for schemes beyond striking the PLO in southern Lebanon. As for the Palestinians, the PLO "mini-state" in Lebanon was a false option: it provoked the Israelis without providing an adequate defense against them, and Syria did not oppose Israel cutting 'Arafat down to size—a lesson to the PLO of the consequences of non-cooperation with Damascus.[99]

Asad, like Bashir, expected to profit from the Israeli incursion predicted by most analysts from late 1981 on. Unlike Bashir, however, he did not reckon on Israel abandoning the whole Israeli-Syrian balance in Lebanon established in 1976 and assaulting Syrian forces. The Syrian leader did not properly calculate the impetus of Sharon and Israeli Prime Minister Begin, did not fully appreciate the collusion of the U.S., which had approved the 1976 Syrian intervention, and did not grasp how seriously Israel viewed the missile challenge, which to the Syrians was a justifiable defensive measure.

The large-scale Israeli invasion of the Biqa' as well as southern Lebanon in June–July 1982 therefore came as a shock to Damascus. In the mid-1980s, however, the miscalculation and damages were outweighed by Asad's success in slowly restoring Syria's almost-shattered strategic position. Critical to this restoration was the crushing of the Muslim Brotherhood in Hama in March 1982. A three week bloodbath, in which up to 20,000 civilians died, broke the back of the insurrection in Syria—just in time, considering the developments in Lebanon.

Implications of the Israeli invasion, 1982–83

The details of Israel's 1982 campaign have been well covered by other authors (for example: Yaniv, 1987; Khalidi, 1986; Schiff and Ya'ari, 1984). My primary intention here is to examine the repercussions for Lebanese affairs.

After the defeats of the Palestinians in 1982–83—in Beirut and the south by Israel and later, in Tripoli and the north, by Syria—the emphasis in Lebanon's wars shifted to the struggle for precedence within and between Lebanon's communities, against the backdrop of the continuing contest between the Christian sector and Damascus. The 1980s saw the Shi'i Muslims, Lebanon's largest and most disadvantaged sect, make their first impact, at least as Shi'is, on Lebanon's power balance. Events in Lebanon in the 1980s reflected the Shi'i assertion and the adjustments of other parties, Lebanese and non-Lebanese, to it.

By this time Shi'i political mobilization was not new. However, through the 1960s and 70s, when poorer rural Shi'is became properly aware of their relative deprivation, the slogans of the secular left and the Palestinian "armed struggle" attracted them into a variety of socialist and Palestinian organizations, including 'Arafat's Fatah. Shi'is comprised much of the rank and file of Palestinian-affiliated militias after 1975 but their real commitment was to the idea of revolt, not to Palestinian causes (Abu Khalil, 1988). In turn the PLO and the Lebanese left—whose management was predominantly Sunni, Druze, or Orthodox Christian—had no serious interest in the Shi'is.

As the war years proceeded with little but misery for the mass of Shi'is, sectarian sentiment increased. Musa Sadr's Amal, founded in 1975, was the first political outcome. Amal became the leading Shi'i force after 1978, when Musr Sadr "disappeared" on a trip to Libya.

Parallels were made with the occlusion of the Twelfth Shi'i Imam, Muhammad al-Muntazar ("the awaited one"), and by this stage not much was needed to induce many to abandon their Palestinian connections. In the early 1980s, open warfare prevailed between Amal and the PLO in Shi'i areas of southern Lebanon, although the Palestinians had greater military strength.

Developments between June 1982 and early 1985 drastically altered Lebanon's political geography (maps 6, 7, 8). For the first few months Israel had the initiative. Israel's military activities, including the siege and brief occupation of West Beirut, ended the Palestinian "mini-state," compelled the departure of 'Arafat and the PLO from Beirut, rolled back the Syrian army almost to the Beirut-Damascus highway, eliminated the Syrian missile batteries in the Biqa', and humiliated the Syrian air force, which lost more than 80 aircraft as against negligible damage to the Israelis. The initiative, however, departed Israeli hands at the time of the September 1982 Lebanese presidential elections, manipulation of which was the key feature of Sharon's "grand plan."

Bashir Jumayyil capitalized on Shi'i and Sunni pleasure concerning the PLO exit. Added to Israel's presence this produced a parliamentary majority for his election as president, which would have been inconceivable in other circumstances. Bashir aimed for support across sectarian divides and so indicated to the Israelis that he had no intention of being their puppet. Also, though Sharon had anticipated East Beirut's participation in the battle, the LF carefully avoided doing anything practical for the Israelis. Israel could live with Bashir's assertion of independence—nobody could have expected a credible Lebanese presidency to operate on a different basis—but the Israeli honeymoon with East Beirut was already finished.

The mortal blow to Israel's strategy came with the assassination of Bashir by a huge car bomb on 14 September 1982, most likely organized by the Syrians, who must have been alarmed by Bashir's inroads into the Islamic sector. Israeli troops immediately moved into West Beirut, from which the PLO had been evacuated by sea under the supervision of an American-organized multinational force, and which became a political vacuum with the death of Bashir. Christian militia personnel linked to the LF intelligence chief,

Elie Hubayqa (later a Syrian favorite in Syrian-sponsored Lebanese governments) entered the unprotected Palestinian refugee camps of Sabra and Shatila behind the Israelis and massacred at least 800 civilians.

For Israel, the Sabra and Shatila massacres were a public relations disaster that shattered the mirage of an Israeli-oriented order in Beirut. International pressure forced the Israelis out of the Lebanese capital, and bitter controversy at home undermined the whole Israeli presence in Lebanon. Israel's Kahan report on the circumstances of the massacre, issued in February 1983, forced the resignation of Defense Minister Sharon. Apart from the responsibility of senior Israeli officials for the behavior of their militia ally, the massacre indicated shocking disdain for Lebanon's realities by Israel's decision-makers.

Overall, senior Israelis had made unwarranted assumptions about Christian orientations—like Israel itself, the Maronite leadership would of course take what it could out of a relationship without limiting its options. Far from learning, Israel proceeded to new errors. After 1982, the Israeli army made an unnecessary enemy out of southern Lebanon's Shi'is. Israel took no more care to comprehend the Shi'is before plunging into their midst than it had with the Maronites.

Most immediately, the Israelis had to accept the election of Bashir's brother, Amin Jumayyil, as Lebanon's president. Amin was a cautious traditionalist much influenced by American officials and he promptly made it plain that he preferred the patronage of the Reagan administration to that of Israel. An enlarged multinational force (MNF), dominated by the U.S. and entirely Western in composition, landed in West Beirut in October 1982. The MNF came ostensibly to provide a security umbrella in West Beirut, especially for the Palestinian population, until confidence existed that the Lebanese government could do the job itself. Instead the Reagan administration drifted into promoting Amin Jumayyil's regime, which encouraged Amin to ignore non-Christian requirements for political reform. Israel's Likud government had to watch the U.S. hijack the role in Beirut that Sharon and Begin had intended for themselves, while Israel was lambasted in the American press. Certainly the Israelis felt no urge to assist a U.S. enterprise in Lebanon which was even more muddled than their own.

Amin Jumayyil and the Americans headed for trouble together. Jumayyil behaved as if seven years of warfare had never happened, or at least as if Lebanon's wars had no Lebanese dimension. Lebanon's viability required that the regime take account of the new collective consciousness of the Shi'is, even if the Shi'i political emergence was precipitated as much by PLO provocations as by Maronite and Sunni "privilege." The fact that Shi'is exhibited deep loyalty to Lebanon and its institutions, while pushing for greater political acknowledgement, gave Amin an opportunity to reconstruct the regime on the basis of a Maronite-Shi'i partnership. Despite the more strident talk of their politicians, ordinary Shi'is simply wanted a measure of "dignity" *(karama)*, not to seize the country or even to displace the Maronite presidency.

Instead Jumayyil chose to look to traditionalist personalities, primarily Sunnis, who had no political relevance in the Islamic sector, as the Muslim wing of his regime. He spurned Amal and its relatively moderate leader, Nabih Barri, while the Lebanese army's bulldozing of shanty-dwellings in West Beirut alienated Shi'is. Further, Jumayyil's government did not discourage Maronite militia penetration of the Shuf mountain, a region of historically accepted Druze supremacy. Druze leader Walid Junblatt had little in common with his father, but did share his distaste for the Jumayyils' Kata'ib party.

The Kata'ib and the LF viewed the areas overrun by Israel as an arena for territorial expansion, at least where there were Christian rural populations, as in the Shuf. The Israelis at first allowed LF militiamen in, but soon tired of them as they tired of the Christian sector in general. Through 1983, Israel reassessed its associations with the Lebanese communities and shifted its emphasis to the Druze. Although a much smaller population than the Maronites, the Druze covered the northern extremity of Israel's military deployment and, uniquely for a major Lebanese sect, had strong ties with coreligionists in Israel and the Israeli army. Sporadic fighting broke out between the Druze PSP and the intruding LF, and Junblatt occasionally shelled East Beirut. The Druze acquired war materials from the Syrians, and the Israelis turned a blind eye. Amin Jumayyil made plans to deploy the Lebanese army in the

Shuf; Junblatt accused the army of being an agent of the Kata'ib and prepared for warfare.

President Reagan's administration made grave mistakes in dealing with Amin Jumayyil. The U.S. sought to capitalize on Israel's devastation of the PLO to reorder the Eastern Mediterranean in line with the American priority of stabilization under exclusive U.S. influence. The Lebanese regime would be brought into a security pact with the Israelis, but under American rather than Israeli tutelage, and the weakened Palestinians would be pressed together with Jordan for a joint arrangement with Israel—the September 1982 "Reagan plan." Syria was considered to be finished as a power, the Soviet Union was to be shunted aside, and the U.S. initially discounted the opposition to the Jumayyil government among Lebanon's non-Christian communities. On 17 May 1983, Israeli and Lebanese negotiators agreed to a security pact that was less than a peace but more than an armistice, and received with no enthusiasm in either Israel or Lebanon. The Lebanese government wanly promoted it to obtain Israeli withdrawal, while Israelis had no faith in Lebanese ability to fulfill security obligations. The agreement was dead on arrival. It merely served as a rallying point for the multiplying opponents of the Lebanese regime.

In one respect, however, the ill-starred U.S. intervention in Beirut of 1983–84 had a longer-term impact on local power relations—the U.S. retrained and re-equipped the Lebanese army, which principally benefited the Christian brigades. Jumayyil and the army command made sure that all the new 155-mm howitzers and most other acquisitions stayed in East Beirut, a factor which helped both the president and the Christian sector to survive the approaching storm.

Israel's June 1982 thrust into Lebanon damaged Syria's local alignment but left it with the basis for recovery. This was because the Israeli army stopped before reaching the Beirut-Damascus highway on the Dahr al-Baydar pass and in the Biqa'. The two-day delay needed to mask conversion of an operation against the PLO into an attack on the Syrians, which lacked an Israeli domestic consensus, sufficed for the Soviet Union to have Israel halted short of decisive results. Syria thus retained access to the coastal side of Mount Lebanon, which meant linkage to the Druze of the Shuf, proximity to West Beirut, and topo-

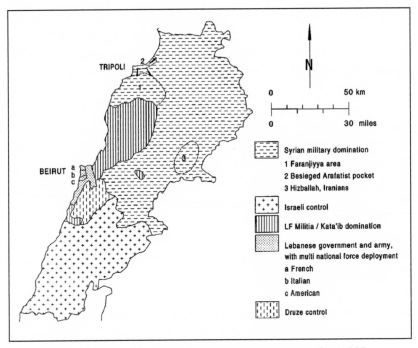

TRIPOLI

N

BEIRUT

0   50 km

0   30 miles

Syrian military domination
1 Faranjiyya area
2 Besieged Arafatist pocket
3 Hizballah, Iranians

Israeli control

LF Militia / Kata'ib domination

Lebanese government and army,
with multi national force deployment
a French
b Italian
c American

Druze control

Map 7. Lebanon: Geopolitical divisions, November 1983

graphic advantage with regard to East Beirut (map 7). If the Israelis had entered Zahla, Syria's whole deployment above metropolitan Beirut would have collapsed and Syria would have been physically severed from Lebanon's political center.

Asad campaigned in 1983–84 to turn the tables on Israel, the Americans, and the Maronites, thus to reassert Syria's authority on its western flank. The campaign proceeded in three theaters along almost the whole length of Lebanon's Mediterranean coast. First, around Tripoli in the north, Syria needed to foil a PLO attempt to re-enter Lebanon by a back door using Syrian controlled territory. Second, in the center, the requirements were to get rid of the Americans, to bring East Beirut and Amin Jumayyil to heel, and to restore Syrian primacy in the Islamic sector. Third, regarding southern Lebanon, Syria intended to have its revenge by subverting the Israeli occupation. Damascus had to be careful about direct confrontation with its adversaries, particularly with respect to Israel and the U.S., because of its military vulnerability. The Syrians resorted to visible involvement only under the most favorable circumstances, or against lesser opponents, meaning 'Arafat and East Beirut.

Asad built his campaign on the blunders of those facing him and on the strategic support of the Soviet Union. Moscow had disapproved of the 1976 Syrian operations in Lebanon against the PLO and Lebanese leftists, disliked Asad's expectation of its backing while disregarding its advice, and had its own connections with Lebanese factions. However, Syria's military humiliation in the June 1982 air battle involved Soviet equipment, and the American arrival in Beirut, together with the "Reagan plan" for Arab-Israeli affairs, seemed the genesis of a new "NATO base" in the Eastern Mediterranean. For several years after 1982 the Soviet Union generously replenished Syria's arsenal, temporarily breathing new life into the Syrian dream of strategic parity with Israel; stationed thousands of "advisors" in Syria; and assisted the Syrian army with surface-to-air defenses in Mount Lebanon, above the Americans in Beirut.[100] Soviet support, reflecting mutual interests more than a patron-client relationship, made Syria confident about its ability to remove the U.S. from Beirut.

Otherwise Syria could maneuver behind an array of local allies and profit from a valuable connection with the Islamic revolutionary regime in Iran. To deal with 'Arafat and quiet the Sunni radicals of Tripoli, Asad had several groups of proxies. Corruption in the PLO and discontent about the conduct of the 1982 fight against Israel led, in early 1983, to a split in 'Arafat's Fatah movement and to the establishment of a Palestinian "opposition" in Damascus under Palestine National Council (PNC) chairman Khalid Fahhoum. Syria nourished the new "Palestine Salvation Front," with its military arm under the Fatah rebel Abu Musa. Abu Musa's units were combined with Syria's older Palestinian subordinates—Sa'iqa and the Yarmouk brigade of the PLA—and sent into battle against 'Arafat from mid-1983 onwards. Around Tripoli they were joined by the local 'Alawi militia and other Lebanese clients of the Syrians, including the SSNP and the Ba'th.

In Beirut, President Jumayyil's insensitivity regarding non-

Christian political forces, particularly Druze and Shi'is, and American entanglement with the regime, left the Islamic sector wide open to the Syrians. As early as June 1982, Syria allowed an Iranian Revolutionary Guard contingent to establish itself in the central Biqa', and thereafter Syrian military intelligence worked alongside the Iranians to encourage the militarization of Shi'i Islamic radicals, violently hostile to the West, to Israel, and to Maronite political supremacy. Syria also took advantage of the rift between the Lebanese government and the Shuf Druze to upgrade its links with the PSP, attenuated since Kamal Junblatt had defied Asad in 1976. Through 1983 the Shi'i Amal movement kept its distance from Damascus, hoping for accommodation with Jumayyil, although Amal's ideas about the abolition of political sectarianism were anathema to the regime. The government never really tried to entice Amal into compromise, and the Americans tried only after they had become too much associated with Jumayyil. Amal drifted into confrontation with the government by late 1983, and therefore entered the Syrian orbit. At that stage, before the disillusion of subsequent years, Amal reached its peak as the foremost populist party in the Islamic sector, and Asad viewed it as his most valuable "catch."

Israel, once it had left Beirut, was not Syria's main target although it was Syria's primary enemy. The interaction of the two regional powers in the Lebanon of 1983–85 involved enmity tempered by a gradual restoration of tacit understandings about "red lines" and limits to confrontation (Evron, 1987; Avi-Ran, 1991). Syria's assault on 'Arafat in Tripoli continued Israel's unfinished work, although with a different objective. Israel aimed to destroy the PLO; Syria wanted mastery over the Palestinian organizations.

Syria profited from the estrangement between Israel on the one hand and Jumayyil and the Americans on the other. From an Israeli perspective the latter parties benefited from Israel's work while denigrating its author, and Israel's sudden September 1983 withdrawal from the Shuf mountain gave Syria and its allies topographic command of Beirut.

Syria intended to upset the Israeli alignment in southern Lebanon via proxies, but the Israelis alienated the Shi'i population so rapidly and comprehensively that Damascus hardly needed to exert itself. In

1982–83, Israel created a surrogate militia in southern Lebanon by adding Shi'i racketeers to Maronite clients and Sa'd Haddad's border zone force. This potpourri of Israeli agents interfered with the lives of a population which, after only a few months, strongly suspected that Israel planned to stay and had claims on Lebanese land and water.

People became more recalcitrant toward the occupying power, the Israelis began to detain militants, Islamists encouraged by Syria and Iran gained in popular sympathy, and on 16 October 1983, displaying monumental insensitivity, an Israeli convoy entered Nabatiyya during a Shi'i *'Ashura* procession, causing a riot. *'Ashura,* the annual commemmoration of the martyrdom of the Imam Husayn, grandson of the Prophet Muhammad, marks the conclusive historical estrangement of Shi'is from Sunnis.

A car bomb attack on the Israeli military headquarters in Tyre on 4 November 1983, probably involving Islamic radicals with Syrian intelligence back-up, and other incidents, caused the Israelis by early 1984 to curb most movement between southern Lebanon and Beirut. Israel hoped to "secure" southern Lebanon along the "defensible" line of the Awali river; instead the economic dislocation and harsh military measures only further enraged most inhabitants of the occupied area and completed the trend to civil insurrection. The Amal movement, which could not afford to leave itself open to criticism because of its early reserve toward Syria, vigorously promoted "resistance" to Israeli occupation from early 1983 on.

After the elimination of Bashir Jumayyil had ended the threat to Syria's strategic alignment in Lebanon, Syria's opening moves in 1983 came as responses to the Israel-Lebanon 17 May pact and the provisional agreement between 'Arafat and King Husayn for a Palestinian-Jordanian confederation. The Syrians were not overly bothered by the 17 May pact, because in mid-1983 their rearmament was well advanced and they could sense the weakness of the American position in Beirut following the 18 April demolition of the U.S. Embassy by a car bomb. In any case, the Israelis indicated they would not fulfill their obligation to leave southern Lebanon without parallel withdrawals by Syria and so Syria knew that it could scuttle the accord simply by refusing to move. The Israel-Lebanon agreement provided a convenient casus belli against the Lebanese regime and the MNF. Also, after mid-1983 the Syrians and opposition militias may have felt some urgency about stirring events in Beirut because of the growing military potential of the Lebanese army (Deeb, 1985).

'Arafat's flirtation with the "Jordanian option" began to produce results about the same time as the signing of the 17 May pact, and represented a more serious challenge to Syria's pan-Arab standing. Damascus agreed with many Palestinians who suspected a "sell-out"—abandonment of the requirement for a Palestinian state.[101] Anyway, if the PLO was looking for "federation," Syrian officials laid down that it be with Ba'thist Syria—not with a lesser entity like Hashemite Jordan.[102] After meeting senior PLO personalities in Kuwait, 'Arafat pulled back from his understanding with King Husayn, but Asad was now determined to wipe out 'Arafatist influence in Lebanon. In June 1983, 'Arafat was expelled from the Syrian capital and Fatah rebels pushed 'Arafat loyalists out of the Biqa'. In September, the PLO chairman joined his troops in Tripoli and the neighboring Palestinian refugee camps (map 7), which were put under siege by Syria's proxies and savagely bombarded by Syrian artillery. By November 'Arafat had no choice but to accept a French offer of evacuation. It was the first victory of Asad's campaign.

In November 1983, I made two excursions with the *Guardian* correspondent, David Hirst. The first was to Ba'albak in the Biqa', after an Israeli air force raid on a nearby Hizballah base. On arrival in Ba'albak, we tried to find the Islamic Amal leader, Husayn Musawi. He was unavailable, and we were stopped by a large and choleric militiaman who told us we were spies and only fit for the Ba'albak jail. After some argument in front of a gathering crowd of teenagers and small children he simply ordered us out of town, which was fortunate as a few days later the Israelis bombed the building in which we were to be detained.

We then headed south to the local hospital, hoping that this might provide more concrete journalistic material. The scene there was chaotic, with dozens of wounded militiamen and loudspeakers delivering verses from the *Qur'an*. After we met briefly with the hospital manager, suspicious Hizballah personnel ordered us into a small room. Just as it seemed the situation might become difficult, the Hizballah commander was diverted by the sudden arrival of the international Red Cross. While he loudly berated the Frenchman leading the Red Cross column outside the window of our room, accusing him of wishing to poison the wounded—*mish damm, samm* ("it's not blood, it's poison")—we slipped out of the building. We hurriedly moved David's white-painted car into the Red Cross column, and a few minutes later departed under de facto Red Cross cover.

On our way back to Beirut over the Dahr al-Baydar pass, we noted Syrian soldiers lining the Beirut-Damascus highway. During the day Syrian Foreign Minister 'Abd al-Halim Khaddam had visited his Lebanese counterpart in Ba'abda, as part of the Syrian campaign to abrogate the 17 May 1983 Lebanese-Israeli agreement. The same evening, naturally after Khaddam's return to Damascus, East Beirut was subjected to bombardment by Syria's Lebanese allies in the Shuf and Matn hills above the city.

Our second excursion—the next day—was to see Yasir 'Arafat in Tripoli, where the PLO boss was besieged by Palestinian dissidents and Syrian artillery. Syrian howitzers in the Kura district boomed occasionally as we approached the city, where day had been turned into dusk by a vast smoke column from fires in the Tripoli oil refinery. On advice from Sunni fundamentalist militiamen, who gave us a rather warmer reception than their Hizballah counterparts in Ba'albak, we left the car some distance from the building 'Arafat had commandeered as an operations center in the Zahriya quarter. We ran the last few hundred meters through the rubble decorating the streets, spurred on by the knowledge that a Viznews cameraman had been badly injured outside 'Arafat's headquarters a few hours before.

We were effusively welcomed by the PLO chairman and his aides, and immediately treated to lunch—the same chicken, tomato, and potato brew "as for our fighters at the front." 'Arafat, who told us that he was certain Hafiz al-Asad intended to finish him off, beamed at us from behind a desk covered with a battery of telephones. He was tired and I noted that his facial stubble had not received much recent attention, but he put on a good showman's front of military business-as-usual. Desultory crashing and banging proceeded a short distance away, although there was a fortuitous lull in the fighting, compared with heavy shelling earlier in the day. The front was said to be moving closer, and the chairman had obviously seen better days. After about an hour, 'Arafat excused himself, as he was conducting an Arabic telephone interview with Radio Monte Carlo. He hoped that he could get the Saudis to persuade Asad to relent. We were ushered down from his fourth floor redoubt, relatively secure as it was surrounded by higher apartment blocks that absorbed the shell-fire, and repeated our street dash. A few days later the siege was suspended—probably because of the confusion in Damascus after Asad's 13 November heart attack, not because of Saudi or other intervention. 'Arafat survived, sailing away to Egypt.

Syrian resurgence, 1984–85

Syria's opportunity to take the initiative around Beirut arrived on 4 September 1983, when the Israelis pulled back from the Shuf to the Awali river. Israel made no arrangement with the Jumayyil government for the Lebanese army to move into the Shuf, which in any case Junblatt and the Druze rejected. For Israel, Jumayyil and the MNF's 1,200 American marines could sink or swim in Beirut as they pleased. Junblatt was now free to evict the LF from the Shuf and to escalate hostilities against East Beirut. Within two weeks, the well-organized Druze seized the entire Shuf and dealt a crippling blow to Jumayyil's aspirations to be a power beyond the Christian "canton." 150,000 Christians fled the area of Druze control. The Lebanese army managed to hang onto the Suq al-Gharb ridge, a detail important in subsequent years, but the government's dependence on American naval gunfire demonstrated its weakness to the watching Syrians. Damascus supplied the Druze with artillery and ammunition, for use against the Americans at the international airport, and coordinated shelling of East Beirut from the Upper Matn.

A 25 September cease-fire briefly froze the situation. The Jumayyil government maintained its jurisdiction in West Beirut, the Shi'i Amal movement had not yet shifted into the opposition camp, and Junblatt was landlocked in the Shuf mountain. Lebanese regime and opposition personalities agreed to meet in Geneva, under Saudi and Syrian auspices, to discuss political reform and the 17 May pact. On 23 October, Shi'i Islamic radicals shook the already-reduced resolve of the Americans and their MNF partners by simultaneous suicide bombings of the U.S. and French compounds in West Beirut, which killed 300 soldiers.

At the Geneva conference in early November Saudi influence and the Lebanese regime's retreat were enough to achieve a limited consensus between the Maronite, Muslim, and Druze participants.[103] They agreed on the "Arab" character of Lebanon, long conceded by the Kata'ib, and delegated Jumayyil to approach the Americans for revision of the 17 May pact, to make it a purely military arrangement.

On 13 November, at a critical time for Syria in dealing with both 'Arafat and Jumayyil, Hafiz al-Asad suffered a heart attack, precipitating a leadership crisis in Damascus. The crisis lasted for almost six months, until the Syrian president fully recovered and could fend off his insubordinate brother, Rifa'at. In Beirut, Jumayyil had a last chance to save his presidency, by taking advantage of the common ground between moderate reform proposals from West and East Beirut[104] and the breathing space offered by the American naval build-up immediately after the bombing of the U.S. marine compound.

Jumayyil prevaricated disastrously. Presumably constrained by East Beirut hard-liners, he took no lead on domestic political reform and, amid tension and clashes between the army and Amal in West Beirut, this exasperated moderate Shi'i leaders. The U.S. rebuffed Jumayyil's attempt to revise the 17 May pact, and after some hesitation backed Israel's insistence on ratification of the original documents. Jumayyil failed to reconvene the Geneva conference for the necessary consultations on the matter. In the meantime, military exchanges punctuated the cease-fire: the Americans lost two aircraft in a raid on the well-prepared Syrians in the Upper Matn, and Walid Junblatt was impatient to extend his new Shuf "canton" to the sea. For the Lebanese regime the most ominous features of the situation by January 1984 were the army's failing hold in West Beirut and Shi'i fury at being shut out of Amin Jumayyil's *'ahd* (presidential period).

On 6 February 1984, after the army command had attempted to repress Amal and bombarded Beirut's Shi'i southern suburbs, Shi'i and Druze militiamen overran all of West Beirut. The army, reunited for barely a year, split on confessional lines for a second time. Christian units retreated to East Beirut, the Shi'i sixth brigade linked with Amal, and the Lebanese capital returned to the wartime division of 1975–82. Junblatt's forces lunged swiftly for the coast between Khalda and Damur, leaving only a Christian militia enclave in the Kharrub area north of Israel's Awali river line (map 8). The American and French troops of the MNF, surrounded by opposition militias, had no choice but to leave Lebanon. After a final brief shelling of the Shuf mountain

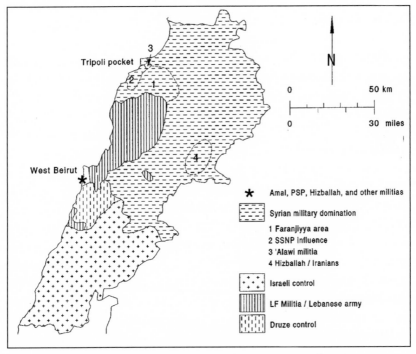

Map 8. Lebanon: Geopolitical divisions, March 1984

by the battleship New Jersey—which, according to one of Syria's allies, "shook no-one except the New Jersey and its passengers"[105]—President Reagan ordered U.S. marines to "redeploy" to the naval task force.

The most significant feature of the February 1984 upheaval was that it was an internal Lebanese development. For the first time Shi'i organizations, with Amal in the lead and the Iranian-backed Islamists of Hizballah (the "Party of God") not far behind, imposed themselves on Lebanese politics. West Beirut came under local militia control, principally Nabih Barri's Amal and Junblatt's PSP, with the Sunnis and Palestinians subordinated and no direct Syrian role. This was a different situation from that of 1975–82 in West Beirut. Syria remained preoccupied with its own regime uncertainties and may well have been as surprised as others by the turn of events. As a result, although Syria made a major strategic advance courtesy of the Lebanese opposition parties, these parties understood their own achievement and were jealous of their autonomy. Even with West Beirut evacuated by both the MNF and the Lebanese army command, Syria acquired only a leading influence—not hegemony—in that part of the city.

Hafiz al-Asad, who was recovering well from his illness, decided that the best way to gain maximum capital out of the changes in Beirut was to bring the hapless Amin Jumayyil to Damascus for a public submission. Abrogation of the Israel-Lebanon pact would be the token of submission but Asad's real purpose was to use the Lebanese president to dominate the Maronite community, which would also increase Syria's weight in dealings with West Beirut. Jumayyil dithered for a few weeks while he made last-ditch appeals to the Americans and Israelis. However, the Americans were already looking afresh at Syria as a factor for stability in Lebanon—their normal outlook before the MNF aberration—and the Israelis answered only with a contemptuous dismissal. Syria tightened the screws by hinting at military action by "allies" against Zahla, encircled by the Syrian army, and Jumayyil's home town of Bikfaya in the Upper Matn.[106] On 29 February, Jumayyil and an official Lebanese delegation traveled to Damascus.

For Asad the occasion coincided with a challenge from his brother Rifa'at over moves to restrict Rifa'at's power base. Jumayyil had to be kept waiting while Asad calmed the atmosphere at an emergency meeting of the Ba'th regional command. In early March, Rifa'at was faced down by his 'Alawi rivals in a mutual show of force in the streets. This marked Asad's full resumption of control of the Syrian military and political apparatus, with immediate reorganization to discipline those who had caused difficulties. Some Syrian officials suspected American and Saudi support for Rifa'at, and within three months he was packed off to exile in Europe (Seale, 1988).

At the working sessions with the Lebanese delegation Asad laid down basic demands but also showed flexibility toward the Christian sector, according to information from Lebanese participants.[107] He requested "full cooperation" with Syria—subordinating Lebanon's external relations to Syrian interests—and reform of the Lebanese constitution to equalize Christians and non-Christians. Asad apparently emphasized the need to satisfy Shi'i political aspirations even at the expense of the Sunnis. In exchange for Jumayyil's "cooperation," Asad indicated readiness to restrain Lebanese opposition pressures. When Syrian Foreign Minister Khaddam required that Jumayyil stop all contacts with Israel, Asad intervened and simply noted that "your links with Israel should be conducted privately and quietly because Syria cannot tolerate or agree to official links." The Syrian leader defined his top priority as reduction of diversions in Lebanon so that he could confront renewed moves for an Arab-Israeli deal involving Jordan and 'Arafat: "I will not permit this process to see the light . . . I say this after our victory over the U.S. in the region, and I will not allow the Americans to put us to the test again." On the matter of Lebanese sovereignty over all Lebanese territory Asad was evasive: "all I can assure you is to enable the [Lebanese] government to gather into its hands a rather extensive tract of land." During the meetings the Lebanese took note of Asad's physical performance. They concluded that although the Syrian president was tired his health seemed "regular."[108]

In Damascus Jumayyil agreed to a new inter-Lebanese conference, this time to be sponsored exclusively by Syria, and on 5 March the Lebanese regime canceled the 17 May 1983 agreement with Israel. Lebanon's warlords assembled in Lausanne in late March and came close to a constitutional compromise. Ironically, the conference suddenly collapsed because ex-president Faranjiyya, Asad's principal Christian confidant, rejected any erosion of the Maronite presidency.[109] The Amal leadership, unhappy about the sectarian nature of the compromise, which benefited Sunnis rather than Shi'is, were grateful to Faranjiyya for sparing them a possible contretemps with Syria.[110]

Military exchanges between the LF, hostile to Jumayyil's new relations with Syria, and Syria's West Beirut allies continued until the end of April when Syrian maneuvers produced a "National Unity Government" under the veteran Tripoli politician Rashid Karami. In this way Syria's allies were brought into the official apparatus and eight months of hostilities around Beirut finally gave way to an uneasy truce between the Christian and non-Christian sectors. Syria moved from playing spoiler against the Lebanese regime, the U.S., and Israel to the more difficult task of stabilizing its primacy. That the new government was "united" only in the sense that its members occasionally assembled at the same table limited its value for Syria.

Between the April 1984 inauguration of the National Unity Government and the scuttling in January 1986 of the Syrian-sponsored Tripartite Agreement, Christians and Druze consolidated their autonomy while Shi'is failed to convert advances in Beirut and southern Lebanon into any change in the Lebanese regime. The most important event was the Israeli evacuation of most of southern Lebanon in early 1985, by which the Israelis admitted the Shi'is were unmanageable but salvaged some strategic advantage. At the same time, 'Arafatist and other Palestinian organizations made serious attempts to reappear in West Beirut and southern Lebanon, which led to hostilities with the Shi'is. Nabih Barri's Amal, acting as a proxy for Syria, largely restricted the PLO to the Palestinian camps, but at considerable political and economic cost. The strain of confronting the Palestinians fragmented the Shi'i community. For many Sunnis and Druze, whose fear of Shi'i numbers had come to exceed their indignation at Maronite "privilege," Shi'i misfortune was a source of satisfaction.

Until the 1985 Israeli retreat, which transformed the Islamic sector, Syria's attention turned—unprofitably—to East Beirut. Asad's scheme to operate through Jumayyil to subordinate the Maronites was unviable, not just because of Jumayyil's slipperiness but also because Syria had humiliated the Lebanese president. After February 1984, Jumayyil irrevocably lost any authority outside the Christian sector, and even among Christians his legitimacy became precarious. In East Beirut he was forced, for the remaining four years of his presidency, to share the political stage with LF militia chiefs and the army command. The militia leadership favored ties with Israel, opposed concessions to Syria, and had no interest in rescuing a pluralist Lebanon. Its outlook on Israel and Syria was stiffened by ex-president Camille Chamoun, widely respected in East Beirut as an elder statesman.

Jumayyil maintained his modus vivendi with Damascus for a while to make the regime appear to be functioning under his chairmanship, to hold off Druze and Shi'i pressures, and to deter his East Beirut opponents. Through 1984, he used his base in his father's Kata'ib party to undermine LF leader Fadi Frem. In November 1984, Jumayyil's nephew Fuad Abi Nader replaced Frem after the president had also installed a loyalist as Kata'ib leader following Pierre Jumayyil's death. Syria supported extended presidential power over Maronite institutions and the Damascus armed forces daily *al-Thawra* termed Frem's removal "a success for Kata'ib moderation as represented by the president"[111]—a far cry from references in the recent past to "the fascist Kata'ib regime." Earlier in 1984, Lebanese army chief Ibrahim Tannous was forced to resign at the insistence of Barri and Junblatt, being replaced by Michel Aoun, an obscure brigade commander who had held the Suq al-Gharb ridge. It was an appointment Syria would later regret.

Sourness re-entered Syria's relations with the Lebanese president in early 1985 after stalling by Jumayyil over the limited constitutional adjustment proposed in the policy statement of the National Unity Government. 'Abd al-Halim Khaddam, now a Syrian vice president, attended special cabinet sessions in Bikfaya which produced no satisfaction for Syria's allies in West Beirut; Jumayyil pointed to the "Christian opposition" in arguing that he had little room for maneuver on constitutional matters. None of this mollified prominent figures in the LF and Camille Chamoun's NLP who believed that Jumayyil would sell out to Syria to stay in office. In February 1985, the Kata'ib leadership visited Damascus, the first such public contact since the collapse of the previous Kata'ib-Syrian connection in 1978. The response educated the Syrians about the fragility of Jumayyil's position in his own community, even if they preferred to ignore the wider Maronite enmity toward Syria itself. On 12 March 1985, anti-Syrian elements in the LF led by Samir Ja'ja' removed Abi Nader from the LF leadership and, by mobilizing on the streets, demonstrated that the LF—not the presidency—controlled the ground in East Beirut.

This coup in East Beirut coincided with Israel's second and larger retreat from territories occupied in 1982. Through 1984 Israel found that the Awali line offered it no real defense, as its main problem was the rising rebelliousness of the Shi'i population within the occupied area. Israel's attempt to create a militia network in Shi'i villages was rejected by the inhabitants, and Hizballah outbid Amal in "resistance" activities.

After the July 1984 Israeli elections, the Likud shared government with the Labor party, which felt no attachment to the leftovers of Israel's 1982 adventure. Between January and June 1985 the Israeli army withdrew in stages from most of southern Lebanon and the southern Biqa' to a "security zone" along Israel's northern border (map 8). Defense Minister Yitzhak Rabin covered the retreat with an "iron fist" campaign against "Shi'i terrorism," intended to impress upon Amal the costs of not ensuring quiet for Israel. It certainly perpetuated Shi'i hostility toward Israel.

The new LF leader, Samir Ja'ja', who had evidently not learned much from the consequences for the Christians of Israel's earlier retreat from the Shuf mountain, commited the LF to holding a "Christian" area that combined the LF's surviving foothold on the Shuf coast with the Christian villages east of Sidon (map 8). It is unclear whether or not the Israelis encouraged this unwise involvement; it could be seen as a counter to the Palestinians and Sunni Nasirites who took over Sidon in January 1985 as soon as Lebanese politicians celebrating the Israeli departure returned to Beirut. However, once the Israeli army disappeared to the south the LF deployment was surrounded by enemies and hostile populations. In April 1985, an assault by Druze, Nasirites, and Palestinians caused a Christian collapse and almost the whole local Christian population of about 50,000, more

Greek Catholic than Maronite, fled inland to Jizzin or by sea to East Beirut.

In the Maronite town of Jizzin a retired Lebanese army general, Antoine Lahad, who had consented to help organize the remnants of Israel's proxy militias into a new South Lebanese Army (SLA) to guard Israel's "security zone," insisted that the SLA also shield the refugees around Jizzin. Despite Jizzin's geographical advantages, which included access to the Shuf from the south, oversight of Sidon and its Palestinian refugee camps, and containment of southern Lebanon's Shi'is, it was not part of Israel's projected "security zone." This was because Israel conceived the "security zone" in defensive and bargaining terms, not as a bridgehead into Lebanon's domestic politics. Also, the Israelis felt the single main road from the "security zone" to Jizzin was too vulnerable and regarded the Christian population as unreliable.[112] Israel, however, could not detach itself so easily from the mess it had helped to create in southern Lebanon: Lahad received assent for the SLA to hold Jizzin, meaning an Israeli security umbrella, although unlike the "security zone" without an Israeli presence.

As for East Beirut, the Israeli withdrawal and the shock of events around Sidon emphasized unfavorable realities of power. Syria may not have been omnipotent but it did overshadow Beirut, and arguments for an accommodation with Damascus gained strength within the LF now that it had registered its autonomy vis-à-vis the presidency. Ja'ja', weakened by the Sidon affair, had to step aside in May 1985 in favor of the militia's intelligence chief, Elie Hubayqa. After Hubayqa became LF leader, Syria decided to sideline Jumayyil and deal with the militia as the "effective force."

On 9 September, Hubayqa visited Damascus and established a personal rapport with Khaddam. Thereafter Asad and Khaddam revised Syrian policy for Lebanon. They abandoned trying to get agreement within the Lebanese government on constitutional reform and decided to promote an accord between the three main militias—the LF, Amal, and Junblatt's PSP—which would then be presented to the "legitimate institutions" for implementation.

Syrian frustration, 1985–86

Despite acquiring Hubayqa, Syria could not command Beirut in the mid-1980s because of its deteriorating position in the Islamic sector. Interestingly, the Israeli retreat of January–June 1985 intensified developments unfavorable to Syria in West Beirut as well as dealing a blow to Syria's opponents in East Beirut. Lebanon's crisis, at least before the world changed at the end of the 1980s, rarely had the simplicity of a "zero-sum" game.

Between February 1984 and early 1985 Amal's paramountcy in West Beirut slowly decayed. Shi'i supremacy represented a novel twist for the cosmopolitan bourgeois society of Hamra and Ra's Beirut. Sunnis, Christians, and Druze instantly disliked it. Poorer Shi'is spilled out of the southern suburbs behind the militia and squatted where they could in the former "fashionable" quarters, changing their population composition. Anarchy and an atmosphere of social confrontation prevailed. Incidents multiplied between the various Lebanese militias, which had West Beirut to themselves for the first time in Lebanon's war. For a few months some cohesion existed between Amal and Junblatt's PSP. PSP militiamen in West Beirut included many Kurds and members of the urban underclass who had social interests in common with the Shi'i poor, although this soon turned to competition. The main Druze component stayed in the Shuf mountain. Amal and the PSP cooperated in 1984 in the bloody dismantling of the Sunni Murabitun militia, a priority Syrian target because of its links with 'Arafat.

Amal did not lack goodwill toward non-Shi'i Lebanese, but it was a sectarian party and its meteoric rise encouraged its political ambitions. Amal's main difficulties stemmed from a deficient infrastructure in both its military and civilian wings—in this respect it was much inferior to the LF and the PSP—and the movement's lack of expertise for controlling a large segment of a major metropolis. Inability to provide public security, increasing frictions with the PSP and smaller militias over spheres of influence in Beirut, and growing fears about Palestinian infiltration made Amal leaders too dependent on their connections with Syria.

Added to the impotence of the National Unity Government, the capricious nature of militia rule led Sunni and Shi'i personalities to seek Syrian intervention, even a return of the Syrian troops expelled by Israel in 1982. Syria had no intention of exposing itself to the risks of a reappearance in Beirut at this stage, and planned to operate through local clients—Amal, other militias, and Syrian-oriented Palestinians—to confront challenges to its influence. If rough times resulted for the bourgeoisie, that was their problem. Thousands of Christians, some of whom had in the past poured scorn on the Maronite "canton," headed for East Beirut. Militiamen and squatters occupied their West Beirut apartments.

Israel's 1985 retreat opened southern Lebanon to Amal, potentially offering the sort of base that the PSP and the LF possessed in the Shuf and Kisrawan mountains. However, the retreat also set the scene for a vicious contest in the enlarged no-man's land separating Israeli and Syrian lines, involving Amal, the Palestinians, the PSP, and Hizballah. The ensuing upheavals wrecked Syria's policy of remote-control management and in 1987 forced the Syrian army to return to West Beirut.

From the outset of militia rule in West Beirut, 'Arafat loyalists began reorganizing among the Palestinian population, while armed elements of different Palestinian factions resurfaced in the battered refugee camps of Sabra, Shatila, and Burj al-Barajina. The situation was complicated for Syria by the difficulty of disentangling Palestinians supposedly allied with Syria from 'Arafat's personnel. For Amal all were a danger to Shi'is, evoking bitter memories of pre-1982 PLO behavior. With the "reopening" of southern Lebanon in early 1985, 'Arafatist infiltration became a determined scheme for the reconversion of the refugee camps of Sidon and Beirut into PLO fortresses. 'Arafat's agents also subverted Amal's leading role in West Beirut by encouraging Shi'i factionalism and Druze and Sunni unease. Amal's amorphous structure, and the fact that many members had been associated with Palestinian groups in the 1970s, assisted 'Arafatist penetration.

Apart from the Palestinian issue, conditions created by the Israeli withdrawal inflamed competition among Lebanon's non-Christian parties. First, Amal's land communications from Beirut to its new domain in southern Lebanon traversed the coastal margin of the PSP "canton" and the Sunni Nasirites and Palestinians of Sidon (map 9). Amal resented this vulnerability, whereas the Druze were worried about Amal encroachment from both north and south. Second, Hizballah, which detested the secularism and compromising tendencies of Amal, regarded southern Lebanon as its own prize and intended not just to thwart Amal but to extend its own power base among the Shi'is. At this point the Iranian revolutionary regime chose to emphasize sponsorship of Hizballah rather than act as a general patron of Shi'i political parties, and its relations with Amal quickly deteriorated. Much more than the Palestinians, Hizballah, as a Shi'i faction with sympathizers in Amal's hierarchy, threatened to sap Amal from both inside and outside.

For Amal and Syria alike the PLO challenge became an obsession. Syria had an eye on Arab states which would intrude more effectively if the 'Arafatists re-established themselves—Iraq, Egypt, Saudi Arabia, and even Libya and Algeria. Amal thus moved from being outside the circle of Syria's allies, as in 1983, to being Syria's leading non-Christian ally for the rest of the 1980s. Only Amal had the motivation and capacity to stand against the 'Arafatists on Syria's behalf—otherwise the Syrian army would have to take direct action.

Syria, however, had a perspective on the coexistence of Amal, Hizballah, and the PSP that did not fit well with Amal interests. All three parties were needed for Syria's regional policies. The PSP's position on the Shuf mountain ridges was vital to control of Beirut. Syria sought to use Hizballah, in combination with its alliance with Islamic Iran, for continued pressure on the West, Israel, and conservative Arab states. Syria stood aloof when Shi'i militants kidnapped a number of Western citizens in Beirut in 1984–85. Overall, Asad balanced between factions and options; while arming Amal against the Palestinian camps, Syria allowed the PSP and Hizballah to constrain Amal. Amal could not cope with these crosscurrents and, although the PLO was blocked, Syria found itself unable to coordinate West Beirut's parties.

On 20 May 1985, after mounting frictions on the perimeters of West Beirut's Palestinian refugee camps, Amal and the Shi'i sixth brigade of the Lebanese army laid siege to Sabra, Shatila, and Burj al-Barajina. A month of vicious fighting ensued, during which Amal razed much of Sabra but suffered heavy casualties, for which it retaliated with atrocities against Palestinians inside and outside the camps. Amal also tried to hunt down 'Arafatists throughout West Beirut, producing a reign of terror for all Palestinians in the urban area.[113] Palestinian factions, including those aligned with Syria, temporarily came together against Amal, and multiple rocket launchers in the hands of the Damascus-based Palestinian National Salvation Front (PNSF) bombarded Amal and the Shi'i southern suburbs from Druze territory in the Shuf mountain. Syria sent Syrian-aligned Palestinians to Beirut despite Amal warnings that those who were "Abu Musa [anti-'Arafat] in the Biqa' become Abu nothing in the Shuf and Abu 'Ammar [with 'Arafat] on arrival in Beirut."[114] Junblatt and the PSP chose ostentatious neutrality, interpreted by Amal as hostility; many Shi'is viewed Syrian failure to stop the shelling from the Shuf as a Syrian double game; and Asad faced Arab accusations that he was promoting Amal against the Palestinian cause. Amal checked 'Arafat, but this was only the opening round of an intermittent "war of the camps" that lasted from 1985 to 1988, spread south to Sidon and Tyre, and exacerbated conflicts of interest among Lebanon's "Islamic and nationalist" factions. The opening round cost at least 1,000 dead on the two sides.

Barely had the Amal-Palestinian hostilities petered out into momentary exhaustion, marked in mid-June by a Syrian-organized conciliation between Syria's Palestinian allies and Amal, than Damascus had to busy itself with the fate of a hijacked American TWA passenger aircraft brought to Beirut by Hizballah operatives. Amal leader Nabih Barri took charge of the passengers, but could not give them security or freedom until Syria intervened with Hizballah, after Israel released some of its hundreds of Shi'i detainees. For Barri the TWA hijacking represented a humiliating demonstration of Amal's limitations within the Shi'i community. It was an important milestone on the road to the 1988–90 showdown between Amal and Hizballah.

For Syria the implications were contradictory. On the one hand, Asad could demonstrate his services to the West in settling such an affair, and show the value of his connections with Iran and Hizballah. This encouraged the West to look to Syria as a go-between regarding Westerners kidnapped in Beirut. On the other hand, the TWA hijacking threatened to bring an American military strike into West Beirut with uncertain consequences—for example, it might reinvigorate Maronite defiance. Media attention during two weeks of wrangling also highlighted Syria's difficulties in imposing itself on West Beirut.

Chaos in West Beirut and a flare-up between the LF and the non-Christian militias after the resolution of the TWA hijacking impelled Syria to urgency in using the opening to Hubayqa in East Beirut to tie the three big militias together. Negotiations supervised by Khaddam went ahead through late 1985. Junblatt objected to dealing with Hubayqa, whom he accused of responsibility for the September 1982 Sabra and Shatila massacre; Junblatt and Barri had to be compelled to sit together when tension between the PSP and Amal led to clashes in West Beirut in November; and Hubayqa had to watch rumblings of discontent in East Beirut. Nonetheless, by 28 December 1985 Khaddam managed to get the leaderships of the LF, the PSP, and Amal to give their assent to an extraordinary document known as the Tripartite Agreement.[115]

The importance of the Tripartite Agreement is as a frank written statement of Ba'thist Syria's ambition for long-term command of Lebanon, to be buttressed by political reform and economic and cultural "integration" *(takaamul)* between Lebanon and Syria. Some in the LF delegation, like Hubayqa and Michel Samaha, had reason to expect prominent positions in a new regime; others had a somber view of the future of the Maronites and felt the Christian sector had very limited choices.[116] Walid Junblatt commented to me before going to Damascus for the signing that there was no point in opposing the Syrians, because the agreement had no chance of being implemented—both it and Hubayqa would shortly be rejected by the Maronites. According to Junblatt, Khaddam had misread Lebanese realities.[117]

Travel between the Christian and Druze cantons, or through the Upper Matn to the Biqa', was always an adventure in the the mid-1980s. One soon discovered that Walid Junblatt was not particularly popular with the Syrians or supposedly fraternal militias. On one occasion I heard a Syrian officer at a checkpoint refer to Junblatt as

---

wazir az-zift (minister of ashphalt or hell—Junblatt was minister of public works at the time). On another occasion I and two students from the University of Exeter, whom I took with me on a visit to Junblatt in Mukhtara, were briefly detained at a Syrian Social National Party post in Duhur al-Shuwayr. The militiamen used various expletives to make it clear what they thought of Junblatt's Progressive Socialist Party.

Otherwise it was fascinating to observe the antics of Syrian military units, especially the "special forces" in their colorful "pink panther" uniforms. Once, when telling a Syrian infantryman at a checkpoint that I was from *nuwzeelanda* (New Zealand) I was asked whether that was a village near Tripoli. On a trip in a service taxi to Zahla in 1985, I watched a changeover of Syrian units in the Upper Matn. One group of soldiers pulling out of a local house was even removing the doors. On another trip to Zahla our service taxi driver was taken away at a Syrian checkpoint for speaking in an "insolent" tone. I and the other passengers were told that we had better continue to Zahla by other means. We refused to move and, after a short delay, the Syrians reproduced a very shaken driver.

I went to lunch with Walid Junblatt once in December 1985. The British ambassador was also there, and the conversation turned to the matter of a British citizen being held hostage by Palestinian radicals. The radicals were linked to Libya, and the ambassador hoped that Junblatt might be helpful as a channel. Junblatt was in a slightly flippant mood and wondered aloud about the advantages to the Druze of British Harrier jump-jets, given the lack of airstrips in the Shuf hills. He dwelt a little on the unfairness of a situation in which the Christian sector—the "other side"—had helicopters and Hawker Hunters.

Junblatt managed such asides while acting as a gracious host, plying the guests with liberal quantities of food and drink. He was also careful in his comments about the Syrians, balancing reservations about Khaddam's handling of the Lebanese "file" with praise of Asad. This brought to mind a tale I heard from several sources. Apparently on one of Junblatt's visits to Asad in Damascus, the Syrian president advised the Lebanese Druze leader not to sit in a certain chair because his father had sat in that chair, and it might mean bad luck given what had happened to his father (the Syrians were widely suspected of responsibility for Kamal Junblatt's death in 1977).

As regards constitutional change, the Tripartite Agreement covered ideas that had already been debated at the 1983/84 Geneva and Lausanne conferences: equalizing Christian and non-Christian representation in parliament and reducing the powers of the presidency in favor of the prime minister and cabinet, as part of a transition toward abolishing sectarian political allocations. However, President Jumayyil had not been consulted about the shrinkage of presidential prerogatives. He had a good incentive to play a Faranjiyya-style role as defender of Maronite political "rights." The provisions for "privileged relations" *('alaqaat mumayyiza)* between Lebanon and Syria were even more controversial. They included "complete coordination" of foreign policies, perpetuation of the Syrian military presence in Lebanon, establishment of joint committees to prepare an "integrated" approach in education, and prevention of any media "distortion" *(tashwish)* of "privileged relations." The Lebanese were explicitly warned about "Arab-Palestinian axes designed to embroil Syria on the political, security, and military levels" and against leaving any opening for Israel to challenge Syria. These provisions made the majority of LF members oppose Hubayqa, and alienated the Maronite church, which perceived a threat to Maronite cultural autonomy. Further, the agreement brushed aside aspirations in the LF for a federation of cantons, which was anathema to Syria, and emphasized a restored unitary state. Finally, a significant section about reorganization of the Lebanese army after its "confinement to barracks" infuriated the army command. Like President Jumayyil, army chief Michel Aoun was kept in the dark. Aoun viewed the attempt by militias and the Syrians to determine the fate of Lebanon's official army as deeply insulting.[118]

Hubayqa found himself isolated in East Beirut when he returned from Damascus. Memories of Christian disasters in the Shuf and Sidon areas were fading, Syria was in trouble in West Beirut, and anger with the "Tripartite Agreement" intensified with contemplation of the text. President Jumayyil, the Maronite patriarchate, and the army command came together in their rejection. Within the LF, Hubayqa's enemy Samir Ja'ja' gathered his supporters to retake the militia leadership, this time backed by both Israel and East Beirut's traditional leaders. On 12 January 1986, Ja'ja' deposed Hubayqa in a ferocious insurrection. Hubayqa and his followers were expelled from East Beirut to Syrian-controlled territory and the Tripartite Agreement collapsed.

Despite its recovery in Lebanon after 1983, Syria on this occasion overreached itself. Asad, Khaddam, and West Beirut politicians responded to the shock from East Beirut by severing communications with President Jumayyil, splitting Lebanon's official apparatus, but the Syrian project to "coordinate" Lebanon with Syria was temporarily thwarted.

Traffic restriction for tanks, East Beirut, 1986

"War games"—Israel in Lebanon (Ze'ev in *Ha'aretz,* 11 June 1982)

CHAPTER SIX

MILITIAS AND CANTONS, 1986–89

The political and economic environment

Between the demise of the Tripartite Agreement in early 1986 and General Michel Aoun's assault on the Syrians in early 1989, Lebanon's fragmentation seemed to be a permanent feature of the Middle Eastern scene. It was not a time of peace. Syria sought to undermine East Beirut, whether by political or military means, and upheavals shook West Beirut. It was, however, a time of stalemate. The Maronites had lost their pre-eminence in Lebanon, but they could still deny pre-eminence to anyone else. The Shi'is had registered their significance, but they possessed no political coherence and their self-assertion only emphasized the sectarian divisions of Lebanon's non-Christians, between Shi'is, Sunnis, and Druze. The Syrians had regained their role of the late 1970s as the leading external influence on Lebanese politics, but their allies in West Beirut could not be mobilized to any effective purpose and Syria was greatly constrained by other powers. After 1984, the U.S. returned to viewing Syria as a stabilizing influence, as in the late 1970s, but as long as the Soviet Union gave Asad strategic patronage there could be no Syrian-American convergence.

It was the heyday of cantons and militias. The Lebanese state, with the exception of part of the army, survived only as a ghostly backdrop to anarchy and warlord exactions. In January 1986, executive government, already of little relevance to Lebanon's population, was crippled when Syria insisted that Prime Minister Rashid Karami and the non-Christian ministers cut themselves off from Amin Jumayyil's presidency. In East Beirut the LF militia consolidated its infrastructure in its self-appointed function of leading a Christian mini-state, although it faced opposition from Lebanon's army command. At the same time Walid Junblatt's PSP established more effective machinery for Druze autonomy in the Shuf mountain (J. Harik, 1993). The Shuf and East Beirut "cantons," superficially opponents, in fact buttressed each other, although the smaller Druze entity's need was the greater. For East Beirut, Druze autonomy diverted Syria by complicating its management of the non-Christian arena. For the Druze, East Beirut's defiance of Damascus made the PSP a valuable Syrian ally in a useful location, which forced the Syrians to be tolerant of Junblatt's fiefdom. Hafiz al-Asad was aware of the nuances of this situation and Syria watched suspiciously for collusion between the Druze and East Beirut. The Druze "canton" had a centralized leadership unlike the unstable political structure of East Beirut, but had too little economic and demographic weight to survive if its Christian counterpart disappeared.

Beyond the Christian and Druze redoubts, whether in the bitterly contested territories of "Islamic and nationalist" West Beirut and southern Lebanon or in the zones of Syrian and Israeli military domination, militias thrived in the late 1980s. Amal and Hizballah struggled for supremacy among the Shi'is of Beirut's southern suburbs, southern Lebanon, and the northern Biqa'. In Jizzin and the Israeli "security zone," SLA commanders supervised the population on Israel's behalf and their own. In the Syrian-dominated areas of northern and eastern Lebanon, Damascus sought control at minimal cost through a weird amalgam of its own troops, local protection rackets, and Lebanese armed groups.

Militias, of whatever political color, had common interests in preserving sectarian identities, protecting the "black economy," and infiltrating the official bureaucracy. Though militias clashed violently with one another they shared a hostility toward the traditional political class, at least while their bosses felt they were regarded as parvenus. Militias also cooperated financially, and generally respected one another's turfs.[119] The drug trade from the Biqa', involving opium and hashish, drew together the Syrian army (in some ways simply a big militia), Hizballah, the Christian city of Zahla, various Syrian-aligned militias, and elements in East Beirut.

This "Indian summer" of the militias could not be sustained because of socioeconomic changes within Lebanon and shifts in the international balances affecting Lebanon when the Cold War ended.

Lebanon's intermittent economic boom of the 1960s and early 1970s had been broken by the first year of warfare, in 1975–76. Official gross domestic product (GDP) (as expressed in 1974 prices) almost halved between 1974 and 1976,[120] the country's physical infrastructure was shattered, and a debilitating out-migration of skilled workers began. GDP never recovered to the 1974 level, although between 1977 and 1982 the economy was buoyed by periods of relative quiet and the financial injections of the PLO "state within the state." Militias were able to draw financial support from the diaspora by playing on sectarian loyalties, and Beirut's connections as the great cosmopolitan entrepôt of the Middle East assisted the expansion of "black market" operations in drugs, arms, and other contraband, even as more legitimate entrepôt functions fled elsewhere. Up to 1984, the Lebanese lira maintained a reasonably stable exchange rate of 2–3 to the U.S. dollar and the 1975–84 average annual inflation rate of about 17% was not extraordinary, given Lebanon's wartime circumstances and the inflationary international economic climate of the period.

More ominous economic features of the first eight years of the war included the loss of the whole pre-1975 growth, which condemned the bulk of Lebanon's population to declining living standards, and the highly concentrated benefits of the "black economy," which skewed income distribution even more than before 1975. At first the militias and radical political parties could extend their popular legitimacy by exploiting the economic grievances and insecurities of the population—grievances on the part of the Muslim lower class and insecurities on the part of their somewhat better-off Christian equivalents. However, popular support derived from such resentments could only be capricious; the militias had no answer to Lebanon's economic deterioration, especially as they themselves were a prominent source of instability.

In 1984, the national economy and currency cracked under the strain. First, the 1982 Israeli invasion caused considerable additional infrastructural damage, and the PLO evacuation from Beirut meant a diminution of Palestinian financial input. Second and probably more significant, the resumption of large-scale hostilities in the Beirut region and elsewhere from September 1983 on disrupted the industrial and commercial sectors for an unprecedented length of time, even compared to 1975–76. At this point businessmen as well as the population abandoned their long-held hopes that Lebanon might somehow recover its pre-1975 status, and the psychological slump reinforced the physical one. Between 1984 and 1987 the Lebanese lira collapsed, sliding from 3 to 430 to the U.S. dollar, and inflation soared to over 100% per annum. The upper levels of society, including militia and mafia leaders, promptly shifted to using the U.S. dollar as the local medium of exchange and treated the lira as a speculative plaything. Such behavior by the high bourgeoisie only worsened conditions for the majority of Lebanese, Christians and Muslims, who were imprisoned in a "lira society" of rapidly depreciating incomes.

> When I taught at the Haigazian University College in East Beirut in 1987 I regularly took a small backpack to the bank to collect my monthly salary. The highest-denomination bank-note—250 lira—was at that time worth not much more than fifty U.S. cents. I once had to collect about 15,000 lira in fifty and one hundred lira notes. The process at the bank counter took easily a quarter of an hour, even with fast money counting machines, and did not encourage careful checking of what one was receiving.

What were the implications for militia power in the Lebanon of the late 1980s? On the one hand, the various geopolitical fragments of the country maintained a ramshackle financial viability despite the national economic disaster. Remittances from the diaspora, subsidies from interested foreign powers, agricultural and drug trading from the Biqa', light industrial exports assisted by the collapsed exchange rate, especially from East Beirut, and miscellaneous smuggling activities all combined to make life tolerable for the wealthy and to keep everyone else from starving. For the moment militias could pursue their affairs with only passing attention to the wider population. Well before the late 1980s the "black economy," meaning the whole range of illicit commercial operations (such as arms and drug trades, militia taxes at illegal ports, sales of war booty, "commissions" taken by officials, protection money, and fraud in the retail and wholesale sectors), had an annual turnover exceeding the official GDP.

An excellent and entirely credible analysis in October 1990 by the daily *al-Nahar* estimated the Lebanese profits on these operations—obviously only a fraction of the total turnover of the "black economy"—at a minimum of $14.5 billion for the 1975–90 period: an average of $900 million per annum.[121] Dividing the "black economy" into 14 segments, the analysis suggested annual proceeds for the three largest components—drugs, arms trafficking, and protection money—at $600 million, $150 million, and $200 million, respectively. "This has helped a substantial number of Lebanese to feed money into [the country's] economic arteries." Lebanon's bank secrecy regulations, introduced by President Camille Chamoun in 1956, facilitated the "laundering" of such earnings.

However, a random trickle-down from the "black economy" could not mask the fact that militias and cantons could offer no decent economic future for the middle and lower classes of their communities. In the late 1980s, the social buffer between rich and poor—the salaried and professional middle class and small businessmen—was devastated by currency depreciation. As never before, even in Lebanon's laissez-faire economic environment, a vast and almost empty space separated the upper class, with its flamboyant new warlord dimension, from the disadvantaged masses. The militias afflicted the population with illegal financial impositions and such obviously empty slogans as "the security of Christian society comes before all else." I recall such phrases plastered on walls in East Beirut at times when bodyguards of LF personalities shot up civilians on mountain roads and interfactional disputes led to bodies appearing in the Beirut River. Militias, at the height of their arrogance after a decade of encouraging sectarian bigotry, failed to heed a shift in public attitudes in the mid- and late 1980s that precipitously reduced their precarious legitimacy.

In East Beirut, the slippage of many Maronites to socioeconomic

conditions not far removed from those of the Shi'i and Sunni poor eliminated the charms of the "canton" and highlighted its more irksome features, such as the displacement of many Christians from their homes
elsewhere in Lebanon. The LF never recovered the public following it
lost after its military disasters in the Shuf in 1983 and the east Sidon
hills in 1985, which wiped away the sentimental legacy left by the charis-
matic Bashir Jumayyil. The Lebanese army, reorganized and re-
equipped in 1983–84 and with all the advantages of legitimate legal status, pulled more strongly on the loyalties of Lebanon's Christians.

Among the Shi'is, Amal always rested its claim for political legitimacy on its support for a unitary Lebanon and for state institutions,
reformed to accommodate greater Shi'i participation, which did not mix
well with Amal's own usurpation of state authority. In addition, com-
petion between Amal and Hizballah for command of the Shi'i community alienated many ordinary Shi'is from both organizations.

As for Sunnis, after the departure of the PLO from Beirut and
Tripoli in 1982–83 they had no serious militia "cover" and naturally
detested the depredations of the militias of other sects. Tripoli residents
developed a special hatred of Syrian Ba'thists and Syrian-aligned
groups during the sieges of their city in 1983 and 1985, which caused
about 2,000 deaths.

Overall, economic conditions after 1985 encouraged popular rejection of militias by most Christians, Shi'is, and Sunnis—in other words,
by most Lebanese—and popular exasperation with the geopolitical status quo, despite the lack of consensus about the character of a new
Lebanon. In 1988, at the end of Amin Jumayyil's presidency, a seductive
answer presented itself—the romantic secular nationalism of General
Michel Aoun, backed by the only remaining embodiment of national
unity for ordinary Lebanese: the army and its high command.

Transformation in international politics in the late 1980s, with the
rapid decay of the Soviet Union and consequent global strategic
supremacy for the U.S., also presaged change in Lebanon. However,
whereas the popular mood inside Lebanon favored a revolution against
militias and foreign occupations, American policy favored "stabilization" in the Eastern Mediterranean, which for Lebanon meant a new
central regime incorporating the militias and under a Syrian security

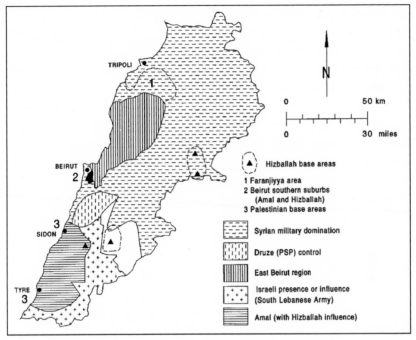

Map 9. Lebanon: Geopolitical divisions, 1987

umbrella. Hence, the impulses for change from inside and outside Lebanon contradicted each other and promised a violent catharsis. For the U.S., the Soviet disengagement from world affairs opened the way to American sponsorship of Arab-Israeli negotiations, without great power interference, and to drawing Syria into a Western-oriented new Middle East "order."

Lebanon was critically important to the implementation of U.S. post–Cold War policy in the Middle East: it was a base for disruptive elements and thus needed to be neutralized, and its disposition was the main test for an American-Syrian rapprochement. In brief, from the U.S. perspective, Lebanon's fragmentation between militias and cantons was incompatible with post–Cold War opportunities for Middle East stabilization, but the impetus was toward a solution that Damascus might find tolerable—there was no interest in satisfying Lebanese populist aspirations.

Though the militia heyday was brief, it is worth constructing a detailed profile of the Lebanon of the late 1980s. The geopolitical pattern of the time represented the outcome of the 1983–85 upheavals, and the temporary stalemating of Syria, and it influenced events during Michel Aoun's wars in 1989–90. The pattern may be simplified into a threefold division (map 9): The zones of Syrian and Israeli domination, together about 70% of the country; the patchwork of Shi'i, Druze, and Palestinian armed factions, which overlapped with the Syrian zone and provided the principal arena of local fighting; and the compressed but still formidable East Beirut redoubt, where the Lebanese presidency and army coexisted uneasily with the main Christian militia.

Syrian and Israeli occupation

Whereas in 1982 Israeli power extended over about one-third of Lebanon while Syria was forced out of West Beirut and all of southern Lebanon, in 1984–85 the reverse occurred: Israel contracted to an area in the far south that comprised 10% of Lebanese territory, while the Syrian presence re-expanded in the southern Biqa' and consolidated in central and northern Lebanon. Israel, under pressure from the Shi'is and with its domestic constituency weary of Lebanon, sought to divest itself of troublesome populations while retaining a minimal defensive buffer. Withdrawal to the post–June 1985 "security zone" reduced the population under Israeli control from the 965,000 estimated to live in Lebanon south of the Awali river in 1984, 8% of whom were Palestinians from near Sidon and Tyre, to less than 200,000, almost none of whom were Palestinians.[122] Thus, in the late 1980s Israel supervised 6% of Lebanon's people compared with 30% in 1984.

Syria's approach through the mid-1980s was more complex because Syria set itself the more difficult objective of strategic hegemony in all of Lebanon except Israel's residual sphere of influence. In some critical locations, most prominently the Sunni city of Tripoli and the Christian city of Zahla, Syria worked to extend its military presence to encompass an additional and plainly unfriendly population of about

210

600,000, thereby doubling the number of Lebanese within the zone of Syrian military deployment between 1984 and 1986. Elsewhere the Syrians preferred to extend their influence without a direct military presence. Syria cautiously inserted a few outposts and intelligence personnel as Israel retreated from the southern Biqa', but otherwise left the neighborhood of the new Israeli lines to its Lebanese allies. As regards West Beirut, after the bitter experiences of 1977-82 Syria was wary of the expenses and risks of placing its army inside the Lebanese capital. The Syrians wished to steer the politics of the "Islamic and nationalist" sector at the lowest possible cost, and from 1983 to 1987 tried to operate through clients and large numbers of military intelligence agents. However, West Beirut proved not to be manageable by such devices and in February 1987 the Syrian army was again deployed in the area. As a result the Syrian military deployment came to cover at least 50% of Lebanon's people in the late 1980s.

Both Syria and Israel aimed to control security in their respective areas, but to avoid the distractions of an occupation regime. Israel had General Lahad's SLA to administer the Lebanese of the "security zone," although into the 1990s the militia remained a Christian-run organization within a population that was 55% Shi'i.[123] After what they regarded as an unfortunate relationship with the East Beirut Maronites the Israelis resolved never again to rely on one Lebanese community,[124] but many Shi'i recruits only joined the SLA to collect a salary. A notorious SLA-run prison at Khiyam, feared and hated by Shi'is because of regular human rights abuses, did not help matters.

Despite their original intention not to have a permanent Israeli presence in the "security zone,"[125] the Israelis found that the SLA needed stiffening from the Israeli army. The militia doubled in size between 1985 and 1990, to about 2,500 personnel, with a considerably enlarged arsenal, but Hizballah was a far more sophisticated opponent after 1990 than in the 1980s.

Syria had the advantages of familiarity with Lebanon's internal affairs and acceptability to some segments of the population that dated back to Syria's 1976 intervention as a peacemaking force, invited by the Lebanese regime. The standard Syrian modus operandi was to have local Lebanese officials and militia proxies handle what passed for administration, while Syrian troops overawed the population at highway checkpoints and the Syrian intelligence apparatus monitored bureaucratic and political activity. Syrian military intelligence proved adept at exploiting the antagonisms within and between the Christian, Shi'i, and Sunni populations of the Biqa' and northern Lebanon to make Syria indispensable as protector and mediator among the factions. Examples of local quarrels requiring Syrian intervention ranged from inter-Shi'i clan problems in Ba'albak and Hirmil to a 1988 land dispute between Maronites and Shi'is near Qubbayat in the 'Akkar, which degenerated into an artillery exchange. Syrian army officers also intruded into local commerce: merchants in the 'Akkar, for example, had to share profits from imported consumer durables with a protection racket run by the Syrian army from Shtura.[126] Together with the drug trade, this kind of activity reflected a Syrian determination to ensure financial returns from Syria's "sacrifices" in supporting its "sister" state—by living off the land.

Aside from West Beirut, Syria's main preoccupations within its zone involved Ba'albak, Zahla, and Tripoli. The Shi'i fundamentalist enclave in Ba'albak and its surrounds—host to several hundred Iranian revolutionary guards as well as containing Hizballah's rearward infrastructure for operations in Beirut and southern Lebanon—was easily coordinated to Syrian purposes. It was dominated by the primary Syrian military concentration in Lebanon, aligned across the central Biqa', and occasional frictions were outweighed by continuing common interests against East Beirut, Israel, and the West.

As for the Zahla Christians, after their disappointment at not being "saved" by the Israelis in 1982 they slowly became more amenable to Damascus (Harris, 1985). Up to 1985, Syria allowed Amal and Hizballah to maintain roadblocks around the Zahla pocket, in addition to its own supervision of access, and the youth of the city were virtually imprisoned. Syria needed the banking and commercial expertise of Zahla, and Zahla merchants could profit from more interactions with Syria. In September 1985, the Greek Catholic bishop negotiated a "security plan" with the Syrian military intelligence commander in Lebanon, Ghazi Kana'an, by which the Syrian army entered the city, the LF armed presence was ended, and access restrictions were eased.

After early 1986, Zahla became a base for Syrian pressure on East Beirut, via the dissident LF faction of Elie Hubayqa, and an important asset in the Syrian game of balancing between the Christians and Shi'is of the Biqa'.

In northern Lebanon, from 1978 on, Syria had a firm hold on rural areas that included part of the Maronite heartland of Mount Lebanon. The Marada militia of ex-president Faranjiyya took care of the Zgharta-Ihdin area as a private fiefdom, helping Syria to prove that East Beirut leaders did not speak for the whole Maronite community. Similarly, the Syrian Social Nationalists (SSNP) had a foothold in the Orthodox Kura but had to share it with the Syrian army. Close to Tripoli, Syria could rely on the 'Alawi suburb of Bab al-Tabbani and its well-armed Arab Democratic Party.

Tripoli itself was outside the Syrian deployment for two years after the 1983 'Arafatist episode. Finally, in late September 1985, Syria's allies battered the Islamic Unification Movement of Sa'id Sha'aban into accepting a Zahla-style "security plan," only two weeks after implementation of the Zahla model. Syrian intelligence monitored the city scrupulously after 1985, using blackmail to acquire local informants,[127] and Sunnis felt threatened by 'Alawi immigration. Tripoli was spared further hostilities in the late 1980s, but economic conditions for the middle and lower classes were almost as bad as in West Beirut. Not surprisingly, General Aoun's nationalist campaign gained a widespread following in the city after 1988, as evidenced by the resounding local Sunni boycott of the Syrian-sponsored 1992 Lebanese parliamentary elections.

"Islamic and nationalist" Lebanon

West Beirut's fragments

From late 1986, when Syrian-sponsored efforts to destabilize East Beirut and resurrect the Tripartite Agreement by violent means faded away, to the opening of Michel Aoun's "war of liberation" in March 1989, warfare in Lebanon was restricted to factional fighting within West Beirut and southern Lebanon and sporadic clashes between Israel and its opponents. Since 1983, Syria had tried to promote an alliance of the Druze PSP, the Shi'i Amal movement, Syrian-oriented Palestinians, and other leftist parties, to confront East Beirut and demolish the 'Arafatists. The alliance lasted only as long as the Maronites and the Jumayyil regime were the main target; the shift of attention toward the Palestinians exposed the contradictions among the "Islamic and nationalist" militias. Through 1985 and 1986 Syria found itself forced more and more to rely on Amal as its main instrument in West Beirut and southern Lebanon. However, Amal was constrained by its multiplying local enemies.

First, the 'Arafatist Palestinians re-established bases in the refugee camps of Beirut, Sidon, and Tyre by early 1986, having merely been checked in the inaugural round of the "war of the camps." 'Ayn al-Helwa in Sidon became the 'Arafatist command center, with numbers of Palestinian fighters expanding from a minimal level at the time of the 1985 Israeli withdrawal to approximately 6,000 at the end of 1986, equivalent to Amal's entire strength in southern Lebanon. Only in Sidon did Palestinian control spread beyond the camps, and 'Arafat's Fatah had to share its bases with competing Palestinian factions. Nonetheless, Amal had to cope with a series of new fronts along the coast, and the Fatah break-out into the hills around 'Ayn al-Helwa threatened Amal's land link between Beirut and southern Lebanon.

Second, Amal was estranged from its West Beirut "allies" by 1985. Once the Druze had secured their Shuf mountain autonomy, their access to the sea, and a siphon into revenues from West Beirut's "black economy," their main interest was to hold their gains—not to serve Syria in more military operations. Walid Junblatt refused to be seen in the Arab world as going against the Palestinians, and his aides did not bother to hide their apprehensions about the Shi'is.[128] In addition, Amal viewed Junblatt's Communist associates as competitors for secular Shi'i support and his Sunni Nasirite friends—Mustafa Sa'ad's Popular Army in Sidon—as 'Arafatist agents.[129]

Third, Amal had to cope with the Iranian-backed Hizballah challenge within the Shi'i community. On this matter Amal found the Syrians unhelpful; the alliance with Iran was too valuable to Damascus to be endangered for the sake of a Lebanese militia ally. Syria wanted

Amal to serve its purposes but also wanted to keep the Shi'is divided. In 1987, Syria encouraged Iran to dispatch a contingent of Iranian revolutionary guards from Ba'albak to southern Lebanon to increase pressure on Israel and depended on Amal to provide a local control on Hizballah's improved position. Iran acted in favor of a stronger Hizballah but also felt sufficiently embarrassed by conflict between Shi'is and Palestinians to mediate a 1987 PLO-Amal truce that freed Amal to face Hizballah. For its part, Hizballah exploited Syrian laxity and Iranian aid to undermine and provoke Amal. Syrian and Iranian maneuvering thus helped set the scene for the 1988–90 inter-Shi'i war which succeeded the 1985–88 "war of the camps."

In 1986, West Beirut was a no man's land in which militias and armed gangs jostled for command of the streets. Amal's disorganization and preoccupation with the Palestinians allowed the Druze PSP to assert itself in bourgeois Ra's Beirut and Hizballah to subvert Amal in the southern suburbs. Sunni politicians and Shi'is connected to Amal repeatedly appealed for Syrian military intervention, the former in despair and the latter for reinforcement. Syria, however, still wished to avoid involvement; Asad preferred not to have Syrian troops absorbed in police functions in West Beirut while East Beirut continued to be defiant, and direct management of local affairs implied responsibility for Hizballah and Western hostages held by Shi'i radicals. Syria did contribute some hundreds of personnel to a July 1986 "security plan" arranged by Syrian military intelligence, but the operation quickly fell apart and the episode must have confirmed the reluctance of the doubters in Damascus. In consequence there were no restraints on the drift toward conflict between Amal and the PSP, or on a Hizballah takeover of much of the southern suburbs. Although Amal wanted the leftist parties cut down to size and perhaps desired a dramatic deterioration to test Syrian reliability, the PSP and Hizballah were the dynamic elements.

Syria's crisis came in the battles of 16–21 February 1987, when the PSP and its leftist partners worsted Amal in much of Ra's Beirut, the heart of West Beirut. Junblatt may have sensed that Syrian vacillations through 1986 would permit him to establish a strong foothold in Beirut, which was economically and politically important for the PSP. The

215

fighting was preceeded by a big Lebanese Communist gathering in the Druze town of Ba'aqlin, away from Syrian monitoring and attended by a senior Soviet official. At about the same time Hizballah indicated its independent-mindedness to Damascus by briefly seizing a dozen Syrian special forces soldiers and a Christian envoy closely associated with Syria. The February 1987 crisis presented Syria with the danger that its principal ally, Amal, would be displaced in Beirut by less amenable parties with non-Syrian external connections, and that 'Arafatist penetration would become uncontrollable.

On 22 February, after days of debate in the Syrian high command, 8,000 Syrian troops descended through 'Aley and Dammour to be deployed throughout West Beirut, except in the Palestinian camps and the southern suburbs. This was a premature move for the Syrian leadership, which regarded its hand as having been forced. The Syrian army hinted that it might enter the southern suburbs and curb Hizballah, an indication to the US of a "contract" if Syrian requirements were satisfied elsewhere, starting with reduction of East Beirut. Israel was delighted to see the Syrians become so enmeshed in Beirut, especially against 'Arafat, and only warned against any move south of the Awali.[130]

On 24 February, as part of a drive to remove militias from Ra's Beirut, a Syrian detachment invaded the Hizballah headquarters in Basta, killing 24 people. Hizballah mobilized large demonstrations against "the massacre" and Iran warned that it could make Syria's presence in West Beirut untenable. Damascus promptly retreated, denying any intention to enter the southern suburbs, and Syrian-Iranian relations resumed their normal course with a check for Syria. In a March 1987 interview[131] Hizballah's spiritual guide, Muhammad Husayn Fadlallah, criticized "those" who raised the subject of "security in the suburbs" and wished to strike at "particular factions."

For Syria, punishment of the Druze and leftists for their insubordination represented a top priority after Syrian deployment in West Beirut. This would also curtail 'Arafatist influence outside the camps. Amal was restored as the leading local force, but as an outright Syrian agent.[132] Clearance of militia arms and offices from Ra's Beirut was particularly directed against the PSP and its associates, and PSP access to its ports was squeezed,[133] causing Junblatt financial problems. The Syrian army occupied a corridor for its communications through the Shuf to Beirut and spread down the coast to the Awali river, in a notable territorial encroachment on Junblatt's "canton." Syrian forces detained many PSP and Communist operatives, and Syria's military intelligence chief, 'Ali Duba, gave Junblatt four foolscap pages of names of people for immediate delivery to Syria.[134] Junblatt's humiliation continued in the following months. Syria blamed the PSP for attempts to disrupt Syrian security measures. In June 1987, PSP officials in West Beirut hurriedly left for Mukhtara. Junblatt was forced to hand over a senior aide to the Syrians and to purge his command in favor of party members acceptable to Damascus. This caused severe discontent among the Druze population. Junblatt gloomily defined his choices as "the sea, Israel, or Syria."[135]

West Beirut under Syria

Asad's objective in West Beirut through 1987 and 1988 was to stabilize Syrian control at the least possible cost—to hold the situation until the end of President Jumayyil's term in September 1988. By April 1987, about three-quarters of the 8,000-man Syrian contingent that had entered West Beirut had been pulled back to the Aramun hills overlooking the airport, from where they could intimidate the Druze and reinforce units left in the urban area. Secular and religious Sunni leaders got, for a time, the quieter streets they had long demanded, but new orders went out for suspension of flirtations with East Beirut—no repeat, for example, of a meeting between the Chief Mufti and the Maronite patriarch. However, the Syrians carefully avoided hostilities on the main front with East Beirut. In the southern suburbs, excluded from Syrian deployment into 1988, Amal was expected to guard the status quo but Hizballah was left to its own devices. In June 1987, Syria re-emphasized its alliance with Iran[136] and apparently told Tehran not to take contrary indications seriously. As for the Palestinian camps, the Syrians wished to take decisive action but were constrained by Soviet and Arab pressures; Asad visited Moscow in April 1987 and found Gorbachev unforthcoming on aid to Syria and unhappy with

Syrian policy in Lebanon.[137] The survival of significant 'Arafatist pockets containing 1,000 fighters in Shatila and Burj al-Barajina nagged at Asad, and Syrian troops made a tight cordon around the two camps.

Syria's "waiting game" was interrupted on 1 June 1987, when Prime Minister Rashid Karami was assassinated in a bomb explosion on a Lebanese army helicopter. A few weeks earlier Karami had indicated his unhappiness with the paralysis of the regime by declaring his intention to resign. At the time, Karami was involved in secretive contacts about ending the 1969 Cairo agreement, which legitimized the Palestinian military presence in Lebanon, and resolving the government deadlock. On the latter subject Karami had reportedly reached an understanding with Dani Chamoun, son of ex-president Camille Chamoun and a leading East Beirut political personality, on the council of ministers being established as an institution autonomous from the presidency.[138] Such a contact, if not coordinated with Damascus, would have violated the primary Syrian directive to West Beirut leaders. For their part, the LF and the Palestinians suspected Karami's attempt to resurrect the regime. The army command regarded itself as the target of a scheme to discredit the military institution, as Karami was killed while under army protection.[139] East Beirut elements and the Syrians could both have had an interest in such a scheme.

Whoever was responsible for the assassination, Syria seized the opportunity to force together West Beirut's squabbling factions against East Beirut. Contacts between President Jumayyil and the traditionalist Sunni-Shi'i establishment, by which Salim al-Huss became acting prime minister, brought a furious Syrian reaction. At a meeting in Tripoli after Karami's funeral Syrian Vice President Khaddam subjected both Huss and Shi'i parliamentary speaker Husayn al-Husayni to stinging rebukes,[140] and West Beirut's go-between to Jumayyil, Muhammad Shuqayr, was shot dead in his apartment shortly thereafter. West Beirut leaders agreed that Jumayyil must pinpoint blame for Karami's death, implying the LF, and purge the army command for negligence before any renewed communications between themselves and the presidency.

Otherwise, however, Syria's impetus soon fizzled. Damascus could not impose extreme measures, for example a succession of resignations to make the presidency unviable,[141] as traditional Islamic leaders feared these would cause formal partition. Junblatt loudly attacked Jumayyil and the army, earning an accolade from Khaddam, but his agenda had nothing in common with that of Syria—he kept his "back door" to East Beirut through his friend Dani Chamoun.

The Amal-Hizballah war complicated West Beirut politics from early 1988 on. After Amal's pre-emptive attack against Hizballah positions around Nabatiyya in April 1988, a Hizballah response in Beirut's southern suburbs was inevitable. Coordinating with powerful radicals in Tehran through the Iranian embassy, Hizballah plotted to overrun Beirut's Shi'i areas, where it had a military advantage over Amal's poorly disciplined forces, and then to demand a restoration for itself in southern Lebanon. Hizballah quietly brought reinforcements from the Biqa' and linked with 'Arafat's network in the neighboring Burj al-Barajina camp, developments apparently not properly monitored by the Syrians. Hizballah struck without warning on 6 May and achieved most of its objectives within three days. Amal found itself restricted to the northern quarters of Ghubayra and al-Shiyya, and Hizballah slowly eroded this residual presence over the next two weeks. Syria was caught off balance and wanted a peaceable outcome—relations with Iran must not be upset, especially as the U.S. still offered no pay-off for a Syrian crackdown on "extremist [i.e. Hizballah] activities." [142]

On 13 May, Amal, its commanders disgusted by the lack of Syrian back-up,[143] abandoned responsibility for the outer perimeter of the southern suburbs, which allowed Hizballah fighters to surge into the area of the Syrian deployment, stimulating street disturbances. Syria now had no choice about taking action, but both it and Hizballah edged toward a cooperative approach. In late May, Asad took the unusual step of inviting Hizballah leaders to Ladhiqiyya, where they agreed not to oppose Syrian entry to the suburbs in exchange for preservation of Hizballah assets.[144] 3,500 Syrian soldiers then moved into the southern suburbs, although they were soon replaced by an ineffectual Lebanese internal security force.

Syria maintained its authority in Beirut, kept its alliance with Iran, and quietened the suburbs. Badly shattered, even before two further rounds of inconclusive internecine fighting in southern Lebanon in

1988–90, the Shi'i community faced calamity in the Lebanon of the late 1980s—the promise of the Shi'i surge of 1984 was unfulfilled.

As the emergency in the suburbs subsided, Syria lost no time in eliminating the residual 'Arafatist presence in West Beirut. Only months remained of Jumayyil's presidency and Asad wanted no distractions. Fortuitously, Syria did not need Amal on this occasion; 'Arafat's 1988 "peace strategy" toward Israel ensured that Palestinian dissidents could be relied upon for the last push. Clashes in the camps during May broke months of calm, and through June Abu Musa's Fatah rebels ate into Shatila and Burj al-Barajina. A novel feature of these events was Syrian success in isolating the 'Arafatists from other Lebanese and Palestinian groups. After his 1987 experience Junblatt did not dare cross Asad, and the PSP condemned "the 'Arafat rightist deviation."[145] PLO affiliates like the PFLP and the PDFLP took a neutral stance and the Fatah commander in Burj al-Barajina remarked bitterly: "We fought alone as our allies had their own calculations . . . until now they are not aware of the full dimensions of the conspiracy."[146] Shatila and Burj al-Barajina, deserted by civilians and largely pulverized, fell to Abu Musa's troops on 28 June and 8 July respectively, and hundreds of 'Arafat's loyalists left for the PLO stronghold in Sidon.

In the event, quiet in West Beirut did not help the Syrians to impose a Syrian-oriented Lebanese president. As long as East Beirut maintained its cohesion, West Beirut had only limited relevance. Trouble in West Beirut could wreck Syrian maneuvering against the Maronites, but even a unified front of "Islamic and nationalist" forces could not decisively help Syria. East Beirut checkmated Syrian-American arrangements for a new president and on 23 September 1988 Amin Jumayyil departed office with no successor. Lebanon now had no president and two governments: a military council in East Beirut, appointed by Jumayyil as an interim authority and headed by the army commander, General Aoun, and a West Beirut rump of the pre-existing civilian council of ministers under Salim al-Huss, who claimed the right to continue in office.

Syria looked ahead to a long tussle with Aoun and made it plain that it expected the West Beirut parties not just to behave themselves, but to put pressure on East Beirut. Iran's summer 1988 defeat in the Iran-Iraq war freed Iraq to make trouble for Syria in Lebanon, via the Christians, but also advantaged Syria in the Iranian-Syrian relationship. For the moment Iranian passivity gave Syria a freer hand with Lebanon's Shi'is. As a result, Amal-Hizballah disturbances in Beirut bothered Syria less and less. In late November 1988, the Syrians even allowed an outburst of street fighting in West Beirut—the first serious disruption in the bourgeois districts since February 1987—to persist for several days before restoring order. This reminded the Sunnis and others of their need for Damascus.

Apart from overseeing the Shi'is, Syria was concerned to keep the PSP and Sunni traditionalists in line. As a first challenge to Aoun and a "loyalty test," Syria insisted that the Huss cabinet appoint a new army commander. Syria wanted to reorganize Lebanese army units outside East Beirut as a surrogate force, as militias had proved themselves unreliable. Junblatt, who viewed a formal splitting of the army as a boost for cantons, was happy to promote the idea; Acting Prime Minister Salim al-Huss and Muslim conservatives tried to stall. However, they soon bowed to intimidation. In mid-November 1988 the Huss cabinet made Brigadier Sami al-Khatib provisional army chief, although without formally dismissing Aoun. Aoun's military council reacted angrily. Syria thus drew the battle lines for the next stage of the Lebanese drama.

East Beirut and the Christian sector

East Beirut as the leading "canton"

By the late 1980s East Beirut, which had been hard pressed in 1983–84, had regained some of its self-confidence. The alignment of its Lebanese opponents had fallen apart and it survived as the strongest of Lebanon's sectarian citadels. The difference with respect to 1982, when it had seemed that the Israeli invasion might renew Maronite political supremacy, was that East Beirut was now permanently on the defensive. The Syrian resurgence and the collapse of the Christian presence in almost the whole southern part of Mount Lebanon—the Shuf and Sidon hills—meant that the old days of Christian primacy were gone for good, even apart from the relentless shift in Lebanon's demography.

The combination of East Beirut's strong strategic position and Maronite political decline encouraged the LF militia to press its federalist project on the Christian population. "Federalism" in the late 1980s meant Christian political separatism based on East Beirut, shorn of the militia's earlier ambitions to dominate other parts of Lebanon. The LF paid lip service to Greater Lebanon as a federation of cantons, a concept they shared with the PSP after the Druze had secured the Shuf—Junblatt asserted privately that "the reality of this country is cantons."[147]

The Christian population of East Beirut, despite Maronite phobia about subordination to Muslims, was never converted to Christian separatism and swung decisively against it when Michel Aoun entered the political arena. First, the militia advocates of "federalism" faced an uphill battle for popular sympathy after the LF's military fiascos in the mid-1980s, and because of the plainly self-serving character of the project. Second, the LF's extralegal status compromised its acceptability to Christians, who endured the militia because of its defensive military function but who otherwise preferred rule by "legitimate" authorities. Third, Christian separatism was of no interest to most of the 40% of East Beirut's inhabitants who were refugees from elsewhere in Lebanon. Many of the refugees, who squatted in substandard accommodation, hated their enforced sojourn in the "canton." Fourth, the currency collapse of the 1980s made cantons an unattractive economic option.

According to the population estimates based on the 1988 Hariri Foundation food distribution "head count" (Faour, 1988) the East Beirut area then had a population of 827,183, which was 99.3% Christian. This represented almost two-thirds of Lebanon's total resident Christians, up from considerably less than half before 1975. In East Beirut the Hariri Foundation was not permitted to collect data other than household addresses, in contrast to other areas, so there may have been some undercounting; East Beirut sources claimed a population of one million. A slightly higher East Beirut population than the Hariri count would of course only accentuate the wartime geographical concentration of Lebanon's Christians. Outside East Beirut in 1988 about 26% of Lebanon's Christians lived in the Syrian-controlled zone, including West Beirut; 4% were in Israeli-dominated territory; and 3% were in the Shuf and "liberated" southern Lebanon.[148] Overall East Beirut contained about one-quarter of Lebanon's people in the late 1980s, on 20% of the country's territory.

Despite being only a small segment of Lebanon, East Beirut was the most important internal element in Lebanon's crisis in the late 1980s. In economic terms it had become Lebanon's industrial core, with 80% of national manufacturing capacity[149] and the bulk of service facilities. From the political perspective it contained the main surviving apparatus of the Lebanese regime, centered on the presidency at Ba'abda, the defense ministry at Yarza, and the foreign ministry in Ashrafiyya. East Beirut, as the redoubt of the Maronite community, also highlighted the main issue in Lebanese politics—the privileged constitutional position of Christians in general and Maronites in particular. In strategic terms East Beirut was the base of the two most powerful Lebanese military forces—four intact brigades of the Lebanese army, and the LF militia. Its very existence blocked Syria's campaign to control Lebanon.

East Beirut presented an often misinterpreted face to the outside. It was an unattractive entity, its structure riven with competing mafias. It had a certain respectability only by comparison with the more dismal conditions prevailing in "Islamic and nationalist" Lebanon. However, as long as East Beirut preserved a minimal coherence among its power centers, it was much less vulnerable to internal disruption than its opponents supposed. Syria hoped that the political boycott imposed on East Beirut after the latter's coup against the Tripartite Agreement would cause sufficient financial chaos to bring capitulation; Khaddam reportedly observed to a Zahla notable: "Syria can wait . . . Let's see who will pay your salaries."[150] Economic deterioration continued, but it did not have the political effects anticipated in Damascus. West Beirut suffered more than East Beirut and in both the Christian and Islamic sectors sentiment trended against Syria and the militias, and in favor of radical options—General Aoun and Hizballah.

East Beirut had a multipolar political structure, which was to be its downfall, but until September 1988 the Lebanese presidency played a restraining role. The most powerful military element—the Lebanese army—was the least visible political factor until 1988. The defense ministry at Yarza emerged from the stormy years of the mid-1980s with an armed force of about 16,000 men, rotating its four combat brigades between the fronts facing the Syrians and the Syrian-allied militias in the Matn, Suq al-Gharb, and West Beirut (map 10). Its main assets were about 50 new 155-mm howitzers and about 120 tanks—kept in East Beirut since their importation from the U.S. in 1983. The army command under General Aoun was in theory subordinate to Defense Minister Adil 'Usayran, a Shi'i traditional politician in West Beirut, but in practice coordinated with President Jumayyil as its "commander-in-chief."

The army command's concept of East Beirut had little in common with that of the LF militia—the "canton's" other armed force. Particularly for General Aoun and his closest colleagues, East Beirut simply represented a territory from which legitimate state authority, meaning the army, would seek to reach out again to the rest of Lebanon. In the late 1970s, when the army had fragmented, Christian officers had collaborated with Bashir Jumayyil against the Palestinians and others, and the army chief of the early 1980s, Ibrahim Tannus, had the reputation of defender of the old-style Maronite-dominated regime. Aoun, however, was a Maronite who carefully shunned identification with his community's political privileges. After 1983, up to 20% of army manpower in East Beirut was Sunni or Shi'i and much of the Christian 80% came from peripheral rural areas outside East Beirut—the northern Biqa', the 'Akkar, and southern Lebanon. In addition, the army command maintained professional and personal links with the largely non-Christian brigades in the rest of Lebanon. Most of these units were moribund and under heavy militia and Syrian pressure, but they still represented a nationwide network. Aoun and his circle were committed to the indivisibility of the army, thought in terms of Lebanon as a whole, and regarded themselves as the sole remaining official institution not compromised by connections with militias or foreign powers.

Until 1988, Aoun was content to keep a low public profile and to leave the political role to President Jumayyil, on the understanding that the presidency would not sign away Lebanon's independence to Syria and would stay aloof from the LF. The LF, on the other hand, was politically aggressive and regarded the East Beirut Christian base as its own creation, to which it had a proprietary right. The LF and its old parent organization, the Kata'ib, remained a formidable political-military apparatus. The militia slipped out of the hands of the Jumayyils between 1982 and 1985 when Bashir and Pierre died and Amin became president of the republic. Leadership passed to Bashir's militant young lieutenants, while Amin Jumayyil retained influence in the Kata'ib party and a small private militia in the Matn district.

In the late 1980s, the LF under Samir Ja'ja' had perhaps 10,000 armed members and an artillery capacity not much inferior to that of the army. It was the most sophisticated of the illicit armed organizations that flourished in Lebanon after 1975 (Snider, 1984). The LF intruded on the daily lives of the people: it ran ports, took taxes from houses, restaurants, and crossing points to other parts of Lebanon, had a lucrative interest in the Junya casino, and established a popular television channel. It tried to extend itself as a social and political movement but came up against the increasingly chilly attitude of the population toward it and its sectarian emphasis. At this time the Kata'ib diverged somewhat from the LF as a vehicle for more cautious, conservative Christian politicians who looked to pluralism rather than to sectarian mini-states. In June 1986, Dr. George Sa'adah was elected Kata'ib leader with LF support, which was interpreted as a defeat for President Jumayyil's loyalists, but the party proved resistant to Ja'ja's aspirations to coordinate it with the LF.

For the army command, the LF was at best a nuisance. Through the mid-1980s the attitudes of senior Christian officers toward the Christian militia became less tolerant than in the days of Bashir Jumayyil. The army reorganization of 1983 and the successful defense of Suq al-Gharb inspired confidence that the army could protect the fronts by itself, while the feud between Hubayqa and Ja'ja', together with the Tripartite Agreement, led the army command to perceive the LF as a destabilizing influence. When Hubayqa set up a Syrian-backed operation in Zahla in 1986, the army worried about Syrian sabotage in

East Beirut via Hubayqa's LF channels. Later, when Ja'ja' aspired to extend the LF as a "state within the state," the army command became suspicious about what it saw as LF attempts to infiltrate its brigades.[151] The smaller East Beirut parties such as the National Liberals, the Tanzim, and the Guardians of the Cedars, forced together with the Kata'ib in the late 1970s, found the army a more congenial associate than the militia in the late 1980s, which complicated political interactions.

Aside from the army, the LF, the Kata'ib, and their associates, several traditional political elements also played their part in the workings of East Beirut. Most prominently, the presidency of Amin Jumayyil served as a buffer between the army and the LF. Two experienced and capable Orthodox presidential advisors—former foreign minister Elie Salem and *al-Nahar* publisher Ghassan Tuwayni—acted to calm the army command and the LF leadership at difficult moments and to ensure that President Jumayyil pursued his contacts beyond East Beirut in such a way as not to cause internal crises. Their objective was to preserve East Beirut's stability in the wait for a compromise on reintegrating Lebanon—they opposed the LF's federalism. Also, Jumayyil's maneuverings to block Ja'ja's designs on the Kata'ib in 1987–88 caused occasional firefights between Jumayyil's militiamen and LF personnel. Probably the most tense episode inside East Beirut came in June 1987 after the assassination of Prime Minister Rashid Karami, when senior officers became convinced there was an LF plot to discredit the military institution among Muslims. Presidential advisors were involved in defusing the situation.

The Maronite church—the patriarchate, the bishops, and the monastic orders—had great moral and material weight within the largest Christian community, but its influence depended on a delicate balancing act between factions. In April 1986, Maronite bishops elected Nasrallah Butros Sufayr to replace Cardinal Quraysh as Maronite patriarch—spiritual head of the community—but neither personality was viewed by the East Beirut factions as being of much political consequence. Some in the monastic orders, most visibly Abbot Bulos Na'aman, had political involvements, but this was an individual more than an institutional activity. Overall, there was no possibility of the church or patriarch replacing the presidency as a "switchboard" between East Beirut's two military power centers after President Jumayyil left office in 1988.

Most personalities from the bourgeois Christian establishment, including leaders of prominent families, religious dignitaries, ex-ministers and members of parliament, were not much noticed in the late 1980s. The establishment had been eclipsed with the rise of Bashir Jumayyil in the late 1970s; the "Lebanese Front" ceased to be relevant in 1978 when Sulayman Faranjiyya took most northern Christians out of it, and the young militants of the LF took control of a truncated Christian enclave. Conservative politicians and religious figures tended to be adjuncts of the presidency. They preserved ties with their Sunni and Shi'i counterparts, also sidelined through the 1980s.

The deaths of Pierre Jumayyil in 1984 and Camille Chamoun in 1987 removed true leaders, even if they were men whose vision was unacceptable to non-Christians, and left an assortment of lesser bourgeois personalities, whose chief motivation was the maintenance of privilege by whatever means. Their political significance was that they and their Islamic equivalents comprised the Lebanese parliament, which had extended its own mandate every four years since the last elections in 1972, and which voted for a new president of the republic every six years. When Amin Jumayyil's 'ahd drew to a close in September 1988 and the presidency became vacant, the parliamentarians assumed a salience they had not attained in the presidential elections of 1976 and 1982, when new presidents had been installed relatively swiftly. In 1988–89, the old parliament became viewed by the Syrians, Americans, and Saudis as the appropriate instrument for rewriting the constitution and undercutting the inconvenient General Aoun.

Developments, 1986–89

For East Beirut the course of events in the late 1980s was dominated by the continuing tussle with Syria over the orientation of Lebanon and its regime, as illustrated by Christian repudiation of the Tripartite Agreement and the presidential contest of 1988.

For nine months after the January 1986 demise of the Tripartite

Agreement, Syria campaigned to crack East Beirut. President Jumayyil's home town of Bikfaya was heavily bombarded, Hubayqa's agents tried to subvert Ja'ja's command of the LF, a succession of car bombs terrorized civilians, and in September 1986 Ashrafiyya was briefly seized in an unprecedented militia incursion from West Beirut, masterminded by Hubayqa and Syrian military intelligence. These activities, however, strengthened East Beirut's cohesion, while West Beirut bosses failed to back Syria. For the first time, Syrian forces had to engage the Lebanese army directly in artillery duels[152]—an embarrassing development.

Jumayyil, Ja'ja', and Aoun were forced to coordinate their policies, and a rare combined response of the army and the LF stopped the September incursion into Ashrafiyya: the army closed the front behind the invading militamen and the LF finished them off. Ja'ja' contained disaffection within the LF by importing more of his own circle from the north—from Jubayl and his home town of Bsharri. The Ashrafiyya incursion also exposed Hubayqa's agents, which enabled a purge. By late 1986, the Syrians gave up their siege and fell back on the political boycott of President Jumayyil.

Syria did not try to break the stalemate until the last months of Amin Jumayyil's presidency. However, at the November 1987 Arab summit meeting in Amman, Hafiz al-Asad refused mediation by the Jordanian and Moroccan monarchs and articulated his frustration with East Beirut: "No meeting with President Jumayyil can be profitable in the last nine months of his term when he didn't give anything in our discussions with him over five years[153] . . . We met more than eleven times [and] we agreed every time on steps to bring the reunification of Lebanon and to achieve political reform . . . He went back on everything afterwards . . . I fear he will exploit [a meeting] and explain it according to his taste when he returns to Lebanon, distorting it as he does every time."[154]

In East Beirut a consensus on political reform was brokered by the Maronite patriarchate and transferred to Damascus as Jumayyil's final "constitutional proposal" in early 1988. It adopted ideas from the 1976 Faranjiyya document and the national conferences of 1983–84, such as Christian/non-Christian equality in parliament. It also suggested reduction of sectarianism in the allocation of official functions and adjusting the balance between the presidency and the council of ministers. It did not budge on a powerful Maronite presidency, or on resistance to Syria's concept of "privileged relations" with Lebanon.

In February 1988 the U.S. intervened in this unpromising environment with a visit to Damascus by Undersecretary of State for Middle East Affairs Richard Murphy, after Syria indicated interest in American involvement. By 1988, the Syrians had redone their calculations and concluded that a Syrian-American deal over the heads of the Lebanese was the only way to establish Syrian hegemony; when U.S. Secretary of State George Schultz stopped in Damascus in March 1988, the Syrians carefully separated failure to reach an understanding on Middle East issues from the Lebanese question.

The U.S. was concerned to avoid Jumayyil's departure from office causing an upheaval, with regional implications, at a time of concentration on Arab-Israeli issues as the Palestinian *intifada* developed. The U.S. had fully returned to its 1976 stance of viewing Syria as a useful policeman. The difference between the two occasions was that in 1976 the U.S. perceived the problem as secular political radicalism backed by the Soviet Union, whereas by the mid-1980s U.S. fears about militant Islamic revivalism became the overriding consideration. In both 1976 and 1988, the U.S. saw Lebanon as a hotbed of "radical" forces. Likewise, in both 1976 and 1988, the U.S. grappled with the contradictions of making concessions to Syria's power in Lebanon while claiming to support Lebanon's independence, and protecting communities while pressing for a fairer distribution of powers in the political system.

Syria's view of any deal with Washington was limited and hardheaded. In exchange for Syrian restraint of "terror," delivery of foreign hostages held by Shi'i Islamists, and discouragement of provocations against Israel, the U.S. would endorse Syrian primacy in Lebanon, support Lebanese presidential candidates with "programs" acceptable to Damascus, and restrict Israeli activity in southern Lebanon. Syria hoped that strain within East Beirut over the presidential succession and forceful American mediation with Christian bosses might at last "deliver" the Maronites, and lead to the election of a Syrian-inclined president.

In 1988, however, neither East Beirut nor the U.S. satisfied Syrian expectations. In April, Jumayyil and the LF rejected American-Syrian ideas for reforms to be implemented by the incoming president,[155] perceiving a phased imposition of the hated Tripartite Agreement. East Beirut exuded confidence through the summer—Syria was diverted by the inter-Shi'i war, no credible military threat existed, and a presidential vacuum had partitionary implications attractive to LF "federalists." With 25 of the surviving 77 parliamentary deputies resident in East Beirut, attempts to compel the election of a Syrian-oriented president could be instantly aborted, and one presidential source dismissed consideration of political reform for the foreseeable future.[156] As for the Americans, non-activation of "understandings" reached with the Syrians in April led to a cooling in Syrian-American exchanges until only a week before the presidential conjunction in September.

Syria's electoral tactic in August–September 1988 was to promote ex-president Faranjiyya for the presidency, to put pressure on the U.S. to accept an already ·prepared substitute candidate[156]—'Akkar deputy Mikhail Daher, whose "program" satisfied Syrian and West Beirut requirements. Army commander Michel Aoun also showed his hand as a presidential aspirant, seeking to raise his nationwide credibility with sharp criticism of the LF.[158] Jumayyil and Ja'ja' drew together to block him, but the frigid Syrian reaction to Aoun's emergence ensured that the three East Beirut personalities quickly repaired their relations. Iraq, more free to pursue its vendetta against Asad following the August 1988 cease-fire in the Iran-Iraq war, promoted East Beirut's rejection of Syria—the first big Iraqi arms shipment to the LF was unloaded in Beirut port on 16 August.[159]

On 13 September, Undersecretary Murphy headed an American delegation to Damascus after appeals by the Vatican, Saudi Arabia, and even the Soviet Union for a bid to break the deadlock. The U.S. had its own purposes. On the one hand, collaborating with Syria on a joint candidate for the Lebanese presidency would improve relations with the Syrian regime and might shock East Beirut into a review of the Christian position in Lebanon. At the same time, the certain collapse of the joint candidacy would ensure that Syria gained nothing practical and would need Washington again. After three days of discussions,

Murphy told Khaddam that if Damascus gave up Faranjiyya, whom the Americans regarded as unsuitable, it could have whatever candidate it wanted. The Syrians promptly proposed Mikhail Daher and the Americans departed to inform Christian leaders about the Syrian-American "name."

The entire East Beirut leadership—army command, militia, presidency, and patriarchate—condemned the "imposition" as a trangression of Lebanon's sovereignty and made clear their intention to wreck Daher's candidacy by boycotting the 22 September parliamentary session. The Americans disappointed the Syrians by not dragooning the Maronites and the electoral process fell apart. President Jumayyil made a surprise move as a power broker by visiting Damascus a day before leaving office, but only ensured his own political burial—the Syrians were scornful and East Beirut was furious. On the same day, Iraqi and Egyptian efforts brought a public linkage between General Aoun and LF chief Samir Ja'ja'—noteworthy considering the tension between the general and the militia. Jumayyil spent his last hours as president trying to avoid appointing a military government by sounding out various Maronites and Salim al-Huss. Every avenue was closed by vetoes from West or East Beirut and literally at 10 minutes to midnight Jumayyil issued a decree establishing a temporary military administration headed by Aoun as prime minister.

Lebanon's two prime ministers—Michel Aoun in East Beirut and Salim al-Huss in West Beirut—naturally refused to recognize each other. Aoun's military council, entirely Christian due to the refusal of the three appointed non-Christian officers to participate after warnings from Damascus, based its authority on presidential decree. Huss's cabinet, minus two of its three remaining Christian ministers, asserted that the decree flouted custom and constitutional requirements: the prime minister should be a Sunni, and the president could not by exclusive fiat create a government or have the same person simultaneously army commander and prime minister. However, Aoun and Huss shared an aspiration for a united Lebanon; certainly they had more in common with each other than they had with the militia chiefs. Circumstances rather than goals were to keep them apart.

After September 1988, a much less stable relationship of forces existed within East Beirut. The army command now regarded itself as the legitimate government of Lebanon and intended to use East Beirut as the base from which to reach out to all Lebanese, especially Sunni and Shi'i Muslims, and from which to reassert government authority in broader territories. The problem was that the army command's "partner" in East Beirut, the LF militia, saw the presidential vacancy as an opportunity to make the Maronite territorial redoubt a distinct political entity, and had no interest in reaching out to Muslim Lebanese. Both the army and the LF termed East Beirut "the liberated area," but for the former it was a starting point and for the latter the end point. The communications exchange that Jumayyil's presidency had provided for several years disappeared.

Developments in East Beirut in the first few months of the presidential vacancy help explain the violent upheavals that rocked Lebanon in 1989–90. Aoun felt pressed for time in registering himself as a Lebanese national leader and soon saw his temporary understanding with the LF, a tactic to compel Jumayyil to establish the military council, as a liability that damaged his reputation among Muslims. For its part the LF, fearful of Aoun's populism, sought to imprison Aoun in their camp and to erode his credibility. In October 1988, Ja'ja' took over Jumayyil's area of influence in the Matn, absorbing the former president's militia followers and media assets into the LF. At first Aoun tried to ignore the challenge, asserting in an October interview with *al-Majalla* that LF leaders had accepted a "total [national] solution" encompassing an end to militias and separate political projects.[160] Nonetheless the military council, which claimed sole legitimacy in all Lebanon, could not indefinitely coexist in its base area with a militia that controlled the ports, collected taxes, and generally behaved like a state apparatus.

Aoun's dilemma was that he could not sustain limitations on the LF, for example closing their ports, without parallel limitations on militias in the rest of Lebanon. This required Syrian cooperation. Aoun therefore made an early attempt to open a dialogue with Damascus, referring to Syria as the "nearest neighbor" whose interests Lebanon was "committed to guard."[161] Syrian leaders, however, viewed Aoun's "coup" in succeeding Jumayyil as an insult and the Syrian media urged the

Lebanese "to overthrow this government, and so destroy the Zionist project which it carries and works to implement."[162] Aoun responded by equating the Syrian and Israeli "occupations" of Lebanese territory. Aoun's deepening difficulties with the militia within East Beirut and Syria's blockage of relief from those difficulties put him on the path toward his 1989 "war of liberation" against Syria, and toward a disturbance of the status quo in the Eastern Mediterranean.

PART THREE

Lebanon after the Cold War

The regime, corruption, and the ordinary citizen
(Yasin al-Khalil in *al-Safir,* 6 November 1993)

bas yizoob at-talj wa yibayyan al-khara'
Just let the snow melt and the shit will appear
—LEBANESE SAYING

Neither Syria's achievement of full command of the Lebanese in October 1990 nor its enforced military withdrawal from Lebanon in April 2005 could have occurred without the decisive role of the United States. In 1990, Washington conceived Lebanon as a trouble spot in the Levant and Syria as a convenient stabilizer, whereas after the March/April 2003 Anglo-American occupation of Iraq Syria presented itself as a threat to U.S. interests. The difference had much to do with the quality of leadership in Damascus. Hafiz al-Asad, Syria's ruler from 1970 to 2000, was shrewd and subtle, able to appear simultaneously as frustrating and cooperative. He adjusted skillfully to the global supremacy of the U.S. when Syria lost its Soviet patron in the late 1980s. In contrast, his son Bashar, Syrian president after June 2000, quickly proved rigid and provocative, with a gambling streak in the style of Iraq's Saddam Husayn.

Iraq featured prominently in both the imposition and termination of Syrian hegemony in Lebanon. The U.S. allowed Hafiz al-Asad to overthrow the defiant General Michel Aoun and extend Syrian control over the East Beirut Christian enclave in late 1990 in exchange for Syrian involvement in the international coalition mobilized to reverse the Iraqi occupation of Kuwait. In late 2004, Bashar al-Asad's forcing an extended term for the Lebanese president, Emile Lahoud, provided Washington with the opportunity to reply decisively to Syrian support for the insurgency against the U.S. army in Iraq and the new Iraqi authorities. The first President George Bush thus covered Hafiz al-Asad in 1990, and his son George W. Bush removed the cover from Hafiz al-Asad's son fifteen years later.

Through the 1990s, Israel was the most important prop for Syria's domination of Lebanese domestic affairs and coordination of Lebanon's foreign policy. First, Israel's continued occupation of a "security belt" in southern Lebanon delivered the Shi'i Muslims, who by the late twentieth century constituted about one-third of Lebanon's population and the country's largest sectarian community, into Syrian hands. Hafiz al-Asad patronized the Shi'i Islamic radicals of Hizballah, who resisted the Israelis and whose popularity inflated with each new Israeli bombardment. Hizballah had a degree of autonomy, but Syria controlled its geographical link to its Iranian backers. Together with the weight of Syria's military and intelligence presence in Lebanon, this gave Syria the pivotal position in the Hizballah/Syrian/Iranian alignment.

Further, Israeli occupation justified indefinite maintenance of the Syrian presence. While the Israelis remained in southern Lebanon, any Lebanese criticism of Syria could be smeared as serving "the enemy," and no possibility existed of Lebanese dissent from the proposition that the Lebanese and Syrian "tracks" in peace discussions with Israel were inseparable. Also, both Israel and the U.S. hoped that Syria would tame Lebanese and Palestinian militants as part of a Syrian-Israeli deal— hence Israel and the U.S. favored the perpetuation of Syrian authority in Beirut. Both countries were disenchanted with the Lebanese Christians and fearful of the Lebanese Shi'is. Hafiz al-Asad knew how to play on Israeli and American ambivalence by occasional "good offices" in calming southern Lebanon.

What did Syria gain from its command of Lebanon after 1990? Despite Ba'thist Syria's lack of respect for Lebanon's existence as an independent state, evidenced by refusal to have normal diplomatic relations, Hafiz al-Asad's main concern was strategic predominance on Syria's western flank. The Syrian regime worried about unsettling external influences in Lebanon, whether the West through the Christians, Saudi Arabia through Sunni Muslims like Rafiq al-Hariri, one of the architects of the 1989 Ta'if Agreement, or Iran through the Shi'is. Lebanon also provided lifelines for the ramshackle Syrian economy after the resuscitation of the Lebanese state in the early 1990s. Profiteering and protection racket opportunities for Syrian officers and their Lebanese partners multiplied as Lebanon's reconstruction boomed on borrowed money in the mid-1990s. Lebanon became flooded with unregulated Syrian laborers, who competed with poorer Shi'is and remitted their earnings to Syria. This relieved the strain on Syria's labor market arising from its demographic bulge in younger age groups. Overall, command of Lebanon fed the power, prestige, and greed of the Syrian elite, as well as offering space to influence Islamic and militant organizations while maintaining deniability.

At the end of the 1980s, was Lebanon a "failed state" that required external control to recover stability and functioning government institutions? Certainly Lebanon needed assistance to negotiate an adjusted "national pact," but there were trends in the country in the late 1980s that indicated that, if permitted autonomy, it might have reestablished itself more easily than pessimists allowed. First, there was a strong, re-assertive civil society demanding restored central democratic authority, expressed in street protests by unions and other associations (Johnson, 2001, 227 and 257). Second, economic deterioration for the middle and lower classes in all communities through the 1980s, along with lawlessness and militia depredations, made the public extremely hostile to sectarian warlords. Third, the government and legislature remained intact, with the army continuing to attract respect as a "legitimate" institution, as demonstrated by the popularity of army commander Michel Aoun's call for state resurgence and an end to militias and foreign occupations.

What Lebanon actually received in 1990 was unique in the post–Cold War world. It can be summarized as domination by an authoritarian neighbor that had manipulated sectarian and political divisions through Lebanon's war period since 1975, domination sanctioned by the global superpower with the international community sidelined. The abortive December 1985 "tripartite agreement" among Lebanese militias, by which Syria sought to shackle Lebanon to Damascus without recourse to the Lebanese government, illustrated the contempt of Lebanon's aspirant overlord for the Lebanese state. Damascus responded to Maronite blockage by forbidding West Beirut politicians from interacting with the Lebanese president in East Beirut, thereby paralyzing the government until the end of President Jumayyil's term in late 1988. Such behavior made confronting Damascus or accepting Syrian dictation the only alternatives to militia fragmentation for the Lebanese.

Syria was initially embarrassed by General Michel Aoun's March 1989 "war of liberation" against it, but soon turned the affair to its advantage. Aoun's demand for Syrian withdrawal before political reform alienated Muslim and Druze leaders, while his supra-sectarian Lebanese nationalism terrified Maronite politicians and infuriated the Christian militia. The U.S. resented Lebanon's reappearance on the international agenda, considered Aoun a nuisance, and looked for the cheapest means of consigning Beirut to oblivion. Hafiz al-Asad was delighted to step forward as the solution. The U.S., Saudi Arabia, and Syria patronized a meeting of Lebanese parliamentarians in October 1989 in the Saudi resort town of Ta'if, away from Aoun. They agreed to reform the Lebanese constitution, and invited Syria to assist the Lebanese state in "extending its authority." There was no mention of Syrian withdrawal— simply "redeployment" after two years. As regards Syria's role in Lebanon, the Ta'if accord was a watered-down version of the 1985 "tripartite agreement," but it was adequate for Syrian purposes.

On 5 November 1989 the parliamentarians met again, in northern Lebanon, and elected Rene Mu'awwad as president. Mu'awwad was more an American/Saudi candidate than a Syrian one, and hinted at openness to Aoun. On 22 November, he was killed by a large car bomb. The parliamentarians then elected Ilyas al-Hirawi, a second-rank Maronite politician from the Biqa' and more convenient for Damascus. In consultation with Syria, Hirawi announced a government and appointed Emile Lahoud to replace Aoun as army commander.

1990 was a good year for Syria. Further violence made the Lebanese ready for any sort of peace, and Saddam Husayn's seizure of Kuwait made the Americans anxious to court Asad. Internecine fighting exhausted Shi'is and Maronites, Lebanon's leading communities of the 1980s. After two years of clashes the Amal secularists and the Hizballah Islamists confirmed their stalemate in a final convulsion in July 1990, with Syria teaching Iran its inferiority in Lebanon and much misery among Shi'is. Meanwhile, in February 1990 the Lebanese Forces militia of Samir Ja'ja' struck at Aoun within the Christian heartland. Months of fighting shattered East Beirut and reduced Aoun to a fraction of his 1989 strength. Nonetheless, Asad could not administer the coup de grâce to Aoun without U.S. acquiescence, which he extracted after attaching himself to the U.S.-led coalition against Iraq, and making a go-between trip to Iran for the Americans. He implemented the decisive assault on the Lebanese presidential palace at Ba'abda on 13 October 1990.

Syrian maritime siege of East Beirut, 1989
(photo by Dani Sfeir)

CHAPTER SEVEN

THE ADVENTURE OF MICHEL AOUN

Zahirat 'Awn (the Aounist phenomenon)

In the late 1980s, with Lebanon debilitated by more than a decade of warfare, it was not surprising that the country should produce the sort of convulsive reaction represented by the nationalist campaign of General Michel Aoun, commander of the Lebanese army after 1984. Because Aoun rose out of the ordinary Lebanese population, spontaneously expressed the mood of that population, had little interest in sectarian boundaries, and had a "clean" personal background in a legitimate state insitution, he was an aberrant political personality in late twentieth century Lebanon.

Aoun came from a lower-middle-class family in the mixed Maronite-Shi'i neighborhood of Harat Hurayk in Beirut's southern suburbs, which gave him a combination of popular and cross-sectarian personal associations unusual for a Maronite leader. From high school he went straight to the military academy and entered the officer corps during Fuad Shihab's term as army commander, in the late 1950s. Shihab's translation from the army to the presidency, in the style of Charles de Gaulle, and his use of the state to promote national cohesion undoubtedly influenced the young Aoun. Certainly Shihab was singular among Lebanese presidents although, unlike Aoun, he was not from the "popular" level of society. In late 1988 Aoun was reported as remarking that "Generals make the best presidents." [163]

Aoun steadily climbed in rank through the 1960s and 1970s, did artillery training courses in France and the United States during which he added competence in English to his French and Arabic, and became commander of the eighth brigade in the early 1980s. He achieved a strong rapport with his soldiers and put President Jumayyil in his debt when he held the Suq al-Gharb hill above the presidential palace during the 1983 mountain war. At the same time he had limited involvement with the East Beirut militias, unlike some other Christian officers, and so preserved his bridges to Shi'is and Sunnis through the difficult times of the army's disintegration after 1975. Aoun's apolitical professional military reputation earned him West Beirut's acquiesence for his appointment as army chief in 1984 and it was the central element in his political appeal four years later.

Aoun's secular nationalism reflected the Lebanese patriotism of the army's officer corps, or at least of that part of the officer corps not subordinate to militias or occupying powers. This was a source of both strength and weakness. Even after the renewed division of Beirut in 1984, with the army's nerve center in East Beirut partially severed from other regions, most officers and soldiers regarded themselves as a single organization under a unified command—despite sectarian segmentation of the brigades.

Equally important, as the Jumayyil presidency foundered and officialdom became a plaything of militias and mafias, the majority of the Lebanese people of all sects looked to the army as the only surviving repository of national legitimacy and public honesty. When the predominantly Christian brigades of the army in East Beirut came into confrontation with either the LF militia or the Syrian army they represented a Lebanese plurality, however briefly or imperfectly. For Aoun, such sentiment meant that the army in the late 1980s was the spearhead of a popular yearning for a restored Lebanese dignity and that it must lead a struggle against internal and external enemies. Just before plunging into his campaigns of 1989–90 he asserted: "Only [the military] together with the living force of our people can shatter the cell bars and release our captive country from the prison of foreign interests."[164]

The problem with the nationalism of Aoun and his senior officers in the late 1980s was that despite the secular tone the priorities betrayed a sectional outlook—that of military personnel with a predominantly Christian background. The emphasis went to removing foreign armies, especially the Syrians, before consideration of constitutional reform, and Aoun apparently saw no urgency about translating his personal preference for non-sectarian politics into a distinctive reform package. Certainly Aoun claimed to be Lebanese rather than Maronite, said he didn't care if the president was a Muslim, and scorned conservative Christian reformers.[165] When added to the popular dislike of the Syrians among non-Christians,[166] who had day-to-day experience of Syrian arbitrariness, this was enough to make West Beirut attentive and to give Aoun a cross-sectarian following. However, it was not enough to dissolve the suspicion separating Christians from non-Christians and to enable Aoun to head a united Lebanese movement above and beyond sectarianism, rather than being a Maronite leader who happened, uniquely, also to have a Muslim popular base.

To transcend sectarianism, Aoun would have had to propose specific constitutional adjustments to establish equity among Lebanese. He never did this, arguing that an understanding could not be achieved while West Beirut was constrained by a Syrian presence and while its leaders were not free agents—an argument rejected by West Beirut politicians. As a result, Damascus could still play on resentments of Maronite "privilege" and the army's historical association with the "Maronite regime." For all their own divisions, the non-Christian political bosses came together on one point, as expressed by Walid Junblatt: "It is impossible to reach a common denominator with Aoun . . . He wants to skip the internal conflict."[167] Most of the non-Christian leadership ranked priorities in the order: reforms, elections, Syrian withdrawal—the reverse of Aoun's priorities. This may not have reflected exactly the attitudes of the non-Christian population, but even the population wanted to see defined objectives for the Aounist enterprise. Aoun's real dilemma perhaps lay deeper in Lebanon's sectarian fabric: What would have been the impact on his mass Christian support if he had tried to energize his Muslim following with a constitutional proposal abolishing Maronite prerogatives? The inhabitants of Greater Lebanon may have become distinct from other Arabs, but could they ever be truly united under a new political dispensation?

Aoun's military background and approach also raised questions concerning his political competence and management of civil-military relations in a country that did not share the widespread Arab experience of interventions in politics by soldiers. When he moved into the Ba'abda presidential palace in September 1988 after his appointment as prime minister by the outgoing president, he surrounded himself with an "inner circle" of East Beirut associates of mainly military pedigree and dangerously limited political expertise.[168] He tended to distrust civilians, had little tolerance for the traditional political class, whether Christian or Muslim, detested militias, and had virtually no familiarity with the intricacies of international diplomacy.

Although his dismissal of Lebanese politicians as craven and corrupt was understandable, Aoun's distaste for civilian politics had serious consequences. First, a considerable East Beirut reservoir of experience in dealing with the outside world went unused; perspectives such as those of Jumayyil's former advisors were seen as too cautious and made little impact in Aoun's Ba'abda.[169] His "inner circle" held an image of the Middle East conditioned less by realistic analysis than by conspiracy theories concerning Syria and Israel and inflated views of likely international responses.[170] Second, the traditional political class staffed the Lebanese parliament which, although moribund, remained the only internationally recognized organ of constitutional change. Aoun's derisive attitude towards the old parliamentarians made it easier for the Americans and Saudis later to mobilize them against him.

Nonetheless, despite his failings, Aoun deserves note as the only democratic populist in the contemporary Arab world. Despite his reluctance to clarify his own relatively radical attitudes on constitutional reform—a strategic error in 1989–90, when he had to take risks with his Christian followers to undermine the Syrians in the Islamic sector—Aoun's declared purpose in trying to provoke international action to remove foreign forces from Lebanon was to clear the way for free elections, impossible under the "shadow of occupation," for a provisional assembly. This assembly, unlike the existing parliament, would have the popular legitimacy to determine political reforms. Aoun wanted to weaken the old ruling class and felt that the existing parliament had no right to make decisions for the people after almost two decades without elections. At the same time he always asserted his adherence to constitutional legality and his goal of resurrecting a democratic and sovereign Lebanese state.

How does Aoun compare with two other populists of Lebanon's war era—the Maronite Bashir Jumayyil and the Shi'i Musa Sadr? First, Aoun acquired a reputation for frankness and approachability—an empathy with ordinary people—unequalled by any other political personality since Lebanon's independence in 1943. Second, Aoun consistently put forward a nonsectarian commitment to the whole Lebanese people that had not been seen in Lebanon, at least not with any credibility, since the presidency of Fuad Shihab. Both Bashir Jumayyil and Musa Sadr were very much sectarian figures, who galvanized segments of Lebanon's population and whose legitimacy was grounded within those segments. Third, Aoun emerged from a state institution—the army—not from a militia (Jumayyil) or a sectarian religious hierarchy (Sadr). As army commander, Aoun had advantages of national institutional legitimacy over a lengthy period. Bashir Jumayyil only acquired such legitimacy for a few weeks after being elected president, and for many Lebanese this was compromised by Israel's involvement.

Finally, because Aoun survived the Syrian assault on Ba'abda in October 1990 he remained an active political influence in Lebanon even when not physically present. His following—tested in the popular boycott of the August/September 1992 parliamentary elections—persisted as the Lebanese people chafed under the Syrian-controlled regime.

Collision with Syria

Between September 1988 and March 1989 Aoun drifted erratically but steadily toward a showdown with the Syrians. Considerations of physical viability and nationalist ideology impelled Aoun's military council to seek to extend itself beyond East Beirut. Most immediately, this was necessary if the army was to sustain its political primacy over the LF militia within East Beirut. In consequence, there was no avoiding either a deal or an early confrontation with Syria, whose military presence encircled East Beirut.

On the regional level, the prospect of formal partition of Lebanon after the collapse of the 1988 presidential elections led to an Arab diplomatic intervention in Lebanon's crisis unprecedented since the mid-1970s. Principally, Iraq and some conservative regimes saw an opportunity to restrict Syria; in January 1989, Arab foreign ministers established a six-state committee chaired by Kuwait to survey solutions for Lebanon. The Iraqi foreign minister observed: "It is not permissible to leave one Arab state—Syria—to operate by itself in Lebanon."[171] Arab intervention angered Damascus and upset intra-Lebanese balances. Iraq encouraged Aoun's ambitions to bait Asad, and Iraqi arms shipments were accelerated with a new emphasis on Aoun's brigades as well as supplies for the LF militia. Iraqi largesse significantly augmented the military weight of East Beirut, forcing West Beirut elements, especially the Druze "canton," into greater dependence on Syria. It also strained the already difficult relations between the army and the LF within East Beirut—each resented the increased armed capacity of the other—an effect not appreciated by the Iraqis.

Arab committee activities exacerbated tensions. At the beginning of February 1989, Aoun made his only venture outside East Beirut during the lifetime of the military council when he, rival premier Salim al-Huss, and parliamentary speaker Husayni travelled to Tunis for sessions with the committee. Aoun made a better impression than Huss, received a measure of recognition, and registered his insistence on giving priority to a Syrian pullback, thus "freeing the Lebanese decision."[172] He also met 'Arafat, who talked about "putting the Palestinian gun" at Aoun's disposal "as a representative of the legality."[173] Syria, with Husayni's help, rejected all criticism, setting the pattern of diplomatic deadlock for the following months. On return to East Beirut, Aoun neglected to inform LF leaders of the results of the Tunis discussions and stalled on including the LF in his government, in deference to an American request to avoid partitionist measures. Aoun's Arab contacts caused rumors about "bazaars" at LF expense[174] and the LF provoked the army by founding a "National Development Council."

Damascus played on problems between Aoun and the LF. Meetings allegedly occurred between army officers and subordinates of Ghazi Kana'an, Syria's military intelligence commander in Lebanon, on the possibility of a "deal"[175]—suppression of the LF in exchange for Syrian acquiescence in a national role for Aoun. On 14 February 1989 the Syrians got the army-militia fight they had been seeking, when Aoun struck at the LF in the Matn and urban East Beirut, but the aftermath was not to their taste. The army gained the upper hand in two days of clashes and Aoun strengthened his position without any benefits for Syria. In East Beirut he achieved an improved modus vivendi with the LF by which the militia surrendered its main illicit port, the Beirut "fifth basin," gave up its major taxes, evacuated some urban installations, and formally acknowledged the military council's political supremacy, but the LF remained a strong autonomous entity.

From the Syrian perspective, Aoun also made a worrying public relations advance in Syrian-dominated territory: traditionalist Muslim politicians and northern Christians welcomed Aoun's assault on the LF and the takeover of Beirut port, with Huss and West Beirut army commander Sami al-Khatib moving for similar measures in their sector.[176] Damascus promptly indicated its displeasure to the more forward West Beirutis, and by early March 1989 the uniform message from Syria and West Beirut was that even a "partial opening" to Aoun depended on submission of an acceptable proposal regarding constitutional reform.

Aoun came to feel thwarted on several levels. Despite his improved authority in East Beirut, the LF had a score to settle, and traditionalist Christian politicians and religious leaders angered him by treating the army and militia as equivalent. This unsympathetic atmosphere increased the urgency of momentum elsewhere; it was difficult to sustain the reduction of the LF on the ports issue without a parallel retreat by West Beirut militias. The initial reaction of Huss and others encouraged Aoun to believe that he could "stampede" an extension of the military council's writ beyond East Beirut. On 24 February 1989, even before his settlement with the LF, he took the fateful decision to close all "illegal ports" and to compel shipping to use the army-controlled Beirut port.[177] Aoun considered that he had made a maximal beginning regarding the LF, which should be answered by gains for "legitimate authority" in West Beirut.

Druze leader Walid Junblatt took the lead in disappointing Aoun's expectations. Junblatt felt squeezed from all sides in early 1989: Syria already watched his ports; he feared Shi'i and Palestinian inroads in the Druze Shuf; and he suspected that the 9 February murder of his aide Anwar Futayri[178] was the work of East Beirut elements trying to sabotage his new proposal for a return of Christian refugees to the Shuf, which Junblatt had hoped would reduce the vulnerability of his "canton." Junblatt was thus in a nervous mood when Aoun hit the LF and trespassed on West Beirut politics. The PSP ports at Khalda and Jiyya, Druze lifelines to the outer world, together with an Amal landing point at Awza'i, were among Aoun's targets. On 5 March Junblatt abandoned his refugee proposal and denounced both the army and Salim al-Huss, who worked "to please some Beirut traders . . . Aoun gives an order in Yarza and they execute it here . . . the war is still at its beginning and we refuse a settlement on the basis of no victor and no vanquished."[179]

For their part, the Syrians were infuriated by Aoun's bid to accelerate events and perturbed by the trend in the Arab committee, with the Kuwaitis appearing partial to Aoun.[180] At a meeting of Lebanese religious notables sponsored by the committee in late February, Maronite patriarch Sufayr demanded that priority be given to presidential elections before reforms. Syria and West Beirut "nationalist" parties responded by hinting at a boycott of the committee. Aoun took the Junblatti and Syrian attitudes badly and on 6 March activated the army's "marine operations room," inaugurating the blockade of West Beirut militia ports. Escalation inevitably followed.

Heavy bombardments began on 14 March 1989 and thereafter there was no going back for Michel Aoun. In his confinement to East Beirut and in the frustration of his plan to impose "legitimate authority" on "illegal ports" Aoun saw only the hand of Damascus. He immediately elevated the hostilities to a "war of liberation" (*harb al-tahrir*) from Syria and answered Syrian participation in the shelling of East Beirut with an unprecedented targeting of Syrian military installations, from Beirut to the central Biqa'. Aoun was urged on by Iraq, was heartened by Syria's unpopularity with other Arab states, and believed that an assault on "smuggling, terrorism and piracy"[181] would bring Western support.

Because he could not hope to move the Syrians with his own resources, Aoun built his military approach on forcing Syria to expose itself as a primary and aggressive party in Lebanese hostilities, in order to precipitate international action. Within a few days he declared: "The question is no longer one of ports . . . we have passed this and defined the ceiling—Syrian withdrawal from Lebanon."[182] In April he publicly attacked Hafiz al-Asad: "What remains to be broken is the head of Asad—Lebanon will be his graveyard and that of his regime."[183] Asad avoided a personal reply until early May, when he referred to "those raising the slogan of liberation from Syria" as "enemies of Lebanon" and "a small gang within a minority."[184]

Aoun certainly pulled the Syrians into open view and aroused international concern about Lebanon, but international intervention—in which the U.S. was the decisive element—favored Syria, not Aoun. In consequence, he has been criticized by some analysts for not taking alleged opportunities to relieve the crisis before March 1989, for launching an adventure with no hope of success, and for antagonizing the Americans.

According to Augustus Norton,[185] Aoun could have made a promising opening to rival premier Huss and to "potential allies" in Amal instead of "imperiously" decreeing port closures. This, however, credits both Aoun and Huss with more freedom of maneuver than they in fact possessed. It also assumes that the Syrians would have tolerated a coming together of Aoun and Huss which, given Aoun's attitude toward "foreign forces," could only have had disturbing implications for Damascus. On the matter of Aoun's entry to hostilities with Syria, it is true that he made a crucial miscalculation regarding the international environment and compounded the error by his subsequent capricious behavior. On the other hand, Norton is unfair not to take into account the severely constraining circumstances Aoun faced in East Beirut and with regard to Syria, which presented him with a "Hobson's choice" of either armed confrontation or giving up the project that motivated him.

Paul Salem[186] refers to Aoun making a "sworn enemy" of the U.S., but as already discussed Aoun was never compatible with American plans for the Middle East after the Cold War. Aoun's bitter reactions when he finally realized that he had no chances with the Bush administration made it easier for the U.S. to work against him, but Washington had decided to work against him anyway.

From the outset of Aoun's tenure in Ba'abda the U.S. demonstrated rigid opposition to any reappearance of "Lebanon" as a subject of international discourse. American officials aimed consistently for an understanding with Syria and for containment of Aoun's challenge to the status quo. The Bush administration stood against U.N. Security Council involvement and resented Aoun's mobilization of the French, the Vatican, and a lobby in the U.S. Congress. One State Department official even observed to the Senate Foreign Relations Committee that "if Syria withdraws I expect the situation would worsen rather than improve."[187]

Aoun's "war of liberation" became a six-month epic of static artillery duels, blockades, and limited frontal probing, in which 850 people died and about 3,000 were wounded. Local conditions and the regional situation, including Syrian-Israeli considerations, dictated siege-style warfare and military stalemate—a disadvantage to Aoun, who was trying to register gains. In 1989, East Beirut possessed a solid defensive base but nothing to encourage an offensive project. The 16,000 troops in the East Beirut brigades were the Lebanese army's effective core, and Iraqi aid increased Aoun's strike capacity by at least 30%, raising his tank strength to almost 200 and his heavy artillery pieces to a similar number.[188] For defense against an external threat one could add the LF's 10,000 men to the army's capacity, giving a total of about 25,000 troops in East Beirut, 300 tanks and more than 300 heavy artillery pieces. The Syrians and their allies and proxies could not realistically bring into play a manpower of more than 40,000. The Syrian army would have to provide more than three-quarters of this, given Shi'i noninterest, Druze fears about losses, the diversions of the south, and West Beirut's internal antagonisms. Assembling two divisions could only be briefly sustained—it meant logistics problems and bringing large armored reinforcements from Syria—and would still be below the 3:1 military ratio theoretically required for a general assault

252

on East Beirut, provided East Beirut was internally united. Air power would make a difference, but an Israeli veto continued to apply in this case.

Local physical and human geography increased the likelihood of stalemate. On both sides of the fronts difficult topography, extensive vegetation, and a sprawl of reinforced concrete apartment buildings militated against easy penetration. In the south the Syrians and Druze held the higher ground and Aoun was forced to concentrate his main forces in a relatively restricted pocket containing East Beirut's vital facilities, the army brigades holding a semicircle of fronts from Duhur al-Shuwayr to Beirut port (map 10). Aoun, with numerical inferiority and facing a Syrian artillery firepower double his own, had no offensive option apart from commando raids. From the defensive perspective, however, East Beirut was compact, had good internal communications lines, and its southern pocket was filled with a forbidding urban maze. A large commitment of Syrian regular forces would be required for even a limited operation to reach Ba'abda via Suq al-Gharb, and in 1989 Aoun had the capability to make sure that such an exercise could not be kept limited.

Both the Syrians and Aoun faced difficulties in their Lebanese "base areas," but Aoun's difficulties were more serious given that American hostility, which implied international isolation, encouraged the LF and Christian traditional politicians to look to break with him as soon as an opportunity appeared. For a few months the LF had no option but to stand with Aoun, as it had always made a slogan out of "liberation," but it resented its secondary status, had no enthusiasm for a campaign that proposed to end "cantons" as well as foreign presences, and held back on full military support. In early April, one LF source told *al-Safir* that "if Aoun wins he wins alone, but if he loses all East Beirut loses."[189]

As for the Christian parliamentary deputies and the Maronite patriarch, on 19 April a "broad meeting" at the patriarchate condemned the destruction on both sides, ignored the question of Syrian "occupation," and even recognized a Syrian security role. Large street demonstrations backing Aoun exposed the deputies' lack of popular legitimacy. Syria also assisted Aoun, when it took the "broad meeting" as an invitation

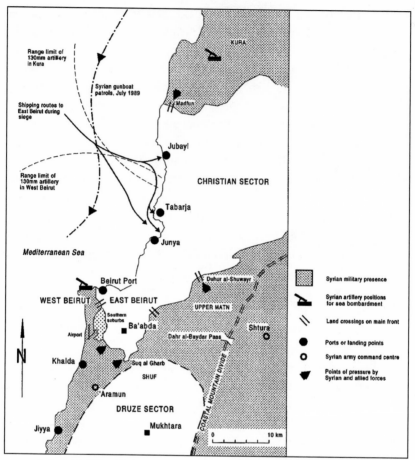

Map 10. The Syrian Siege of East Beirut, May–August 1989

to tighten its screws on East Beirut by refusing to lift its own maritime siege without political capitulation. In these circumstances Aoun's Christian opponents risked appearing as Syrian agents and, for a while, they retired into obfuscation.

Syria had only Junblatt's PSP and its more lightweight clients alongside it in the military line-up, and so had to be the main party even in nonmobile warfare, but otherwise had no real troubles. Lengthy bombardments between East and West Beirut suited the Syrians even when Aoun tried to concentrate on their facilities because non-Christian civilian neighborhoods were badly damaged, which weakened Aoun's nationalist appeal. Here Syrian and LF interests came together even as the LF radio station castigated *al-muhtal al-suri* ("the Syrian occupier"). Some in Amal and the Shi'i sixth brigade of the army, on the other hand, viewed Aoun sympathetically—certainly Syria could not rely on Lebanese army personnel in West Beirut. Amal leader Barri spent as much time as possible out of the capital, although he made the pronouncements Damascus expected from him. The Syrians found some traditionalist Sunni leaders more irksome. Sunni Chief Mufti Hasan Khalid made cease-fire appeals to the Kuwaitis and other Arab states and in early May made secret contacts with Aoun, but on 16 May Khalid was killed by a huge car bomb[190] and thereafter no front-rank Sunni offended the Syrians.

Events during Aoun's "war of liberation" drifted from the opening bombardments of March 1989 through an emergency Arab summit meeting in May to a military climax, U.N. Security Council intervention, and U.S.-Saudi moves to bypass Aoun in August–September. From the outset, stalemate on the land fronts and Iraqi shipments to East Beirut turned Syria's attention seaward. Damascus did not bother to conceal its direct operation of a siege because the issue amounted to a regional confrontation with Iraq. Up to June, however, Syria's seaward blockade involved only inefficient artillery shelling, and East Beirut faced few problems apart from a severe fuel shortage. On the diplomatic front, Syrian implacability crippled the Kuwaiti-chaired Arab committee and killed off ideas for introduction of an Arab observer force into Beirut. In response Iraq and Jordan demanded Syrian military withdrawals. In late May, Arab leaders assembled in Casablanca to consider the impasse.

Syria's trump cards at the summit included its presence on the ground in Lebanon, Egypt's need for Syrian support to re-enter the Arab League, and American unhappiness with Iraq's efforts to Arabize Lebanese affairs. Asad, in a classic performance, treated the conference to a three-hour harangue: "The relationship between Syria and Lebanon has a special historical, geographical, and human character without parallel in Lebanon's relationship with any other Arab state. Syrian forces will not leave Lebanon except by a Lebanese agreement in a national referendum or by a request from a unified central government."[191] The Iraqi president walked out of the summit in a rage a day before the final session.

I was in East Beirut through May 1989. I came into Junya at 3 a.m. on a blacked-out hydrofoil from Cyprus, guided to the wharf by car headlights. Ineffective artillery bombardment to interdict sea access to East Beirut was the main military activity of the month. I obtained a good view of such shelling by going up the hill behind Junya early in the morning. The Syrians used batteries in West Beirut and the Kura, south of Tripoli. I watched trails of splashes accompany ships into port.

Also in May I went to see General Aoun at Ba'abda. The general sat in a well-appointed basement room to receive visitors. Outside there was only some occasional noise from the Suq al-Gharb front, up the hill from Ba'abda. The general was relaxed and confident, dressed in military fatigues with enthusiastic staff members coming and going. Aoun acknowledged Syria's military advantages but explained his feeling of optimism as stemming from being on one's home ground, defending one's home.

As for reactions to Aoun's stand from Muslim politicians, a few months later I visited a political personality in West Beirut who expressed irritation at what he saw as Aoun's attempt to monopolize nationalist virtue. He noted that "nobody likes the Syrians" *(ma fi hada' yihibb as-suriyin),* but that one could not ignore the realities of the world.

The 28 May communiqué was in line with earlier American-Syrian and Saudi-Syrian consultations,[192] setting an order of priorities for a Lebanese settlement gratifying to Damascus: political reform via the old parliament, presidential elections, establishment of a unity government, and measures to implement territorial sovereignty. Only an Israeli withdrawal was explicitly demanded. The summit created a new committee for Lebanon, this time under the auspices of the heads of state of Morocco, Saudi Arabia, and Algeria. The positive feature for Aoun was that a firm project would be presented only after "tripartite committee" contacts involving all sides.

Events in July impelled both Aoun and the Syrians toward military escalation. Aoun wanted to break the maritime constriction of East Beirut, which now threatened his political viability, and Syria felt pressed by financial costs and rising international concern.[193] In early July reports of a large Iraqi consignment to Aoun, including Frog-7 surface-to-surface missiles which could be used against the Syrian capital,[194] led Syria to impose a gunboat blockade on Junya. Using Tripoli as a base, up to six gunboats at any one time cruised 10–15 kilometers offshore (map 10), shelling and arresting incoming vessels. By late July the civilian population of East Beirut faced strangulation, raising doubts in Ba'abda for the first time as to whether Aoun could continue.[195] At this point LF chief Samir Ja'ja' finally agreed with the army to coordinate artillery fire to help ships enter, and Aoun, who had shown relative restraint since May, energetically pursued escalation, including commando raids, to force immediate internationalization.

Desperation also led Aoun to look toward Israel, the real counter-force to Syria in Lebanon. Overall, Aoun preferred to steer clear of the Israelis because he was anxious to bring Arab sentiment to his side against Syria and because he was worried about the impact of dealings with Israel on his Lebanese popular following—on the other hand, his "Arab path" was not producing results, and his Iraqi backers could not compete with Syria's proximity to Lebanon.

Israeli officials were not impressed by the "war of liberation"—one senior personality defined Aoun's performance up to July as "obtuse."[196] Aoun, with no prior consultation, was trying to change the regional strategic environment without realistic prospects for success, in the Israeli view, and in ways that might face Israel with difficult choices in relation to Syria. Aoun's connections with Iraq and 'Arafat aroused concern, and the Americans indicated that Israel should not get involved with Aoun's affairs.[197] Nonetheless Israel did not share the Bush administration's animus against Aoun or its indulgence of Syria, and still preferred that East Beirut survive as a nuisance for Asad, as long as

Israel only had to make a minimal investment. Hence the Israelis used some low-profile psychological devices to keep Damascus unsure of Israeli intentions; during one Syrian invasion "scare" in late May, Israeli aircraft carried out mock bombing raids over West Beirut and south of Suq al-Gharb. Aoun's ambiguous overtures could not elicit more than this, but it helped to deter any Syrian thoughts of assault.

On 31 July Aoun received a brief morale boost, when the foreign ministers of the states forming the Arab tripartite committee on Lebanon surprised the U.S. and angered Syria by issuing a report expressing sharp differences with Damascus on two issues: extension of Lebanese authority over all Lebanese territory and the relationship between Lebanon and Syria.[198] On the first, the committee favored a "comprehensive security plan," including a timetable for contraction of the Syrian presence. Syria demanded that the matter be left undetermined until after formation of a Lebanese national unity government. On the second, the committee indicated that the Syrian alignment facing Israel in the Biqa' should be defined in a rigorous fashion and that other dimensions of Lebanese-Syrian relations be coordinated in a loose manner to respect Lebanese sovereignty. Syria maintained the "strategic integration" concept of the 1985 Tripartite Agreement, covering "strategic, economic, social, and other aspects," which would significantly erode Lebanese sovereignty.[199] Radio Damascus condemned the report, voicing "astonishment" at its "political errors in ignoring the stand of the isolationist band."[200]

The Syrians resorted to the battlefield to sideline the committee report. Syria stepped up its shelling of East Beirut and brought armored reinforcements across the Dahr al-Baydar pass. Residents fled many parts of metropolitan Beirut; by 10 August up to 350,000—at least 40% of the population—had left West Beirut and the southern suburbs for Sidon and the south,[201] while many East Beirutis headed for the mountains. On 14 August, the Syrian command experimented with an attack on Suq al-Gharb, the only bid to seize territory in the six months of fighting. To reduce Syrian political exposure, Druze militiamen and Palestinians were given the front-line role, with stiffening by Syrian special forces.[202] This attempt to reconcile a military operation with diplomatic constraints flopped badly—Aoun trumpeted a victory and the international community reacted sharply. With urgent French pressure and a Soviet-American concord, the U.N. Security Council met on 15 August and called for an immediate cease-fire—the first and last Security Council move during the "war of liberation."

Thereafter fighting subsided, with Syria retreating behind Lebanese surrogates, giving West Beirut Lebanese army officers formal control of siege shelling. Gunboat operations and plans for frontal assaults were terminated, as these were Syrian matters. Damascus was restricted by Israeli warnings, the arrival of French warships, and the late-August movements of Soviet and French envoys. Aoun's brigades attracted some attention from those who had long discounted the Lebanese army—Israeli Defense Minister Rabin remarked: "Growing international pressure and the strength of the Lebanese army are enough to stop action by the Syrian army . . . the restraints which Israel imposes by land, sea, and air are well known to the Syrians and there is no need to restate them daily."[203] Late August 1989 marked Aoun's high tide.

However, although the Syrians were checked on the fronts, the military climax helped them to force Arab diplomatic activity back into the framework of the Casablanca summit communiqué, after the deviation of the "tripartite committee" report. The vehicle for the Syrian rebound was the U.S. administration, which viewed the initial Arab committee report as impractical and regarded the events of August 1989 as confirming the judiciousness of its hostility to Aoun.

The U.S. agreed to the U.N. Security Council resolution only to defuse the immediate crisis and to enable a retooling of the Arab diplomatic involvement, for internal stabilization of Lebanon backed by Syria. Among other things, Washington was ever hopeful about Syrian aid with releases of Western hostages. Aoun's success in embarrassing Damascus internationally was as inconvenient as every other aspect of Aoun's enterprise, and his stimulation of a French-Soviet agreement noting the need "to convince the Syrian leadership to withdraw its forces from Beirut and the mountain according to a fixed timetable"[204] represented just another tiresome complication.

After the Suq al-Gharb battle the U.S. de-emphasized any Syrian role in hostilities and blocked further recourse to the Security Council.[205] One American diplomat boasted to a Lebanese deputy that "the U.S. administration has more influence on Syria than the Soviet Union has."[206] On 6 September the Americans, who had apparently been considering closure of their embassy in Lebanon for some weeks,[207] used an alleged offhand reference by Aoun about the efficacy of Hizballah-style hostage-taking as a pretext to evacuate all U.S. staff from the embassy compound in East Beirut.

Aoun commented that the U.S. "has sold Lebanon to Syria,"[208] and subsequent developments demonstrated that this was not far from the truth. Early September also saw the resuscitation of the Arab tripartite committee, in abeyance since rejection by Syria a month earlier. U.S. officials apparently told committee members that Washington had no pressing interest in [Syrian] "withdrawals" and wanted the committee's initial report "passed over."[209] The U.S. planned to progress directly to laying constitutional reform proposals before a conference of Lebanese parliamentary deputies, as recommended by the Casablanca Arab summit meeting.

Syria adjusted cleverly to the U.S. impetus, which opened a new route for eliminating Aoun. As the July Arab report had gone against Damascus in part because of Syria's Iranian connection and a meeting of Syria's Lebanese allies in Tehran, Asad personally contacted Gulf state leaders to "clarify" the limited nature of the connection. Syria also raised the scare of a "security vacuum" if there were Syrian withdrawals without an "alternative security force,"[210] and became more cooperative regarding the cease-fire. On the committee Saudi Arabia and Algeria pulled Morocco into line on giving priority to Lebanese internal reform, and by mid-September France and the Soviet Union had both abandoned an independent approach. Inside East Beirut the international and Arab trend against Aoun encouraged his critics to reemerge, while the U.S. encouraged restiveness in the Christian political and religious establishment.

The Ta'if Agreement and its aftermath

On 17 September 1989 the Arab "tripartite committee" produced a draft "National Unity Charter" to be discussed by Lebanese parliamentary deputies meeting in Saudi Arabia. In contrast to the July report, the putting together of the "National Unity Charter" was closely supervised by the U.S. It involved major concessions to Syrian strategic requirements, combined with consitutional reform proposals that could be accepted by Christian politicians. Criticism of Syria thus collapsed in favor of an Arab-American deal with Syria.

The draft, strenuously pressed by Arab and American officials, was accepted almost unchanged by the Lebanese deputies on 22 October, after three weeks of sterile haggling at the Saudi resort city of Ta'if. It then became known as the "Ta'if Agreement" and was billed as the basis of a "second Lebanese republic." Aoun had little choice but to let the East Beirut parliamentarians go to Ta'if; he warned them against "any treason" but he had no illusions about their behavior once out of Lebanon.

At Ta'if the Saudis and Americans quickly got to work on the Christian deputies. Saudi foreign minister Sa'ud al-Faysal told them that Syrian acceptance of the Arab draft, including relatively moderate political changes, hinged on a clause regarding Syrian participation in extending the authority of the new Lebanese regime (bizarrely termed "extension of sovereignty"), formulated after long negotiations with Damascus.[211] An American diplomat transferred the same message: the clause was immutable. West Beirut deputies refused any linkage of Syrian withdrawals to reforms, while the more radical "Islamic and nationalist" parties gathered in Tehran to attack the emerging Ta'if compact as "consecrating sectarian privileges." Some said Syria allowed such a gathering to highlight its own "moderation."

Toward the end of the conference Sa'ud al-Faysal traveled to Damascus to consult with the Syrians. Syria conceded a reduction in the size of the new Lebanese parliament, at the expense of its Druze and Shi'i allies, but rejected any alteration in the favorable provisions for its own strategic interests. The Saudis concentrated on converting Kata'ib chief George Sa'ada, deploying the draft's substantial retention of

Christian and non-Christian traditionalist prerogatives, "secret" oral assurances about eventual Syrian withdrawals, and even hints about the presidency for Sa'ada. Sa'ada finally decided that the draft document represented the best available deal. At the closing ceremony 58 of the 62 deputies signed the accord, including all 31 Christians.

Several features of the Ta'if Agreement[212] established the basis for Syrian hegemony in Lebanon. First, the precedence given to constitutional adjustment in advance of any Syrian pullback facilitated Syrian manipulation. Executive authority would shift from the Maronite presidency to the national unity cabinet headed by the Sunni prime minister and based in West Beirut, an area in which the Syrian army would remain for at least two years after the government's formation. Aoun did not object to change regarding the presidency, but he opposed its implementation while Syrian forces sat in Beirut.

Second, the "state sovereignty" clauses—authorizing Syrian military intervention against opponents of the government whenever requested by the regime (which would be militarily impotent in the crucial formative period), and setting the date for any Syrian redeployment 18 months after "dissolution of militias"—immediately gave Damascus the high ground in relation to Lebanese parties. Regarding Syrian redeployment, the Ta'if Agreement only suggested Syrian positioning on "the Hammana–Mudayraj–Ayn Dara line" two years after execution of political reforms, perpetuating a Syrian presence well down the seaward side of the coastal mountains, Syrian control of the Dahr al-Baydar pass, and Syrian topographic domination of Beirut. This was what the Americans liked to refer to as "withdrawal to the Biqa'." Beyond the vaguest wafflings about a "joint Lebanese-Syrian committee" for consultations on the location of Syrian forces, the agreement did not mention any further Syrian movement.

Apart from limiting Lebanon's sovereignty, the Ta'if Agreement reconciled Syria to the traditional Christian and Muslim political class. Equalization of Christian and Muslim-Druze representation in the parliament and cabinet was a long overdue response to the internal demographic evolution—it was the best holding position the Christian elite could expect in the early 1990s. The agreement provided for eventual abolition of sectarian political quotas, a sine qua non for Shi'is, but left further consideration to a "national commission" to be established by the first elected parliament of the new regime. In the meantime, the chief individual beneficiaries of the Ta'if "reforms" were the Sunni prime minister and the Shi'i parliamentary speaker. The agreement extended the speaker's term from one to four years, and gave him greater influence over submission of legislation to the chamber of deputies.

In general terms, what came out of Ta'if was a sanitized version of the 1985 Tripartite Agreement, the differences being those one would expect between a product of Syrian-Saudi-American consultation with Lebanese upper class personalities and a product of Syrian coordination with militias. The crude language in the Tripartite Agreement regarding such matters as Syrian-Lebanese "integration," "privileged relations," and elimination of media "distortion" was absent from the Ta'if document, but from the Syrian perspective, international cover and explicit provision for more detailed Lebanese-Syrian pacts compensated for the dilution. Both agreements treated the Lebanese army as an object rather than an actor. Hatred of Aoun and Saudi financial enticements brought some to accept in 1989 what they had refused in 1985.

Despite international endorsement the Ta'if Agreement did not face an easy passage in Beirut. The Druze and Shi'i communities saw almost nothing to celebrate; Druze aspirations for an upper house of parliament (a house for the communities) and administrative decentralization were ignored, and convergence of the Sunni and Maronite elites curtailed Shi'i ambitions for numerical democracy. In answer to Sunni West Beirut premier Huss's welcome of the Ta'if result, Druze leader Junblatt accused Huss of "sabotaging the nationalist cause," observing that Ta'if "carries the seed of new civil wars . . . The Maronite-Sunni alliance triumphs . . . Tomorrow political Maronitism will remove Aoun in one way or another."[213] Hizballah, next to Aoun the main U.S. target, attacked Saudi Arabia and the traditionalist politicians but without any reference to Syria: "The people will ignore all those who filled their stomachs with the fattening Saudi meals . . . Sooner or later these deputies will have to pay the bill for their treason."[214] Even Amal's Nabih Barri referred to the "Ta'if scandal," but the

Syrians soon persuaded him to be more amenable.

Aoun was isolated as never before in the Lebanese and international arenas, but his hold on the Christian masses only strengthened. In contrast, the more conservative Christian politicians had international backing but no popular legitimacy. After Ta'if, large crowds congregated daily at Ba'abda, reaching tens of thousands by the end of October, to applaud Aoun's pronouncements that the Ta'if Agreement negated Lebanese sovereignty and was "repair to a rotten regime."[215] Most Christian deputies did not dare to return to Beirut, moving from Ta'if to Paris to await the call to a parliamentary session to ratify the agreement and to elect a new Lebanese president. In early November Aoun abruptly declared parliament dissolved, but outside East Beirut his "transitional government" decree was dismissed as having no effect.

Worried that the Ta'if Agreement might founder without immediate follow-up steps, the Americans and Saudis wanted to reassemble the Lebanese deputies in Lebanon for a presidential election, even if the session had to be held on Syrian-controlled territory. The session took place on 5 November at the Qulay'at airstrip, in the Syrian-dominated north, and the deputies elected their colleague Rene Mu'awwad, a frontrank political figure from the northern town of Zgharta. Mu'awwad was one of three possibilities already discussed between the Syrians and the Saudis.[216] He was the preferred American-Saudi candidate—his local power base, which gave him a little buffering against pressure, his conciliatory approach to Aoun, and his international backing were mild disadvantages from the Syrian perspective. The shift of executive authority to the cabinet made the Syrians more relaxed about such matters than might otherwise have been the case.

Mu'awwad lived only 16 days after his election, a tense time with strange political cross-currents. The Syrians pushed for a government under Huss, and dragooned Junblatt, Barri, and even Hizballah into compliance with Ta'if. Syrian Vice President Khaddam invited himself on a tour of the north only two days after the election and warned that Syrian assistance to enable the "National Unity Government" to extend its authority "will not be small," a comment aimed at Aoun. Mu'awwad, on the other hand, exhibited a little autonomy in pledging himself to form a broad government, with the hint of a door left ajar for Aoun.[217]

Inside East Beirut the LF itched to cut away from Aoun, but were not given any serious incentive to attach themselves to a Mu'awwad administration; it was a frustrating time for the East Beirut militia. Aoun's supporters angrily confronted patriarch Sufayr regarding his endorsement of Ta'if and compelled him to flee to the north while Aoun himself threatened to occupy the Kata'ib headquarters and did not slacken in his public rejection of the new order: "Do you believe in a Syrian withdrawal in the presence of a government and a [new] parliament formed by Syria?"[218]

Nonetheless, indirect contacts proceeded between Mu'awwad and Aoun on Aoun's integration into the new structure and on promoting a Syrian pullback in the rural north.[219] Information from Aoun's side implies that Mu'awwad was not coordinating with Syria on the subject.[220] On 22 November conditions were suddenly transformed when Mu'awwad was assassinated in West Beirut by a car bomb.

Syria now did not waste a moment in ensuring that its favorite candidate became president and in producing an amenable government. With American cooperation the deputies were promptly summoned to Shtura, the Syrian military nerve center, and Ilyas al-Hirawi, a little-known Zahla deputy chiefly interesting for his connections to both Syria and the LF militia, was elected president without opposition. Unlike Mu'awwad, Hirawi had no personal power base, being eclipsed in the Zahla social scene by the Greek Catholic Skaff family. Further, the integrity of the family business and lands in the Biqa' obviously depended on Syrian goodwill. According to a Zahla source,[221] Hirawi's path to Damascus was smoothed by a nephew closely involved with the Ba'thist apparatus. As for the LF, Hirawi had long-standing links with the militia—he had become a Zahla contact for Bashir Jumayyil in the early 1980s. On 26 November, Hirawi announced a government headed by Huss and consisting largely of parliamentarians. This time there was no pretense about consultations: some government members, for example Kata'ib leader Sa'ada and Amal's Barri, only heard about their appointments on the radio.

Syria's immediate purpose was to crack East Beirut psychologically with a series of political and military moves. As soon as the first "Ta'if" government was formed it dismissed Aoun as army commander, replacing him with Emile Lahoud, who had left East Beirut some months earlier. Lahoud's command called on Aoun's brigades to transfer allegiance and, before the end of November, more than 7,000 Syrian troop reinforcements crossed Dahr al-Baydar amid talk of a military operation to capture Ba'abda and end Aoun's "rebellion."

However, the Syrian bubble soon burst. Evidence suggests that Syrian commanders seriously considered a military strike, including attack helicopters and air power,[222] but Asad stepped back in the face of various deterrents. First, Aoun kept his full military capability and the LF did not dare go against him in the context of such a blatant Syrian challenge; East Beirut had not yet split, and hence the additional Syrian troops were not enough for a credible ground move. Second, popular demonstrations unprecedented in Lebanon's history created a human wall around Ba'abda—by early December the numbers exceeded 150,000, including people from outside East Beirut, which apparently unnerved Syrian leaders.[223] Third, international approval of Ta'if was not yet convertible into an appropriate background for a Syrian military offensive. The U.S., according to some reports not against a "limited military move" after Hirawi's election,[224] soon feared a "massacre" and discouraged the idea; the Vatican and the French made clear to Hirawi that any call for a Syrian attack contradicted "the spirit of Ta'if"; and, most significantly, Israel reasserted its veto of Syrian aerial support for a ground push. In contrast to their view of Mu'awwad, Israeli officials had no doubt about Hirawi's status as a Syrian "stooge."[225]

The collapse of East Beirut

At the beginning of 1990 the "Ta'if process" was stalled. The first elements of Syria's new Lebanese regime existed in West Beirut, as an outgrowth of the Huss cabinet which had perpetuated itself since President Jumayyil's departure from office. Ilyas al-Hirawi was installed as president and little more could be done while a defiant

Michel Aoun held out in East Beirut, controlling the most important government installations. It had become plain to the Americans, the Syrians, and Hirawi's government that a "surgical military operation" to remove Aoun was not practical in prevailing conditions—not without attrition of his still substantial material strength. This left the option of encouraging trouble within East Beirut.

East Beirut entered 1990 with a dangerous double stand-off between the main elements of a hopelessly segmented Christian leadership, with Aoun in a pivotal position. Aoun had mass Christian support and retained a cross-sectarian appeal, but he had lost international legitimacy and lacked competent advisors. On the government level he faced much of the Maronite elite, which had accepted Ta'if and contributed a vital component—most of its parliamentary deputies—to the Hirawi-Huss regime. Buoyed by international recognition and anxious to enjoy the fruits of office, these people sought any lever to get Aoun out of Ba'abda. Within East Beirut, Aoun faced the LF-Kata'ib complex, which had a large organization but had lost popular credibility to Aoun. As already seen, the LF had no sympathy for Aoun's nationalism and had scores to settle with him. None of the three Christian "power centers" had a stable base, so conflict was likely. The main meeting of interests was between the LF and the Christian wing of the "Ta'if regime," as both were exposed by Aoun's capture of the street.

The LF stayed with Aoun after Ta'if only because it was not offered an alternative, and its positive noises about the Ta'if Agreement were at first ignored by the Syrians. Damascus was cautious toward the LF, which was an older enemy than Aoun, but after November 1989 Syria turned to manipulating the LF against Aoun. In contrast to the Americans and Christian members of the new government, who wanted to bring the LF and the Kata'ib into the regime to restrict Syrian weight, the Syrians simply aimed to have Aoun and the LF reduce each other, with no payoffs.

The LF hoped that collaboration with the Ta'if parties would give it international respectability and that once Hirawi was brought into East Beirut he could be detached from Syria and used as cover for restoring LF domination of the enclave—an updated version of the 1976–82 Sarkis period. Through January 1990, the LF made no secret either of its option of linkage with Hirawi "if things don't work out with the general" or its derision for the "circus" of pro-Aoun demonstrations.[226] Syria, which was well aware of the LF scheme,[227] encouraged Hirawi to entice the militia.

Also in January 1990, rumors surfaced in East Beirut about alleged LF contacts with American officials and Syrian officers regarding an LF ditching of Aoun.[228] Whether these reflected reality or disinformation, they certainly raised tensions. The daily *al-Safir* later quoted a reference by Christian deputies to "the capitals that were behind encouraging the LF to go into the battle with Aoun."[229] Only Washington and Damascus could have had this interest.

For his part, Aoun felt under mounting pressure in January. The Hirawi government used its control of the financial machinery, especially the Central Bank, to cut money flows to officials and institutions in East Beirut. Diplomatic isolation tightened. In addition, Aoun's necessarily ad hoc means for storing financial contributions received unwelcome publicity when a French newspaper uncovered a $15 million private bank account in the name of the general and his wife.[230]

Aoun refused to bend to anyone. His confidence was sustained by the daily stream of thousands of people to the Ba'abda presidential palace, and on 16 January he ordered the local media to cease using the titles of president, minister, or deputy to describe participants in the Ta'if regime—for Aoun the military council remained the sole legitimate authority. Apart from West Beirut media organs, magazines, radio and television stations associated with the LF had employed the offending terminology since Hirawi's election as president.

LF radio and television suspended all news broadcasts, two East Beirut newspapers rejecting Aoun's decree were closed, and the standoff ended after a week in a compromise involving a climbdown by the general. By this point the LF was probably already plotting a surprise military strike to paralyze army communications to coincide with a "security plan" proposed for West Beirut in early February. On 30 January, Aoun intervened after army and LF mobilizations in a clash over LF use of school buildings in a Beirut suburb—he announced a compulsory "uniting of the rifle" in East Beirut, meaning absorption of the LF into his army brigades. For the LF it was a declaration of war—

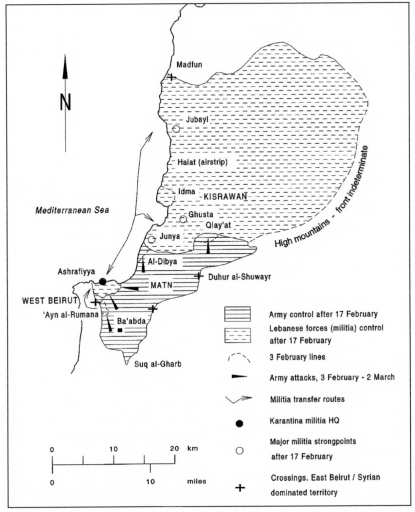

Map 11. The Army/Militia War, 1990

a war for which it had been readying itself.

Aoun had been concentrating on his enemies outside East Beirut and was not well prepared for a sudden flare-up within his base area. After the media standoff there were even moves for a rapprochement between Aoun and the Kata'ib party, with George Sa'ada confirming

269

his resignation from the Hirawi government, and the army took no precautionary measures with regard to its scattered barracks, ammunition dumps, and other assets in the LF heartland north of Beirut. The big Idma base in the Kisrawan, which was exposed to encirclement, had only limited ammunition, and no provision was taken for dispersing the helicopter fleet, destroyed by the LF on the first day of fighting. Aoun made no preparations for the swift blitz necessary if he wished to demolish the militia.

In contrast, immediately after Aoun's "unification of weapons" speech, the LF invaded army facilities in Junya and the Kisrawan, made sure of almost all the coastline, spread through the urban area, and secured the Ashrafiyya hill, adjacent to the militia "war council" (map 11). The army did not respond to militia advances for many hours. Aoun apparently believed that the LF would fall apart within two days[231] because it lacked popular support beyond its own dependents—a serious miscalculation.

The ferocity of the army-LF war of February–May 1990 was determined by the fact that the army started from a much eroded geographical position—the Matn—and faced the task of "conquering" more than 80% of the East Beirut enclave. A new Iraqi arms shipment in early 1990, "to be divided equally between the army and the LF"[232] and intended by Saddam Husayn for trouble-making against Asad and the Ta'if parties, meant East Beirut's weapons stocks were at an all-time high. The Maronite community could thus blow itself apart in grand style. The LF's arsenal was not much inferior to that of Aoun and it had the less arduous task of holding ground in urban and mountain terrain favoring the defense, especially in winter weather. Awareness of its unpopularity merely made the militia more ruthless.

The war evolved in two phases, with frontal assaults degrading into brutal artillery poundings and the Christian enclave becoming a latter-day Stalingrad. Bombardments matched anything seen before in Lebanon, and in the first 18 days the casualty toll climbed to 615 dead and 2,128 injured,[233] almost equalling the totals for the whole six months of the "war of liberation." Unusually, at least half were military casualties.

I was at the Ba'abda presidential palace the day before the outbreak of fighting, but did not see General Aoun as he was much preoccupied. I walked back to Hazmiya; the atmosphere was quiet and tense. In Sin al-Fil unusual numbers of people were out on their balconies, watching and waiting.

The next morning I went to Ashrafiyya to see a friend. School children were all hurrying home by 10 a.m., as the militia had ordered the area's schools closed. Fighting had already started across St. George's Bay, in Antelias. I was near a militia station, and the militia rolled out a tank to block the access road. Bombardment was expected imminently. My friend and I headed for home [Antelias area] through the Armenian suburb of Burj Hammoud, between the army and the Lebanese Forces. Bullets whined overhead, and we kept our heads low while speeding down the Dowra highway, literally the front line.

Where I was staying we had sandbags piled up around the kitchen and salon. In the afternoon I counted shells for a while, but gave up when it went into the hundreds. Neighbors visited, and commented that the grid pattern of initial shelling corresponded closely to the pattern of Syrian targeting during the previous year.

The third day of warfare saw ferocious bombardments in our area, which had the misfortune to be a front line for a brief period. Shrapnel whizzed and tinkled everywhere. A 130-mm projectile destroyed an upstairs room and collapsed part of the kitchen ceiling, together with the water supply, a couple of meters from where we were standing. The number of artillery projectiles rose into the tens of thousands; for four hours there was no break in the noise, and the house shuddered and swayed like a ship at sea.

The next day the army pushed the front northwards, and shelling in the immediate vicinity slackened somewhat. The army continued to pound the militia headquarters across the bay. Large white columns of smoke rose from the bursting of 155-mm phosphorous shells. A young soldier proclaimed joyfully: *ramadna ooyehim* (we have incinerated them). The proclamation was premature, but indicative of the hysterical atmosphere. Neighbors inspected the shell damage to the house, sipped coffee, and offered their sentiments—*hamd illah al salaama* (praise God that you're safe).

Through the first month the army launched attacks with increasing desperation to crack the LF. In early February Aoun cleared the LF from the coastal Matn, seizing the militia barracks at al-Dibya. This almost brought a morale collapse in the militia,[234] but the destruction in the battle zone, which in three days matched the landscape created by years of shelling in old central Beirut, deterred Aoun from marching into Junya. Instead the army tried to outflank Junya and split the Kisrawan in a mountain push—a much longer distance in worse terrain and weather. This gave the LF time to recover its balance.

The push petered out and Aoun turned to Beirut. He drove the LF out of its Ayn al-Rumana pocket in an artillery firestorm. For each of these assaults the army used about 1,000 men and 40 to 100 armored vehicles.[235] Finally, on 1 March, Aoun tried to overcome the LF's defenses around its "war council," to bring the surrender of Ashrafiyya and shatter the LF's apparatus. However, the army had to break off the engagement—the 400 commandos who had spearheaded successive battles were exhausted and an ammunition shortage silenced the army's American howitzers. Aoun had to fall back on Iraqi-supplied Soviet artillery pieces. The initiative now passed out of his hands permanently.

The second phase was a standoff, with shelling exchanges continuing until late May when an Iraqi-sponsored truce brought an uneasy calm. The old East Beirut, where power centers had cohered against strategic challenges, was gone for good. In its place was a shell containing two tiny entities (map 11), each anxious to blot out the other but unable to do so. The population faced intolerable disruptions and up to 320,000 people fled the enclave by May;[236] the Syrians instructed their allies not to interfere with the outflow.

Syria aimed to have the LF and Aoun reduce each other to a point at which the LF would have to submit to the Ta'if arrangement without a quid pro quo, and Aoun would be so emasculated that he would either have to surrender or suffer a swift military blow. Damascus had to play a waiting game: the Americans would not give Syria cover for military intervention after February 1990. The U.S. was unhappy about Asad's rigidity toward Israel and his continuing associations with Palestinian and Islamic militants; the Syrians declined to budge on these matters.

According to some sources,[237] Aoun was reduced by April to half of his original military capability. He had lost his air and naval bases, major stocks of 155-mm shells, and 25% of his tank force. Of his 16,000 troops, up to 2,000 either were in LF hands or had been forced to cross to West Beirut. At the same time, Iraq was losing interest in East Beirut as Saddam Husayn began, from early 1990 onward, to drum up grievances against Kuwait. For Iraq, Aoun had lost his utility for goading Asad, and access to him had become almost impossible.

Aoun's only answer to his supply and ammunition difficulties was to turn to Lebanese army officers in West Beirut and those Christian allies of Syria most hostile to the LF of Samir Ja'ja'—Elie Hubayqa's group, the Faranjiyya family, and the Syrian Social Nationalists. Syria approved a drip-feed of necessities, so that internecine attrition could continue and to contain the LF, which after March had firepower superior to that of Aoun.

Aoun's anxiety to retain his curious new prop for as long as possible led him to make gratuitous verbal attacks on the Israelis. In May 1990, Aoun announced that he was "in confrontation with those who collaborate with Israel"[238] and spoke of "Zionist plots." The Israeli official in charge of connections with Lebanon, Uri Lubrani, noted that "Aoun has joined those who are digging their own graves."[239] Whatever was left of the Israeli aerial deterrence that had helped to buttress East Beirut for years may have evaporated even before Iraq's August 1990 invasion of Kuwait.

All attempts in February and March 1990 to achieve a settlement between Aoun and the LF, whether by local mediation or by France, the Vatican, the PLO, Iraq, and Israel, came to nothing. In any case, they were undercut by the Americans, who told Ja'ja' that any East Beirut arrangement ignoring the Ta'if regime was unacceptable.[240] The LF rejected Aoun's bottom line: subordination to the military council in an East Beirut "political authority."

Similarly, all efforts in mid-1990 to squeeze Aoun into a peaceful surrender to the Hirawi regime collapsed. Even when reduced to linking with Syria's Lebanese allies, Aoun refused to adapt to the Ta'if project and searched the world for any means to escape from his predicament. A three-week bid through July by the Arab "tripartite committee" envoy,

Lakhdar Ibrahimi of Algeria, to persuade Aoun or even to buy him off with Saudi money,[241] proved fruitless. Aoun correctly surmised that his Lebanese popularity depended on staying outside the Ta'if Agreement, and he held out in the hope of change in the international environment. Saddam Husayn, his old backer, stimulated such a shift in August 1990, but it spelled disaster for Aoun.

Without Samir Ja'ja', the Ta'if regime might well have been permanently limited to West Beirut, but the LF's crippling of Aoun enabled Syria to exploit the Iraqi-American confrontation to expel Aoun from Ba'abda in October 1990. In its dealings with Hirawi after February, the LF sought to trade commitment to the Ta'if document for a powerful position within the new "National Unity Government." The Syrians intended to extract the former without conceding the latter. The LF cultivated the Arab "tripartite committee" and the U.S., which embarrassed Syria by advancing the opinion that the LF had done enough to join the new regime.

In mid-April, Asad and Khaddam had Hirawi dispatch a letter to Ja'ja' on "the necessity of joining the peace process unreservedly, and abandoning any illusions or bets on foreign and regional factors, illusions that conceal a desire for continued hostility to Syria and its role in Lebanon."[242] Ja'ja' observed that "Syria wants to get rid of Aoun, but also to injure us along the way."[243] Nonetheless Damascus had the stronger hand in the bargaining—Syria's manipulation of openings by its allies to Aoun to force the LF towards the Hirawi government began to work in late May when the LF allowed Kata'ib ministers George Sa'ada and Michel Sassin to abandon their boycott of cabinet sessions "to stop Aoun's attempts to expand relations with some in West Beirut and Syria."[244] Regime-LF negotiations through June finally brought LF acceptance of the Ta'if reforms and a downgrading of the LF's "federalism" satisfactory to Syria.[245]

Impact of the Iraqi-American confrontation

In July 1990, Syria turned to a "surgical operation" to eliminate Aoun, to be implemented as soon as opportunity offered, at the same time as Saddam Husayn fixed on Kuwait as the target for his own military surprise. It is a great irony that Saddam, who in 1989 had devoted his regional policy to inciting and provisioning Aoun against Syria, in late 1990 gave his arch-rival Hafiz al-Asad a chance to consecrate hegemony in Lebanon that Asad could not have dreamed of a few months previously.

In any case, by July Syria's drip-feed to Aoun had accomplished its purpose of impelling the LF to submit to Ta'if, and Aoun was plainly irreconcilable. Syria thus ordered its allies to end their relations with him. The most interesting of these relationships was a warm connection that developed with the Druze PSP, mediated by Junblatt's friend and fellow Shuf *zai'm* Dani Chamoun—one of Aoun's closest confidants—and by Jubran Tuwayni, whose father was *al-Nahar* publisher Ghassan Tuwayni and whose mother had been a Druze. Junblatt remained suspicious of the Lebanese military institution, but he had no personal problems with Aoun and he was deeply dissatisfied with the Ta'if arrangement. He did, however, stress to visitors from Aoun's New Lebanese Front that there could not be an anti-Ta'if alignment. Aoun was deaf to the warning.

Iraq's 2 August 1990 seizure of Kuwait, the Iraqi-American confrontation, and the infusion of Western forces into the Persian Gulf transformed Middle Eastern political calculations. The U.S. now needed—or, more accurately, imagined itself as needing—the broadest possible Arab military participation, and Syria suddenly found itself the object of the most flattering Western attentions. Asad tested the winds of the world for a week or so, calculated that his Iraqi enemy was headed for catastrophe, and offered himself as a partner in the American-led coalition. By mid-August, as the daily *al-Safir* noted, it was obvious that "Gulf events have removed foreign barriers standing against the [Hirawi] government asking Syria to strike at the unnatural situation in East Beirut."[246]

Intensified Syrian-American consultations culminated in the 13

September visit of Secretary of State James Baker to Damascus. Asad provided troops to sit in Saudi Arabia and in late September, clearly at Baker's request, made his first personal visit to Tehran to "secure continuation of Iran's adherence to [U.N.] sanctions [against Iraq]."[247] In exchange for involvement in the Gulf, Damascus expected and got approval to settle things in Beirut, by whatever means.

In late August the U.S. ambassador to Syria gratified Syrian officials and the Hirawi regime by publicly stating that "we [the U.S.] want to see immediate implementation of Ta'if."[248] American reservations about Syria's association with "terrorism" temporarily vanished. The only American requirements, completely coincident with Syria's own approach, were that the operation must be swift and by invitation of the Hirawi government, to counter comparisons with Iraqi behavior concerning Kuwait.[249] Curiously, in mid-September the Israelis seemed convinced that Syria was too busy with the Gulf crisis to open "an additional front" in Lebanon[250]—this after the U.S. had already assured Lebanese officials, and by extension the Syrians, that Israel would not interfere "provided there is no movement southward."[251] The question arises as to whether the U.S. sought to neutralize Israel by deliberately misleading the Israelis about American-Syrian understandings.

Coordinated activities by the Hirawi government and Syria went ahead slowly—Asad wanted to give Aoun a last chance to submit. The LF-Kata'ib camp in East Beirut threw in its lot with the regime: Asad was so pleased with Kata'ib leader George Sa'ada at a late July audience that he asked him "not to stay away from us too long."[252] On 21 August, parliament met with the necessary two-thirds quorum, courtesy of the LF, and voted through the Ta'if constitutional amendments. This completed the formal legal base of the regime, at least to the satisfaction of its partisans. On 23 September, LF and Syrian delegations had a productive session in the Biqa',[253] and on 26 September the LF handed over the crossing points on Aoun-LF fronts to Hirawi government troops.

On 28 September, the Ta'if regime committed its prestige and existence to a successful showdown by imposing a siege on the Aoun area, blocking food supplies to the population. Some West Beirut parties exhibited their unhappiness about the implications for themselves.

Junblatt expressed opposition and hosted an anti-regime demonstration from Jizzin and the Israeli occupied "security zone." The Syrians summoned him to Damascus to explain himself. There was even fraternization between Aoun supporters and Hizballah. None of it made any difference to Aoun's fate: on 9 October, the Ta'if regime made the official written request, as required by the Americans and Syrians, for Syrian military intervention. Very large Syrian armored and infantry concentrations then formed around the Matn, with Lebanese regime units as an appendage. Almost to the end Aoun believed that Syria would not be allowed to attack.

Immediately before the assault, Syrian aircraft overflew the Matn to test the efficacy of American intervention with Israel. In the early morning of 13 October the Syrians made a large-scale ground invasion of the Aoun area, accompanied by air strikes on the Ba'abda presidential palace (map 11). LF artillery joined the Syrians.[254] At Suq al-Gharb, Aoun's Lebanese army units, with only a fraction of their pre-February 1990 hardware, killed about 400 Syrians before the front was overrun. Aoun saw that prolonging the agony was pointless, ordered his troops to surrender to the Ta'if regime, and took sanctuary in the French embassy. Within three hours the Syrian army occupied Ba'abda, and thereafter spread throughout the Matn.

The Syrians perpetrated serious human rights abuses,[255] which the U.S. ignored. One hospital received 73 bodies of Lebanese army soldiers, each executed at close range with a bullet in the lower right side of the skull. This was only the most notable example of a series of small massacres carried out as the Syrian army entered the Aoun area, another case being the murder of 15 civilians by the Syrians in Bsus. A week later, Aoun's most prominent Lebanese champion, National Liberal Party leader Dani Chamoun, was assassinated with his wife and two children by professional killers in his Ba'abda apartment. Widespread looting by the Syrian army took place in the mountain suburbs of Bayt Mirri, Brummana, and Mansuriyya. As Syrian troops stripped the Ba'abda presidential palace of Lebanese state property,[256] President Hirawi could only comment "that snatching an earring from here and a car from there should not be allowed to hinder government efforts to promote national reconciliation with the sisterly assistance of

Syria."[257] Such was the new Lebanese order.

The military crushing of Aoun was a significant event in Lebanon's modern history. The significance did not lie so much in the removal of the East Beirut enclave as a block to Syrian strategic aspirations, as the Aoun-LF war had already done most of the work in that regard. It lay in the unprecedented shock dealt to all Lebanese elements with autono-mist ambitions, a shock well placed and timed by Asad, that cleared the way to a reordering of Lebanon's political geography. The Druze and Hizballah Shi'is instantly understood the magnitude of the shift; the LF-Kata'ib camp seemed less perspicacious. In the shadow of the Iraqi-American confrontation, adroitly exploited by Damascus, the Ta'if Agreement was both pushed ahead and completely Syrianized.

August/September 1996 Lebanese parliamentary elections
(Habib Haddad in *al-Hayat*, 10 August 1996)

278

CHAPTER EIGHT

LEBANON AND SYRIA, 1990–2005

The inauguration of Syrian hegemony, 1990–92

Hafiz al-Asad picked the reliably loyal 'Umar Karami of Tripoli (brother of the assassinated former prime minister Rashid Karami) as prime minister for Lebanon's new "National Unity Government" formed in December 1990, and packed both its Christian and Muslim halves with Syrian allies. The Lebanese Forces and the Kata'ib expected to be rewarded for going against Aoun, but instead were marginalized. Ja'ja' abandoned his cabinet post in March 1991. Syria also oversaw the disbandment and disarmament of the militias by mid-1991, the main targets being the Christian LF and the Druze "canton." The dissolution of militias did not encompass Hizballah's armed wing, the vanguard of resistance against Israeli occupation. Damascus rushed discussions on concretizing the Tai'f reference to "privileged relations," overriding complaints from within the new Lebanese regime about disregard for Lebanese sovereignty.[258] Syrian domination was so blatant that even Prime Minister Karami felt obliged to make such statements as: "It is clear to all that Syria has no ambitions in Lebanon and does not wish, as some see it, to swallow Lebanon and to colonize it and take its revenues."[259]

The Treaty of Brotherhood, Cooperation, and Coordination, signed on 22 May 1991, provided a framework for deep Syrian intrusion in Lebanon's policy-making.[260] It established a semi-federal Higher Council between the two countries, with committees for prime ministerial "coordination," foreign affairs, defense and security, and economic and social policy. The Syrians dropped the word "integration" because of U.S.

objections;[261] Syrian Foreign Minister Faruq al-Shar'a commented that: "The majority of people in Lebanon and Syria are with unification, but [Damascus] is content for the present with coordination."[262] A detailed Defense and Security Pact followed on 1 September 1991, committing Lebanon to "the highest level of military coordination" and "banning any activity or organization in all military, security, political, and information fields that might endanger or cause threats to the other country."[263]

In late 1992, according to the Ta'if accord, Syria was supposed to redeploy its forces in Lebanon out of Beirut to the vicinity of the main pass in the coastal mountains above the Lebanese capital. Asad, who wanted a prolonged Syrian military presence in Beirut to emphasize Syrian power while Syrian-Lebanese "coordination" was gradually consolidated, ignored this provision with ease. The Lebanese defense minister obligingly indicated that the Lebanese army could not yet take over security duties,[264] and Asad rejected any requirement for redeployment ahead of Lebanon's first postwar parliamentary elections.[265] The elections went ahead in August–September 1992, with the Ta'if stipulation for governorates as constituencies abandoned in favor of a gerrymander to give maximum advantage to Syria's allies. General Aoun, from his exile in France, backed a boycott call that reduced voter turnout to less than 25%, but this only assisted Syrian and Lebanese regime domination of the new parliament.

The major weakness in Syria's Lebanese arrangements in the early 1990s was the comprehensive economic incompetence of 'Umar Karami's government, stalling Lebanon's reconstruction and leading to a virtual collapse of the Lebanese currency in early 1992. General strikes promoted by the union movement expressed rising public fury, and on 6 May 1992 there was a near-revolutionary moment when rioters marched on the prime minister's residence in Beirut and sacked the finance minister's house in Sidon. Karami, protected by a Syrian-Lebanese security cordon, promptly resigned.

Despite its suspicions of the Saudi and Western associations of the billionaire Sunni Muslim businessman Rafiq al-Hariri, Damascus acknowledged the advantages of "a prime minister capable of bringing foreign aid and loans to help stabilize Ta'if," in the words of Syrian

Vice-President 'Abd al-Halim Khaddam.[266] The Syrian concept was that Hariri would have freedom to manage Lebanon's reconstruction and finances, keeping both Lebanon and Syria afloat, as long as he left security and foreign relations to Damascus, accepted Syrian vetting of official appointments, and tolerated a financial rake-off for Syrian personalities and their Lebanese associates. Hariri appeared amenable, and in October 1992 he became prime minister, initially without a parliamentary seat.

High hegemony, 1993–2000

Hariri alone had the vision, energy, contacts, and resources to set Lebanon on the path to recovery. However, he could not operate without bowing to Syria's terms and Asad's supremacy, given that both the Americans and the Europeans accepted Syrian command of the Lebanese. Hariri and his partners in the Solidere Company pushed ahead the demolition and rebuilding of central Beirut, the centerpiece of wide-ranging infrastructural investments. Through the mid-1990s, at the cost of massive expansion of public debt and a highly skewed income distribution, Hariri stabilized the currency, lowered inflation, sponsored a construction boom, and achieved GDP annual growth rates of 5–7%. This made Lebanon secure and profitable for the Syrian regime.

In July 1993, Israel added its contribution to entrenching Syria's position in Beirut when it unleashed a large-scale bombardment of southern Lebanon in response to Hizballah rocket attacks into the Galilee. Much of the Shi'i population fled north, and the U.S. turned to Asad to produce a cease-fire. Syria oversaw an arrangement by which Hizballah would not fire into northern Israel if Israel did not shell Shi'i villages, but Hizballah was free to continue raiding the Israeli-occupied "security zone."[267] Even the Israeli prime minister, Yitzhak Rabin, had recognized that Hizballah worked within "the ideology of liberating Lebanese sovereign lands."[268] The episode extended Hizballah's support among Shi'is and demonstrated Syrian influence on the party. No one now dared question Syria's strategic interests in garrisoning Lebanon, and Syria could play between the Lebanese government and a more muscular Hizballah, using each to restrict the other. Later, in April 1996, Israel confirmed Syria's gains and further inflated Hizballah with an equally futile and more brutal bombardment, at the outset of which Israel advised 400,000 people to leave southern Lebanon. On 18 April, Israeli artillery, in an exchange of fire with Hizballah, killed 102 Lebanese civilians sheltering at a U.N. post, the worst casualty toll in a single incident in two decades of Israeli-Hizballah clashes.

Lest Hizballah feel too sure of itself, Syria endorsed the Lebanese authorities when the army shot dead nine party demonstrators at a rally on 13 September 1993. General Ghazi Kana'an, Syria's military intelligence chief in Lebanon, summoned and dressed-down Hizballah leaders after they labeled Lebanon's defense minister "an Ariel Sharon."[269] The party's parliamentary position, the main feature of its desire to represent itself as Lebanese rather than an Iranian agent, was precarious, with only twelve seats out of 128, these part of an electoral alignment with Amal enforced by Syria. Damascus arranged for this quota to be trimmed to nine in the 1996 elections when Hizballah tried to decouple from Amal and rejected alignment in Beirut with Syria's Maronite ally Elie Hubayqa. The latter was previously a friend of Israel and responsible for the 1982 massacre of Palestinians and Shi'ites in the Sabra and Shatila refugee camps.[270]

Between 1993 and Hariri's temporary exit from power in 1998, his government coerced opponents who either attacked its policies or embarrassed it by refusing to accept the new Syrian-sponsored order. It therefore served Syrian security goals at the same time as the Syrians and their other allies regularly frustrated the prime minister. In March/April 1994, the government banned the Lebanese Forces and arrested Samir Ja'ja', who was arraigned on a succession of charges and spent the next eleven years imprisoned in the basement of the defense ministry. Ja'ja' had a dubious record in the war years, but so did many whom Syria backed as government ministers. For Syria, the LF was an old problem, and Ja'ja' sealed his fate by declining to serve in the new regime. In July 1995, the regime faced down a general strike with emergency powers and army deployment. In November 1996, riot police dispersed protests against a restrictive media law limiting radio and TV licenses to stations in the hands of regime personalities (with Hizballah's

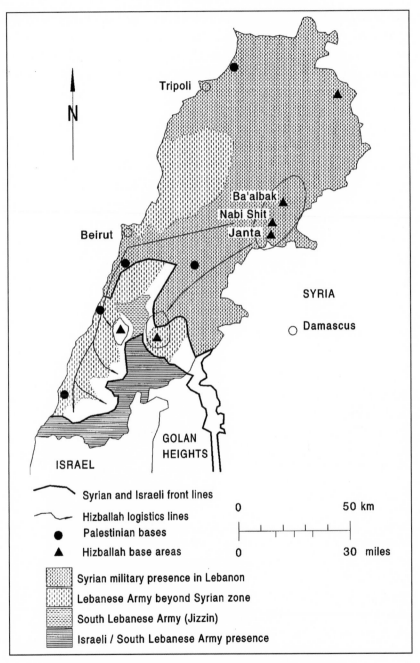

N

Tripoli

Ba'albak
Nabi Shit
Beirut   Janta

SYRIA

Damascus

GOLAN
HEIGHTS
ISRAEL

⌒ Syrian and Israeli front lines
⌒ Hizballah logistics lines
● Palestinian bases
▲ Hizballah base areas

0   50 km

0   30   miles

Syrian military presence in Lebanon
Lebanese Army beyond Syrian zone
South Lebanese Army (Jizzin)
Israeli / South Lebanese Army presence

Map 12. Lebanon: Geopolitical conditions, 1995

media later exempted), while in December the authorities detained scores of Aoun supporters and Tripoli Sunnis after an assault on a Syrian mini-bus.[271] The respected U.S.-based Human Rights Watch (HRW) reported the "torture" of detainees in the Syrian military intelligence base in Beirut (the Beau Rivage Hotel), and their transfer to Syria.[272]

I was in southern Lebanon on 19 July 1995, the day of the general strike. The government declared gatherings of more than three people illegal, and service taxi drivers reported that cars with more than three passengers on the way to Sidon were being turned back by the army, because they were transporting "illegal assemblies." Ordinary people expressed themselves in fierce terms. A couple of days later I heard a Shi'i driver in East Beirut observe to another motorist who was sounding his horn: *Intibee, rah b'thizz amn al-dawla* [Careful! You might shake the security of the state].

Despite his cooperation, the Syrians still distrusted and contained Hariri. They manipulated the jealousies of the Maronite president and the Shi'ite parliamentary speaker against him, and dissension reigned in the affairs of the "troika" of regime heads. President Hirawi and Speaker Barri defended their patronage networks and "shares" of the bureaucracy, wrecking the prime minister's project for administrative reform. According to one commentator, politicians recognized "that the present republic is fragmented and that what links its pieces is the Syrian thread."[273] Hariri's personal relations in Syria were more with prominent regime Sunnis—Khaddam and chief of staff Hikmet Shihabi—than with the Asads. Asad's son Bashar, first in line for the succession after the 1994 death of his brother Basil, developed relations with the Lebanese army commander Lahoud. When Hariri consulted with the U.N. about sending the Lebanese army south after the July 1993 Israeli-Hizballah flare-up, potentially cramping Hizballah, Hafiz al-Asad rebuked him for "concealment."[274] Similarly, Syria reportedly forced Hariri to cancel a May 1998 meeting in Paris with the U.N. secretary-general, Kofi Annan, because of unwarranted suspicion about him wavering on Lebanese-Syrian coordination vis-à-vis Israel.[275]

Even government ministers could be victims of swindles within the state apparatus—poetic justice, from the public perspective. On 19 January 1995 *al-Nahar* reported: "Two days ago a minister complained to the Ministry of Posts and Communications, submitting a set of accounts for his home telephone for September 1994 amounting to 54 million lira [about $34,000]. It had become evident to this minister, whose telephone had been out of order throughout September, that his line had been appropriated by a 'mafia,' which had used it for overseas calls. The Ministry of Posts had told him, when he had reported the 'fault,' that there was a technical problem with the cable."

Through these years, Syria pressed the extension of Syrian-Lebanese coordination beyond the political and security spheres, as envisaged in the Orwellian 1991 Brotherhood Treaty. Khaddam looked ahead to economic union as a "humble experiment" to "serve the interests of the two countries."[276] The Brotherhood Treaty's Syrian-Lebanese Higher Council had annual meetings from 1993 on, and its secretary-general, Nasri Khuri, referred to "reaching the stage of integration [*takamul*]."[277] A cascade of detailed accords ensued, including labor arrangements to ease the flow of Syrian workers into Lebanon, a water agreement under which Syria took 78% of the Orontes River flow, a transit agreement that outraged Lebanese truck drivers, and a proposed customs union that meant little to the Lebanese in view of the facts that Syrian goods already flooded into Lebanon and Syrian industrial and administrative regulations nullified free trade.[278] As early as 1995, several hundred thousand Syrian workers remitted more than $1 billion to Syria, equivalent to 10% of Lebanon's GDP.[279]

Revealing indicators of Syrian impatience with Lebanese constitutional proprieties and residual traces of Lebanese democracy appeared with the extension of President Hirawi's term in 1995, the massaging of the 1996 parliamentary poll, and Asad's 1998 selection of the army commander Emile Lahoud as president.

Asad was sufficiently pleased with Hirawi to see no need for a successor when the latter's single constitutionally allowable six-year term ran out in late 1995. Ghazi Kana'an, Syria's senior official in Lebanon, chose the September 1995 engagement party of 'Umar Karami's son in Tripoli to announce that Lebanese parliamentarians were to override their constitution and give Hirawi three more years. "Kana'an then raised his hand, saying that the vote would take place by a raising of hands and would not be secret. . . . Karami stood and his color changed. . . . The party broke up early. Presidential hopefuls departed with their wives, one complaining of tiredness, another saying he had a headache."[280] Asad's view of the Lebanese constitution was made clear in his comment, "I don't see altering one or two clauses as being of such importance as to justify debate."[281]

The Syrian concept for the July/August 1996 parliamentary elections was clear-cut, and the outcome was exactly as choreographed. Prime Minister Hariri and Speaker Barri would get substantial blocs to ensure government stability; the Christian opposition would be enticed to participate in Mount Lebanon and then crushed by gerrymandering and irregularities; Syrian nominees would sweep Mount Lebanon, North Lebanon, and the Biqa'; and Hizballah would be modestly cut back to please the Americans. *Al-Nahar* columnist Sarkis Na'um commented that Damascus deserved an Oscar for its performance, and his newspaper noted that the 1996 result put the infamous 1947 elections in the shade for "intimidation, forgery, and abuses."[282] Thousands of "new citizens," many from Syria, were bused to polling stations for supervised voting, ballot boxes appeared and disappeared, and the dead woke up "after 4 pm" to have their say.[283] When a voter in East Beirut complained that someone had already used his ballot, a polling station officer told him: "You are not the first. They have voted for you and you are alive, but they also voted for others that are dead."[284] Ghazi Kana'an finalized the division of shares in the south and the Biqa' at a lunch with Barri and Hizballah leader Hasan Nasrallah.[285] A senior U.S. official effusively welcomed the Lebanese exercise of "democratic principles,"[286] a low point in the Clinton administration's pandering to Syria.

In late 1998, Asad reshuffled the Lebanese leadership. Syria was nervous about the continuing alienation of the Maronite community, and tried unsuccessfully in 1997–98 to woo the Maronite patriarch Nasrallah Butros Sufayr, who made scathing remarks about the Syrian presence in Lebanon. The impressive crowds that greeted Pope John Paul II in Beirut in May 1997 also indicated that Maronites and other Catholics remained an important part of the country, regardless of claims about their demographic slippage. For Asad, the army commander Lahoud was the ideal Maronite to replace the ineffectual President Hirawi when the latter's term expired in November 1998. First, he would give the Christians the impression of revitalized presidential weight vis-à-vis the Sunni prime minister and the Shi'i parliamentary speaker. Second, he had proved his complete subservience to Damascus in reorganizing the Lebanese army and associated security forces in subordination to their Syrian counterparts. Third, he would combine civilian and military leadership in one personality, making an excellent Maronite partner for Hizballah in furthering Syria's strategic interests on its Lebanese flank.

Hariri and Barri received Syria's "secret word" on Asad's choice of Lahoud on 16 September 1998.[287] Hirawi went to Damascus to hear directly from Asad on 5 October, after which Lebanese presidential palace sources publicly referred to Lahoud as Lebanon's next head of state.[288] Once again, the constitution had to be changed to allow Lahoud, as a senior state employee, to proceed directly to the presidency. Parliament dutifully followed its orders and elected Lahoud president on 15 October 1998.

Lahoud made it clear that Hariri would have reduced authority if he took up a new mandate as prime minister. Lahoud intended to boost his popularity among estranged constituencies—the poor, the middle class, and the Maronites—by anti-corruption campaigns against Hariri's ministerial bloc.[289] Lebanese parliamentary deputies linked to Asad's son Bashar also reportedly maneuvered to have Hariri removed.[290] Hariri read the writing on the wall and withdrew from contention. His Beirut rival Salim al-Huss became prime minister and launched a reform offensive to curb "waste" and seek out those who had allegedly abused public trust. This dovetailed with moves inside Syria to boost Bashar al-Asad as a young "new broom" to wield against the misdemeanors of

287

entrenched personalities who might endanger his succession. The Lebanese Druze leader Walid Junblatt sarcastically asked if Huss's austerity would include "the numerous and various military, security, and intelligence agencies,"[291] and joined Hariri in the parliamentary opposition.

For two years, Lahoud and Huss hounded Hariri's circle with allegations of embezzlement and misuse of public funds. In June 1999, "sources" from within Lahoud's entourage made an abusive personal attack on Hariri, accusing him of running the state while prime minister as a "private company whose dividends are distributed to those who do his bidding" and colluding with Israel to curb Hizballah.[292] Meanwhile the Huss cabinet of technocrats failed dismally to arrest the economic deterioration heralded by slowing economic growth before Hariri left office. Tax hikes and moral posturing had no impact on soaring debts and deficits. Lahoud and Syria's Ghazi Kana'an engineered a new electoral law that split Beirut to weaken Hariri's parliamentary bloc, but public disenchantment with the Lahoud regime together with Hariri's financial power enabled Hariri and Junblatt to triumph in the July/August 2000 poll. For Damascus, this was all within the compass of Syrian alliances. Whether or not Hariri became prime minister depended on Syria, not on election results, and Junblatt owed his success to the Syrian-promoted carve-up of Mount Lebanon, defying the Ta'if provision for governorates as constituencies.

For Syria, Lahoud's military background enabled the Lebanese presidency to become the anchor of a Lebanese "security state" on the Syrian model, in which security service bosses increasingly overshadowed civilian authority. Syria's chief behind-the-scenes Lebanese intelligence agent through the 1990s was Jamil al-Sayyid, a Biqa' Shi'i who ran President Hirawi's personal security at the outset of his term in 1989 and became deputy head of military intelligence in 1992.[293] Sayyid spearheaded Lahoud's bid for the presidency, but also monitored Lahoud as well as Hariri for his Syrian masters. Hariri regarded Sayyid as the coordinator of "all the political, media, and labor movements against him."[294] In January 1997 Hariri tried to block Sayyid's promotion from colonel to brigadier; Damascus promptly instructed the prime minister "to leave the soldiers to decide the affairs of their institution."[295] At the same time, Sayyid kept Damascus informed about Lahoud's foreign contacts as army commander, particularly with the Americans.[296] Later, when Lahoud and Huss tried to have Sayyid removed from his post as head of Lebanon's General Security Directorate, Syria's Ghazi Kana'an stopped them and reportedly told Lahoud that "Jamil al-Sayyid is my eye and my ear."[297]

On becoming president in October 1998, Lahoud elevated Sayyid to the General Security directorship and appointed the Maronite Raymond Azar as head of military intelligence. These two were the Lebanese extension of Syrian military intelligence, watching each other and playing among Syria's allies.[298] Their real supervisor, Syria's military intelligence commander in Lebanon, General Ghazi Kana'an, was based in the Biqa' Armenian town of Anjar, near the Syrian border. From there he coordinated his senior subordinates in Beirut, for example his eventual successor Rustum Ghazale, and Lahoud's security heads. Apart from Sayyid and Azar, Lahoud appointed his crony Mustafa Hamdan, connected by marriage to Sayyid, as commander of the presidential guard, and promoted Michel Suleiman, brother-in-law of Asad's official spokesman Jebran Kurriyeh, over the heads of higher-ranking officers to be army chief. The Syrian-Lebanese "security regime," in its mature form after 1998, variously moved against Hariri, maneuvered between Hariri and Lahoud, arranged reconciliations of Lebanese leaders, and liaised with Hizballah as Syria's other local instrument. The Syrian leadership termed such manipulations "stability."

At the end of the 1990s, the "security regime," representing consolidated Syrian hegemony, faced uncertainties. It was alien to Lebanon's freewheeling traditions—an import from a state that followed a fundamentally different line of political development after the 1950s. Presidents Fuad Shihab and Camille Chamoun fell back on the security services to win elections or promote reforms in the 1950s and 60s, but such experiments produced severe reactions and proved unviable. Lahoud's nastier version added the provocative element of direction from outside Lebanon by a neighboring authoritarian regime. Walid Junblatt's hostility after 1998 was fully in the mold of his father's opposition to Chamoun and Shihab. By 2000, Junblatt's stance represented the first serious challenge to Syrian intervention in Lebanon from outside the Christian sector.

In parallel, Hafiz al-Asad's deteriorating health raised questions about the future competence of the "security regime" in coordinating Lebanon's fractious leaders and factions. Hafiz al-Asad had the prestige, experience, and skill both to divide the Lebanese and to prevent resulting personal resentments and sectarian competition from getting out of hand. Even so, Lebanon paid a high price through the 1990s in political paralysis and administrative chaos.

Israel also injected a new element into the equation. In May 1999, the Israeli Labor Party leader Ehud Barak defeated Binyamin Netanyahu and the Likud in general elections, promising Israeli withdrawal from southern Lebanon within twelve months of forming a government. Syrian nervousness at having one of the props of its presence in Lebanon removed lay behind "security regime" moves to reconcile with Hariri and Junblat in late 1999. Jamil al-Sayyid arranged a Junblatt-Lahoud meeting on 28 October, and Hariri went to see Lahoud on 7 November, describing the encounter as "more than excellent."[299]

In early 2000, Israeli Prime Minister Barak conceived Israel's redeployment to the international boundary as pressure on Lebanon and Syria to become more amenable to general peace arrangements, noting "if there is not an agreement [with Lebanon and Syria] by April or May, and we don't see an agreement on the horizon, we know what to do."[300] Syrian officials hoped Israel was not serious, preferring to believe that "Israel will not withdraw . . . in a unilateral manner because it will create a vacuum."[301] Nonetheless, the March 2000 collapse of U.S. efforts to produce an Israeli-Syrian breakthrough regarding the Golan Heights cancelled all options apart from unilateral Israeli withdrawal from Lebanon.[302]

The last few months of Israel's occupation of the "security zone" witnessed a bizarre procession of events. Israel's local ally, the South Lebanese Army (SLA), had already abandoned the Christian Jizzin area under Hizballah pressure in May 1999. Thereafter the Israelis stiffened their proxy militia with raised pay and upgraded equipment even as they prepared to pull the carpet out from under the SLA. In January and May 2000, on the eve of departure, Israel responded to Hizballah raids with military escalation, twice bombing Lebanese electricity facilities to demonstrate the consequences of disturbing the border after their abandonment of the "security zone." The Lebanese regime, after years of demanding that Israel implement U.N. Security Council Resolution 425 and leave, suddenly seemed not to want to cope with a new environment. Defense Minister Ghazi Zu'aytar, seconded by deputy parliamentary speaker Elie al-Firzli, threatened that Lebanon might invite the Syrian army into places evacuated by Israel, putting "Tel Aviv within range of Syrian missiles."[303] This embarrassed Damascus, which hastened to curb such ludicrous posturing by its Lebanese clients.[304]

For its part, Hizballah parted company with its allies in the regime and looked forward enthusiastically to Israeli departure without any arrangement with Lebanon or Syria, thereby enhancing the party's claim to a famous unilateral victory. On 16 April 2000, Israel officially notified the U.N. of its intention to fulfill Resolution 425. In late April, the Lebanese parliamentary speaker Nabih Barri, endorsed by Syria,[305] demanded that Israel's withdrawal include the Shab'a farms, land on the Lebanese-Syrian border captured by Israel in its June 1967 conquest of the Golan Heights. The matter had never been raised before; the U.N. regarded the area as Syrian territory, despite Lebanese land ownership. The demand was plainly a device to enable Hizballah to continue "resistance to occupation," thereby justifying its perpetuation as an armed movement above and beyond Lebanese state authority. Hizballah leader Hasan Nasrallah boasted: "The party has outgrown the country [Lebanon] and the [Shi'i] community."[306] For Syria, Hizballah could persist both as a check on the Lebanese regime and as a means to bother Israel when convenient.

Israel pulled its forces out of southern Lebanon between 21 and 23 May 2000. Out of 2,500 SLA personnel, 1,000 fled into Israel and 1,500 surrendered, all being turned over to the Lebanese authorities. Hizballah spread its forces through the "security zone" in an orderly manner, and the Lebanese army stayed out. On 16 June, Secretary-General Kofi Annan announced that Israel had fulfilled his requirement for retirement behind a line delimited by the U.N. (the "blue line") as the international boundary. In the meantime, Syria's Hafiz al-Asad died on 10 June. Lebanon thus faced the new millennium with new Syrian management and Israel no longer on its territory, apart from the Shab'a farms dispute.

Stagnant hegemony, 2000–2004

Hariri's return as Lebanon's prime minister after the July/August 2000 parliamentary elections imposed an increasingly clear division in the Lebanese regime. On one side was a large segment of the cabinet, headed by the Sunni Muslim prime minister, loosely aligned with Druze leader Junblatt and moderate Christian parliamentary deputies. On the other side was the security apparatus, headed by President Lahoud and the intelligence agency chiefs, who linked with Hizballah and a group of ministers unfriendly to Hariri and close to Syria's 'Alawi leadership. The Maronite patriarch Sufayr, who was in Aoun's absence the most influential Christian personality residing in Lebanon and a critic of Syria's role through the 1990s, leaned toward the Hariri-Junblatt camp after 2000. The Shi'i parliamentary speaker Barri and his Amal bloc of ministers leaned toward Lahoud and had a Syrian-enforced electoral pact with Hizballah. Aside from Sufayr, all these personalities and factions remained Syrian allies, though Junblatt was adrift and the moderate Christians bowed only out of the lack of any alternative.

As in the mid-1990s, Hariri's function was to promote economic growth, secure inflows of foreign money, and sustain the Lebanese banking system, so that Syria could keep its ramshackle financial affairs afloat and the Syrian/Lebanese security elite could cream off tens of millions of dollars for its private comforts. For example, the brothers of Rustum Ghazale, who succeeded Ghazi Kana'an as Syrian military intelligence overlord in Lebanon in 2002, stand accused of embezzling Madina Bank in Beirut of massive sums, involving more than eight million dollars in 2002 alone.[307] One report has claimed that Ghazale and his brothers siphoned off a total of $200 million from the bank.[308]

Further, in exchange for room for maneuver in economic policy, Hariri had to cede primacy in security and foreign affairs to the president and Damascus, regardless of the economic implications of Syria's regional militancy. Lahoud, the security chiefs, and their allies were under no such constraints in the reverse direction. Lahoud's blockage of privatization, Hizballah's clashes with Israel, and the general prevalence of theft and extortion all threatened Hariri's vision of a new Lebanon, including his considerable personal investment in that vision.

Syria's new leader, Bashar al-Asad, adopted a new approach toward Lebanon. Unlike his father, who kept above the jockeying among Syrian allies, Bashar descended into the Lebanese arena as the associate of President Lahoud and the security apparatus. Bashar maintained a cool attitude toward Hariri, and sought a personal rapport with Hizballah's Nasrallah, violating his father's concept of Hizballah as nothing more than an instrument. Contrary to wishful thinking about Bashar as a reformer, events soon revealed a rigid mentality and a person fond of provocative speeches and impulsive gambles. Within Syria, a very limited political relaxation was shut down within months when criticism became bothersome. During the May 2001 papal visit to Damascus, Bashar made crude anti-Semitic remarks,[309] and he backed suicide bombings within Israel at the March 2002 Arab summit in Beirut.[310] As for Lebanon, Bashar gave the go-ahead for a vigorous crackdown on opposition to the "security regime" as soon as he felt confident about such a move.

Initially, the Israeli withdrawal and the Syrian succession encouraged Lebanese public questioning of Syria's continued domination of Beirut. The new feature was open dissent from prominent Druze and Sunni Muslims. For example, 'Aliah al-Sulh, daughter of independent Lebanon's first prime minister Riyadh al-Sulh, wrote an editorial highly critical of the Syrian Ba'thists.[311] Walid Junblatt slammed Syrian interference in the 2000 elections,[312] and in September 2000 the Council of Maronite Bishops, chaired by Patriarch Sufayr, issued an unprecedented condemnation of Syrian behavior. The communiqué highlighted Syria's "total hegemony," blamed Syria for flooding the Lebanese market with cheap produce and cheap labor, and invited the Syrian army to redeploy as promised in 1989.[313] Junblatt noted that the new Hariri government's November 2000 policy statement did not mention the Ta'if Agreement's requirement for Syrian redeployment.[314] In response, Syrian officials indicated that Junblatt was persona non grata in Damascus, and the Lebanese Ba'thist deputy 'Asim Qansu made a death threat against the Druze leader.[315] The affair provoked protests from Druze within Syria, which further aggravated the Syrian regime. Overall, the new wave of Lebanese grumblings was less easy to dismiss as Christian recidivism stirred by Israel than it had been in the past.

Bashar and Lahoud waited to gauge the outlook of the new Republican administration in Washington. The critical moment came in March 2001 when Secretary of State Colin Powell and other senior U.S. officials declined to meet Maronite patriarch Sufayr during his visit to Washington. The U.S. thereby indicated its indifference, and its continued toleration of the Syrian hegemony. Junblatt faced pressure almost immediately, in the form of deployment of Syrian troops in the Shuf and a mail bomb against the family of his close associate Akram Shuhayyib.[316] Junblatt looked for cover from the segment of the Syrian regime that also had decent relations with Hariri, inviting vice-president Khaddam to Mukhtara in May 2002.[317]

In August 2001, the "security regime" struck hard, after Sufayr visited Junblatt amid excited crowds to re-launch the old Maronite-Druze mountain partnership. Lahoud's security forces arrested hundreds of activists, particularly Michel Aoun's followers, and Bashar sent military reinforcements into Lebanon. The Syrian Defense Minister, Mustafa Tlas, giving Bashar's address at an officers' graduation ceremony, stressed that Damascus "stands beside President Lahoud and brotherly Lebanese army commander Michel Suleiman" in facing "suspicious movements whose linkage with foreign elements hostile to Lebanon and the Arab nation has been confirmed."[318] Neither Lahoud nor Bashar consulted Prime Minister Hariri about the arrests. Hariri complained impotently from the sidelines.

The repression underscored the ascendancy of the "security regime" and set the tone for the rest of Lahoud's presidential term. Through 2002–2003, Lahoud frustrated Hariri's plans to advance privatization with the sale of mobile phone operating licenses, and cultivated the labor federation by opposing Hariri's tax increases. Although the prime minister pushed through a value added tax in 2002, boosting state revenues, and had the advantage in executive authority under the Ta'if Agreement, power really depended on arbitrary Syrian desiderata favoring Lahoud.

Hariri also came off poorly in encounters with Hizballah. The prime minister's reservations about Hizballah's clashes with Israel in March/April 2002, when Hizballah fired almost 1,500 shells in the Shab'a farms sector to support the Palestinians during major Israeli military operations on the West Bank, had no effect. Hariri stood "firmly against escalation and giving the Israeli government justifications to divert international attention from the West Bank,"[319] but found himself compelled to defend Hizballah in Washington. On 26 June 2002, Hizballah supporters roughed up a Hariri aide at a bridge project ceremony.[320] The bridge excited old Shi'i suspicions about a Sunni-led scheme to displace Shi'is from the southern entrance to Beirut.

Hariri had the advantage in foreign relations, and his mobilization of funds was vital to Lebanon and Syria, but his contacts stimulated jealousies and the financial relief only helped his adversaries to stall economic reform. In April 2002, Hariri met senior IMF, World Bank, and U.S. officials in Washington without briefing Lahoud, returning the favor for his treatment in the security crackdown. At a Paris conference of Lebanon's creditors in November 2002, helped by his friend the French president, Jacques Chirac, Hariri obtained aid and debt restructuring worth $7 billion, equivalent to about 40% of Lebanon's GDP.[321] Unfortunately, the injection, which left Lebanon's mountainous public debt little altered, reduced pressure for budget austerity, particularly in Lahoud's security domain, which was the biggest budget item after debt servicing and off-limits to the prime minister.

In early 2003, as the U.S. assault on Saddam Husayn's Iraq loomed, Syria insisted on reduced tension among its Lebanese allies, especially Hariri and Lahoud. Bashar also reshuffled Syria's intelligence commanders in Lebanon in December 2002. Rustum Ghazale replaced Kana'an as overall chief, effectively Syria's high commissioner, and Muhammad Khalouf replaced Ghazale as the Beirut commander. Both were subordinate to Bashar's brother-in-law Asef Shawkat, the real head of Syrian military intelligence under the titular authority of General Hasan Khalil. Kana'an was outside the new elite around Bashar after 2000, drifted apart from Lahoud, and allegedly received money from Hariri. He returned to Damascus, becoming interior minister in November 2004.

Bashar prepared to defy the U.S. in Iraq. Under Bashar, the old rivalry between the Syrian and Iraqi wings of the Ba'th party became transformed into a blossoming commercial relationship. Syria ignored U.N. sanctions on Saddam's regime and by 2002 profited by more than $1 billion per annum from cheap imports of Iraqi oil, enabling it to export equivalent amounts of its own limited production.[322] At the same time, Saddam's Iraq potentially offered Syria geographical continuity with its Iranian "strategic ally." Long U.S. toleration of Syrian maneuvering encouraged the impression in Damascus that Syria could hold off Washington by dangling deals at the same time as it subverted the U.S. position in the Middle East. Bashar apparently believed that he could outlast any U.S. intervention in Iraq and emerge as an Arab hero.

During and after the March/April Anglo-American occupation of Iraq, Bashar therefore allowed Syrian and other "volunteers" into Iraq to fight the U.S.,[323] gave sanctuary to fugitive Iraqi Ba'thists, and vociferously condemned the U.S. president, George W. Bush. For example, at the October 2003 Islamic summit in Malaysia, the Syrian president described the Bush administration as a "group of extremists" with "wicked intentions" who had used the 11 September 2001 attacks on the U.S. "to assault humanitarian values and principles . . . when they revealed their barbaric attitude to human society and began to market the principle of force instead of dialogue, oppression instead of justice, and racism instead of toleration."[324] His foreign minister, Faruq al-Shar'a, termed the Bush administration "the most violent and stupid U.S. government ever."[325] Bashar's father would never have taken such risks with the global superpower.

Predictably, Syria faced mounting U.S. anger through 2003. In March 2003, Secretary of State Colin Powell referred for the first time to the "Syrian occupation" of Lebanon.[326] In December 2003, a hitherto reluctant President Bush signed the "Syrian Accountability and Lebanese Sovereignty Restoration Act" after this legislation received overwhelming support in both houses of Congress. Just as Hafiz al-Asad's cooperation with the U.S. had opened the gate to Syrian command of Lebanon in 1990, so Bashar's provocation of the U.S. in Iraq in 2003–2004 led Washington to revoke its approval of this hegemony.

Ironically, within Lebanon, Syria's hegemony never seemed so conclusive as in 2003. Confidence about the grip of the "security regime" made the direct military presence less essential, and Damascus drew down the number of Syrian troops from more than 30,000 in 2000 to 16,000 at the time of the U.S. invasion of Iraq, with redeployment away from Christian areas. This lowered the visual profile of domination, its most irritating aspect to many Lebanese. By 2003, troop levels were probably down to the basic level Syria regarded as indispensable to secure its western flank and overawe its more autonomous-minded Lebanese allies, Hariri and Hizballah. Meantime, after being snubbed in Washington in early 2001, the Maronite patriarch Sufayr gradually toned down his criticism of Damascus. In March 2003 he warned of the American "war machine moving in the Middle East" and was so accommodating toward the Syrian regime that Syria's new chief in Lebanon, Rustum Ghazale, toasted him at a banquet.[327] The Syrians thus felt able to increase the number of Syrian loyalists in the Lebanese cabinet via an April 2003 reshuffle, shutting out Christian politicians who had breathed even a breath of dissent.

At first, the U.S. occupation of Iraq produced a Lebanese consensus highly convenient to Syria, with all communities united in disapproval of American "unilateralism." Maronites took their cue from the hostility of the Vatican and France toward the U.S., while Lebanese Shi'is were little affected by the Iraqi Shi'i hatred of Saddam Husayn, their modern communal connections being more with Iran than with Iraq.

A new Lebanese-Syrian souring, at least for Christians, Sunni Muslims, and Druze, came remarkably quickly in 2004, as the end of President Lahoud's single constitutional six-year term in November 2004 approached. Bashar and his inner circle of security bosses preferred to extend Lahoud's term rather than to experiment with another Maronite, especially in conditions of confrontation with Washington. From the Syrian perspective, Lahoud was of proven loyalty and reliability, had warm relations with Hizballah, and represented a convenient fusing of civilian and security authority. No other Maronite could bring such combined advantages, and a civilian politician might drift toward the U.S. and France. As for precedents, there was the warning of Ilyas Sarkis's escape from the Syrian orbit after being promoted by Damascus in 1976, and the incentive of Hafiz al-Asad's easy dictation of Hirawi's extension in 1995.

Bashar's will came up against stiff opposition from Hariri, who was exasperated with Lahoud's sabotage of his policies, and Junblatt, who detested the security machine. Lahoud's subservience to Bashar also meant that by 2004 he had lost virtually all credibility in his Maronite community—six years of relentless fawning to the Syrian regime made a joke of the original selling of Lahoud as a "strong" new Maronite president vis-à-vis Sunni and Shi'i leaders.

The final Syrian decision on Lahoud hinged on the situation in Iraq. Through 2004, Damascus juggled appeasing the U.S. regarding border supervision and coordinating with Iraqi Ba'thists, Sunni militants, and criminal gangs against the U.S. in western Iraq.[328] The August 2004 rebellion of the young Shi'ite firebrand Muqtada al-Sadr in the holy city of Najaf opened a mediation possibility. Bashar enrolled Hizballah leader Nasrallah to assist in pacifying Sadr and doubtless felt he was doing the U.S. a major good turn. From the U.S. perspective this was simply Syrian opportunism, and a sideshow compared with the peace-making of Grand Ayatollah Ali al-Sistani, no friend of Nasrallah. Nonetheless, according to an informed commentator, the Syrians imagined that the Americans owed them freedom in Lebanon in exchange for such grace and favor in Iraq.[329]

On 27 August 2004, brushing aside American and French appeals for a normal vote in the Lebanese parliament for a new president, Bashar summoned Prime Minister Hariri to Damascus to order him to have the Lebanese parliament change the constitution and extend Lahoud's term for three years. Bashar emulated Adolf Hitler's dealings with Austria and Czechoslovakia in the late 1930s. According to Hariri, the Syrian president issued physical threats and spoke of "breaking Lebanon over his [Hariri's] head."[330] Thereafter Hariri also had an unpleasant session with Rustum Ghazale in Anjar. The humiliated and shaken prime minister arrived back in his mountain chalet above Farraya proclaiming that "to them [the Syrians] we are all ants."[331]

The Lebanese-Syrian Crisis, 2004–2005

Bashar al-Asad's behavior and reported remarks over Lahoud's extension were in the same inflammatory vein as his support for suicide bombings in Israel and his attacks on the U.S. administration over Iraq. Bashar and his entourage, sure of their power and contemptuous of the West and the Lebanese alike, plunged Lebanon and Syria into a crisis that soon came to rival the Iraqi and Israeli-Palestinian issues in its Middle Eastern and international repercussions.

Back in Beirut, Hariri followed his orders and had the Lebanese government approve the constitutional amendment in a ten-minute session. The 128 member Lebanese parliament was well packed with Syrian allies and clients, but not well enough to guarantee the requisite two-thirds majority to rubber-stamp the will of Bashar and the "security regime." Intimidation and death threats made the difference,[332] lowering the number of opponents from 50 to 29 and ensuring Lahoud his extra three years.

For different reasons, the U.S. and France were both determined that Syria would not get away with such a coup. The U.S. was fed up with what it saw as Syrian promotion of mayhem in Iraq and Syria's continued cozy relationship with Hizballah in Lebanon. American policymakers had not forgotten the 1983 bombings of the U.S. embassy and marine barracks in Beirut, or the procession of kidnappings of Americans that followed in the mid-1980s. U.S. toleration of Syrian hegemony in Lebanon up to 2004 was in part based on hopes that Syria would clamp down on Hizballah, particularly after Israel's withdrawal in May 2000. Instead, Bashar doted on Hizballah. For its part, France wanted an understanding with Bashar involving a degree of Lebanese independence and respect for French influence in Beirut, in exchange for French buttressing of Syria's position in the Levant.[333] The Lahoud extension made it brutally plain that Syria took the latter for granted, and had no intention of conceding the former. This was after the French government had welcomed Bashar on a state visit, forgiven Syrian debts, and sponsored Syria in trade negotiations with the European Union. In sum, Bashar brought the U.S. and France together against him despite their estrangement over Iraq, a signal achievement.

On 2 September 2004, the U.S. and France co-sponsored U.N. Security Council Resolution 1559, calling for withdrawal of all foreign forces from Lebanon, disbandment of remaining militias—principally the armed wing of Hizballah—and holding Lebanese presidential and parliamentary elections free from external pressure. To ensure passage, Resolution 1559 did not mention Syria by name, but the main target was obvious. Syrian officials and their allies in the Lebanese regime reacted by scorning the resolution. The Syrian outlook was that the past showed that Syria could do a deal with U.S. any time it pleased,[334] and the U.S. now desperately needed Syrian cooperation to extract itself from Iraq. Similarly, France had always fallen in line with Syrian preferences and its new misguided attitude was nothing more than a passing cloud. Syria had no intention of heeding inconvenient Security Council edicts except under *force majeure*, and the U.N. Secretary General's 1 October report on implementation of Resolution 1559 therefore found the Syrian and Lebanese regimes in breach of all its provisions.[335]

Within Lebanon, Lahoud's extension energized opposition to Syria's role in Lebanese politics. Junblatt and Sufayr both condemned the imposition, a fair reflection of the mood of their respective communities and a new turn in their erratic relations with Syria. The most important new recruit was Hariri himself, who resigned as prime minister on 20 October. Hariri's termination of his long and uncomfortable collaboration with Damascus coincided with the lifting of the equally long-lasting U.S. cover for Syria's hegemony. Hariri was bitter about demeaning treatment at the hands of Bashar and Lahoud, and noted that Bashar was "not seasoned like his father."[336] He reportedly advised the drafting of Resolution 1559 in association with his old friend Jacques Chirac,[337] but initially avoided public participation in the opposition leadership to work backstage. He may have hoped for reconciliation with Syria, but Bashar gave this no encouragement.

The Syrian/Lebanese "security regime" at first concentrated on the visible opposition, especially Junblatt's Progressive Socialist Party. In late September, Lebanese security forces mounted dawn raids on Druze villages in the Shuf hills. On 1 October, a roadside bomb badly injured Junblatt's colleague Marwan Hamade, who had resigned from the government to protest Lahoud's extension. This greatly shocked Hariri, and probably removed any illusions that things might be papered over. In November, official security protection around Junblatt's Beirut residence was removed. Bashar sent Hizballah's Nasrallah to persuade Junblatt to behave himself,[338] but the Druze leader escalated his hostility to Lahoud. On 3 December, President Chirac received him warmly in Paris.

Hariri's replacement as prime minister by 'Umar Karami, of proven incapacity from the early 1990s, and earlier departures of other ministers, converted the government into an appendage of the "security regime." A broad opposition coalition including Hariri's Mustaqbal (Future) Movement, Junblatt's PSP, the Qurnat Shehwan bloc of Christian politicians, and the Free Patriotic Movement of Michel Aoun, still in exile in Paris, assembled at Beirut's Bristol Hotel on 13 December. The coalition communiqué censured Syria and Karami's government, but avoided demanding removal of the Syrian army.

As the most dynamic Sunni Muslim politician and a multibillionaire with wide international contacts, Hariri gave the opposition formidable weight. He looked ahead to deploying his resources to rally Sunnis and others to overturn the Syrian-backed government in internationally monitored May 2005 elections. Hariri bought bulk supplies of orange ribbons in Paris for a Ukrainian-style election campaign,[339] and indicated that his goal was "the exit of Syrian forces and the recovery of Lebanon's independence."[340] He also made overtures to Hizballah, telling the Iranian ambassador to France, perhaps unwisely, that his problem "was not Hizballah but the Syrian presence and its operations."[341]

In early 2005, the opposing camps entrenched themselves. Seeking to sidestep Resolution 1559, Damascus rediscovered the Ta'if Agreement call, shelved since 1989, for redeployment to the Biqa' Valley. Junblatt escalated his criticism of the Syrian regime. He dismissed the Syrian concept of "one people in two states," condemned Syria's refusal to have diplomatic relations with Lebanon, and demanded the "sweeping-out" of intelligence agencies.[342] In a 26 January speech at Beirut's St. Joseph's University, he identified "a very dangerous Syrian-Lebanese mafia. . . . Our task is to break up this mafia. . . . We must close the gate of Anjar [Syrian military intelligence headquarters in Lebanon] for good."[343]

To win the May 2005 parliamentary elections, Hariri needed the Lebanese opposition to come on board with Resolution 1559 and build momentum against Syrian dominance. Accordingly, on 2 February 2005 the third opposition Bristol Hotel conclave undercut Syria's Ta'if redeployment maneuver by publicly backing full withdrawal of Syrian forces and intelligence agents from Lebanon.[344] After a 10 February 2005 mission to Damascus, U.N. envoy Terje Roed-Larsen worried that Hariri was in physical danger.[345] On 14 February, a massive bomb explosion on the Beirut seafront killed Hariri and twenty others.

Most Lebanese regarded the Syrian-Lebanese "security regime" as the prime suspect, indeed the only credible suspect, for the murder. The perpetrators presumably wanted to remove Hariri as the main pillar of an opposition electoral challenge to Syrian hegemony. Junblatt reflected wider popular reaction when he asked: "How can you convince a Lebanese from any region that the Syrian intelligence machine didn't kill Hariri, and didn't try to kill Marwan Hamade? We are sentenced to death and Rustum Ghazale or some other [Syrian] officer decides the implementation."[346] Certainly the perpetrators expected that the crime would be unsolved, like previous such crimes in Lebanon, and that any wave of anger would die away. Damascus was not worried about any implications. In the Syrian Ba'thist outlook, Syria's regional weight made it immune from the U.S. and France, and serious Lebanese hostility could never exist. In a 5 March speech to the Syrian parliament, Bashar derided the Lebanese opposition, suggesting that it had no popular depth and was moved by foreign hands.[347]

In fact, the assassination instantly cemented the mass of Sunni Muslims, one quarter of Lebanon's people, in the opposition alignment. When added to the vast majority of Christians and Druze, together at least 40% of Lebanese, simple arithmetic indicated that something close to two-thirds of Lebanon was stirring against Damascus, even if this did not include a single Shi'i. In the event, competitive demonstrations in the month after the assassination showed that forces hostile to Syria had the popular advantage, in line with the above arithmetic. First, there was an impressive Sunni turnout for Hariri's funeral, and Hariri's allies and family asked that representatives of the Lebanese regime stay away.[348] The opposition demanded the sacking of Prosecutor-General 'Adnan 'Adoum and all five heads of Lebanon's security agencies, a new government to conduct the parliamentary elections, and an international inquiry into the assassination.[349] The Lahoud-Karami regime rejected or ignored the demands. On 1 March 2005, street protests forced Karami's resignation, but this had no impact on President Lahoud or the security chiefs.

Syria received a brief boost from Hizballah. Many Shi'is were nervous about Resolution 1559's call for Hizballah disarmament, fearing that it would leave them overshadowed by Israel and the other Lebanese communities.[350] Also, Hizballah was still Syria's ally: Syria backed the party's "regional role" against Israel, and Hizballah underwrote Syria's domination of Lebanon. On 8 March, Nasrallah mobilized almost all the party's following, emptying Beirut's southern suburbs. The party brought about 500,000 demonstrators to central Beirut, more to emphasize Shi'i existence than to endorse Bashar or Lahoud. Nonetheless, Lahoud used the Hizballah show of strength to reappoint Karami, a deliberate insult to the opposition.

They rose to the challenge. On 14 March, the opposition organized the largest demonstration in Lebanon's history; one million people gathered to mark the first month since Hariri's murder. The demonstration expressed a sectarian divide because only limited numbers of Shi'is attended. Comparison with the Hizballah rally therefore indicated that Christians, Sunnis, and Druze together have about double the mobilization capacity of Shi'is. In other words, the sectarian population proportions estimated in chapter 2 for the early 1990s continue to be the rough Lebanese reality in the early twenty-first century, for two reasons. First, there has undoubtedly been a collapse in the Shi'i natural increase rate since the 1980s to a level not much removed from that of Maronites and Sunnis.[351] Second, recent out-migration has affected all communities.

In the international arena, the U.S. and French governments viewed the murder of Hariri as an indictment of the Syrian and Lebanese regimes, and insisted that Syria leave Lebanon immediately, as required by Resolution 1559.[352] According to the Kuwaiti daily *Al-Siyassa*, Crown Prince 'Abdullah of Saudi Arabia (King 'Abdullah after the death of King Fahd in August 2005) gave Bashar the same message: "You don't know who killed him [Hariri] while the whole world knows? We don't believe that an announcement of the names will be in your interest."[353] The rest of the Arab world reluctantly went along with the Franco-U.S. stand, though Egypt showed more interest in protecting the Syrian leader than in Lebanon's emergence from Syrian hegemony. Even "Iranian sources" noted that "Iran will support Syria in its confrontation with Israel, but it is not prepared to support Syria's presence in Lebanon."[354]

Bashar stalled for weeks after ordering a redeployment of Syrian forces to the Biqa' in late February. He pointed to security risks if Syria made a full withdrawal. As if on cue, several small bombs exploded in Christian suburbs of Beirut. Washington, France, and the Lebanese opposition made it clear that they regarded Syria as culpable for such disruption.[355] On 2 April 2005, Bashar bowed to the United Nations and promised full withdrawal by the end of the month. The last Syrian uniformed troops left Lebanon on 26 April, though Syrian intelligence agents plainly stayed behind in defiance of Resolution 1559.

The Syrian retreat came only after relentless U.S. and European pressure and the 27 March release of a U.N. report on the "causes, circumstances, and consequences" of the Hariri assassination, commissioned by the Security Council as its response to the event. Peter Fitzgerald, the Irish deputy police commissioner, headed a small team sent to Beirut by Secretary-General Kofi Annan. His report accused Syria of creating the atmosphere of intimidation preceding the assassination and censured both Syrian and Lebanese security services for negligence, covering up and manipulating evidence, and lack of any seriousness in solving the crime.[356] The Fitzgerald report recommended an international inquiry with sweeping powers. On 7 April 2005, the U.N. Security Council approved Resolution 1595, which called for a comprehensive inquiry to identify Hariri's murderers, brushing aside the Lebanese regime's attempts to emasculate any follow-through.[357] Definition of the assassination as a terrorist crime and the powerful suspicion of non-Lebanese responsibility eased the approval.

Subsequent events pointed the way to a renewal of Lebanese independence, lost since the 1970s, with the international community more enthusiastic than some Arab governments, which feared the lessons for themselves of a demolition of the Syrian-Lebanese "security regime." On 15 April, the Lebanese opposition provided sufficient parliamentary support to compel President Lahoud to appoint the moderate Najib Mikati as prime minister after Karami failed to form a government. Mikati pledged himself to run the forthcoming elections on schedule, welcomed U.N. election assistance and European monitors, and appointed Hasan al-Saba'a, a respected Sunni security official and bitter opponent of Jamil al-Sayyid, as interior minister. Within two weeks, the government removed Sayyid, the military intelligence head Azar, Prosecutor-General 'Adoum, and other security chiefs fingered by the opposition. On 17 May, Secretary-General Annan appointed the Berlin prosecutor Detlev Mehlis to head the inquiry to identify Hariri's killers. Mehlis and a formidable international team arrived in Beirut in mid-June to begin work on their unprecedented assignment.

In June 2005, I went to visit General Michel Aoun, back in Beirut from exile in Paris and newly at the head of a large bloc of parliamentary deputies. Aoun has sensibly located himself amid the posh and spacious villas of the Christian suburb of Rabiya, above the coastal heat and well away from main roads that might bear truck bombs. We reminisced about my visits to him in Marseilles and La Haute Maison, and surveyed the new political scene.

Aoun expressed willingness to work with the other political forces, but was also full of criticism. He condemned Hizballah's "mistake" in issuing a religious injunction (*taklif shara'i*) to Shi'is to vote against him to prop up Junblatt, particularly wounding because it was in his old home area. He commented that Hizballah clinging to its weapons was outdated thinking, and that the party was past its peak. The general expressed a keen interest in an arrangement with Sa'ad al-Hariri despite his anger about insinuations in the Hariri camp that he is "confessional" and what he felt was exploitation of an unfair electoral law against him. Aoun takes fierce pride in reviewing his whole past and program as secular, non-sectarian, and dedicated to reform. Also, whether or not he came back with a nod from Damascus, he wants all the Syrian-Lebanese agreements revisited, revised, and even ripped up—from the Brotherhood Treaty to the Orontes water allocations. He agrees with Junblatt that diplomatic relations must be established between the two countries.

In the run-up to Lebanon's first free parliamentary elections since 1972, the opposition to Syrian hegemony splintered. On 7 May, General Michel Aoun returned from fifteen years in exile, and rallied tens of thousands of youthful enthusiasts the same day to emphasize his claim to a primary leadership role. He needed time to consolidate his position, and indicated lack of interest in forcing the early removal of President Lahoud. Junblatt and others suspected that Lahoud and the Syrians had smoothed Aoun's return to disrupt the opposition front. Aoun felt slighted by the Junblatt and Hariri camps, and resented criticism from those who had been Syria's allies when his Free Patriotic Movement had been the opposition standard-bearer.[358] An acrimonious dispute over allocation of potential seats among Aoun, Junblatt, and the LF in the Ba'abda-'Aley constituency quickly propelled Aoun out of the opposition alignment into an autonomous campaign.[359]

Because of arguments over electoral systems and lack of time to draft a new electoral law, the May–June 2005 elections proceeded on the basis of the deeply flawed 2000 framework, popularly termed "Ghazi Kana'an's law." Most Christians perceived the constituencies as carefully constructed to make Christian deputies subject to Muslim voter majorities everywhere outside the Maronite heartland. Aoun profited from the feeling that the Sunni-Druze opposition leadership took Christians for granted. Paradoxically, in view of his strenuous non-sectarian assertions, Aoun also fulfilled a Maronite desire to have a *za'im* to match the Hariris, Hizballah's Nasrallah, and Junblatt. Aoun wanted the biggest possible showing to boost his claim to the Lebanese presidency, and did not hesitate to ally with pro-Syrian personalities who had useful local electoral machines like Michel al-Murr and Sulayman Tony Faranjiyya. At the same time, he gave these politicians a channel to adjust their alignments.

The election results after the last round in northern Lebanon on 19 June gave mixed signals as to an emerging new face for Lebanon. The alliance of Hariri's son, Sa'ad al-Din, who took on his father's political inheritance, Junblatt, and various second-level Christian factions, including a resurfacing LF, achieved a majority of 72 out of 128 mandates, without Aoun. This was critical as the cornerstone of an alternative Lebanese regime. However, the result involved the gerrymandered electorates left by the Syrian hegemony, extensive vote-buying, and a dubious arrangement with Hizballah, a primary Syrian ally, which kept Junblatt afloat in Mount Lebanon against Aoun. For his part, Aoun defeated Christians associated with the Hariri/Junblatt camp in the

Maronite heartland north of Beirut and, with his partners, gained a bloc of 21 seats. This confirmed him as the primary Maronite leader, with a Lebanese political significance rivaling that of Hizballah.

Shi'i voting, as in every election since 1990, proceeded in a universe different from that of the rest of the country. Hizballah, through its resistance aura and investment in health, education, and welfare services to fill the gap left by an indolent public sector, made itself the main face of the Lebanese Shi'ah by 2000. Through incompetence and corruption, its rival and ally Amal, under Parliamentary Speaker Barri, missed the chance to use superiority within the Lebanese state to serve the Shi'i community. The continued Hizballah/Amal partnership took 35 parliamentary seats in 2005, 23 for Hizballah and 12 for Amal, but the latter's share was largely a concession by the Party of God.

The trend to political monopolization within each of the three big communities—in the hands of the Hariri bloc for Sunnis, Aoun for Maronites, and Hizballah for Shi'is—threatens to accentuate Lebanese sectarianism. It also fuels resentment among traditional leading families and other politicians, especially in the Sunni community. Certainly, the concentration of voters from each community in separated political camps is unhealthy for national cohesion. There is plenty here for Ba'thist Syria to exploit to insinuate itself back into Lebanon if it outlives the Mehlis inquiry.

Formation of a new Lebanese government in the light of the election results took a month. President Lahoud approved a cabinet headed by Fuad Sinyora from Hariri's Mustaqbal Movement as prime minister only on 20 July 2005. This was after Lahoud had named three members, including the minister of justice, and Hizballah and Amal had indicated satisfaction with the Shi'i share of portfolios. Sinyora, Junblatt, and their Christian associates held a majority of posts, but Lahoud, Hizballah, and Barri commanded a pro-Syrian intrusion within the council of ministers. Aoun, whose movement produced the only written reform manifesto in the elections, demanded more than Sinyora could give, and ended up leading the parliamentary opposition to the "new majority." For the first time a Hizballah representative entered a Lebanese government, even as Hizballah made it clear that its armed wing was above and beyond state authority. A Hizballah deputy claimed that the army could not defend the country from Israel, that Lebanese troops should not deploy along the southern border, and that the Party of God would not give up its large private arsenal.[360] Hizballah increasingly ran the risk of appearing more like a threat to other Lebanese than as a bulwark against Israel.

Beirut in mid-2005 exhibited plenty of glitz and bustle. The city had a new face even compared with the 1990s, with the old center again a vibrant hub and redevelopment now diffused through the wider metropolis. I was surprised by an impressive multi-level mall sunk into the crest of the Ashrafiyya hill next to the Sassin square, and by the monstrously opulent Metropolitan Palace hotel in Sin al-Fil. For crossing the city, I experimented with amazingly cheap buses, which proceed at tortoise pace through the miasma of heat, humidity, and pollution that unites the Muslim and Christian concrete jungles from June to October.

In mid-2005, Beirut also featured a darker face of apprehension as it pushed to emerge from the "protection" of the predatory Syrian-Lebanese "security regime." I walked down to the destroyed seaside street, a wasteland of blackened and shattered buildings, where Rafiq al-Hariri was savagely murdered by a ton of TNT. It was rumored that the U.S. had recently uncovered a Syrian death list, and a Lebanese friend in a sensitive position asked me if I could extract any data. The surface calm was punctured that week by the sophisticated killing of George Hawi, ex-leader of the Lebanese Communist party and a vigorous critic of the Syrian hegemony. I came across a gathering of party faithful in Hamra the next day, a sad and subdued little assemblage of red flags and emblems from a bygone era.

In general, Lebanese politics were paralyzed and confused while the Mehlis inquiry proceeded toward its October and December 2005 reports to the U.N. secretary-general and the Security Council. Lahoud clung to the presidency, praised Syria, locked arms with Hizballah, and tried to pretend that nothing was happening. Anything else would be breaking ranks with his Syrian overlords, who hardly needed to spell out the consequences. Lahoud was now a prisoner of his presidential extension. Meantime, Sinyora became a prime minister under siege. Several murders and attempted murders of Syria's critics, along with rumors about Syrian death lists, caused consternation. Prominent members of the "new majority," such as Sa'ad al-Hariri and *al-Nahar* publisher Jubran Tuwayni, left the country for Europe, while others, for example Junblatt and Rafiq al-Hariri's sister Bahiya, rarely ventured out of their houses.

The Syrian regime indicated in advance that it would reject any U.N. findings not to its taste as *tasyis* (politicization).[361] It rationed its cooperation with Mehlis, required under Resolution 1595, to the minimum necessary to keep the U.N. Security Council from taking measures against it, and paraded its spite toward the new Lebanon. In July/August 2005, Damascus closed its borders to Lebanese truck transit for weeks, and in September it permitted infiltration of the Biqa' by armed Palestinians of Syrian-aligned factions like Ahmad Jibril's PFLP-GC. This followed Bashar's declaration that "the power and role of Syria in Lebanon are not dependent on the presence of Syrian forces there," and his information minister's dismissal of the Syrian-Lebanese border as "phony."[362]

On the other hand, Sinyora received the backing of the international community for Lebanon's resurfacing democracy. The U.S., France, and international financial institutions promised major investments, though these depended on Hizballah giving up its military autonomy in favor of the Lebanese army, as required in U.N. Security Council Resolution 1559. Other developments buoyed the prime minister. In late August, at the recommendation of the U.N. inquiry, the Lebanese authorities indicted four top commanders of the Lebanese security apparatus— Jamil al-Sayyid, Raymond Azar, Mustafa Hamdan, and Ali al-Haj—for the murder of Hariri. Mehlis noted that the Lebanese security commanders, key figures in the Syrian-Lebanese "security regime," appeared to be only part of a wider conspiracy. In late September, Lebanese Defense Minister Elias al-Murr, son-in-law of President Lahoud and the sole "pro-Syrian" targeted in the post-Hariri murder plots, disclosed that he had fallen out with Syria's intelligence chief in Lebanon, Rustum Ghazale, before the attempt on his life.[363] The Syrians lashed out at the injured Elias al-Murr as "swimming in corruption."[364] In early October, the Lebanese army surrounded Palestinian positions in the Biqa' and the south, for the first time without consulting Hizballah.[365]

On 5 October 2005, the prime minister attacked the Syrian regime in parliament. He observed: "The whole Lebanese security apparatus was in practice coordinated with the Syrian security machine, which directed Lebanese security to do what it [Damascus] wanted." Sinyora also noted that Lebanon had received "imposed security in exchange for the security regime controlling [Lebanon's] political life and corrupting [its] economic life . . . we have emerged from fake security to national security."[366] Damascus responded menacingly. A commentary in the Syrian economic weekly *al-Iqtisadiyya*, plainly inspired from the summit of the regime, accused Sinyora, Sa'ad al-Hariri, and Junblatt of steering the U.N. inquiry and "preparing to deliver Lebanon to an international protectorate under the U.S. and Israel."[367] The commentary predicted that "Junblatt and his band" would "move to Paris and ask for political asylum," while Sa'ad and his family would stay in Riyadh. If Mehlis could not pin Syrian involvement in the Hariri murder, Bashar and Lahoud aimed to smash Lebanon's "new majority." The program was simple—Syrian hegemony would seep back, Hizballah's armed wing would be secure, and Aoun would be reduced to satellite status.

On 12 October, one week before Detlev Mehlis submitted his progress report, the Syrian regime announced the "suicide" of Interior Minister Ghazi Kana'an, Syria's former intelligence chief in Lebanon. As a prominent 'Alawi who knew the secrets of Syrian-Lebanese affairs, Kana'an was potentially a key witness for the U.N. inquiry. Rumor hinted that he had not been enthusiastic about the Lahoud extension.[368] Question-marks hung over his relations with Syria's ruling clique, especially Bashar's brother Maher and brother-in-law Asef Shawkat, who formally took over Syrian military intelligence on the day of Hariri's assassination. Had Kana'an been part of a group interested in change in Damascus as well as in Beirut? Or did he simply know too much about Bashar, Maher, and Shawkat? Few took the "suicide" at face value.

Mehlis's report on four months of U.N. investigations, delivered to Secretary-General Annan on 20 October, marked a turning point for both Lebanon and Syria. Although not conclusive, the report presented a detailed, damning picture in which every lead pointed toward inner circles of the Syrian regime as well as the Lebanese security apparatus.[369] Mehlis noted "converging evidence" of Syrian and Lebanese involvement in the murder of Hariri, observing: "There is probable cause to believe that the decision to assassinate former Prime Minister Rafik Hariri could not have been taken without the approval of top-ranked Syrian security officials." He stated: "The Government of Syria's lack of substantive cooperation has impeded the investigation and made it difficult to follow leads established by the evidence collected from a variety of sources." An unedited version of the report featured a witness naming Shawkat, Maher al-Asad, and Jamil al-Sayyid as participants in planning the murder.

U.N. Security Council Resolution 1636, sponsored by the U.S., France, and Britain, endorsed the report on 31 October, rebuking Damascus by unanimous vote. The resolution demanded that the Syrian regime produce whomever Mehlis wanted to interview wherever and under whatever conditions the German prosecutor stipulated. Resolution 1636 invoked chapter VII of the U.N. charter, meaning that non-compliance could lead to sanctions including military action. The security council looked ahead to a further Mehlis report on 15 December, with the possibility of extending the inquiry's six-month mandate, and would assemble to consider punitive measures if Mehlis complained of deficiencies in Syrian "cooperation."

The Syrian regime responded with a torrent of belligerent self-righteousness. According to Bashar al-Asad, in a rambling tirade at Damascus University on 10 November, Syria was under assault because of its Arab identity and its defense of Arab rights.[370] He sneered at Lebanese Prime Minister Fuad Sinyora as "the hired slave of a hired slave," the latter being Sa'ad al-Hariri. He accused the new Lebanese government of making Lebanon "a passageway, factory, and financier" for conspiracies against Syria. He scorned Lebanon's May 2005 elections as "moving Lebanon from its Arab role into an international protectorate [*tadwil*], meaning toward Israel under international cover and through instruments dressed up in Lebanese citizenship." Bashar railed against Hariri's Future Movement as "blood merchants who created a stock exchange for money and positions out of Hariri's blood." Never before had leaders of Lebanon's Sunni Muslim community been subjected to such vitriol from Damascus.

If top Syrian officials had ordered Hariri's murder, belligerence, diversion tactics, and stonewalling were probably the Syrian regime's sole options by late 2005. After Resolution 1636, engagement of the international community had gone too far for "deals." This left destabilizing Lebanon and/or the Israel-Lebanon border, in order to derail the Sinyora government and disrupt the U.N. inquiry, frustrating the inquiry over information from Syrian suspects, and a smear campaign against Mehlis and his team. It also left playing on international crosscurrents, for example with Russia, and on Lebanese Shi'i and Maronite suspicions of Saudi influence through the Hariri camp, while Ba'thist Syria fueled Sunni extremists in Iraq and warned darkly of "instability" for Sunni Arab regimes if the 'Alawi Asads faced downfall.

Within Lebanon, weak points included divisions among the government majority headed by Sinyora, the Hizballah/Amal Shi'i camp, and the Aoun bloc, while President Lahoud exploited Maronite sensitivity about the presidential succession to cling to office as Syria's tool. Increased Shi'i political weight in Lebanon had accompanied Syrian hegemony, which meant that many Shi'is retained a tolerant view of Ba'thist Syria. In late October 2005, Hizballah's Nasrallah reacted badly to a U.N. report on implementation of Security Council Resolution 1559, in which U.N. envoy Terje Roed-Larsen criticized the party's military autonomy.[371] Prime Minister Sinyora strove to head off a Sunni-Shi'i rift over Hizballah's continuing close relations with the Syrian regime, emphasizing to the U.S. that the party represented a "substantial slice [*shariha wasi'a*] of Lebanon...with internal legitimacy,"[372] and that issues like its weaponry needed to be resolved through a Lebanese consensus. Nonetheless, Hizballah remained suspicious of Sinyora's adherence to international decisions, especially Resolution 1559. Sinyora also sought to defuse difficulties with armed Palestinians, another target of Resolution 1559, by an understanding with Palestinian Authority President Mahmoud 'Abbas. The latter appealed to the 350,000 Palestinians in Lebanon to behave as "guests." As regards Aoun, Bashar's outburst against Sinyora induced the general to support the prime minister, while both Sinyora and Walid Junblatt took initiatives for reconciliation with the general.[373] Aoun went to Washington in mid-November, pursuing his presidential aspirations, while Junblatt looked to "fortify Lebanon's independence and Arabism against sabotage by the Syrian regime."[374]

In late 2005, the futures of Lebanon and Syria hinged on whether or not a U.N.-commissioned German prosecutor would tie senior Syrian officials to an assassination in Beirut. The early twenty-first century history of the northern Levant thus became a detective thriller, with prospective international court dramas and public exhibitions of Ba'thist Syria's "dirty linen." This was the extraordinary end product of Bashar al-Asad's August 2004 forcing of an extended term for Lebanese President Emile Lahoud.

How might Lebanese Shi'is react to the Syrian regime unsettling Lebanon to stay afloat? Parliamentary Speaker Barri's Amal colleagues were already wavering, and a loyalty test loomed for Hizballah. For their own purposes, Hizballah's hard-line Iranian friends looked to preserve Bashar and Lahoud even by detonating Lebanon. Discourse within Hizballah still did not appear to exceed the horizons of the Syrian security machine and various Iranian-aligned tendencies looking to command Lebanese Shi'is. However, if the international community persuaded Israel to cease violating Lebanese air space and satisfied Lebanese claims to the Shab'a farms, what oxygen would be left for Hizballah's regional pretensions?

Overall, the new Lebanon emerging from the clutches of the Syrian-Lebanese security regime remained defective. Many members of the political elite still had scant respect for the concept of accountability, and the country teetered between being a jumble of statelets and a coherent state. Lebanon's future depended on the political choices of Fuad Sinyora, Sa'ad al-Hariri, Michel Aoun, Hasan Nasrallah, Nabih Barri, Walid Junblatt, and Maronite patriarch Nasrallah Sufayr. It also depended on the commitment of the international community, especially the U.S. and France, to buttressing Lebanon's still far-from-solid "cedar revolution."

CONCLUSION

Lebanon's story has involved a distinctive assemblage of Arab sectarian communities, Christian and Muslim, jumbled together in and around a great mountain massif, strategically positioned on the crossroads of Europe, Asia, and Africa. Mount Lebanon, the summit of the coastal hills of the Eastern Mediterranean and the major mountain range of the Fertile Crescent, is placed midway between the Nile valley and Anatolia, historical heartlands of major Middle Eastern states, and dominates access between the sea and the Syrian interior. It has thus been both a frontier zone and a gateway. As a frontier, Mount Lebanon attracted minority religious groups, most notably the Druze and Maronites in the days of the Fatimids and Byzantines; as a gateway, it invited interest from across the Mediterranean, especially from the great powers of industrial Europe in the nineteenth century. In particular, Lebanon's Maronite Christian community became established because of the mountain's frontier function in early Islamic times, and this same community enhanced the gateway role of the mountain for nineteenth century Europe.

The European connection, added to the sectarian complexity of the population in the vicinity of the mountain, created a hybrid culture that intermingled Western and Middle Eastern elements and in which Islam and Christendom faced each other in rough equivalence. This situation led to increasing sectarian tensions in the nineteenth and early twentieth centuries. The hybrid culture was also a fragmented culture: European penetration advantaged some elements, especially Christians, and disadvantaged others, especially non-Christians. The population, including Muslims, became more differentiated from its Middle Eastern neighborhood, because of the local interactions of the sects and the Western impact, but it could not establish a common understanding of its identity.

Greater Lebanon's creation in the 1920s enforced an unsatisfactory "pluralist" compromise, for the benefit of a small multicommunal upper class. The compromise could not endure: the "merchant republic" exacerbated social divisions, and demographic change delegitimized political arrangements between the Maronite Catholic and Sunni Muslim elites.

315

War came in 1975 because of a conjunction of Arab-Israeli intrusions and catastrophic regime incompetence under President Sulayman Faranjiyya, but the basic reality was that the Maronite-Sunni National Pact of 1943 was no more viable for the long term than had been the règlement organique of 1861.

Ironically, fifteen years of violence and chaos after 1975 proved that, far from being an artificial territorial unit, Greater Lebanon was almost indestructible. Unlike Yugoslavia in the 1990s, Lebanon's communities did not and could not escape from their post–First World War "cage." The country was too small for fragmentation to be economically or institutionally conceivable, and generally the communities did not think in such terms. Even among Maronites, despite some nostalgia for a Christian-dominated Little Lebanon, most of the leadership and populace did not want to dismantle Greater Lebanon, while the Shi'i Muslims firmly committed themselves to its maintenance, as the prospects for political change to their advantage increased.

The war period did, however, convert Lebanon into an environment virtually uninhabitable for decent people. "Politics," in any normal understanding of the word, ceased to exist. Competition for power became little more than the human equivalent of a perpetual feeding frenzy—the "nasty, brutish and short" sort of life depicted in Thomas Hobbes' "state of nature." Despite the shared suffering of most of the Lebanese population, people became physically and psychologically separated into communal compartments to an extent that made the nature of their undoubted joint identity a riddle almost beyond comprehension. As for attitudes toward neighboring states and peoples, the great majority of Lebanese felt more and more hostile to the Syrians, Israelis, and Palestinians as the war period lengthened. Syrian manipulations aroused the special antipathy that comes with familiarity, while Israeli interventions seemed like alien invasions from another planet. The fact that such attitudes became part of Lebanon's sense of distinctiveness was hardly a healthy phenomenon.

An important feature of the historical record discussed in this book, which readers will have noticed, is the fact that only one woman—the Druze matriarch of the 1920s, Nazira Junblatt—registered as a prominent individual in Lebanon's story, right up until the late twentieth century. For both Christians and Muslims, it has been a story of unrelenting male domination of the public arena. Even the war years and their shabby aftermath did not provoke any sustained assertion of women's perspectives and protests. Women received the vote in 1953, but there has not yet been much sign that they can make a serious political impact. The two women who have emerged in the contemporary scene— Layla Mu'awwad (Maronite) and Bahiya al-Hariri (Sunni)—are respectively the wife and sister of murdered male politicians.

The war ended in 1990, but Lebanon's crisis continued. Indeed, Greater Lebanon's reformulation under the Ta'if Agreement added new regressive features: Syrian overlordship and a new Lebanese regime intended to service Ba'thist Syrian agendas rather than the Lebanese people. Shamefully, U.S. administrations of the 1990s endorsed both features. Subordination to the Syrian interior contradicted the whole direction of Lebanon's modern history. It went against Lebanese aspirations for independence, led much of the Lebanese diaspora, with its skills and resources, to turn its back on post-war Lebanon, and stimulated smoldering street-level resentment.

If there is a revenge of history in contemporary Lebanon, it has two main dimensions—one positive, and one negative. First, the popular upsurge against Syrian hegemony in 2005 indicates the continuing influence of Lebanon's confessional democracy and civil society from the "first republic" of 1943–75. The 1943 National Pact may have been ultimately unviable and mid-twentieth century civil society hostage to sectarianism, but the traditions they consolidated proved stubbornly resistant to Damascus after 1990. The new Lebanon appearing in 2005 resembled nothing so much as the Lebanon that supposedly disappeared in 1975. There was some change in sectarian balances and in the composition of the bourgeoisie, but nothing revolutionary. Hizballah represented a new force, but it was contained in one-third of the population. Overall, Lebanese cosmopolitanism and pluralism looks likely to trump Syrian Ba'thism.

Sectarian identities and jealousies, however, are also in good health in 2005. Confessional friction went with confessional pluralism, and Lebanon could not escape its longer past. Sectarian polarization began with internal demographic and social change in the late eighteenth century, principally the increasing assertion and cohesion of the Maronite Catholics. Such polarization was more an indigenous development than a product of European intrusion, though the latter had an exacerbating effect. Sectarian differentiation became a central element of Lebanon's modern history. It survived effortlessly into the twenty-first century, assisted by Syria's divide-and-rule methods, a photocopy of European imperialism. Its latest permutation is the prickly defensiveness of the Shi'i third of Lebanon. Many Shi'is have resented the Christian-Sunni-Druze coalescence after the February 2005 murder of Rafiq al-Hariri as potentially targeting the Shi'i community. Sectarianism, like the 1975–90 war period, is not a subject Lebanese like to hear about, but making diversity an asset rather than a curse for Lebanon's future cannot be built on denial of history.

LIST OF MAPS, FIGURES, AND TABLES

IDF   Israel Defense Force

LF   Lebanese Forces

MNF   Multi-national Force

NLP   National Liberal Party

PDFLP   Popular Democratic Front for the Liberation of Palestine

PFLP   Popular Front for the Liberation of Palestine

PLA   Palestine Liberation Army

PLO   Palestine Liberation Organization

PNC   Palestine National Council

PNSF   Palestinian National Salvation Front

PSP   Progressive Socialist Party

SLA   South Lebanese Army

SSNP   Syrian Social Nationalist Party

UAR   United Arab Republic

UNIFIL   United Nations Interim Force in Lebanon

■ NOTES ■

Notes to the Introduction

1. *Al-Nahar*, 26 April 1994.
2. Hélène Carrère d'Encausse, *The End of the Soviet Empire: The Triumph of the Nations.* London: Basic Books—English translation, 1993.
3. Lauro Martines, *Power and Imagination: City States in Renaissance Italy.* London: Peregrine, 1983, pp. 36–37.
4. Samuel Huntington, "The Clash of Civilizations?" *Foreign Affairs.* Vol. 72, 3, 1993, pp. 22–49.
5. Hilal Khashan, *Inside the Lebanese Confessional Mind.* New York: University Press of America, 1992.

Notes to Chapter 1

6. Salibi, 1988, p. 3.
7. Comnena, trans. Sewter, 1969, p. 312.
8. Runciman, 1980, pp. 269–276.
9. Comnena, trans. Sewter, 1969, p. 354.
10. Kennedy, 1994, pp. 54, 67.
11. Marshall, 1992, p. 232.
12. Marshall, 1992, pp. 135, 206.
13. Tadmuri, 1978, p. 446.
14. Ziadeh, 1953, p. 66.
15. Salibi, 1988, p. 141.
16. Abu Husayn, 1992, p. 664.
17. Abu Husayn, 1992, p. 667.
18. Abu Husayn, 1992, p. 671.
19. Van Leeuwen, 1994, p. 38.
20. Akarli, 1993, pp. 190, 192.
21. Abu Manneh, 1992, pp. 17–22.
22. Dubar and Nasir, 1976, p. 24.
23. Ibid.
24. Statistics from 1921 and 1932 censuses as cited in Buheiry, 1986, p. 11.
25. Ibid.
26. My interview with a senior Turkish Foreign Ministry official, May 1999.

Notes to Chapter 2

27. Barakat, 1979, p. 10: République Libanaise, Ministère du plan, *Besoins et possibilités du dévelopment du Liban,* Beirut, 1961.
28. *The Lebanon Report,* April 1992.
29. *Al-Safir,* 27 June 1992.
30. Data collected during distribution of food parcels by the Hariri Foundation. See Faour, 1991, p. 636.
31. *Tübinger Atlas des Vorderen Orients (TAVO),* Sheet A VIII 7— Lebanon: Religions, Tübingen University, 1979.
32. J. Harik, 1994, p. 469.
33. *Risala maftuha alati wajaha hizballah ila al-mustada'fin fi lubnan wa al-'alam,* Beirut, 16 February 1985, p. 15.
34. Hizballah program for 1992 parliamentary elections—*al-Anwar,* 6 August 1992.
35. Dubar and Nasir, 1976, p. 24.
36. For example, Dr. Anis Abi Farah to *al-Safir,* 20 June 1992.
37. Maronite patriarch Nasrallah Butros Sfayr claimed there were half a million wartime emigrants—*al-Anwar,* 30 March 1992.
38. Remark to author, West Beirut, May 1985.

Notes to Chapter 3

39. Betts, 1988, p. 69.
40. Salibi, 1988, p. 125.
41. Dubar and Nasir, 1976, p. 26.
42. Van Leeuwen, 1994, p. 52.
43. I. Harik, 1968, pp. 31–32.
44. I. Harik, 1968, pp. 178–199.
45. Halawi, 1992, p. 33.
46. Van Leeuwen, 1994, pp. 42–43, 57.
47. Van Leeuwen, 1991, pp. 609–613.
48. Dubar and Nasir, 1976, p. 31.
49. I. Harik, 1968, p. 241.
50. I. Harik, 1968, p. 245.
51. Fawaz, 1983, p. 96.
52. Johnson, 1988, p. 14.
53. Khalaf, 1979, p. 108.
54. Fawaz, 1983, p. 105.
55. Khalaf, 1979, p. 128.

56. Rizq, 1992, p. 64; Khalaf, 1979, p. 90.
57. Fawaz, 1994, p. 54.
58. Fawaz, 1994, pp. 164, 226.
59. Fawaz, 1983, pp. 48–52.
60. Rizq, 1992, pp. 217, 221.
61. Hottinger in Binder, 1966, p. 60.
62. Nantet, 1986, p. 11.
63. Nantet, 1986, p. 14.
64. Akarli, 1989, pp. 165–172.
65. Gulick, 1967, pp. 177–183.
66. Halawi, 1992, pp. 36–37.
67. Johnson, 1986, p. 26.
68. Khoury, 1987, pp. 464–468.
69. Goria, 1985, p. 22.

Notes to Chapter 4

70. Zamir, 1985, p. 73.
71. Zamir, 1985, p. 75; Burke, 1973, pp. 175–176.
72. Zamir, 1985, p. 186.
73. Hottinger in Binder, 1966, p. 95.
74. Longrigg, 1958, pp. 161–162.
75. Longrigg, 1958, pp. 169–170.
76. Salibi, 1965, p. 178.
77. Spagnolo, 1977, pp. 228–229.
78. Chamoun, 1963, pp. 86, 87.
79. Goria, 1985, p. 22.
80. Longrigg, 1958, p. 130.
81. Johnson, 1986, p. 122.
82. Hudson, 1968, p. 274.
83. Seale, 1986, pp. 289–302.
84. Alin, 1994, p. 77.
85. Hudson, 1968, p. 312.
86. Hudson, 1968, p. 308.

Notes to Chapter 5

87. Goria, 1985, p. 128.

88. I heard this while listening to President Hirawi's interview with MTV Television, Beirut, 8 January 1995.

89. Johnson, 1986, p. 165.

90. Johnson, 1986, p. 182.

91. Goria, 1985, pp. 179–180.

92. See Pakradouni's own account of his involvement in East Beirut's interactions with Damascus, principally as a go-between for President Sarkis (Pakradouni, 1983).

93. As subsequent problems between East Beirut and Damascus demonstrated, Syria did not do its "homework" very well regarding Sarkis. Brigadier Sami al-Khatib, a senior Sunni army officer who took part in Syrian-Lebanese contacts during the war period, later observed that Asad never met Sarkis before the 1976 Lebanese presidential election. Further, Sarkis never visited Damascus (Sami al-Khatib interview with *al-Wasat*, 26 December, 1994).

94. Rabinovich, 1984, pp. 183–218. Translation of Asad's speech from Radio Damascus by FBIS, Daily Report, 20 July 1976.

95. Lebanese Front membership: Camille Chamoun, Pierre Jumayyil, Bashir Jumayyil, Abbot Bulos Na'aman (then head of the Maronite monastic orders), Charles Malik (foreign minister under President Chamoun), Fuad al-Bustani, Edward Hunayin.

96. Rabinovich, 1984, pp. 183–218. Translation of Asad's speech.

97. Johnson, 1986, p. 195.

98. My interview with Sulayman Faranjiyya, Zgharta, 12 April 1984.

99. My interview with Muhammad Haydar, chairman of Foreign Relations Committee, Ba'ath party National Command, Damascus, March 1984.

100. I heard of the presence of Russian advisors in the Upper Matn from Syrian soldiers stationed in the area, November 1983.

101. My interview with Palestine National Council (PNC) chairman Khalid Fahhoum, Damascus, March 1984.

102. My interview with Muhammad Haydar, Damascus, March 1984.

103. Full transcript of deliberations of Geneva conference in T. Salman, ed., *Al-Muhadir al-Sirriya al-Kamila*, Arab Center for Information, Beirut, 1984.

104. For example, see report of the follow-up committee of the Geneva conference, *Al-Mahadir al-Sirriya al-Kamila*, pp. 209–219.

105. PNC chairman Khalid Fahhoum on Radio Damascus, 7 April 1984—monitored by me in Beirut.

106. My discussion with Lebanese foreign ministry officials, Beirut, 29 February 1984.

107. Information transferred to a *Ha-aretz* correspondent, *Ha-aretz*, 4

March 1984.

108. Ibid.

109. My interview with Sulayman Faranjiyya, Zgharta, 12 April 1984.

110. My conversation with Ghassan Siblani, Amal command member, Beirut, 4 April 1984.

111. *Al-Thawra*, 10 November 1984.

112. My discussion with Amos Gilboa, Israeli representative at Israel-Lebanon Naqura talks and former deputy director of Israeli military intelligence (AMAN), Jerusalem, April 1984.

113. Amal's dragnet involved "flying" checkpoints on main roads and visits to apartments. My observation, West Beirut, May 1985.

114. My conversation with Ghassan Siblani, Beirut, May 1985.

115. Arabic text in Lebanese Center for Documentation and Research, 1986, Vol. 2, pp. 342–353; English translation in Lebanese Information and Research Center, 1986.

116. My discussion with Charles Ghustin, LF command member, Beirut, December 1985.

117. My conversation with Walid Junblatt, Mukhtara, December 1985.

118. The outlook of the army command was relayed to me at a meeting with a senior officer, Beirut, April 1986.

Notes to Chapter 6

119. A typical tale from the late 1980s, perhaps apocryphal but illustrative of Beirut's nuances, was that of a commercial traveller who avoided paying "taxes" to the LF on passage through East Beirut, but was later visited in West Beirut by Amal and ordered to pay the LF charges.

120. Saidi, 1986, p. 5.

121. *Al-Nahar*, 13 October 1990.

122. Israel Foreign Ministry Research Office, 1984; Israel Defense Ministry, Office of the Coordinator for Lebanon, 1993.

123. Israel Defense Ministry, 1993.

124. My interview with Uri Lubrani, Israeli coordinator for Lebanon, Tel Aviv, July 1984.

125. My conversation with an Israeli foreign ministry official, Jerusalem, April 1985.

126. People from Qubbayat discussed the arrangement with me, Beirut, 1987.

127. In early 1986, I was asked to provide testimony concerning the situation in Lebanon for a U.S. immigration case involving a person who

had fled to the U.S. to escape such pressure. I successfully rebutted a very strange State Department opinion that the Syrians would soon be reducing their presence in Lebanon, and that the young person from Tripoli would therefore not be in physical danger back at home!

128. My discussion with a PSP personality, Beirut, April 1987.

129. Relations between the Sidon Nasirites and Amal were always cool and Sa'ad suspected Amal as having been responsible for a bomb attack in which he was severely injured. My visit to Sa'ad in Sidon, November 1987.

130. Israeli perspective as outlined to me by Uri Lubrani. At the time of the preliminary Syrian entry in July 1986, Lubrani's reaction was to hope they would send more personnel. Interviews, Tel Aviv, July 1986 and October 1987.

131. *Al-Safir*, 31 March 1987.

132. A Shi'i personality close to the Amal leadership told me that the war of the camps was a Syrian-Palestinian issue; the fact that Amal did the fighting had no relevance! Further, if Asad did a deal with 'Arafat, Amal would have to put up with it. Interview, Beirut, April 1987.

133. Reports of the United Nations Truce Supervision Organization's Beirut Observer Group indicated an almost complete cessation in traffic at the PSP's Khalda port, March–May 1987. I noted a very obvious Syrian military presence around the port installations six months later, in November 1987.

134. *Al-Nahar*, 2 February 1987.

135. Harris, 1988, p. 100. Junblatt was fond of this phrase, and repeated it in an 18 October 1994 interview with *al-Nahar*.

136. *Al-Safir*, 1 July 1987.

137. An Eastern European ambassador in West Beirut whose views one would expect to reflect Soviet outlooks was reported to me as saying: "We support Syria against imperialism and as regards the Arab-Israeli conflict, but we do not agree with Syrian policy in Lebanon." Beirut, May 1987.

138. My conversation with Salim al-Huss, Beirut, July 1987.

139. My interview with General Michel Aoun, Beirut, November 1987.

140. *Al-Afkar*, 8 June 1987. Also reported to me by a U.S. diplomatic source, Beirut, June 1987.

141. Elie Salem, advisor to the presidency, to me, July 1987. Apparently a prominent Sunni advisor of President Jumayyil reported to Ba'abda that Syria intended to operate the most extreme political pressures.

142. Muwaffaq Madani column, *al-Safir*, 16 May 1988.

143. *Al-Nahar al-'Arabi wal-Duwali*, 6 June 1988.

144. Hizballah spokesman Ibrahim Amin quoted Asad as having told the delegation: "You represent the true Islam in Lebanon as against the Islam deputed by imperialism to hit Islam; you are the Islamic struggle in Lebanon that I have remembered in my speeches"—*al-Safir*, 28 May 1988.

145. *Al-Safir*, July 1988.

146. *Al-Safir*, 6 July 1988.

147. My conversation with Junblatt, December 1985.

148. Calculations from data presented in Faour, 1988.

149. *Al-Nahar*, 8 October 1990.

150. My interviews during visit to Zahla, September 1986.

151. My interview with Michel Aoun, November 1987.

152. Junblatt refused a request from Khaddam and Nabih Barri indicated that Syria already had Amal's hands full with the Palestinians. The Lebanese army estimated that about 30 Syrians were killed in a 27–28 March 1986 artillery exchange between the two regular forces (which I personally witnessed on the Upper Matn front). My interview with a senior army personality, Beirut, April 1986.

153. *Al-Safir*, 16 November 1987.

154. Walid Shuqayr column, *al-Safir*, 2 December 1987.

155. *Al-Safir*, 23 April 1988.

156. *Al-Safir*, 16 June 1988.

157. *Al-Safir*, 5 August 1988.

158. *Al-Safir*, 5 and 11 August 1988.

159. *Al-Majalla*, 7 September 1988.

160. *Al-Majalla*, 12 October 1988.

161. *Al-Nahar*, 29 September 1988.

162. *Al-Thawra*, Damascus, 25 September (quoted in *al-Safir*, 26 September 1988).

Notes to Chapter 7

163. *Al-Safir*, 1 October 1988.

164. Aoun to *al-Nahar*, Beirut, 6 January 1989.

165. Aoun's interview with *al-Ra'y*, Amman, 30 August 1989—FBIS Daily Report, 31 August 1989:

Q. Can we conclude that you are more Lebanese than Maronite?

A. Yes, because I have a different view of authority. My concept of reform also differs from the current one and from that of the school of thought that has dominated Lebanon since 1920 or 1943.

166. Senior PSP official to me, West Beirut, January 1990.
167. Junblatt's interview with Voice of the Mountain, 8 April 1989—FBIS Daily Report, 10 April 1989.
168. Aoun's "inner circle" comprised such people as Kalas (commander of the eighth brigade); Sassin (head of the military police); Shahin (commander of the commandos); Shihab (chief of military intelligence); Fawzi Abu Farhat, Fu'ad Aoun, 'Izzat Haddad (senior officers); and Simon Khoury (a lawyer).
169. Elie Salem to me, Beirut, June 1989.
170. My impressions from Ba'abda, May 1989.
171. *Al-Nahar*, 12 January 1989.
172. *Al-Nahar*, 14 February 1989.
173. *Al-Nahar*, 1 February 1989.
174. *Al-Nahar*, 15 February 1989.
175. I heard this from a source close to the army, Beirut, January 1990.
176. Huss on Radio Lebanon, 23 February 1989—FBIS Daily Report, 24 February 1989. In the north Robert Faranjiyya spoke of transferring Sila'ta to the "legitimate authority."
177. *Al-Safir*, 25 February 1989.
178. My interview with senior PSP official, Beirut, January 1990. Also see *al-Safir*, 6 March 1989. In a speech Junblatt asserted that Futayri had been killed "to keep the Druze in the mountain on the same path as the Maronites," *al-Nahar*, 8 March 1989.
179. *Al-Safir*, 6 March 1989.
180. *Al-Safir*, 13 March 1989.
181. Aoun's "address to the nation," Voice of Lebanon, 17 March 1989—FBIS Daily Report, 21 March 1989.
182. *Al-Nahar*, 7 March 1989.
183. Aoun's interview with the Voice of Lebanon, 18 April 1989—FBIS Daily Report, 18 April 1989.
184. *Al-Safir*, 5 May 1989.
185. Norton, 1991, p. 465.
186. Salem, 1991, p. 73.
187. Assistant secretary of state Lawrence Eagleburger, quoted by *al-Nahar*, 189 March 1989; see *al-Nahar*, 18 March 1989, for Aoun's angry reply.
188. *The Economist*, 24 February–2 March 1990. Also, my field work in Beirut.
189. *Al-Safir*, 10 April 1989; Kata'ib leader George Sa'ada is quoted as observing: "Aoun's decision was spontaneous, and furthermore he is alone in it."

190. Aoun recalls envoys from Khalid visiting Ba'abda only two days before Khalid's death—discussion with me, Marseille, September 1992.

191. *Al-Safir*, 26 May 1989.

192. The Murphy-Asad agreement of September 1988; *al-Safir*, 29 May 1989: Madani column on the Fahd-Asad and Saudi-Syrian understandings regarding parallelism of reforms and elections, December 1988.

193. *Al-Nahar*, 8 August 1989.

194. *Al-Nahar*, 6 July 1989—Syrian demands through Western and Arab channels for removal of any missiles that might have arrived. Aoun found the uncertainty of the affair useful for morale and propaganda purposes, although later investigation by Western intelligence agencies could not establish physical evidence for the presence of the missiles.

195. As indicated to me by a source close to Aoun.

196. Observation to me.

197. Senior Israeli official to me, July 1989.

198. *Al-Nahar*, 1 August 1989.

199. Arab committee communiqué specifically noted the points of disagreement—FBIS Daily Report, 1 August 1989.

200. *Al-Nahar*, 9 August 1989.

201. *Al-Nahar*, 17 August 1989; *Ha-aretz*, 17–18 August 1989, reported the influx of 600 refugees per day from Beirut into the "security zone" in early to mid-August.

202. *Al-Nahar*, 17 August 1989, gives a preliminary survey from various viewpoints.

203. *Al-Nahar*, 18 August 1989. Ze'ev Schiff analyzed the evolution of Israeli "red line" definitions in "Weekly Round-up," *Ha-aretz*, 17–18 August 1989. Intelligence assessments prepared for the 19 August Israeli cabinet meeting agreed that "Syria froze its attack in Lebanon due to international pressure, but Syria would renew its military activities if international pressure ceased," *Ha-aretz*, 24–25 August 1989.

204. *Al-Qabas*, 29 August 1989—FBIS Daily Report, 31 August 1989.

205. *Al-Nahar*, 21 August 1989.

206. *Al-Nahar*, 2 September 1989.

207. Jim Hoagland, *International Herald Tribune*, 9–10 September 1989 (referring to "reliable sources" on the matter of prior discussion about withdrawing the embassy staff); *al-Nahar*, 7 September 1989 (Sarkis Na'um's analysis on reasons for embassy closure).

208. *Al-Nahar*, 2 and 4 September 1989.

209. *Al-Nahar*, 16 September 1989—Emile Khoury column, quoting political sources close to Damascus.

210. Ibid.

211. *Al-Nahar*, 7 October 1989.

212. Arabic text in *al-Safir*, 23 October 1989; English translation of agreement and associated amendment of the Lebanese constitution in *Beirut Review*, Vol.1, 1, pp. 119–172, 1991; critical commentary in Maila, 1992 and Institute for Human Rights in Lebanon, 1990.

213. *Al-Nahar*, 24 October 1989.

214. Voice of the Oppressed, 24 October 1989—FBIS Daily Report, 26 October 1989.

215. *Al-Nahar*, 25 October (on demonstration numbers) and 26 October 1989.

216. *Al-Nahar*, 27 October 1989.

217. *Al-Nahar*, 6 November 1989. Perhaps significantly, the Syrian-influenced *al-Safir* did not report some of Mu'awwad's remarks (*al-Safir*, 6 November 1989).

218. Aoun's interview with *al-Anwar*, 18 November 1989—FBIS Daily Report, 21 November 1989.

219. My discussion with Abbot Bulos Na'aman, East Beirut, January 1990.

220. My discussion with Aoun, Marseille, September 1992. Aoun named Mu'awwad's envoy.

221. Observations to me, January 1990.

222. Certainly this was the Israeli view, as I heard personally. Sarkis Na'um gives an interesting analysis of factors deterring the Syrians in *al-Nahar*, 25 December 1989.

223. As reported to me, Beirut, January 1990.

224. *Al-Nahar*, 1 December 1989.

225. My discussion with senior Israeli source, February 1990.

226. LF command member to me, East Beirut, January 1990.

227. *Al-Nahar*, 23 February 1990.

228. I heard this in East Beirut, January 1990.

229. Wahhab column, *al-Safir*, 14 March 1990.

230. *Le Canard Enchaîné*, 3 January 1990.

231. My information from a diplomatic source, East Beirut, February 1990; a "spiritual leader" quoted in Shuqayr column, *al-Safir*, 6 March 1990.

232. LF command member to me, East Beirut, January 1990.

233. Radio Monte Carlo, 18 February 1990, as recorded by me.

234. Immediately after Aoun's success, the Kata'ib radio station, the Voice

of Lebanon, fabricated a tale about a fire at the Zuq power station, which was said to threaten a vast explosion at the hydrogen tanks. This was obviously intended to deter an Aoun advance toward Junya—Voice of Lebanon, 8 February 1990, as recorded by me. Junya sources told me that LF personnel were in a state of panic at that time.

235. 1,200 men, 100 tanks in Qulay'at attack—*Voice of the People* (West Beirut), 10 February 1990, as recorded by me. 900 men, 40 tanks in 'Ayn Rumana attack—Radio Monte Carlo, 15 February 1990, as recorded by me.

236. Madani column, *al-Safir*, 9 April 1990, estimating that 250,000 fled to West Beirut and 70,000 to Damascus.

237. *Al-Safir*, 26 March 1990. Also *al-Safir*, 5 March 1990, reported the following army losses up to 1 March: 32 officers and 251 soldiers dead; 40 tanks, 10 APCs, and 11 helicopters destroyed; 20 tanks and 15 APCs damaged.

238. *Al-Safir*, 8 May 1990.

239. *Al-Anwar*, 7 July 1990.

240. *Al-Safir*, 15 March 1990.

241. My discussion with Aoun, Marseille, September 1992.

242. *Al-Safir*, 14 April 1990, after "secret" Asad-Hirawi summit.

243. *Al-Safir*, 15 March 1990.

244. Madani column, *al-Safir*, 28 May 1990.

245. The LF climb-down was clear in the shift from the position enunciated by LF Chief of Staff Fuad Malik to *al-Anwar*, 2 June 1990 ("our support for Ta'if does not mean accepting all its clauses or contents ... As long as Syria occupies Lebanese land, we cannot be friends") to allowing the constitution vote to go ahead unopposed on 22 August. *Al-Safir*, 12 July 1990, indicated that LF-regime negotiations had been in progress for six weeks.

246. *Al-Safir*, 14 August 1990.

247. *Al-Nahar*, 15 September 1990, quoting a U.S. official at the end of the Baker-Asad talks.

248. *Al-Safir*, 21 August 1990.

249. Sarkis Na'um reporting the U.S. requirements, *al-Nahar*, 11 and 13 September 1990.

250. Comment by senior Israeli source to me, 14 September 1990.

251. *Al-Nahar*, 3 September 1990. Also see *al-Safir*, 30 August 1990.

252. *Al-Safir*, 28 July 1990.

253. Delegations led by Ghazi Kana'an and Nadim Sukr, *al-Nahar*, 24 September 1990.

254. Dagher, 1992, pp. 325, 332.

255. *The October Debacle*, Foundation for Human and Humanitarian Rights (Lebanon), 4 November 1990.

256. *Al-Nahar*, 15 October 1990, reports Syrians taking furniture, even kitchen utensils, from the presidential palace, "all as planned" according to a Syrian soldier. *Al-Nahar*, 19 October 1990, Syrian army withdraws from palace, "taking all its contents."

257. Hirawi audience of Kahhala village delegation, reported in *The October Debacle*, 4 November 1990.

Notes to Chapter 8

258. *Al Nahar*, 6 May 1991.

259. Ibid.

260. For full text, see William Harris, "Lebanon," in Ami Ayalon, ed., *Middle East Contemporary Survey, Vol. XV, 1991* (Boulder, Colo.: Westview, 1993), pp. 570–72.

261. Sarkis Na'um in *al-Nahar*, 21 May 1991.

262. *Al-Nahar*, 24 May 1991.

263. For full text, see William Harris, "Lebanon," op. cit., pp. 572–73.

264. *The Lebanon Report*, April 1992, reporting Michel al-Murr interview with *al-Masira*, 20 March 1992.

265. Niqula Saykali in *al-Anwar*, 29 March 1992.

266. Fuad Da'bul in *al-Anwar*, 23 March 1992.

267. Sarkis Na'um in *al-Nahar*, 5 August 1993; Yoel Markus in *Ha'aretz* international edition, 22–27 August 1993.

268. *Ha'aretz*, 28 October 1992.

269. Nicola Saykali in *al-Anwar*, 19 September 1993.

270. *Al-Hayat* and *al-Safir*, 5 September 1996; *Lebanon Report*, Fall 1996.

271. *Lebanon Report*, Winter 1996.

272. For graphic depiction of the behavior of Syrian military intelligence in Lebanon, including systematic abuse of human rights, see the Human Rights Watch report "Syria/Lebanon: An alliance beyond the law," http://hrw.org/reports/1997/syria/.

273. Ghassan Charbel in *al-Wasat*, 3 February 1997.

274. Nicola Saykali in *al-Anwar*, 15 August 1993.

275. *The Lebanon Report*, Summer 1998, p. 51.

276. Khaddam to delegation of Lebanese commercial and banking representatives, *al-Safir*, 14 January 1995.

277. *Al-Nahar*, 27 January 1996.

278. See, for example, *al-Diyar*, 22 September 1994, Reuters News Service, 15 January 1997, and *al-Hayat*, 14 February 1998.

279. *Al-Nahar*, 24 July 1995.

280. *Al-Hayat*, 2 October 1995.

281. Hafiz al-Asad interview with the Cairo daily *al-Ahram—Al-Hayat*, 11 October 1995.

282. Sarkis Na'um in *al-Nahar*, 22 August, and *al-Nahar*, 19 August 1996.

283. *Al-Nahar*, 19 August, and Andrew Tarnowski in Reuters News Service, 30 August 1996.

284. *Al-Hayat*, 2 September 1996.

285. *Al-Hayat*, 30 July 1996.

286. *Al-Hayat*, 26 August 1996.

287. *Al-Safir*, 28 September 1998.

288. *Al-Hayat*, 6 October 1998.

289. Hariri could see what was coming, and in October 1998 tried unsuccessfully to rush through a law to protect any "unfairly accused person" holding public office—*al-Hayat*, 31 October 1998.

290. *Al-Hayat*, 30 November 1998.

291. *Al-Hayat*, 17 December 1998.

292. *Mideast Mirror*, 16 June 1999.

293. Daniel Nassif, "Dossier: Jamil al-Sayyid," *Middle East Intelligence Bulletin* 2, no. 3 (March 2000), http://www.meib.org/articles/0003_ld.htm.

294. Sarkis Na'um in *al-Wasat*, 27 January 1997.

295. Ibid.

296. Daniel Nassif, "Dossier: Jamil al-Sayyid," *Middle East Intelligence Bulletin* 2, no. 3 (March 2000), http://www.meib.org/articles/0003_ld.htm.

297. Former minister Isam Na'aman to *al-Ra'i al-'Am*, 5 September 2005.

298. Both Sayyid and Azar operated with Kana'an in maintaining contacts with Lebanese politicians estranged from Lahoud in 1999–2000, particularly Hariri and Junblatt. See, for example, *al-Hayat*, 19 May 1999.

299. *Al-Hayat*, 8 November 1999.

300. *Ha'aretz*, 13 February 2000.

301. *Al-Hayat*, 10 February 2000.

302. *Ha'aretz*, 28 March 2000 ("The assessment in the IDF is that the failure of the [Clinton-Asad] Geneva summit greatly increases the prospect of a unilateral withdrawal from southern Lebanon."). Also see Dan Margalit in *Ha'aretz*, 30 March 2000.

303. *Al-Hayat*, 2 April 2000.

304. Syran Foreign Minister Faruq al-Shar'a publicly rebuked Zu'aytar—*al-Hayat*, 3 April 2000.

305. *Al-Hayat*, 30 April and 7 May 2000.

306. Report by Ibrahim Bayram, *al-Wasat*, 23 October 2000.

307. *Al-Hayat*, 19 May 2005.

308. *Al-Siyassa* (Kuwait), 4 October 2005.

309. *Al-Hayat*, 6 May 2001.

310. *Al-Hayat*, 28 March 2002.

311. *Al-Nahar*, 20 March 2001.

312. *Al-Hayat*, 26 August 2000. Walid Shuqayr noted "Syrian anger" with Junblatt's courting of Syria's Christian opponents, and an appeal from the Lebanese Ba'th party to Hizballah to support Junblatt's Druze rival Talal Arslan.

313. *Al-Nahar*, 21 September 2000.

314. *Al-Hayat*, 7 November 2000.

315. Ibid. (front-page headline: "Damascus furious with Junblatt's positions, and Ba'thist deputy accuses him of being an agent and threatens him").

316. Gary Gambill and Daniel Nassif, "Walid Jumblatt—Head of the Progressive Socialist Party," *Middle East Intelligence Bulletin* 3, no. 5 (May 2001), http://www.meib.org/articles/0105_ld1.htm.

317. *Al-Hayat*, 22 May 2002.

318. *Al-Hayat*, 20 August 2001.

319. *Al-Hayat*, 5 April 2002.

320. *Al-Hayat*, 27 June 2002 ("Crisis between Hariri and Hizballah with the beginning of work on the Awza'i bridge project").

321. Economist Intelligence Unit, Economist Publications, London: *Country Report*, Lebanon, April 2003, p. 18.

322. Economist Intelligence Unit, Economist Publications, London: *Country Report*, Syria, August 2002, pp. 26 and 30.

323. In late September 2003, the U.S. civilian administrator in Iraq, Paul Bremer, said that of the 248 captured foreign fighters held in Iraq by the U.S.-led coalition, 121 were from Syria—*Al-Hayat*, 18 September 2003.

324. *Al-Hayat*, 17 October 2003.

325. As reported by Ibrahim Hamidi, *al-Hayat*, 28 July 2003.

326. For details and analysis, see Gary Gambill, "The American-Syrian Crisis and the End of Constructive Engagement," *Middle East Intelligence Bulletin* 5, no. 4 (April 2003), http://www.meib.org/articles/0304_s1.htm.

327. Gary Gambill, "Nasrallah Boutros Sfeir—76th patriarch of the Maronite Church," *Middle East Intelligence Bulletin* 5, no. 5 (May 2003), http://www.meib.org/articles/0305_ld.htm.

328. See, for example, Salim 'Arif in *al-Zaman*, 24 February 2005, on the Iraqi capture of a Syrian military intelligence officer in Mosul, and on Syrian coordination of Iraqi insurgents from Mosul to Ramadi.

329. Walid Shuqayr in *al-Hayat*, 9 September 2004.

330. Peter Fitzgerald, *Report of the U.N. Fact-Finding Mission to Lebanon* (New York: United Nations, 25 February–24 March 2005), p. 5.

331. Nicholas Blanford, Richard Beeston, and James Bone in *The Times* (London), 18 March 2005.

332. *Al-Nahar*, 1 and 3 September 2004.

333. *Al-Dustur* (Amman), 9 September 2004.

334. Ibrahim Hamidi in *al-Hayat*, 6 October 2005 ("Syria flaunts its regional 'cards'—and the options are open for a 'deal' in preparation for the Mehlis report") gives good data regarding the Syrian regime's seemingly unshakeable perspectives.

335. *Report of the Secretary-General pursuant to Security Council Resolution 1559* (New York: United Nations, 1 October 2004), p. 8.

336. Comments to *Irish Times* correspondent Lara Marlowe, quoted in *al-Nahar*, 26 February 2005.

337. *The Times* (London), 18 March 2005, *The New York Times*, 20 March 2005.

338. *Al-Safir*, 27 November 2004.

339. Randa Taki al-Din in *al-Hayat*, 18 February 2005.

340. *Al-Hayat*, 21 February 2005.

341. Ibid.

342. *Al-Quds al-Arabi* (London), 6 January 2005; *Al-Nahar*, 11 January 2005; *Al-Mustaqbal*, 16 January 2005.

343. *Al-Nahar*, 27 January 2005.

344. *Al-Nahar*, 3 February 2005.

345. *The Times*, 18 March 2005. Also see *al-Qabas* (Kuwait), 29 October 2005, on Roed-Larsen's testimony to the Mehlis inquiry, held back from publication in the 20 October 2005 report ("Bashar al-Asad said to me that Hariri is playing dirty roles against Syria").

346. *Al-Nahar*, 25 February 2005.

347. *Al-Hayat*, 6 March 2005.

348. *Al-Hayat*, 16 February 2005.

349. *Al-Hayat*, 15 February 2005; *Al-Nahar*, 3 March 2005.

350. *Le Monde*, 7 March 2005.

351. A Hizballah official interviewed by *al-Nahar*, 28 June 1995, estimated that the family average of 6–7 children in Beirut's southern suburbs had fallen to about five in the "new generation." This was more significant than immediately apparent because of a parallel drop in the marriage rate. My own personal observations in the southern suburbs in 1998, 2001, and 2004 are that the average family size has fallen further because of economic circumstances and changed social expectations.

352. Joint statement by President Bush and President Chirac, White House news release, 21 February 2005.

353. *Al-Siyassa*, 2 April 2005.

354. *Al-Hayat*, 21 February 2005.

355. For example, David Satterfield, U.S. deputy assistant secretary of state, on a visit to Beirut, *al-Hayat*, 26 March 2005.

356. Peter Fitzgerald, *Report of the U.N. Fact-Finding Mission to Lebanon*, p. 20.

357. *Al-Hayat*, 6 April 2005.

358. My interview with Michel Aoun, 24 June 2005.

359. My interview with Free Patriotic Movement deputy, 20 June 2005.

360. Hizballah deputy Hajj Hassan cited in *The Daily Star*, 19 August 2005.

361. Ibrahim Hamide in *al-Hayat*, 15 August 2005 ("Damascus fears 'politicization' of Mehlis work"); Walid Shuqayr and Ibrahim Hamidi in *al-Hayat*, 28 August 2005 ("Damascus warns of 'politicization' of the Mehlis report).

362. *Al-Nahar*, 6 and 7 March 2005.

363. Elias al-Murr interview with LBC television, 27 September 2005.

364. *The Daily Star* (Beirut), 1 October 2005.

365. According to *al-Nahar*, 11 October 2005, "a powerful party has expressed its indignation about recent measures that the army has taken in the vicinity of Palestinian positions, and has said that for the first time this is a step not coordinated with it."

366. *Al-Mustaqbal* and *al-Nahar*, 6 October 2005.

367. As reported in *al-Mustaqbal*, 10 October 2005.

368. Sami Nazih in *al-Ra'i al-'Am*, 15 October 2005, reports that "Several Lebanese and Syrian officials have indicated in private that Kana'an was not basically enthusiastic about extending Lahoud's term. At a particular stage animosity had arisen between them [Lahoud and Kana'an], which caused Kana'an's recall from Lebanon to Syria and the withdrawal of the Lebanon file from his hands." Nazih also notes: "This, however, did not preclude Kana'an from participating in a meeting between Asad and Hariri in 2003 attended by other officers. Kana'an and the other Syrian officials and officers present comprehensively attacked Hariri, including accusing him of secretly meeting a high-ranking American official in Lebanon and working against Syria. . . . A close former aide of Hariri says that the former prime minister felt ill and went to hospital before returning to Lebanon."

369. Detlev Mehlis, *Report of the International Independent Investigation Commission established pursuant to Security Council Resolution 1595 (2005)* (Beirut: United Nations, 19 October 2005).

370. Full Arabic text in *al-Hayat*, 11 November 2005.

371. *Al-Safir*, 29 October 2005.
372. *Al-Safir*, 14 November 2005.
373. *Al-Nahar*, 17 and 18 November 2005.
374. Junblatt to *al-Mustaqbal*, 20 November 2005.

■ BIBLIOGRAPHY ■

References cited in Part One

Abu Husayn, Abdul-Rahim. 1992. "Problems in the Ottoman Administration in Syria during the Sixteenth and Seventeenth Centuries: The Case of the Sanjak of Sidon-Beirut." *International Journal of Middle East Studies.* Vol. 24, pp. 665–675.

Abu Manneh, Butrus. 1992. "The Establishment and Dismantling of the Province of Syria." In J. Spagnolo, ed., *Problems of the Modern Middle East in Historical Perspective: Essays in Honour of Albert Hourani,* pp. 7–26. Reading: Ithaca.

Ajami, Fouad. 1985. *The Vanished Imam: Musa al-Sadr and the Shi'a of Lebanon.* Ithaca: Cornell University Press.

Akarli, Engin. 1993. *The Long Peace: Ottoman Lebanon, 1861–1920.* Los Angeles: University of California Press.

Barakat, Halim. 1979. "The Social Context." In E. Haley and L. Snider, eds., *Lebanon's Crisis: Participants and Issues.* Syracuse: Syracuse University Press.

Betts, Robert. 1978. *Christians in the Arab East: A Political Study.* London: SPCK Press.

Betts, Robert. 1988. *The Druze.* New Haven: Yale University Press.

Buheiry, Marwan. 1986. *Beirut's Role in the Political Economy of the French Mandate, 1919–39.* Oxford: Centre for Lebanese Studies— Papers on Lebanon, 4.

Chamie, Joseph. 1977. "Religious Differentials in Fertility: Lebanon, 1971." *Population Studies.* Vol. 31, No. 2, pp. 365–382.

Chevallier, Dominique. 1971. *La Société du Mont Liban à l'Époque de la Révolution Industrielle en Europe.* Paris: Geuthner.

Comnena, Anna. 1969. *The Alexiad of Anna Comnena.* English translation by E. Sewter. London: Penguin.

Dubar, C., and S. Nasir. 1976. *Les Classes Sociales au Liban.* Paris: Presses de la Fondation Nationale des Sciences Politiques.

El-Khazen, Farid. 1991. *The Communal Pact of National Identities: The Making and Politics of the 1943 National Pact.* Oxford: Centre for Lebanese Studies—Papers on Lebanon, 12.

Faour, Muhammad. 1991. "The Demography of Lebanon: A Reappraisal." *Middle Eastern Studies.* Vol. 27, No. 4, pp. 631–641.

Fawaz, Leila. 1983. *Merchants and Migrants in Nineteenth Century Beirut.* Cambridge, Mass.: Harvard University Press.

Fawaz, Leila. 1994. *An Occasion for War: Civil Conflict in Lebanon and*

Damascus in 1860. London: I.B. Tauris.

Gordon, David. 1980. *Lebanon: The Fragmented Nation.* London: Croom Helm.

Gulick, John. 1967. *Tripoli: A Modern Arab City.* Cambridge, Mass.: Harvard University Press.

Halawi, Majed. 1992. *A Lebanon Defied: Musa al-Sadr and the Shi'a Community.* Boulder, Colo.: Westview.

Harik, Iliya. 1968. *Politics and Change in a Traditional Society: Lebanon, 1711–1845.* Princeton: Princeton University Press.

Hottinger, Arnold. 1966. "Zu'ama in Historical Perspective." In L. Binder, ed., *Politics in Lebanon,* pp. 85–104. New York: John Wiley and Sons.

Kennedy, Hugh. 1994. *Crusader Castles.* Cambridge: Cambridge University Press.

Khalaf, Samir. 1979. *Persistence and Change in Nineteenth Century Lebanon.* Beirut: American University of Beirut.

Khalaf, Samir. 1987. *Lebanon's Predicament.* New York: Columbia University Press.

Khoury, Phillip. 1987. *Syria and the French Mandate: The Politics of Arab Nationalism, 1920–45.* Princeton: Princeton University Press.

van Leeuwen, Richard. 1991. "Monastic Estates and Agricultural Transformation in Mount Lebanon in the Eighteenth Century." *International Journal of Middle East Studies.* Vol. 23, pp. 601–617.

van Leeuwen, Richard. 1994. *Notables and Clergy in Mount Lebanon: The Khazin Sheikhs and the Maronite Church.* Leiden: E.J. Brill.

Ma'luf, Isa. 1907–08. *Diwani al-Qutuf fi Ta'rikh Bani al-Ma'luf.* Ba'abda, Lebanon: Ba'abda Ottoman Press.

Marshall, Christopher. 1994. *Warfare in the Latin East, 1192–1291.* Cambridge: Cambridge University Press.

Moosa, Matti. 1986. *The Maronites in History.* Syracuse: Syracuse University Press.

Psellus, Michael. 1966. *Fourteen Byzantine Rulers.* English translation by E. Sewter. London: Penguin.

Rizq, Karam. 1992. *Les Événements de 1860 et le Premier Mutasarrifiya: Tenants et Aboutissants du Grand-Liban.* Kaslik, Lebanon: Bibliothèque de l'Université Saint Esprit.

Runciman, Steven. 1951. *A History of the Crusades, Volume 1: The First Crusade.* Cambridge: Cambridge University Press.

Salibi, Kamal. 1965. *The Modern History of Lebanon.* London: Weidenfeld and Nicolson.

Salibi, Kamal. 1988. *A House of Many Mansions: The History of Lebanon Reconsidered.* Los Angeles: University of California Press.

Shehadi, Nadim, and Dana Haffar-Mills, eds. 1988. *Lebanon: A History of Conflict and Consensus.* Oxford and London: Centre for Lebanese Studies and I.B. Tauris.

Shorrock, William. 1970. "The Origin of the French Mandate in Syria and Lebanon: The Railroad Question, 1901–1914." *International Journal of Middle East Studies.* Vol. 1, pp. 133–153.

Soffer, Arnon. 1986. "Lebanon—Where Demography is the Core of Politics and Life." *Middle Eastern Studies.* Vol. 22, 2, pp. 197–205.

Spagnolo, John. 1977. *France and Ottoman Lebanon, 1861–1914.* London: Ithaca.

Tadmuri, Umr 'Abd al-Salam. 1978. *Ta'rikh Tarabulus: al-Siyasa wa al-Hidara 'abr al-Usur.* Tripoli, Lebanon: Dar al-Bilad Press.

Ziadeh, Nicola. 1953. *Urban Life in Syria under the Early Mamluks.* Beirut: American University of Beirut—Oriental Series, 24.

Primary sources for Parts Two and Three

NEWSPAPERS, NEWS MAGAZINES, AND NEWS AGENCIES

(a) Arabic and Hebrew
Al-Anwar daily newspaper, Beirut
Al-Diyar daily newspaper, Beirut
Al-Hayat daily newspaper, London and Beirut
Al-Majalla weekly newsmagazine, London
Al-Mustaqbal daily newspaper, Beirut
Al-Nahar daily newspaper, Beirut
Al-Nahar al-'Arabi wa al-Duwali weekly newsmagazine, Beirut
Al-Qabas daily newspaper, Kuwait
Al-Quds al-Arabi daily newspaper, London
Al-Ra'i al-'Am daily newspaper, Kuwait
Al-Safir daily newspaper, Beirut
Al-Siyassa daily newspaper, Kuwait
Al-Thawra daily newspaper, Damascus
Tishrin daily newspaper, Damascus
Al-Wasat weekly newsmagazine, London
Al-Zaman daily newspaper, London and Baghdad
Ha-aretz daily newspaper, Tel Aviv

(b) English and French
Le Canard Enchainé daily newspaper, Paris
The Daily Star daily newspaper, Beirut

341

The Economist weekly newsmagazine, London
International Herald Tribune daily newspaper, Paris and Zürich
L'Orient le Jour daily newspaper, Beirut
Le Monde, Paris
The New York Times, New York
Reuters News Service, London
The Times daily newspaper, London

PERIODICALS AND SINGLE PUBLICATIONS

The Lebanon Report, monthly, January 1990–July 1995, and quarterly, Fall 1995 onward—Lebanese Center for Policy Studies, Sin al-Fil, Beirut.
Country Reports (Lebanon), quarterly—Economist Intelligence Unit, Economist Publications, London.
The October Debacle. Foundation for Human and Humanitarian Rights (Lebanon), November 1990.

MONITORING SERVICES

Foreign Broadcast Information Service (FBIS). *Daily Report: Near East and South Asia.* Monitoring published in English translation, U.S. Government.

RADIO AND TELEVISION STATIONS (other than reports, news items derived from monitoring services)

Lebanese Broadcasting Corporation, independent television station (Arabic).
Radio Monte Carlo, independent radio station (Arabic).
Voice of Lebanon, Kata'ib radio station (Arabic).
Voice of the People, Lebanese Communist Party radio station (Arabic).

INTERVIEWS

Author's interview records—interviews with Lebanese, Syrian, and Israeli personalities, 1983–2005, as detailed in chapter notes.

References cited in Parts Two and Three

Abu Khalil, Asa'ad. 1988. "The Palestinian-Shi'ite War in Lebanon: An

Examination of its Origin." In R. Gauther, ed., *Third World Affairs, 1988,* pp. 77–89. London: Third World Foundation for Social and Economic Studies.

Alin, Erika. 1994. *The United States and the 1958 Lebanon Crisis: American Intervention in the Middle East.* Lanham, Maryland: University Press of America.

Avi-Ran, Reuven. 1991. *The Syrian Intervention in Lebanon since 1975.* Boulder, Colorado: Westview.

Bou-Nacklie, N. 1993. "Les Troupes Spéciales: Religious and Ethnic Recruitment, 1916–46." *International Journal of Middle East Studies.* Vol. 25, pp. 645–660.

Chamoun, Camille. 1963. *Crise au Moyen-Orient.* Paris, Gallimard.

Dagher, Carole. 1992. *Les Paris du Général.* Beirut: FMA.

Deeb, Marius. 1985. "Lebanon's Continuing Conflict." *Current History.* Vol. 84, pp. 13–15, 34.

El-Khazen, Farid. 2000. *The Breakdown of the State in Lebanon, 1967–1976.* London: I. B. Tauris.

El-Khazen, Farid, and Paul Salem, eds. 1993. *Al-Intikhabat al-uwla fi Lubnan ma ba'd al-Harb: Al-Arqam wa al-Waqa'i'wa al-Dalalat.* Beirut: Lebanese Center for Policy Studies.

Evron, Yair. 1987. *War and Intervention in Lebanon: The Israeli-Syrian Deterrence Dialogue.* London: Croom Helm.

Fadlallah, Muhammad Husayn. 1994. *Fi Afaq al-Hiwar al-Islami al-Masihi.* Beirut: Dar al-Malak.

Goria, Wade. 1985. *Sovereignty and Leadership in Lebanon, 1943–1976.* London: Ithaca.

Hamzeh, Nizar, and Hrair Dekmejian. 1994. "The Islamic Spectrum of Lebanese Politics." *The Beirut Review.* No. 7, pp. 115–134.

Harik, Judith. 1993. "Change and Continuity among the Lebanese Druze Community: The Civil Administration of the Mountain, 1983–90." *Middle Eastern Studies.* Vol. 29, 3, pp. 377–398.

Harik, Judith. 1994. "*Shaykh al-'Aql* and the Druze of Mount Lebanon: Conflict and Accommodation." *Middle Eastern Studies.* Vol. 30, 3, pp. 461–485.

Harris, William. 1985. "The View from Zahle: Security and Economic Conditions in the Central Beqa'a, 1983–85." *Middle East Journal.* Vol. 39, 3, pp. 270–286.

Harris, William. 1988. "Syria in Lebanon." In R. Gauther, ed., *Third World Affairs, 1988,* pp. 90–106. London: Third World Foundation for Social and Economic Studies.

Harris, William. 1993. "Lebanon." In A. Ayalon, ed., *Middle East Con-*

temporary Survey, vol. 15, 1991, pp. 540–576. Boulder, Colorado: Westview.

Harris, William. 2005. "Bashar al-Assad's Lebanon Gamble." *Middle East Quarterly* 12, no. 3: 33–44.

Hudson, Michael. 1968. *The Precarious Republic: Political Modernization in Lebanon.* New York: Random House.

Institute for Human Rights in Lebanon. 1990. *Muqarrarat al-Ta'if wa Huquq al-Insan.* Beirut: Institute for Human Rights in Lebanon.

Johnson, Michael. 1986. *Class and Client in Beirut.* London: Ithaca.

Johnson, Michael. 2001. *All Honourable Men: The Social Origins of War in Lebanon.* London: I. B. Tauris.

Kassir, Samir. 1994. *La Guerre du Liban: De la Dissension Nationale au Conflit Régional.* Paris: Karthala.

Khalidi, Rashid. 1986. *Under Siege: PLO Decisionmaking During the 1982 War.* New York: Columbia University Press.

Lebanese Center for Documentation and Research. 1986. *Al-'Alaqat al-Lubnaniyya al-Suriyya, 1943–1985: Waqa'i', Bibliografiya wa Watha'iq.* Beirut: CEDRE (two volumes).

Lebanese Information and Research Center. 1986. *Full Text of the Syrian Sponsored Peace Agreement for Lebanon* [The Tripartite Agreement]. Washington: Lebanese Information and Research Center.

Longrigg, Stephen. 1958. *Syria and Lebanon under the French Mandate.* Oxford: Oxford University Press.

Maila, Joseph. 1992. *The Document of National Understanding: A Commentary* [The Ta'if Agreement]. Oxford: Centre for Lebanese Studies.

Mansur, Albert. 1993. *Al-Inqilab 'ala al-Ta'if.* Beirut: Dar al-Jadid.

Norton, Augustus R. 1991. "Lebanon after Ta'if: Is the Civil War Over?" *Middle East Journal.* Vol. 45, 3, pp. 457–473.

Owen, Roger. 1976. "The political economy of Grand Liban." In R. Owen, ed., *Essays on the Crisis in Lebanon,* pp. 23–32. London: Ithaca.

Pakradouni, Karim. 1983. *La Paix Manquée.* Beirut: Editions FMA.

Partner, Peter. 1995. "The Rebirth of Beirut." *The New York Review.* 22 June, pp. 38–42.

Quandt, William. 1991. "American Policy toward Lebanon." In *State and Society in Lebanon,* pp. 75–83. Oxford: Center for Lebanese Studies.

Rabinovich, Itamar. 1984. *The War for Lebanon, 1970–1983.* Ithaca: Cornell University Press.

Saidi, Nasser. 1986. *Economic Consequences of the War in Lebanon.* Oxford: Centre for Lebanese Studies—Papers on Lebanon, 5.

Salem, Paul. 1991. "Two Years of Living Dangerously: General Awn and

Lebanon's 'Second Republic.'" *The Beirut Review.* No. 1, pp. 62–87.

Salibi, Kamal. 1976. *Crossroads to Civil War: Lebanon, 1958–1976.* New York: Delmar.

Salman, Talal, ed. 1984. *Al-Muhadir al-Sirriya al-Kamila.* Beirut: Arab Center for Information.

Schiff, Ze'ev, and Ehud Ya'ari. 1984. *Israel's Lebanon War.* London: Allen and Unwin.

Seale, Patrick. 1987. *The Struggle for Power in Syria.* New Haven: Yale University Press.

Seale, Patrick. 1989. *Asad: The Struggle for the Middle East.* Los Angeles: University of California Press.

Snider, Lewis. 1984. "The Lebanese Forces: Their Origins and Role in Lebanese Politics." *Middle East Journal.* Vol. 38, 1, pp. 1–33.

Yaniv, Avner. 1987. *Dilemmas of Security: Politics, Strategy and the Israeli Experience in Lebanon.* New York: Oxford University Press.

Zamir, Meir. 1985. *The Formation of Modern Lebanon.* London: Croom Helm.

INDEX OF NAMES